Russia and the Soviet Union

John M. Thompson

Universities Field Staff International

Russia and the Soviet Union

An Historical Introduction

CHARLES SCRIBNER'S SONS
New York

5/XII/86

To Ron —

With warm regards and memories of times together in the bush leagues.

Joel

Copyright © 1986, Scribner Book Companies, Inc.,
an affiliate of Macmillan, Inc.

Printed in the United States of America

Macmillan Publishing Company
866 Third Avenue, New York, New York 10022

Collier Macmillan Canada, Inc.

Library of Congress Cataloging in Publication Data

Thompson, John M.
  Russia and the Soviet Union.

  Includes index.
  1. Soviet Union—History. I. Title.
DK40.T48 1986   947   85-10807
ISBN 0-02-420720-9

Printing: 1 2 3 4 5 6 7 8   Year: 6 7 8 9 0 1 2 3 4 5

ISBN 0-02-420720-9

Contents

List of Maps _____

Preface _____

This book grew out of dissatisfaction with longer, more detailed histories of Russia that my students and I experienced at the University of Hawaii in spring 1983, when I taught a survey course treating the entire history of Russia in one semester. Such a course, difficult in the best of circumstances, becomes almost impossible for both instructor and students when the latter must try to master in fourteen weeks the complex material of a six-hundred-page textbook designed for a two-semester course. In my view, there is no up-to-date, clear, short history of Russia that gives approximately equal attention to earlier Russian history and to the modern period since 1801. This is the book I attempted to write in the hope it will fill a need for teachers and students at the upper secondary and college levels.

At the same time, I was aware of the interest in Russia and its past on the part of many individuals not enrolled in courses in Russian history—those in other fields or with a general curiosity about foreign cultures or international affairs. Friends of my children, acquaintances, members of the audience at public lectures I give, and others frequently ask me, "I would like to learn something about Russia and its history; is there a good short book I can start with?" Unfortunately, I cannot recommend any single book as an introduction to the subject. Consequently, although I wrote this volume primarily for students, I also had in mind general readers, with the goal that this brief account might both provide them basic information and whet their appetites for further reading and study of Russian history.

To some extent this book is also the outgrowth of my career as a student and teacher of Russian history for almost forty years. The story of the Russian people—their tribulations and courage, their tragedies and triumphs, and their remarkable contribution to world culture—remains just as fascinating to me today as when I first encountered it in 1946 in the undergraduate classroom of Professor E. Dwight Salmon of Amherst College. I hope that the personalities, excitement, and drama of Russian history can be glimpsed even in this introductory account.

A work of this circumscribed compass has obvious limitations. In this preface and throughout the book I occasionally use the term *Russia* or *Russian* to mean the whole territory and collection of peoples in the tsarist empire or the Soviet Union. The reader needs to keep in mind that this terminology is for brevity and convenience, that in fact Russia is only part of a much larger state, and that Russians are barely half the population of the Soviet Union. Although the book tries to make clear that the tsarist empire was multinational from at least the 1600s and that non-Russians made important contributions to Russian and

Soviet history, a longer volume would be needed to provide adequate treatment of the non-Russian aspects of this story.

Similarly, a number of significant topics, such as religious history, could be dealt with only cursorily, and no subject could receive full and definitive treatment. Moreover, many questions in Russian history are still matters of lively historiographic debate. Although I have tried to note the most significant of these disputes, lack of space made it infeasible to present contending positions in detail or to take account of the Marxist views of Soviet historians as fully as is probably warranted.

The book is designed for the introductory survey course that treats Russian history from Kiev to the present in one semester or fourteen weeks. If the instructor desires, one chapter can be assigned for student reading each week. Since the chapters are short, averaging about twenty-five pages, the instructor can require corollary reading as well. The book can also be used in two-semester survey courses, in which the instructor wants students to acquire a basic chronological structure and framework of information from a textbook but also seeks to expand their acquaintance with Russian history and culture by asking them to read primary sources, selected articles, contemporary documents, or fiction (poetry, short stories, novels, plays). To assist both students and general readers who wish to delve more deeply into a topic that interests them, a brief list of recommended readings in English follows each chapter. Maps and illustrations have been chosen to relate directly to the text.

This history is predominantly a straightforward narrative. Its aim is to give the reader a logically organized, lucid, unembellished account of the main events and developments in the history of Russia from its origins to today. No particular theory about the evolution of Russia is espoused; no special or novel interpretations are advanced. Within the limits of space the reasons why important events happened are analyzed, and for certain questions readers are challenged to think through their own answers. Whenever a conclusion is put forward that is not widely accepted among Western scholars or that represents a new point of view, I have noted it as my own opinion.

Dates and Names

Beginning in 1700 and continuing until February 1918, dates in Russia were calculated according to the Julian calendar, or in the Old Style (O.S.). In the eighteenth century that calendar was eleven days behind the Gregorian calendar (New Style [N.S.]) used in the West; in the nineteenth century it was twelve days; and in the twentieth century, thirteen days. Because students are familiar with Western dates, I have given all dates in New Style, or according to the Gregorian calendar.

Since some Russian names are familiar to Western readers (Nicholas for the last tsar, Leo Tolstoy for the novelist), it would be confusing to transliterate all names according to strictly followed rules. I have tried to use common sense, seeking clarity and trying at the same time to avoid excessive anglicization.

In an effort to assist students and readers with the pronunciation of Russian names, I have given rough phonetic equivalents for the more difficult names when they are first used.

Acknowledgments

I am indebted to my first graduate teachers of Russian history, Professors Philip E. Mosely and Geroid T. Robinson, for providing the enthusiasm and insights on which I began to build my own understanding of Russia and the Soviet Union. My students at the University of Hawaii and my colleagues there, Professors Don Raleigh and Rex Wade, empathized with my complaints about the difficulty of the course I was teaching and the lack of suitable text material for it, and all of them strongly encouraged me when I was seized by a determination to try to write the book I needed. My employer, the Universities Field Staff International, generously released me half-time between May and September 1984, so that I could begin this book. My first editor, Alex Holzman, reacted enthusiastically when I first suggested this volume and assisted me with heartening support in the initial stages of planning and writing it.

Invaluable help was furnished by Professor John T. Alexander of the University of Kansas, a distinguished scholar of seventeenth- and eighteenth-century Russia, who acted as my consultant and meticulous first reader. He not only caught many errors and awkward expressions but was willing to discuss with me points of befuddlement and interpretation. I am most grateful for his cheerful assistance. Needless to say, he is in no way responsible for whatever mistakes and infelicities remain.

This book was written at home, and I thank my wife warmly for her constant support and understanding.

J. M. T.
SEPTEMBER 1985

1

Ancient Russia and the Kievan State

The Russian Land

Most Americans, even those accustomed to the transcontinental stretch of their own country, find it difficult to comprehend the vast expanse of territory encompassed in the Russian state, known formally as the Union of Soviet Socialist Republics (USSR). To be sure, we learn such numbing facts as that the Soviet Union covers one-sixth the land surface of the entire earth, or that Russia has literally stretched, at least since the late 1600s, all across Eurasia from "sea to shining sea," from the Pacific Ocean on its eastern border to the Baltic Sea, an arm of the Atlantic Ocean, on its western boundary (see Map 1). But it requires a specific experience to make concrete the enormous sweep of the Russian land.

For me this happened one evening in the 1960s when I boarded a train to travel from Kiev, an ancient city in the southwestern republic of the Ukraine, to Moscow, the old and present capital of the country in central western Russia. I would travel only overnight, but I found occupying at least 80 percent of the space in the Pullman compartment I had been assigned a large and voluble Soviet woman (sleeping cars on Russian trains traditionally accommodate both sexes) accompanied by what seemed like a hundred suitcases, bundles, packages, and even a small trunk. Friendly conversation soon revealed that her husband was a colonel in the Soviet air force stationed in Vladivostok, a main port and base on the Pacific Ocean. She had been home visiting relatives in the Ukraine and had stocked up on a few supplies to make her life on the distant frontier of the Soviet Far East a bit more comfortable. As I tried to wedge myself in among the boxes and bags, I asked her how long a trip she would have. When she replied, "Eight nights and seven days," my jaw dropped and I stared at her. Seeing my surprise, she admonished me, "Yes, it *is* a big country, much bigger than yours." (And, in fact, bigger than the United States and Canada combined.)

Six thousand miles and eleven time zones from east to west, three thousand miles from north to south, with the world's longest coastline (much of it on the frozen Arctic Ocean), the Soviet Union has every sort of terrain: desert, semitropical beaches and fruit groves, inland seas, sweeping semiarid plains, rugged mountains, fertile treeless agricultural fields (the famous steppe), thick forests, long rivers, and the ice-locked tundra of the far north.

Russia's size alone, now as the Soviet Union and for over two hundred years before the Communist Revolution of 1917 as the Russian Empire, has created special challenges for the people living there. How is such a huge territory to be managed and its riches extracted and used efficiently? How can its inhabitants stay in touch with one another and develop a sense of common identity and purpose? How can power be exercised and the state administered over such vast distances? These problems, which plagued the Russian tsars, still vex the Soviet leaders today. What should be the balance between control from the center and local decision making? Should new industry be developed where a majority of the people live but where there are few resources, or where there are lots of raw materials but few inhabitants? How can diverse peoples, so widely scattered, have a common belief, or even agree on what language all should speak?

In addition, the great extent of the Russian land mass has had important strategic consequences. Paradoxically, Russia has been both hard to conquer and hard to defend. Today Soviet generals worry about a possible two-front war, against the United States and its allies on the Soviet Union's western border and against the People's Republic of China in the east. Earlier, the Russians had, at various times, to cope with enemies on three, four, and occasionally even five fronts. Thus, the Russian government has always had to allocate much of its effort and resources to defending its large territories. On the other hand, Russia's opponents have had trouble invading and occupying the country. Although the Mongols succeeded in conquering and ruling most of Russia from the 1200s to the 1400s, the Poles, the Swedes, the Turks, the French under Napoleon, and the Germans, twice in the twentieth century, have had less luck, being turned back in part by the enormous distances to be traversed.

In assessing the influence of Russia's natural environment on its history, its location is as important as its size. For example, if you lived in Washington, D.C., and were suddenly transported by magic to a city in the Soviet Union with a comparable location, where do you think you would end up: Moscow? Kiev? Not at all; you would miss the Soviet Union entirely because it is located so far north in Eurasia that most of the country lies in latitudes parallel to those of Canada and Alaska. Leningrad, for example, is just a bit farther north than Juneau, Alaska.

This northerly position on the earth's surface has caused recurring hardships for Russia's citizens. In most of the country, winters are long and cold, and the growing season for food is short. Besides, much of

Russia's huge territory is so far north that it can't be farmed, and living there is unpleasant and expensive. One result has been that Russia has never been rich agriculturally, despite its huge size.

Although situated in the northern part of the great Eurasian land mass, the Soviet Union stretches south, east and west so that it touches most of continental Asia, the Middle East, and Europe (see Map 1). Consequently it has always been a crossroads of cultures and ideas. Russia has been affected by European, Asian, and Islamic civilizations and has absorbed something from all of them. In turn, and increasingly in the past two hundred years, it has influenced and, on occasion, dominated its neighbors.

In the 1930s an elaborate theory of "geopolitics" concluded that Russia was ideally located to rule the world. Although such a notion is clearly rubbish, there is no doubt that the central location of the country in Eurasia has contributed strongly to the mix of cultures and values in it today and to its important role in contemporary world affairs. Even though it is linked to both Asia and the West, Russian society has evolved in distinct and complex ways. It need not be characterized as exotic, Asian, or "Mongol"; nor should it be interpreted as a stunted offshoot of western civilization. It has had a unique history that has produced a modern society unlike any other. The Soviet Union must be understood on its own terms.

Without venturing into geographical detail, we need also to note the effects on Russia's historical development of several topographical features of the Russian land. Partly because of its northerly location and partly because it is situated far from the major oceans, Russia has a forbidding climate in most regions: very hot and dry in the summer, and bitterly cold in the winter, with a spring marked by deep mud that makes travel on unpaved roads almost impossible. Since most of the rain comes across Europe from the Atlantic Ocean, it peters out as it moves over the Russian agricultural plain from west to east. Some of the best soil receives insufficient rainfall, and almost all the farming in Soviet Central Asia requires irrigation. The result is that less than 15 percent of Russia's land is used for growing food, another feature that limits the country's agricultural potential and strength.

The borders of the Soviet Union have contradictory characteristics. In the north the country is well protected by the frozen expanse of the Arctic Ocean and in the southeast by some of the highest mountains in the world (see Map 1). Modern bombers and missiles have made these barriers obsolete, but it is still true that to invade Russia from either of those directions would be almost impossible. On the other hand, along its borders in the east, the southwest, and the west Russia has virtually no natural defenses, and at different times it has suffered invasions from all those points of the compass.

Moreover, the heart of the country is one vast plain, broken only

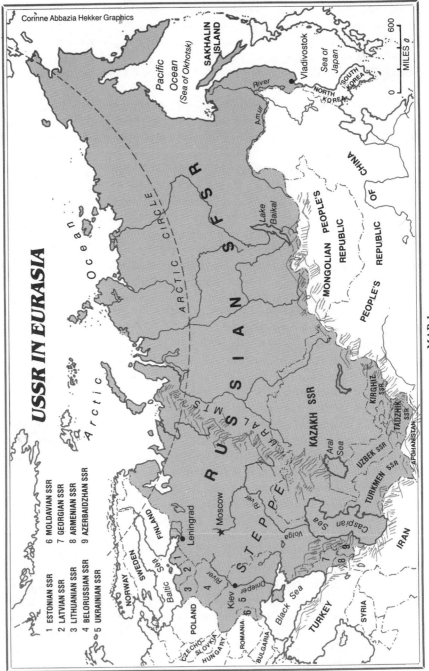

MAP 1

by the Ural Mountains, which are not very high and which in any case do not reach all the way to the Caspian Sea. The effect of this plain has also been two-edged. Russia has been open to attack across this terrain, but the extent of the plain has made it easy for Russians, and the Russian state, to expand and to bring surrounding nationalities under Russian rule. Thus, when I flew for the first time from Moscow to Tashkent in Soviet Central Asia, looking down hour after hour at the endless semidesert, or when I took the train from Czechoslovakia to Moscow and gazed for almost two days across rolling Russian steppe, I could easily visualize Asian horsemen, Russian traders, and modern armies moving back and forth across the flat expanses.

But Russians have historically traveled as much by water as by land. Although the country is largely landlocked and has limited access to the sea—the Arctic shore opens primarily on ice, and the Baltic and Black seas and the Sea of Japan in the Far East lead to the Atlantic and Pacific oceans only through narrow straits subject to closure by enemy military action—Russia possesses a widespread system of interconnecting rivers, "the roads that run," as folk wisdom puts it. Up to the last one hundred years, when railroads, motor vehicles, and planes appeared, Russians moved extensively by boat, up and down the rivers, which generally flow in a north-south or south-north direction, or along the tributaries that touch each other along an east-west axis. Thus, the earliest inhabitants, using river routes, traveled to and traded with Europeans and Vikings in the northwest, Greek Christians of Byzantium in the southwest, and Asian merchants and artisans in the south. Later, Russia's expansion across Siberia, led by fur trappers and traders, was carried out primarily by water. Even in modern times river transport has played an important role in moving goods and people throughout the country (see Figure 1).

The contemporary Soviet Union is rich in natural resources, in fact virtually self-sufficient, despite a recent dependence on imports of grain. But much of this wealth, such as oil, natural gas, and other abundant minerals, has been exploited only recently. Historically, Russia has been a very poor country, its people struggling to survive and improve their way of life while supporting, with limited resources, a government-organized defense against recurrent enemies. Unfortunately, carrying the burden of the state and the army has too often meant that the people have lived in harsh poverty. Recently, progress in raising the quality of life has been made, and the resources exist for Soviet citizens to live better in the future.

Nevertheless, problems remain. Much of Russia's wealth, as in the past, is being eaten up in defense expenditures. The economy, now as often before, is sapped by inefficiencies and irrationalities. A major dilemma is that the most important and abundant natural resources are in the eastern part of the country, where the fewest people live and where

Figure 1. *Barge traffic in the 1890s on the Volga River, an important commercial artery in Russia from earliest times.*

the climate is generally inhospitable. It is expensive to transport these raw materials to factories in western Russia, where the bulk of the population lives. On the other hand, it is unlikely that many people, even with attractive material inducements, will be persuaded to move to Siberia.

Finally, the Soviet Union confronts, as Russia did throughout its history, a major problem of food supply. Crop yields, especially per capita, have always been low. In the past this has meant a constant battle to survive and a coercive pattern of economic, social, and political institutions in society. Today, it is a brake on the further development of the Soviet economy and creates an unwanted dependence on foreign imports. Much of the Soviet Union's poor agricultural performance can be explained by such natural factors as limited arable land, inadequate rainfall, and a short growing season. But low agricultural productivity also stems in part from the lack of incentives for farmers and from the organization of agriculture under Soviet socialism. Whether this can be changed remains, as we will see in Chapter 13, a moot question.

The Peoples of Russia

The most striking fact about the population of the USSR is its great diversity: there are some one hundred twenty-five nationality groups, of which over twenty include more than one million people. School textbooks are printed in over fifty languages, and a wide variety of religions and cultures coexist inside Soviet borders. The Jews, who number about two and one-half million people, generally speak Russian and live intermixed throughout European Russia (the territory west of the Ural Mountains). All the other large non-Slavic nationality groups speak their own languages, live in geographically separate regions on the borderlands of the country, and have their own republics within the federal state of the Union of Soviet Socialist Republics. Consequently, although it is a multinational society and individuals of many nationalities can be seen in most of the big cities, it is not as racially mixed a society as that of the United States. For example, although a few Estonians might reside in Moscow and Leningrad, the great majority of them lives in the Estonian Soviet Socialist Republic on the northwestern periphery of the Soviet Union. As we will see later, this gives them a sense of cohesiveness and identity but also raises important issues about their relationship to the dominant nationality, the Great Russians, and about their ultimate loyalty to the Soviet state in a time of crisis. Whether the Soviet leaders can satisfy the aspirations of the national minority groups for greater autonomy and a larger share of the material benefits of Soviet socialism is one of the major challenges for the Soviet government in the next decade.

Out of a total population of almost two hundred eighty million, the largest groups and their estimated size in 1985 are as follows:

1. Eastern Slavs: 202 million
   a. Great Russians: 145 million
   b. Ukrainians: 45 million
   c. Belorussians: 12 million
2. Turkic and Tatar Peoples (Bashkirs, Azerbaijani, Uzbeks, Turkmens, Kazakhs, and others): 48 million
3. Caucasian Peoples (Armenians, Georgians, and others): 10 million
4. Finno-Ugric Peoples (Estonians, Karelians, and others): 5.5 million
5. Baltic Peoples (Latvians and Lithuanians): 4.5 million
6. Jews: 2.5 million

The Great Russians, who today make up just over half the population, formed the core of the Russian state established in northeastern Russia in the 1100s, and have largely dominated the government and society ever since. They are the bulk of the population in the largest republic, the Russian Soviet Federated Socialist Republic, which extends from the northwest part of European Russia all across the great Eurasian plain and Siberia to the Sea of Japan. The Ukrainians are descendants of the Slavs who formed the first Russian state based at Kiev and they have their own Slavic language and their own republic in the southwest. The Belorussians live in the west bordering Poland and speak a form of Russian. Most of the Turkic and Tatar peoples are Moslems, which makes Islam the second largest religion in the Soviet Union, after Orthodox Christianity.

Only in the last three hundred years has Russia become predominantly a multinational society. The Muscovite state founded by the Great Russians in the 1300s expanded to incorporate the Ukrainians in the 1600s and the other major non-Russian nationalities between 1700 and 1850. With the rise of nationalistic and religious feeling among these groups in the past one hundred years, their integration into the Russian Empire before 1917 and into the Soviet Union after 1917 has created special problems. Today, as the non-Russians, who have a higher birth rate than the Russians, become a larger percentage of the total population, the relationship between the dominant Great Russians and the other nationality groups remains a thorny issue (see Chapter 13).

If you visit the Soviet Union, you will be intrigued to see, in the major cities, the great variety of individuals, with a wide range of body types, facial features, and hair and skin colors (see Figure 2). You will certainly have an opportunity to meet non-Russians and to learn at first hand the diversity of cultures, ideas, and experiences represented among the peoples of the Soviet Union.

As this short overview has tried to show, geographic and demographic factors are important in understanding the development of Russian society. A word of caution is in order, however. History is made by individuals interacting with each other and with their neighbors, and it would be a misleading oversimplification to conclude that Russian institutions, such as a centralized authoritarian system of government, or Russian values, such as a concern for the group or the collective unit in society, resulted primarily from the harsh conditions of Russia's natural environment.

Even worse, it is utter nonsense to predetermine the future of the Soviet people on the basis of their past. To say that history has made the Russians inherently "subservient" or insensitive to the rights of individuals or naturally militaristic is as silly as the old axiom "Scratch a Russian; find a Mongol." Certainly no American would accept the conclusion that because the history of the United States is filled with instances of discrimination against native Americans and blacks, our institutions and our values condemn us to a future of racial bias and oppression. Consequently, as we begin to trace Russia's historical evolution, we need constantly to bear in mind that this society is a complicated product of the interplay over a thousand years among the land, the people, and outside influences. We will not look for simplified, pat answers but will instead seek sympathetic and broad understanding of who the Russians are and how they came to be that way.

Figure 2. *A typical non-Russian citizen of the Soviet Union: a Kazakh visitor from Central Asia in Red Square in front of the Kremlin. (Courtesy of the United Nations)*

The Slavs Come to Russia

Archeology helps explain the past, but there is a lot it cannot tell us. In the past few decades excavations in the southern part of European Russia have revealed that early human settlements were well established there by at least 3500 B.C. These ancient inhabitants of the steppe farmed and kept domestic animals, but who they were and how they organized their society remain largely unanswered questions.

In the centuries just before the birth of Christ, the region north of the Black Sea (today the Ukraine) was dominated by two talented and well-organized partly nomadic peoples who migrated there from Central Asia: Scythians, who ruled the area from 700 to 200 B.C., and Sarmatians, who held sway from 200 B.C. to A.D. 200. They were only the latest in a succession of loosely organized "steppe empires." The Scythians, who were in contact with the Greeks, were master artisans and created exquisite gold jewelry, which has hardly been matched since. A highlight of any trip to the Soviet Union is a visit to the Treasure Room of the Hermitage Museum in Leningrad, where original pieces of this lovely and delicate Scythian jewelry are displayed.

The Scythians and Sarmatians were linked by language and culture to the Persians, and both groups established militarized states. At the same time they maintained cultural and trading ties with Greek colonies on the north shore of the Black Sea so that the influence of classical civilization reached the territory that was to become Russia as early as it did western Europe.

A series of nomadic invasions disrupted the evolution of this region for almost five hundred years, from about A.D. 200 to the 700s. As was to occur later in Russian history, the invaders came from all directions, first the Goths from the northwest, then the Huns and Avars from the east, and finally the Khazars, who from their bases southeast of Russia extended their control over the northern Caucasus, as well as the area around the lower part of the Volga River and nearby stretches of the great steppe.

Two important characteristics of Khazar civilization influenced the birth and early development of the first East Slav state at Kiev. First, the Khazars were active and successful traders, maintaining lively commercial contacts with the Arabs, the Greek civilization of Byzantium, and various Asian societies to the east and south of them. Second, the Khazars seem to have been open to and tolerant of a variety of cultural and religious influences. Their leaders eventually adopted Judaism, but Christian, Islamic, and pagan ideas circulated widely in the Khazar state. In a similar fashion Kievan society depended heavily on trade and plunder and was in contact with a range of European and Asian societies.

In fact, it seems quite clear that the Kievan state was multinational. It included descendants of previous occupiers of the region north of the Black Sea, as well as Finns and Vikings from Scandinavia, together with a majority of Eastern Slavs. We are not sure, however, where the Slavs came from or how long they had been there. Soviet specialists in prehistory make the case that Slavs had lived on the plains of European Russia hundreds of years before the historic state of Kiev was founded, and they may be right. One difficulty is that the term *Slav* is a linguistic one; it designates a group of people who speak a common language, one of a family of languages called Indo-European, which are today spoken from India and southwest Asia all across Europe to England and the Americas (in the transported languages of English, Spanish, and

Portuguese). *Slav* itself probably comes from *slovo,* meaning in the Slavic language "word"; thus, the Slavs were all those who spoke a common word or language. By contrast the original Slavic term for foreigners apparently was *nemtsy,* meaning "those who are mute": who could not speak the word. (Today *nemtsy* in the Russian language means "Germans.") We know that in modern times speakers of Slavic languages are distributed from Yugoslavia (Serbs, Croats, and Slovenes) in southeastern Europe through the southern Balkans (Bulgarians and Macedonians) to central Europe (Czechs, Slovaks, and Poles: the Western Slavs) and the Soviet Union (Russians, Ukrainians, and Belorussians: Eastern Slavs). But exactly how each group got to its present location and whether they all started from some central point remains a mystery.

The archeological remains of villages in southern Russia unfortunately cannot tell us what language the inhabitants spoke. Nevertheless, by about A.D. 600 references by Gothic, Byzantine, and Arabic authors make it clear that Slavic tribes formed a considerable part of the population north of the Black Sea and that these tribes paid tribute to the Khazars. Putting the written and archeological evidence together, we know that these early Slavs had well-developed agriculture, raised cattle and bees, fished and hunted, and knew how to weave and make pottery. Yet we know little about their social structure, government, customs, or beliefs. Unfortunately, no traveler, no early Marco Polo, penetrated the region, which was on the fringe of the great civilizations of the Mediterranean basin and of Asia, to leave us a detailed description of Slavic life at the time.

The Formation of the Kievan State

The first East Slavic state was founded in the 800s, making Russian civilization just over a thousand years old. It was centered briefly on the northern city of Novgorod, then for several hundred years on Kiev, a city on the Dnieper River in south Russia, and it was soon known as the state of Kiev Rus'. But, as with the origins of the Slavs, how the state was established and the meaning of the word *Rus'*, from which Russia derives, are obscure. The key point of uncertainty is the role of Swedish Vikings, known as Varangians in the first Slavic chronicles, in forming the state and in their relations with the predominant Slavic population of the region.

The most detailed historical source, *The Primary Chronicle,* compiled by monks in the eleventh century, recounts that since there was no order among the Slavic tribes, they invited a Scandinavian named Riurik and his two brothers to come and rule over them. But this chronicle was written several hundred years later, partly for the purpose of legitimizing the claims to power of Riurik's alleged descendants, making the story suspect in itself. In addition, there is a growing body of archeological and other evidence to suggest that the role of the Vikings, or Varangians, in Russia was a good deal more complex than the picture the chronicle paints.

In this period long-distance trading flourished, and the Vikings participated in it. They certainly knew that silver and gold, as well as other valuable articles, existed in Asia and were traded by the Khazars and by Arabs. They were also well acquainted with the trading route from Scandinavia to the advanced Byzantine (formerly Greek) civilization at Constantinople ("the road from the Varangians to the Greeks," as it was called) that passed through Russia, primarily down the Dnieper River and across the Black Sea. Finally, the Vikings' travels into Russia, primarily by boat across the Baltic Sea and then via lakes and rivers, were motivated in part by their recognition of the value of the furs, honey, and wax that existed in the areas of Slavic settlement.

Consequently it is quite clear that the Vikings, though occasionally plundering and conquering as they did in western Europe a short time later, entered Russia primarily as traders and mercenaries. It seems logical to assume that in these roles they worked closely with local Slavic leaders to increase order and security, to protect trade routes, and to encourage regular payment of tribute by rural peoples to the commercial and military leaders of the towns in Russia. Thus, although in certain times and places Slavs and Varangians undoubtedly clashed, and even on occasion Vikings may have attempted to assert political control over Slavic groups, much more often the Varangians and the local leaders almost certainly cooperated in pursuit of common objectives. The most sensible conclusion is, not that they set up a state for the hapless Slavs, but that they worked with Slavic chieftains to create a stable government and state system.

Even this interpretation does not entirely satisfy many historians in the Soviet Union who, for understandably patriotic reasons, would prefer to have the role of the Vikings downgraded to insignificance and the contributions of the Slavs highlighted. In a similar vein Soviet writers are unhappy with the theory that the word *Rus'* is of Scandinavian origin. Another explanation links it to a place name in southern Russia. Since the evidence is scanty and inconclusive, we will probably never know where the word came from. But we are certain that it was applied to the first state at Kiev, and that from it came *Russia* and *Russian*.

This first state is important to an understanding of Russian civilization for several reasons. In Kievan Russia the fundamental characteristics of Russian culture and religion took root. The Kievan state also introduced basic and lasting political ideas and social institutions. Finally, it created the tradition of Russia as a major force in international affairs and as a linkage point between Europe and Asia, between East and West.

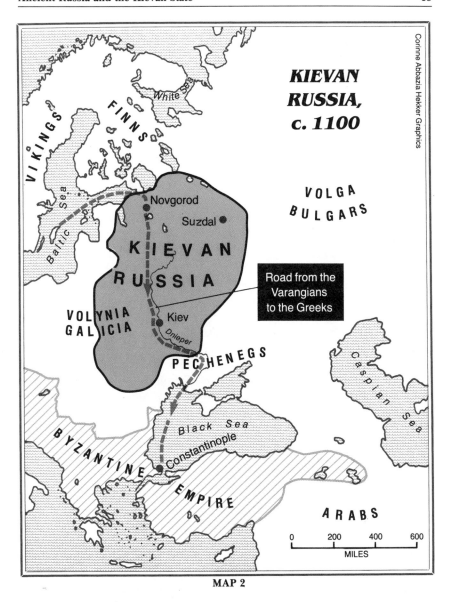

KIEVAN RUSSIA, c. 1100

Corinne Abbazia Hekker Graphics

VIKINGS

White Sea

FINNS

Baltic Sea

Novgorod

Suzdal

VOLGA BULGARS

K I E V A N

R U S S I A

Road from the Varangians to the Greeks

VOLYNIA GALICIA

Kiev

Dnieper

PECHENEGS

Caspian Sea

BYZANTINE

Black Sea

Constantinople

EMPIRE

ARABS

| 0 | 200 | 400 | 600 |

MILES

MAP 2

How Did Kievan Russians Make a Living?

Kiev Rus' lasted from the 800s to the early 1200s, considerably longer than the history of the United States to date. At its largest the Kievan state was long and skinny. It stretched in the 1000s from the Baltic Sea on the north to the Black Sea on the south, including a band of territory of varying width both east and west of its main axis on the Dnieper River (see Map 2). Educated guesses put its maximum population at about seven or eight million, of whom fewer than a million lived in towns and cities. The largest cities, like Kiev, probably contained tens of thousands of people, but in most of the over two hundred fortified centers that have been identified the population was undoubtedly less than five thousand.

Over 85 percent of the people lived on the land as farmers, hunters and trappers, beekeepers, and herdsmen. Most of the farming was small-scale and used primitive implements, such as wooden plows and harrows (though some iron plows existed). Agriculture was often carried out by the slash-and-burn method: when old, cleared ground lost its fertility, a new area of trees and undergrowth was cut away and then burned, with the ashes providing nutrients for the new crops planted there.

Most of what people produced they ate. But some of the output was delivered (or seized) as tribute or taxes to political and military leaders, first representing clans or tribes and later based in towns within the Kievan state. These goods included, besides crops used to feed soldiers and townspeople, furs, honey, hides, and wax, all of which could then be traded to outsiders, primarily to the Byzantine Empire. Since there were frequent military campaigns to collect tribute and recurring wars with outsiders, captives were taken and were often sold or traded as slaves, a convenient commodity since they could walk to market.

Because individual farmers or even farming families of the sort we are accustomed to in Europe and the United States could not muster sufficient labor power to grow crops in the difficult conditions and with the poor methods of that era, most rural people in Kievan Russia banded together in communes. A farming commune, known in Russian as *obshchina* (ohb-shcheena), usually consisted of several extended families, although some apparently included individuals who were not near relatives. The *obshchina* lasted over a thousand years, down to the Revolution in 1917 led by Lenin and the Bolshevik party, and exists today, in much modified form, in the Soviet collective farm. Its advantage is that it permits a pooling of labor and tools to accomplish heavy agricultural tasks. Members of the *obshchina* share not only the work but the products of their labor. It obviously fosters a spirit of group solidarity and collectivism, an attitude that has played a critically important role throughout Russian history.

Historians in the Soviet Union have argued that the economic, social, and political system of the Kievan state was feudalism. This is one of the main categories in Karl Marx's *historical materialism,* or laws of historical development, so applying it to Kiev corresponds with the basic tenets of the Soviet Union's official ideology, Marxism-Leninism. Other historians have denied that Kievan Russia was a feudal society. For our purposes the technical issues in this debate are largely irrelevant. The important conclusion is that the Kievan system was distinctive, quite different in various ways from feudalism in western Europe or feudalism in Japan.

At the same time it is useful to note several aspects of Kievan society related to feudalism that influenced later Russian history. In the first place the system of tribute (and later taxes) did lead to continuing obligations by peasant farmers to various sorts of social, religious, and political overlords. Although in the Kievan period these obligations were not usually in the form of labor nor tied to land ownership (*obshchinas* generally possessed their own land), later on they took the form of service to a particular lord in return for certain use rights to land. Thus, in Kievan Russia a pattern of obligation developed that in later centuries and under different economic and political conditions would help turn essentially free peasants into serfs.

Second, the Kievan state did incorporate concepts of service that resembled some aspects of the relationship between lord and vassal in western Europe. In particular, fighting men in Kiev, who came to be known as *boyars,* served particular princes, although the terms and duties of such service are rather unclear. This service concept later reappeared as a major principle in Russian society at the time of the development of the Muscovite state.

Finally, a key ingredient of European feudalism was largely lacking in Kievan society: the idea of mutuality. In the European relationship between lord and vassal, the lord had definite responsibilities to his subordinate vassals; in return the vassals owed obligations to the lord. Some writers have argued that this sense of a contract, of a mutual responsibility, is a crucial element in the development of representative government and civil rights in Western civilization. Whether they are right or not, the principle of mutual obligations hardly existed in Kiev, and this may have contributed later to the ease with which the Russian tsars were able to assert unlimited authority over all the people, lords and peasants alike.

Not only feudalism has sparked historiographic controversy about Kiev. Historians have also argued whether agriculture or trade predominated in the Kievan economy. The commonsense answer is that although most of the people farmed and most of what they produced were agricultural and forest goods, trade and commercial activity also played an important role, especially in the life of the towns. Their location favored the Kievan Russians in this regard. Situated between northern Europe and Byzantium and midway between central Europe and Asia, they could carry on a lively commerce in several directions.

There were, of course, risks. Small nomadic groups, such as the Cumans and Pechenegs, often attacked trading parties, particularly at rapids, where boats and goods had to be portaged. Terms of trade with the Byzantine Empire were not always favorable, and Kiev sent several military expeditions against Constantinople to compel the opening of better trading opportunities and contracts. Thus, military activity, including the collection of tribute, and trade went hand in hand. As a result, warriors and merchants—often the same persons—ranked high on the Kievan social scale.

The importance of trade to Kievan society was not only in economic benefits. Because the Russians traded with neighbors on all sides, in Byzantium and in Asia, they were exposed to a wide range of ideas, technology, and cultural influences. Kievan Russia was not a "closed" society at all and interacted effectively with Christian Europe, with the Hellenic empire of Byzantium, and with the Islamic civilization of the Arabs. Only later, after the Mongols conquered it, did Russia become largely isolated. In Kievan times it was in the mainstream of world history.

Kievan Society

Because rigid class divisions do not exist in the United States, it is hard for Americans to imagine societies in which every group has a place clearly defined by custom and law. Yet most societies in the world are structured in such a fashion; ours is the exception, not the rule. No evidence exists to tell us when class differentiation began in Russian society, but by the time of the first Russian law codes, compiled in the eleventh and twelfth centuries, the lines were sharply drawn. Russian society remained divided into classes down to the Revolution of 1917, and some observers would argue that even in postrevolutionary and allegedly classless Soviet society, class distinctions remain.

Depending on how you define a distinct class, there were as many as eleven classes stipulated in Kievan law. But these can be allocated among seven main categories: princes, *boyars* (nobles), merchants, artisans, *smerdy* (peasants), semifree persons, and slaves. At the top of the ladder were the princely families. These were allegedly descendants of the legendary Riurik and his brothers, and they exercised military, judicial, and administrative power over most Russian towns and territories. As we shall see shortly, relations among the princes were complicated, and their struggles for political preeminence led to civil war and greatly weakened the Kievan state.

At first each prince had his own band of military servitors, of whom many in the beginning were probably Vikings. But soon they merged with already existing groups of Slavic warriors, and by the 1000s a Slavicized upper class of lords, called *boyars,* had been formed. Their numbers were always small, but their role was crucial since they carried out military service on behalf of prince, town, and state and also assumed administrative and governing responsibilities. Some of them certainly engaged in commerce as well.

In this role they blended with a separate merchant class, the origins of which undoubtedly go back before the formation of the Kievan state. The merchants, though of lower rank than the princely families and the boyars, had considerable influence because of their importance to the economy of Kievan Russia and because in some towns they exercised political power as well. The merchants were among the chief consumers of the goods they imported from Asia and Byzantium: silks, spices, wines, fruits, metals, and jewelry.

Most people in towns were free and fell into a broad group of artisans and workers. Their equivalent in the countryside were peasants, who bore the colorful designation *smerdy* (best translated "smelly ones"). Some were dependent on princes or boyars, but apparently most were free. Through debt or other circumstances both artisans and peasants could fall into a semifree class: people who were bound to another through some sort of obligation.

At the bottom of the social ladder were slaves. How important they were to the Kievan economy is not clear. Some may have been semifree individuals who fell into complete bondage, but a majority were apparently captured in war, and many were therefore not Slavic. In the earlier years of Kievan rule, slaves formed an important item of trading.

Religion and Culture in Kievan Russia

The single most important event in the history of Kiev was the state's official adoption of Christianity in A.D. 988. Although pagan beliefs and practices and earlier cultural attributes of Kievan society persisted long after the conversion, the acceptance of Christian religion fundamentally altered Russian civilization ever after. Adopting Christianity affected not just religious beliefs and practices but also law, education, literature, the arts, attitudes and feelings, and even the political system. To grasp the overriding significance of this conversion you need only think about how completely different the history of Russia would have been if the rulers of Kiev had chosen Judaism or Islam, options open to them and that they apparently considered. Or think about how the United States would have turned out if Hindus from India or Buddhists from China had discovered the New World.

An extremely significant aspect of Russia's conversion was that Christianity came to Kiev from the Byzantine Empire, which practiced what is today called Eastern or Orthodox Christianity. When the Russians were converted, the Christian or Holy Catholic (that is, universal) Church was united, although there were already considerable differences between its western wing based in Rome and its eastern wing centered on Constantinople. A short time later, in A.D. 1054, these divisions became irreconcilable and the Christian Church split in two: the

Latin or Roman Catholic Church, which dominated in western Europe, and the Greek or Eastern Orthodox Church, which was prevalent in the Balkans, the Middle East, and Russia.

This separation had three important consequences: first, the development of Christianity took quite a different form in Russia from that in western Europe. Second, as the hostility between the two main branches of Christianity heightened, Russians were put at odds with their nearest neighbors to the west: Poles, Lithuanians, and later German settlers along the shores of the Baltic Sea, all of whom were Catholic. Finally, Russia was cut off from close intellectual and cultural contact with western European societies for five or six hundred years, almost into modern times when religious differences became much less important. It is true that the Mongol conquest of Russia in the 1200s also acted to sever Russia's ties with central and western Europe, but religious difference was a formidable barrier and a source of suspicion and hostility.

As early as 955 the first woman ruler of Russia, the Regent Olga, chose Christianity for herself, but another three decades elapsed before Vladimir, one of Kiev's ablest princes, decided to adopt Christianity as an official religion for the whole state and all its subjects. To make sure everyone got the message he had the pagan idols smashed and arranged a mass baptism in the Dnieper River for all the inhabitants of Kiev, according to the *Chronicle*.

We do not know Vladimir's reasons for choosing Eastern Christianity but can surmise fairly safely that the close commercial and political ties with Byzantium that Kiev had developed in the preceding hundred years were an important factor. Vladimir (who was later made a saint in recognition of his decision and whose magnificent statue looks out over the Dnieper River in present-day Kiev) was probably also influenced by the fact that two Christian monks, Cyril and Methodius, had developed a written language that, though based on Greek, transcribed quite well the spoken Slavic language. This new literary language meant that people did not need to learn Greek or Latin to become Christians and the average person could understand the mass and other church services. Russian is still written in the Cyrillic alphabet, named in honor of one of those inventive monks.

Finally, geographic and political factors undoubtedly weighed heavily in Vladimir's choice. If he selected Judaism, its nearest adherents, the Khazars, were some distance away to the southeast, and their power was already in decline. If he chose Islam, the Arabs were even farther away, and he would be drawn into wars against their continuing enemy, the Byzantine Empire. As regards Latin Christianity, it had spread only recently to northern Europe and must have seemed quite insignificant to Vladimir, in comparison to the nearby might and magnificence of Orthodox Christianity with its seat at Constantinople.

The Christianity Vladimir adopted had several important characteristics that were reinforced by Russian conditions and that later dif-
ferentiated it sharply from Western Christianity, particularly after the
Latin Church split in the 1500s into Protestant and Catholic branches.
One was the almost mystical concern in Orthodox Christianity with the
collective spirit of the whole congregation. In the religious service itself
and in the spiritual outlook of the faithful the focus is on the group of
believers, rather than on individual souls and their salvation. This attitude, called *sobornost*, or "spirit of the congregation," (*sobor* may also mean
"cathedral"), fitted well with the collective sense of the community that
had already been developed among the Russians through the peasant
institution of the *obshchina*.

Another aspect of Orthodox Christianity that was strongly im-
planted in the Russian Church was an emphasis on outward forms of
religion: the church buildings and decorations, the icons (paintings on
wood of holy figures and saints), and the structure and ritual of the
mass itself. To stress these visible signs of devotion made it easier to
wean the East Slavs away from pagan idols and customs and to convert
an illiterate population, but, together with the concept of *sobornost*, it
encouraged a rather routine and passive practice of the new religion
rather than engaging individuals directly in the process and stimulating personal commitments of faith and belief. Later, in Western Christianity, particularly after the Protestant Reformation, individualism in
religion (and later in other matters) gained ground while collectivism
continued to predominate in Russian Orthodox Christianity.

Finally, Byzantine Christianity was quite otherworldly, stressing asceticism, the importance of a communal monastic life, and the rewards
in the hereafter. Again, this tendency was strengthened in its trans-
plantation to Russia, and later it militated against the Russian Orthodox Church's taking an active role in everyday life as a force for social
betterment.

For a long time Christianity was only thinly superimposed on the
basic animistic beliefs and customs of the Slavic population of the Kievan state. Many old pagan rites and practices were continued or even
adapted to the new religion. As a result, some historians say, many Russians never fully understood the new faith and accepted it only super-
ficially. Only the educated few in the upper classes of society were fully
committed to Christianity.

At the same time there is no doubt the introduction of Christianity
raised the general level of culture, learning, and artistic expression in
Kievan Rus'. Well-educated monks and priests entered Russia, monasteries were established, churches were built, and artisans were trained.
By the middle of the eleventh century, Kievan civilization, though
modeled on Byzantine achievements in most fields, had reached a height
of cultural and artistic splendor that was not to be equaled in Russia

again until some five hundred years later. As the most renowned Soviet historian of Kiev, B. D. Grekov, has recounted:

> There is no need to list all the treasures of Kiev, Novgorod, Chernigov, Polotsk, Galich and other ancient cities of Rus'. Even without such a recital one is struck not only by the high level of Russian culture of the 10th–11th centuries, but also by its wide diffusion over the tremendous expanses of Eastern Europe.[1]

The introduction of a written language, Old Church Slavonic, meant that books were produced and circulated (usually copied or composed by monks). To be sure, only a tiny fraction of the population was literate, but this upper crust was quite sophisticated, aware of intellectual currents and developments in both Byzantium and Europe. In addition, Byzantine masters taught Russians the art of painting icons and introduced church music to them. A magnificent cathedral in Byzantine style, St. Sophia, named after the main church in Constantinople, was built in Kiev and decorated by Russian craftsmen. Russian artisans, who had developed great skill in working with indigenous materials, particularly wood, modified Byzantine forms into a distinctive and charming style. Unfortunately, because almost all the buildings they erected were made of wood and were subsequently destroyed in the frequent fires that plagued early Russian towns, we have descriptions or examples of only a few of their striking architectural achievements.

Education, scholarship, art, architecture, and music were all predominantly religious in motivation and theme. Naturally all these aspects of cultural life followed Byzantine precepts and models. But Russian artists soon introduced local themes and techniques and in icon painting they before long surpassed their Byzantine masters, creating some of the most moving and beautiful religious painting in the world (see Figure 4, page 49).

Nonreligious, primarily folk, art also developed, particularly in songs and stories. The first secular piece of literature, *The Tale of the Host of Igor,* is a stirring pagan saga of the adventures of a Kievan prince and his followers in fighting an array of enemies in order to defend their homeland. In the words of the *Tale:*

> Igor leads his warriors to the Don.
> The birds in oak trees portend his misfortunes
> The wolves howl of the menace in the ravines
> The eagles with their clatter summon beasts to a bony feast
>
> The foxes yelp at the crimson shield.
> O Russian land! You are so far behind the mountains. . . .

---

[1] B. D. Grekov, *The Culture of Kiev Rus* (Moscow: 1947), p. 9.

With their shields the Russians have divided the great field
Seeking honor for themselves and glory for their prince.[2]

Considered as a whole, Russian culture and civilization in the 1000s
and 1100s was probably at a higher level than Western European civilization at the same time. The Russians were definitely not a backward
"strange" race in the panoply of world peoples. Moreover, the upper
classes in Kievan society interacted with the elite of central and western
Europe. In addition to the contacts and travels between Russian and
European merchants, the princely families in Kiev intermarried with
noble and royal families in the Germanies and in Scandinavia.

Power and Politics in Kievan Russia

The impact of Byzantine civilization was felt not only in religion
and culture but also in thought, values, and attitudes. These influences
were made tangible in Kievan law codes of the eleventh and twelfth
centuries and in the political order. Yet in politics Byzantine ideas could
never quite overcome more traditional concepts and institutions and
therefore had their greatest impact quite a bit later, in the Muscovite
period of the tsars.

For example, in Byzantium the state was a clearly defined geographic area over all of which the emperor and his administration exercised control. But the concept of state and sovereignty in the Kievan
system was much less clear. Authority derived originally from the person of the prince, and his jurisdiction ran along trade routes, over scattered areas that paid him tribute, and in certain fortified centers, rather
than over a specific contiguous territory.

Moreover, although eventually it was recognized that the prince at
Kiev was the senior prince and therefore head of the state, princes in
other towns had rights of their own. They also felt free to contest for
the headship with the Kievan prince. Certain towns, particularly the
important northern trading and administrative center of Novgorod, also
seem to have had autonomous rights. In general, therefore, the Kievan
state was much looser and more disjointed than our modern state. The
princes at Kiev possessed little centralized authority or direct administrative and political control but rather led a fluid federation of towns
and tribes.

In the middle of the Kievan period, Iaroslav (1019–54), one of the
ablest Kievan princes, tried to set up a system of rotation of rulership
under which younger brothers to the prince of Kiev held power in towns

[2] From *Medieval Russia: A Source Book, 900–1700* (p. 74) by Basil Dmytryshyn.
Copyright © 1967 by Holt, Rinehart and Winston Inc. Reprinted by permission of CBS
College Publishing.

designated according to their seniority. When the ruler at Kiev died, everyone moved up one notch. This system was designed to avert the bitter and bloody struggles for succession that had plagued the politics of the Kievan state over the preceding hundred years. But such a complicated system, requiring great self-restraint by all the players, soon broke down in practice, and the succession to the princedom at Kiev continued to be settled on most occasions by force and strife.

This meant that the Kievan prince had to spend a good part of his reign fighting off rival claimants to the throne, who were usually jealous brothers or nephews. In addition, he had to defend the state from external enemies on all sides and, particularly, to protect the trade routes to Byzantium from nomadic attacks originating in the southeast. A further major military obligation was to keep sufficient pressure on the Byzantine emperors so that they would grant political concessions and favorable commercial privileges to the prince, his warriors, and merchants. As if all this were not enough, the prince was frequently called upon to wage military campaigns against recalcitrant subjects or neighboring tribes who refused to pay taxes or deliver tribute.

It is little wonder that a good part of a prince's life was spent in warfare. One of Kiev's most successful military leaders, Sviatoslav, who ruled from 962 to 972, is described in the *Chronicle* as follows:

> Stepping light as a leopard, he undertook many campaigns. Upon his expeditions he carried with him neither wagons nor kettles, and boiled no meat, but cut off small strips of horseflesh, game, or beef, and ate it after roasting it on the coals. Nor did he have a tent, but he spread out a horse-blanket under him, and set his saddle under his head; and all his retinue did likewise.[3]

When the princes were at home, they faced other obstacles to their rule. Two political-administrative institutions existed in Kievan Russia to represent the interests of the upper classes: the boyars' *duma* and the *veche*. The *duma* was a body of the highest-ranking nobles advisory to the prince. How much power it had and how regularly he consulted it are not clear. Before major military campaigns and during succession struggles over title to the head principality at Kiev it behooved the prince to get as much support from the boyars as possible, and he probably used the *duma* for that purpose.

The *veche,* a town council dominated by merchants, had considerable influence, particularly in towns in the north of Russia, where it had a stronger and longer tradition. In a few places, such as Novgorod, the *veche* on occasion exercised full political authority and administered the town and surrounding territory. But in other towns it had only a minor advisory role.

[3] Samuel H. Cross and Olgerd P. Sherbowitz-Wetzer, trans. and eds., *The Russian Primary Chronicle, Laurentian Text* (Cambridge: 1953), 84.

As with any series of rulers, the princes of Kiev varied greatly in ability, persistence, and success. The first few were Vikings, though quite Slavicized; all the rest for over two hundred years were Slavs. In our effort to understand the complex nature of politics in Kievan times, three outstanding princes can serve as examples of the challenges Russia's early rulers faced and the victories they won.

Although the legendary credit goes to Riurik, Prince Oleg was the actual founder of the Kievan state. A Varangian from Novgorod, he saw the advantages of linking as many towns as possible along the main trade route from the Baltic Sea to the Black Sea, and he united Novgorod and Kiev by force. Moving his base to Kiev around A.D. 880, he established the primacy of that city, "the mother of Rus towns," which lasted until 1132. In 907, Oleg attacked Constantinople. As a result of his victories, he was able to negotiate an effective commercial treaty with Byzantium in 911. Oleg also merged his Viking and Slavic warriors into a single upper class and established greater control over the Slavic tribes along both sides of the Dnieper River.

Almost a hundred years after Oleg had established and begun to consolidate the state, Vladimir, who ruled from about A.D. 980 to 1015, made remarkable strides in extending its authority east, south, and west and in raising the level of culture and sophistication in Kievan society. As we saw earlier, he adopted Christianity as the official religion and at the same time encouraged and supported the arts and education.

Yet Vladimir's sons fought over the succession, and civil war weakened the state for two decades. Strong leadership was restored under Iaroslav the Wise, who reigned from 1036 to 1054. He extended Kievan authority over new areas and was able to put an end for some time to the constant harassing attacks of the Pechenegs in the east. He also supervised compilation of the first Russian law code and encouraged the building of St. Sophia and other important churches. But within a few decades of his death, interprincely fighting was again widespread, and except for a brief resurgence in the first quarter of the twelfth century Kievan power and cohesion declined steadily in the next one hundred and fifty years.

The Fall and Significance of Kievan Russia

Various reasons have been advanced for the decline of Kiev. As is so often true in explaining major events in history, not one cause but many produced the collapse of the Kievan state. Perhaps the most important was its political weakness. Not effectively centralized nor cohesive in the best of times, by the late 1100s under weaker princes Kievan Russia increasingly disintegrated into rural princedoms and towns that spent more time fighting each other than their common external ene-

mies. As we saw earlier, no institutionalized central government existed, and the struggle to become grand prince became increasingly
divisive. For example, between 1139 and 1169 the throne changed hands
seventeen times. The loose federation that was the Kievan state gradually fractured into its component parts.

A second major factor in the decline of Kiev was its loss of economic strength. The goods it traded became less valuable, and at about
the same time Europeans established new trade routes to the Near East
and Asia, while the position of the Byzantine Empire weakened. As a
result, the trade routes across Russia became less important, and the
Kievan economy declined.

However important political, economic, and commercial reasons for
Kiev's demise were, in the end external factors played the decisive role.
Throughout its history Kiev had struggled, with limited resources, against
foreign foes, particularly various nomads from Asia who constantly attacked the state from the southeast. In the 1100s this effort became increasingly a losing fight, and Kievan Russia was much weakened by recurring battles against the Cumans (also called Polovtsy). These latest
nomadic invaders succeeded on various occasions in cutting the trade
route to the Black Sea and caused much damage, as well as loss of life.
Moreover, in 1169 Andrei Bogoliubskii, prince of Vladimir-Suzdal, an
area in the northeast, sacked Kiev and then chose to reign as grand
prince at Vladimir instead of Kiev. In the thirteenth century the Mongols arrived to administer the coup de grace to the Kievan state.

Although Kievan Russia was overrun and conquered, Kievan civilization was not. The state disappeared but left a powerful legacy on
which much of subsequent Russian civilization was built. Kiev had succeeded in drawing together and blending four elements: the ancient indigenous population, the imprint of successive steppe empires, the influence of the Varangians/Vikings, and the powerful impact of
Byzantium.

A major bequest of Kiev was the tradition of Slavic political unity
and glory. Even today Russians look back on Kiev as a "golden age," an
era of power and accomplishment when Russia occupied a significant
place among the world's societies. It was indeed a civilization of which
to be proud. It was multinational yet tolerant for its time. It was stratified but not unduly oppressive. It produced beautiful art and architecture but was not vainglorious.

The most significant concrete gift Kiev bestowed on subsequent
generations was Orthodox Christianity. As we shall see, the Orthodox
Church and faith played a quite different role in Russia than Christianity did in Western history, but its importance in the development of
Russian society cannot be denied. Even today, after seven decades in
which the Soviet government has attempted to eliminate religion, it is

estimated that there are as many as forty million Christians in the Soviet Union.

Because the Christianity of Kievan Russia came from Byzantium, it developed in Russia quite differently from Latin Christianity in the West. At the same time Byzantine culture, learning, law, and the arts accompanied it. Consequently, Russian civilization developed from the very beginning as a compound of indigenous Slavic values and forms and Byzantine borrowings. The result was quite distinct from Western European civilization.

At the same time it would be a dreadful mistake for a reader to conclude at this point, "Ah, the poor Russians, so that is where they began to go astray, to diverge from the good things that were about to happen in the West. They fell under the influence of Byzantium, with its rather mystical obscurantist religion and its rigid, formal culture." The rejoinder of course is that, indeed, the Russians began to go their own way, to build their own civilization, borrowing to some degree from the Byzantine experience, but what was being formed was not worse or better, only different. A foundation had been laid, but it was only a beginning. Much more, and much of it traumatic, was to happen to the Russians as they struggled to build their unique civilization and future.

FURTHER READING

GEOGRAPHY AND PEOPLES

Chew, Allen. *An Atlas of Russian History*. New Haven, Conn.: 1970.
Hooson, David. *The Soviet Union: People and Regions*. London: 1966.
Lydolph, P. E. *Geography of the USSR*. New York: 1964.

ANCIENT AND KIEVAN RUSSIA

Boba, I. *Nomads, Northmen and Slavs*. Wiesbaden and The Hague: 1967.
Cross, Samuel H., ed. *The Russian Primary Chronicle*. Cambridge, Mass.: 1953.
Grekov, B. *Kiev Rus*. Moscow: 1959.
Mongait, A. L. *Archeology in the USSR*. London: 1961.
Noonan, Thomas. "Kievan Russia." In *Modern Encyclopedia of Russia and the Soviet Union*, Vol. 16, pp. 230–245. Gulf Breeze, Fla.: 1980.
Philipp, Werner. "Russia's Position in Medieval Europe." In Lyman Letgers, ed., *Russia: Essays in History and Literature*. Leiden: 1972.
Riasanovsky, Nicholas. "The Norman Theory of the Origin of the Russian State." In Sidney Harcave, ed., *Readings in Russian History* (Vol. 1). New York: 1962.
Rybakov, B. *Early Centuries of Russian History*. Moscow: 1965.
Sawyer, P. H. *Kings and Vikings*. London and New York: 1982.
———. *The Age of the Vikings*. London: 1962.
Vernadsky, Geroge. *The Origins of Russia*. Oxford: 1959.
———. *Kievan Russia*. New Haven, Conn.: 1948.
Wren, M. *Ancient Russia*. London: 1965.

2

Russia Divided and Conquered, 1054–1462

In the twelfth century internal dissension gravely weakened Kievan civilization. In the thirteenth century Mongol conquest delivered a crushing blow to it. To be sure, some features of the old society persisted and were incorporated into the new Muscovite state that arose in the fourteenth century. But the new civilization was different in a number of ways, many of which resulted from the devastating psychological, economic, and political effects of Mongol invasion and domination.

It is difficult for Americans to comprehend the long-term impact of internal strife and foreign conquest on a society and people. In the past one hundred years we have been spared both. The Civil War between the North and the South was divisive and disruptive, yet four generations later those wounds have largely healed. Imagine, however, what the effect would have been had a foreign power, say, Great Britain or Mexico, invaded and occupied most of the United States shortly after the Civil War and were still ruling the country today. That is what happened to the Russians 750 years ago.

For Russians living in the thirteenth and fourteenth centuries the overriding need was for security. This was at the very time when Europeans, as they emerged from the Middle Ages, were both enjoying increased protection from feudal in-fighting and external attack and benefiting from rising economic well-being provided by improved agriculture and reviving trade. Yet Russia was an occupied country. Trade languished, and agriculture remained primitive. Consequently, the Russians' efforts to protect themselves and to create a stable society were hampered by limited resources. Moreover, the Russians' enemies maintained continuing pressure on the newly forming state. Russian civilization struggled to rise from the ashes of the Mongol conquest in conditions that were far from ideal.

Russia Divided

Despite brief periods of strong, unifying rule by able princes the Kievan state from A.D. 1054 to the Mongol invasion in A.D. 1237 was characterized primarily by internal dissension and political weakness. As we saw in Chapter 1, this was partly because the Kievan state system was inherently unstable, based as it was on rotating authority among princely families and lacking the concept and practice of a homogeneous, centralized territorial government. It was also due to the relentless pressure of foreign enemies, particularly the nomadic tribes to the southeast.

As the unity of Kiev disintegrated, the average citizen reacted in two ways: many fled from the open exposed plains of southern Russia to the thick protecting forests of the north. Although we have no precise numbers, we know that a considerable population shift took place in the eleventh though thirteenth centuries, from southern Russia to the northeast in particular. Mixing with the people already there, the immigrants formed a new strand of the Russian line, called Great Russians.

Second, people throughout Russia sought security from the depredations of outside foes and neighboring princes by placing themselves under the protection of a local boyar, monastery, or prince. This marked a significant step toward development of a social system characterized by privileges for the upper classes and obligations for the lower classes. But a considerable period of transition occurred before Russian serfdom and the Russian service state emerged.

In political terms, when the grand prince at Kiev could no longer command tribute and allegiance from all the towns and tribes over whom Iaroslav the Wise had ruled, the system began to break up into separate principalities and city-states. At the height of this process of disintegration European Russia was divided into dozens of such small units, many of which fought each other. Although only a rough generalization, one can say that different forms of government tended to predominate in three main areas of Russia:

- The southwest (Volynia and Galicia): aristocratic (rule by boyars)
- The northwest (Pskov and Novgorod): democratic/oligarchic (rule by the *veche*)
- The northeast (Suzdal and Moscow): monarchic (rule by a prince)

There were exceptions to this pattern, and in many principalities all three institutions—boyars' duma, *veche*, and prince—coexisted although one was dominant. That Russians developed and practiced each of these systems belies the misleading aphorism that harsh autocratic rule is natural to, and needed by, the Russian people.

To look at each of these areas in turn, the southwest encompassed the territory stretching west and northwest of Kiev to the northern slopes of the Carpathian Mountains and including present-day Belorussia. It contained two important principalities, Volynia and Galicia, and was probably the richest area agriculturally. It had excellent prospects of emerging as the center of a revived Russian state, the logical successor to Kiev, with close ties to Europe. Strategically, the principalities of Volynia and Galicia had certain advantages. They were far enough away from the eastern borders of Russia to be spared the incursions of the Cumans. They were next door to Poland and Hungary, two strong European states of the time, with which Volynia and Galicia had lively commercial and cultural intercourse.

On the other hand, their location created certain disadvantages for these southwestern states. Their trading partners, Hungary and Poland (and later Lithuania), were larger and more powerful and soon began to covet the resources of neighboring Volynia and Galicia. Moreover, Hungarians, Poles, and Lithuanians were all Latin Catholics and looked upon the Orthodox Russians to their east as ripe for reconversion into the fold of true Christianity. Finally, although these small states were on the western border of European Russia, they were, alas, not far enough west to escape the Mongols, who overran and briefly occupied the region in the 1240s.

Another liability to the potential of the southwest's forming the nucleus of a restored Russia was that state power in Volynia and Galicia was quite unstable. Wealthy boyar landholders contended with aspiring princes for political control, and it was the only area of Russia down to the 1500s in which a boyar had the audacity to claim a princely throne. During the period of Mongol overlordship boyar power and prestige continued to grow, and it seems likely that Volynia and Galicia would have ultimately had a full-fledged system of aristocratic rule, had the two territories not been absorbed by Lithuania and Poland, respectively, in the 1300s.

A second area that could have shaped and led a resurrected Russian state was the northwest. As we saw in the first chapter, this was probably where the first towns and organized government were established, even before the founding of Kiev. Its largest town, calling itself Lord Novgorod the Great, had a population of over thirty thousand and ranked in splendor and culture with the major towns of Europe. Any visit to the Soviet Union is incomplete without a side trip from Leningrad to Novgorod, where one can stand amid the beautifully re stored ancient churches and, eyes closed, easily imagine the bustle, excitement, and relative magnificence of the squares and streets of the twelfth-century city.

Novogord, a city-state, controlled a considerable hinterland from which it drew forest and agricultural products. It traded extensively with Scandinavia and the north German towns of the Baltic Sea, exchanging Russian furs, wax, honey, and timber for grains, woolens, wine, metal, and sweets. It also served as a major storage and transshipment point for trade to south Russia down both the Volga and Dnieper rivers. At the same time, small manufacturing and craft work were almost as important to Novgorod as commerce. The town was well known for talented artisans who created not only practical items like tools and corduroy (log-paved) streets but intricate wooden decorations and tall, elegant churches in a distinctive, northern style.

The people of Novgorod were cultured, energetic, and decidedly independent-minded. Despite a number of threats, the Novgorodians preserved their independence for six hundred years, a remarkable record in those times. As we shall see in Chapter 3, they finally succumbed to the rising state of Moscow after A.D. 1470.

It is of course an oversimplification to call Novgorod democratic, just as it is misleading to label ancient Greece a democracy (or the United States in 1776, for that matter). Like those other societies, Novgorod did not permit women, slaves, and certain other classes in society to vote. But most freemen could, so it was a republic in form and provided a considerable degree of representative government. Voters elected both an all-city government and district administrations in five boroughs. For the first few hundred years there was a prince, though with strictly limited powers. In 1136 the *veche* began to elect the prince, who "reigned but did not govern." After the 1290s the post of prince was abolished altogether.

There was also a complex and quite enlightened judicial system as well as an autonomous church, whose archbishop was elected by the townspeople (though confirmed by the highest official of the Orthodox Church in Russia, the metropolitan of Kiev).

The *veche*, a town meeting of all freemen, was summoned by the ringing of a special bell. In the 1470s, when Moscow conquered Novgorod, the bell was carried back to Moscow as a symbol of Novgorod's loss of freedom. In the beginning the *veche*, besides electing officials, decided major issues of policy. Later an elected council, or executive committee, acted in its stead on most matters. Also the wealth, education, and influence of the leading merchants and landowners meant that increasingly they controlled the government and affairs of Novgorod. It became more an oligarchy than a democracy.

As in most medieval towns disease, famine, and fire regularly ravaged Novgorod. Moreover, the *veche* was supposed to act unanimously, and when there were strongly opposing viewpoints, quarreling in the *veche* could turn into fisticuffs and brawls. Finally, as the gap between the boyars (upper-class merchants and landowners) and the rest of the population widened, social strife would occasionally erupt, as *The Chronicle of Novgorod* for A.D. 1418 makes clear:

> And again they [the common people] became enraged like drunkards, against another boyar, Ivan Yevlich . . . and on his account pillaged a great many boyars' houses, as well as the monastery of St. Nikola in the Field,

crying out: "Here is the treasure house of the Boyars." And again the same morning they plundered many houses in the Lyudgoshcha Street, calling out: "They are our enemies. . . ." And they began to ring throughout the whole town, and armed men began to pour out from both sides as for war, fully armed, to the great bridge. And there was loss of life, too. Some fell by arrows, others by arms . . . and a dread fell on the people on both sides.[1]

At its height Novgorod controlled a good part of northern Russia, including the satellite town of Pskov, as well as colonized territories to the northeast, along the shores of the Arctic Ocean. Off and on it successfully battled enemies to the west, including Sweden, Teutonic Knights who occupied the area along the eastern shore of the Baltic Sea, and finally Lithuanians. But Novgorod was not basically a warrior state, and its decentralized system of government made it an unlikely candidate to lead the restoration and unification of the Russian lands.

The honor was to fall instead to the area of the northeast and, ultimately, to a small and obscure principality that was not even founded until the middle of the twelfth century: Moscow. Although the northeast contained old and important cities, such as Suzdal and Rostov, it had fewer resources than either the southwest or Novgorod. The balance of power began to shift there, even before the Mongol invasions, for two reasons. First, it was a relatively secure area, entirely in the forest zone and fairly far removed from Russia's western and southeastern foes. Second, it developed a tradition of princely rule that permitted the beginnings of centralized authority and effective government.

Thus, when the tradition that the most powerful prince should be based at Kiev broke down, his seat was moved to Suzdal, then to a newer town in the northeast, Vladimir. Later, the metropolitan, the chief official of the Orthodox Church in Russia, also migrated from Kiev to the northeast. In this way the tradition of Russian unity was preserved in the states of that region, including eventually that of Moscow.

Moreover, as trade declined and land became a more important resource, the princes of the northeast, dependent primarily on agriculture, were better able to mobilize the limited wealth of the country and to establish viable state power. But before they could do so, they had to endure the sudden smashing intrusion of the Mongols.

The Mongol Scourge

In the woods, glades, and towns of northeastern Russia A.D. 1237 must have seemed like any other year. The seemingly endless winter

---

[1] Basil Dmytryshyn, ed., *Medieval Russia: A Source Book, 900–1700* (New York: 1967), 129.

Figure 3. *A painting of Mongol warriors like those who conquered Russia. (Courtesy of the Freer Gallery of Art, Smithsonian Institution, Washington)*

had at last suddenly erupted into green and luxuriant spring growth. The crops had been sown, tended, and harvested; winter pelts and hides were prepared for market; traders had come and gone; and quarrels among the region's princes had been no worse nor more harmful than customary. To be sure, people still passed about rumors of a new and ruthless band of nomads who had routed the Russian army fourteen years earlier southeast of Kiev, but neither hide nor hair of the intruders had been seen since (see Figure 3).

The autumn had been spent accumulating food and fuel for winter, repairing houses and town walls, and hunting and trapping. No one was prepared for what suddenly occurred in mid-December, as reported, no doubt with some exaggeration, in chronicles and other early sources:

> With irresistible vigor and astonishing speed, the Mongols made their way through the forests of Penza and Tambov, and appeared before the beautiful city of Riazan. For five days they discharged a ceaseless storm of shot from their ballistae [military catapults] and, having made a breach in the defenses, carried the city by assault on the 21st of December, 1237. The prince, with his mother, wife [and] sons, the boyars and the inhabitants, without regard to age or sex, were slaughtered . . . some were impaled, some shot at with arrows for sport, others were flayed or had nails or splinters of wood driven under their fingernails. Priests were roasted alive, and nuns and maidens ravished in the churches before their relatives. No eye remained open to weep for the dead.[2]

[2] Cited from a compilation by Sir Robert Kennaway Douglas in Frank Trippet, *The Emergence of Man: The First Horsemen* (New York: 1974), 139.

Who were these cruel and indomitable despoilers? Today we know much more about the Mongols than the bewildered and hapless citizens of Riazan in the thirteenth century, although the origins of the Mongols—where they first lived and who their cultural forebears were—remain obscure.[3] In any case, they emerge into history in the 1100s, clearly in the same mold as earlier nomadic horsemen, from the Scythians through the Huns, who attacked the main centers of civilization and who invaded Europe, trampling over the Slavs north of the Black Sea as they passed westward from inner Asia.

The Mongols, however, differed from their predecessors in two important respects. First, their impact was even more devastating, both materially in loss of life and physical destruction of towns, churches, and dwellings, and psychologically, in terrorizing their opponents and subjugating them. Second, the Mongols were extremely well organized and disciplined, characteristics that permitted them to establish the largest empire in history. At its height the realm of the Great Khan of the Mongols stretched five thousand miles from the China Sea to the Adriatic Sea in the Balkans and from the frozen wastes of Siberia in the north to the Persian Gulf in the south. The Mongols soon withdrew from Europe, and this huge empire, as a unit, did not last very long. Nevertheless, the Mongols conquered and ruled China and Russia, affected India and Islam, and threatened western Europe (see Map 3). Moreover, they did all this with a relative handful of warriors and administrators; several hundred thousand Mongols held sway over more than one hundred million people in Eurasia.

It is an astounding record and it was due largely to the inspired (or half-mad) genius of one man, Genghis (more accurately, Chingiz) Khan. He was born as Temuchin, around 1165, the son of a minor chieftan among some nomadic tribes living in present-day Mongolia. Reputedly a skilled horseman and archer by the age of eleven, Temuchin worked unceasingly as a young man to unite the quarreling Mongol tribes. Finally, in 1206 at a solemn conclave of tribal leaders, he was proclaimed "mighty ruler," or *Genghis Khan*. He apparently believed he had a divine mission to rule the world. After subduing neighboring regions, he conquered north China, almost all of central Asia, and part of Persia. After his death in 1227, his three sons and his grandson, Batu Khan, extended the empire by overrunning most of the Russian principalities, the Caucasus, southwest Asia, and the rest of China.

The dazzling military success of the Mongols depended on four qualities that characterized almost all their campaigns: surprise, mobility, organization, and discipline. Applied together, these traits permitted the Mongols to overrun armies that were often twice as large as their

[3] In Russia the Mongols were known as Tartars or Tatars, but *Tatar* is more accurately used to designate Turkic groups allied with the Mongols who subsequently settled in southeastern Russia and the Crimea.

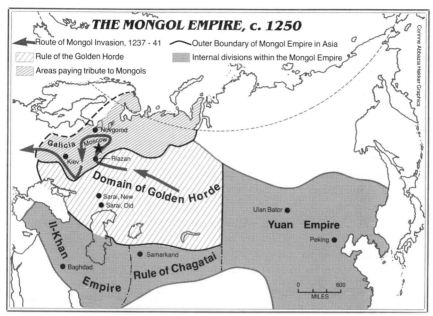

MAP 3

forces. The Mongol generals were carefully selected and trained, usually by the Great Khan himself. They relied on stealth and tactical and strategic surprise to catch the enemy unaware and to confuse him in battle. The army was organized on a decimal basis into units of ten, one hundred, one thousand, and ten thousand, and strict discipline was enforced from the lowliest soldier to the highest general reporting to the Great Khan.

The soldiers were outstanding horsemen and highly skilled with the bow and arrow. They wore cloth, leather, or metal armor and could travel incredible distances, as this account by Marco Polo, who worked at the court of Kublai Khan, shows:

> [The Mongol soldiers] are also more capable of hardships than other nations; for many a time, if need be, they will go for a month without any supply of food, living only on the milk of their mares and on such game as their bows may win them. Their horses also will subsist entirely on the grass of the plains, so that there is no need to carry store of barley or straw or oats. . . .[4]

Finally, the Mongols were skillful adapters. By the time they invaded Russia, they had learned from the Chinese how to use catapults and other siege weapons.

Between the attack on Riazan in 1237 and 1241–42, when their ar-

[4] In L. S. Stavrianos, ed., *The Epic of Man to 1500* (Englewood Cliffs, N.J.: 1970), 241.

mies pushed through central Europe to the Balkans, the Mongols over-ran and destroyed most of the Russian cities. Those in the northwest were spared direct conquest though Novgorod was forced to recognize the overlordship of the Mongols and to pay them tribute. A few towns that offered no resistance were bypassed, but the usual pattern was to raze a town's main buildings, to slaughter or enslave up to a quarter of the population, and to demand future subordination to Mongol rule. Princes and boyars who knuckled under were tolerated, as was contin-uation of the activities of the Orthodox Church. Even after the Mon-gols were converted to Islam in the latter part of the thirteenth cen-tury, they made no attempt to force the Russians to become Moslems.

After the death of Genghis Khan in 1227, his empire was divided among three surviving sons and a grandson. The western territories fell to the grandson, Batu Khan, who planned and executed the invasion of Russia and western Europe. In the spring of 1242 his forces unex-pectedly withdrew from the Balkans, and he returned to his headquar-ters at Old Sarai, a town north of the Caspian Sea along the Volga River. It is unclear whether this voluntary withdrawal occurred because Batu believed he was overextended militarily and politically; because he lost interest in Europe, not finding anything there to justify permanent Mongol occupation; or because he was anxious to be near the center of Mongol power in Asia so that he could participate in the selection of a successor to the Great Khan, his uncle Ugedei, who had died a few months before. Perhaps all of these considerations influenced him.

Whatever his reasons, one result of Batu Khan's pulling back was to consolidate his authority in a western Mongol state that soon became virtually independent and was known as the Khanate of the Golden Horde. (Apparently called *Golden* from the gold-leaf decorations that adorned the felt tents of Batu Khan and some of his leading lieuten-ants.) Batu Khan and his successors established for the Russian lands a system of indirect rule. Russian princes had to recognize the suzerainty of the Khan but were allowed to continue to administer their princi-palities. For example, Alexander Nevskii, a Russian national hero be-cause he defeated the German order of Teutonic Knights, was permit-ted to rule Novgorod and assume the title of grand prince as long as he acknowledged Mongol overlordship. The princes had to go regu-larly to the Khan's capital at Sarai to pledge submission and to receive a *yarlyk*, or charter of authority. The Golden Horde collected taxes among the Russian principalities, based on a crude census of the population that the Mongols carried out. Later, the Mongols permitted Russian ad-ministrators to assess the taxes for them.

Occasionally the Mongols also demanded Russian recruits for their armies, but such levies were relatively infrequent. The Mongol over-lords interfered little in the Russians' daily life and tolerated the Ortho-dox Church. If, however, any Russian town or group resisted their dominion, the Mongols, reacting swiftly, wreaked terrible vengeance on the rebels, leveling villages or towns and killing or enslaving most of the inhabitants.

The Mongols ruled the Russian lands in this fashion until the latter part of the fourteenth century, for about 140 years. Because of Mongol decline and growing Russian strength, as we shall see in the next chapter, after 1380 the Russians, although still obliged to recognize Mongol suzerainty, were increasingly independent, and Mongol overlordship was more symbolic than real.

The Impact of the Mongols

The Mongol invasion of Russia 750 years ago may seem far removed from our contemporary concerns about relations between the West and the Soviet Union. Yet I vividly recall the final argument of a young Soviet history professor several years ago, as we discussed enthusiastically but politely the course of Russian and Western development: "How can the United States fear us? The Russians saved Western civilization in the thirteenth century by taking the brunt of the Mongol onslaught. And look what it cost us!"

As we have seen, there is little truth to this assertion that somehow the Russians, despite being overrun, blunted the Mongol sweep westward toward the Atlantic Ocean, thereby sparing most of Europe the horrors of Mongol conquest and occupation. In fact, the forces of Batu Khan rather easily defeated a Polish-German army and then the Hungarians in 1241, and it is difficult to see who could have stopped them, had they wished to seize all of Europe. The fact that they did not do so and shortly withdrew to their headquarters in southeastern Russia had almost nothing to do with the Russians, who were prostrate and benumbed after the Mongol incursion. Thus, we can hardly accept the reasoning that Russia "saved" the West, although, as we shall see much later in this book, Soviet historians sometimes make an analogous argument concerning the Soviet Union's contribution to the defeat of Hitler and the Nazis in World War II.

That leaves unanswered, however, the more complex and intriguing question raised by the last part of the young Soviet scholar's comment: "And look what it cost us!" As with the role of the Vikings in the founding of the first Russian state, the impact of the Mongols on Russian civilization is a touchy issue. Some writers sympathetic to Russia are anxious to blame characteristics of Russian development since the thirteenth century that they disapprove of, such as autocratic government and serfdom, on the poor example and punishing harassment of the Mongols. Otherwise, they claim, Russia might have evolved democratically, as the West did.

Some Soviet scholars, although eager to discount Mongol influence on Russian society, are nevertheless happy, like the young historian quoted previously, to ascribe Russia's early struggles in Muscovite times and her relative backwardness compared to European civilization to the destructiveness of Mongol rule. Finally, some observers, basically critical of both the tsarist and Soviet systems, argue that the Mongols simply reinforced and brought out negative traits already inherent in Russian civilization before the thirteenth century: cruelty, repression, militarization, and expansionism.

As so often in historiographic debates, a middle ground seems the sensible answer. The Mongols certainly affected the course of Russian history. It would be difficult to dismiss their devastating invasion and two centuries of domination as counting for naught. But it would be equally foolish to decide that Mongol precepts, values, and institutions completely shaped the Muscovite state that emerged in the fourteenth century. In the first place, Mongol rule was indirect; the Mongols made no effort to mold Russia exactly in their image. In the second place, the new Russian society grew organically out of the traditions and three-hundred-year experience of the Kievan state and the conditions and challenges of its times. The Muscovite leaders tried not to imitate Mongol society, since the Mongols were thoroughly detested for what they had done to Russia.

To see how this middle-of-the-road conclusion about the impact of the Mongols works out in practice, we will examine some of the areas in which the Mongols did have some influence and then note those in which they had almost none. In my view, the most important effect of the Mongol conquest was economic. In three key ways, the Mongols' defeat and subjugation of Russia led to severe economic losses: first, and perhaps least important, was the immediate physical destruction: the leveling of towns and villages, the seizing of goods and crops, and the killing of large numbers of people. This was certainly a setback, but these were shortly recouped, and after Mongol dominion was established and acknowledged by most Russian princes and towns, subsequent physical devastation was not extensive.

Second, the Mongols seriously weakened the productive capacities of Russian society. In those preindustrial times most production was agricultural, but there was also a significant output of household goods, clothing, tools, implements, buildings, and other handicrafts by artisans, who, though limited primarily to using human power, displayed a high degree of skill and ingenuity. Most of these goods were consumed locally, in towns and villages, but some were traded regionally and a few internationally. In the Kievan period Russia, like other European and Asian societies, had developed this kind of production to a moderate level. Although the evidence is not clear as to whether artisan work in Russia had already begun to decline before the Mongols's arrival, as part of a general weakening of the Kievan economy, it is patent that the destruction associated with the Mongol invasion was a serious setback to this sector of Russian economic life. Not only were workshops and tools destroyed, but skilled artisans were killed or captured. It was not so easy for Russian society to bounce back from losses of that sort.

Finally, and most importantly, the Mongols sapped the Russian economy by appropriating most of the surplus in it, or, putting it colloquially, by skimming the cream off it. They did this at first by seizing any wealth they could lay their hands on and then, in the subsequent two centuries, by a fairly efficient system of taxation. This was a serious blow to the economy because early agricultural societies like that of Russia had, even in the best of times, little surplus. To have most of it taken away every year by a foreign occupier left the Russians struggling to survive.

Moreover, it is likely that the drain that Mongol taxation represented also thwarted Russia's potential for economic growth, although this is difficult to prove since we do not know what might have been and since economic data from that period are sparse. Even though recent studies suggest that Russian trade and economic activity under the Mongols were less curtailed than was once believed, the essential point is that without the Mongol conquest, the Russian economy might have gone through—and indeed been an easternmost part of—the same economic upsurge that western Europe experienced in the fourteenth century and that undergirded Europe's commercial revolution and subsequent worldwide expansion. An important part of this economic boom was the accumulation of capital (or surpluses) from the production and trading of agricultural and handicraft goods. This stimulated the growth of towns and a wide range of social and political changes in Western civilization. Yet Russians under the Mongols had limited opportunities to expand production, increase trade, and accumulate capital. Whatever surplus was built up, the Mongols took.

At this point you might well say, "but the conditions for this sort of economic expansion didn't exist in Russia anyway, regardless of the Mongols," and you would certainly be right to some degree. We must leave, however, to the next chapter a full consideration of why by the 1400s the Russian economy lagged behind that in the West. The point here is that it seems fair to say that Mongol exactions certainly didn't help.

A somewhat less complex but still quite tangled issue is the political effects of Mongol rule. Some have argued that the Russian princes borrowed Mongol political ideas, particularly the concept of the unlimited, unchallengeable authority of the Mongol Khan, and melded these into the theory and practice of absolute rule in the Muscovite state. Yet this view is not entirely convincing: the Russians had both indigenous and

Byzantine models of autocratic power exercized by a single ruler on which to draw. And these were what they referred to when they wanted to justify the autocracy.

It has also been suggested, even less convincingly, that from the Mongols the Russians took the goal of establishing a universal world empire, that the messianic mission of Slavic (or later Communist) world dominion had its misty origins in Genghis Khan's belief that he was divinely anointed to conquer the universe. But, again, it is much easier to trace the origins of such ideas, as we will do in a subsequent chapter, to the later concept of a special Christian mission for the Russian people and state, rather than to try to find Mongol roots for them.

In fact, in my view, the Russians took little directly from the Mongol political system. They borrowed in some administrative areas, for example, in fiscal matters, in setting up tax and postal systems, and possibly in military organization and technology, but otherwise adopted little else.

To be sure, many policies of the early Muscovite princes were a *reaction against* the Mongol overlordship, designed first to survive and then to overthrow the Mongol yoke. Consequently, in this indirect sense, as we shall see in Chapter 3, the Mongols greatly influenced Moscow's political actions and institutions—but directly, not very much.

An important way, related to politics, that the Mongols affected Russia was psychologically, although such an influence is almost impossible to substantiate. The notion that because of the Mongol yoke and the fact that Russian princes had to humble themselves at the court of Khan, Russians became inherently servile and craved strong rule is of course utter rubbish. But that Russians were shocked, humiliated, and grief-stricken by the suddenness, fury, and cruelty of the Mongol onslaught makes excellent sense. And this certainly made them extremely, if not obsessively, concerned with their own safety and with the security of their society and state. Russians had been battling various foes and invaders thoughout the previous four hundred years of their recorded history, but the Mongol conquest was an experience at an entirely different and traumatic level. It is no exaggeration to say that the excessive fear of the outside world that Russians have displayed over the last five hundred years—and today as well—can be traced in part to the nightmarish devastation of their society in 1237–41 at the hands of the Mongols.

Finally, it is certainly true that the Mongol conquest affected Russian development by making it more difficult for the Russian principalities to stay in close touch with Byzantium and with the states of central and western Europe. Recent research has shown that Russia was not as totally cut off and isolated as we once believed, that some trade and cultural contacts persisted throughout the period of the Mongol yoke. But obviously, personal, intellectual, and commercial ties were much attenuated by Mongol rule at the very time when Europe was beginning to change in a rapid and revolutionary way. Whether Russia, without the Mongols, would have been more fully aware of these changes and would perhaps have shared in them is naturally difficult to estimate. But, as we saw earlier, there were close links between Kiev and Europe in the preceding centuries, and it is logical to assume that the intellectual, social, and economic stirrings and excitement of the High Middle Ages and, particularly, of the Renaissance would have had some spillover and impact in Russia, had Russia not been first under the Mongols' thumb and then bending all her energies to overthrow the Mongol yoke.

It is important to note that the Mongol domination, although perhaps not causing division of the Russian lands, at least accelerated this process. Such a fragmentation would probably have occurred anyway, but the Mongol conquest strengthened the centrifugal tendencies already at work. In west Russia, where Mongol domination lasted only one hundred years, Volynia and Galicia were absorbed by Lithuania and Poland. This marked a point of no return in the branching of the Russian peoples into Belorussians in the east, Ukrainians in the southwest, and Great Russians in the northeast. At the same time the Mongol invasion undoubtedly facilitated the occupation of the lands along the Baltic Sea by Germanic knights and later by Swedes, so that these territories remained outside Russian control for several hundred years.

The list of areas in which the Mongols' rule had little or no effect is much shorter than that just discussed, but it encompasses important aspects of Russian society. First, as we have already noted, because the Mongols governed indirectly, through Russian princes, the daily life of the Russians who survived the first assault and whose princes did not defy the Mongols changed little. Their customs and patterns of living were not affected. Local social and political arrangements and institutions were basically not altered. The peasant commune, the village, the town, the principality, all remained pretty much as before.

Most important, the beliefs and culture of the Russian people persisted unchanged. This continuity permitted gradual reestablishment of a distinctly Russian society and emergence of an autonomous and finally independent and expanding Muscovite state. The Orthodox Church, which the Mongols left untouched, was able to preserve and transmit the essentials of earlier Russian civilization through the period of Mongol domination: religion, education, literature, and values all survived. In the hardest times the people were able to look to and rally around the Church. It carried forward the tradition of unity and uniqueness, on which a resurrected civilization could be built. Consoler and protector, the Church played an indispensable role in preventing the people from abandoning themselves to despair and in holding the society together. Later, with the prince, the Church was able to induce the people to support a new political system that eventually liberated them from the Mongol yoke (though, some would argue, enslaving them to indigenous institutions).

Thus, by retaining their religion and with it the essential attributes of their culture, which was undoubtedly at a higher level than that of the Mongols, the Russians, though set back economically and subjugated politically, were able to outlast their conquerors and rebuild their own state and civilization.

The Decline of Mongol Power

The Russians collapsed under the Mongol onslaught in part because they were divided and had no viable state system. In an ironic turnabout, the Russians were finally able to rid themselves of the Mongols because the latter became disunited and failed to build an effective state structure. The huge Eurasian empire put together by Genghis Khan and his successors split into several parts by the end of the 1200s. And in the 1300s and 1400s the Khanate of the Golden Horde, its westernmost unit and Russia's overlord, gradually weakened as a result of struggles for power among the descendants of Batu Khan and as internal dissension among its component tribes increased. The result was that although nominal Mongol suzerainty over Russia continued until 1480, Mongol power could be brought to bear only sporadically, and the Russian principalities gradually acquired autonomy.

One factor undermining Mongol authority was that although they had developed a discipline, organization, and system of rule that was well suited to expansion and conquest, they did not have a well-developed social or religious system that would enable them to hold together disparate peoples and societies. The Mongols constituted a thin overlay on existing cultures, and they did little to fuse their domains into an integrated civilization. Without linguistic, religious, or cultural unity the Khanate of the Golden Horde could not develop a strong political structure, and the centrifugal tendencies within it gradually began to pull it apart. In the 1400s separate khanates were established at Kazan and Astrakhan, and in the Crimea; this fragmentation made the task of the Russian princes striving for idependence a good deal easier.

Though divided, the Mongols, or Tatars as their descendants were now called, were still formidable foes. Mongol rule over Russia did not collapse of its own weight. The Muscovite princes and the Lithuanians worked hard to overturn it and succeeded only after a long struggle, as we shall see shortly.

Conclusion

In assessing the Mongol period of Russian history it is important neither to dismiss it nor to overplay it. Looked at from the broadest perspective, the Mongol era left three significant legacies for future Russian civilization. First, it heightened a deep sense of insecurity among Russians and within Russian society. The fear of being overrun and subjugated might eventually have faded from the consciousness of ordinary Russians and their leaders, except that subsequent events, as we shall see, kept those anxieties boiling. Thus, time and again in Russian history the people and state struggled, with limited resources, to ward off foreign intruders and to ensure their own safety and security.

Second, the Mongol invasion made unity and cohesiveness a high-priority value in Russian society and the Russian state. The Russians had had no chance against the Mongols, in part because they were divided, with each prince and his followers trying to fend for themselves. Out of that experience and the necessity of building a strong state to overthrow the Mongol yoke came an emphasis on the strength to be found in a common religion, Orthodoxy, and in a common allegiance to the grand prince (later the tsar). Without the Mongols a Russian state or empire might eventually have been formed out of the disparate pieces into which Kievan civilization had separated, but it is at least equally possible that the Russians would have remained divided and would have been absorbed by their powerful neighbors: Poles, Lithuanians, and others.

Finally, whatever specific effects the Mongols had in draining the Russian economy and terrorizing the population, a highly significant fundamental outcome of their rule was to spur the divergence of Russian civilization from the West. As we have discussed, Russia was bound to emerge as a unique society, but at least in Kievan times it was developing along a track parallel to that of western Europe and its Latin Christian civilization. But after the Mongols the distance between them had perceptibly widened, and Russian society evolved along more distinctly different lines than it had a few centuries earlier. As a result, serfdom emerged in Russia just as it was disappearing in western Europe. Trade and commercial capitalism flourished in Europe but languished in Russia. Europe bubbled over with intellectual ferment and social fluidity, particularly during the Renaissance. Thought in Russia remained quite traditional, even stagnant, as Russian society became increasingly rigid and stratified. To be sure, this is not to argue that, but for the Mongols, Russia would have turned out (happily in our view) much like the West. It is simply to underscore that the Mongol era made certain that Russian civilization would follow a markedly different course from that being traversed by Western civilization.

FURTHER READING

Allen, W. E. *The Ukraine: A History.* New York: 1940.

Presniakov, A. E. *The Formation of the Great Russian State.* New York: 1971.

Spuler, Bertold. *The Mongols in History.* New York: 1971.

Tikhomirov, M. N. *The Towns of Ancient Rus.* Moscow: 1959.

Treadgold, Donald. "Russia and the East." in Donald Treadgold, ed., *The Development of the USSR.* Seattle, Wash.: 1964.

Vernadsky, George. *The Mongols and Russia.* New Haven: 1953.

3

Moscow and "The Gathering of the Russian Lands," 1328–1533

A bird's-eye view of European Russia in the mid-1300s would have revealed four major centers of power and civilization: the Mongols in the southeast; the emerging Lithuanian or Lithuanian-Russian state in the west; Novgorod in the northwest; and two contending princely states in the northeast: Tver and Moscow. Any one of these had the potential to become the heir of the Kievan state and the unifier of Russia. Yet by the early 1500s Moscow, which 150 years earlier was the smallest and least promising contender, had emerged as the dominant power. In the words of the *Chronicle,* it "gathered the Russian lands" under its rule and established a strong centralized state. In five generations Moscow defeated all its nearby rivals, such as Tver and Novgorod; threw off the Mongol yoke forever; and seized much of the territory of the Lithuanian state, pushing it westward and into union with Poland.

This remarkable development, almost as sweeping and dramatic as the Mongol conquest itself, also had fateful consequences for the future course of Russian history. In the first place, Moscow's victory meant that the principle of obligatory service to the ruler, a policy that was key to Moscow's success, became a central tenet of Russian society from that time forward. Second, the triumph of Moscow ensured that of the three political concepts that coexisted in Kievan times—princely or autocratic rule, republican or democratic government, and boyar or aristocratic domination—the autocratic system would prevail in the new Russian state. Finally, the rise of Moscow meant that the reemergent Russian civilization would have a strong religious orientation, that of the Orthodox faith, and would be dominated by Great Russians. If, for example, the Lithuanian state had won instead, the resulting society would have been Latinized and subject to Roman Catholic influences and would have had an aristocratic system of governance. Thus, the triumph of Moscow set firmly in place characteristics of a Russian society that would last at least five hundred years, down to 1917.

The Odds Against Moscow

Certainly if you had been sent to Russia as an objective observer in the early 1300s and asked to predict which among the contending factions were destined to unify Russia, you would hardly have picked the tiny principality of Moscow. You might have concluded that other northeastern princedoms, like Suzdal-Vladimir, or Riazan, or Tver, had a better chance. Or, more likely, you would have decided that no one was a good bet to unite all these fractious territories and establish a single Russian state, and that the Russian lands were destined to remain fragmented and weak.

Moscow's disadvantages were several. It was, to begin with, an upstart. First mentioned in the *Primary Chronicle* for the year 1147, it was fortified in 1156 but remained a minor principality and was then ravaged by the Mongols in 1237. Even in the early 1300s as its significance began to grow, Moscow was still small and "second-class" compared to its long-established and more powerful rivals.

Second, the Moscow princes had to fight against the dominant principle of post-Kievan Russian society, the *appanage* system. It is significant that the Latin root of this word gives it a basic meaning of providing "bread" or "nourishment." In medieval Russia appanages were princely holdings of land, or territories, from which the prince and his family were expected to draw economic sustenance and over which the prince exercised considerable administrative, judicial, and political rights. In a sense it was the private property of the prince, but he controlled it for public purposes as well. It is important to note that *primogeniture,* or the inheritance of property by the eldest son, did not operate in Russia. Thus, a prince's appanage and title were divided among all his sons, a system that produced more and more princes with smaller and smaller holdings from generation to generation. Moreover, *boyars,* the aristocratic servitors of the princes, who held *votchinas* (vóht-cheena), that is, hereditary estates for which they owed no service, also divided their lands among their heirs. As a result, the overriding tendency in Russia of the thirteenth and fourteenth centuries was for territory to be cut up constantly into smaller and smaller parcels. The princes of Moscow had to reverse that trend, or at least make it work for them.

Third, the Muscovite rulers had to contend with the Kievan tradition of senior or grand princes and the rotation of people in that office. The princes of Moscow, as we shall see, first had to claim and solidify the title of grand prince and then make sure it was passed on only to their eldest sons.

Fourth, the founders of the Muscovite state had only extremely limited resources with which to defeat powerful rivals. Theirs was not a particularly rich town, they had little accumulated wealth, and they possessed no tangible assets to give them an advantage over others.

Consequently, they had to scrimp and save and then to mobilize and manage what little was available to them more efficiently than their competitors.

Finally, the Muscovites had a level of technology and culture that was certainly no better, and perhaps even lower, than their enemies. To be sure, they had the great spiritual advantage of the support of the Orthodox Church, as we shall shortly see, but otherwise they had no great tradition, no well-educated servitors or general population, no special skills or weapons, no knowledgeable and wealthy merchants or intellectuals, and no ideas or precepts, at least in the beginning, that gave them any edge over other contenders for power in Russia.

Moscow's Advantages

In spite of its liabilities, Moscow also had a number of assets that help explain its rapid ascent to dominion over the Russian lands. Some of these were circumstances that benefited the Moscow princes but over which they had no control. Others resulted from the conscious actions and policies of the princes. We will examine this latter set of advantages for Moscow first.

Security and Internal Order. From our smug modern perspective it is easy to say, "How could the Russians have acquiesced so abjectly in the building of a state and society that was based on centralized absolute rule and that soon instituted an oppressive social system, serfdom?" Yet if we imagine ourselves back in those times, we can at once see how attractive the policies of the growing Muscovite state were for the inhabitants of the Russian lands. For almost three hundred years the people had been buffeted by civil war, invasions, and finally conquest. Their towns and villages had been overrun and razed many times. Apart from the usual medieval disasters of famine, fire, and disease, their lives were in constant danger, and they were afraid and insecure most of the time.

It is not surprising, therefore, that when the Moscow princes said, "Here you will be safe," people flocked to the territory and willingly served the Muscovite rulers. Put in an oversimplified way, the Russian people were happy to trade freedom for protection. It is true, of course, that the Moscow princes could not absolutely guarantee security and tranquility; for example, the Mongols sacked the city in 1382. Moreover, many Muscovites were engaged in fighting external foes of the principality: rival princedoms, the Mongols, and the Lithuanians. Nevertheless, within the territories controlled by Moscow, a rapidly expanding area, peace and order reigned most of the time. In my view, which is based on that of V. O. Kliuchevsky, the leading Russian historian before the 1917 Revolution, the ability of the Moscow princes to provide security for the people was their greatest asset.

Organization and Management. Although sufficient information for making precise judgments obviously does not exist, it seems fair to conclude from what we do know that the Moscow princes were on the whole skillful administrators and proprietors of their domain, probably abler in this regard than most of their rivals. We have already noted that they did not have much to work with, but they made the most of their limited resources. They encouraged agriculture and helped colonize and develop new lands. They built up the city of Moscow and established other towns. They handled their military campaigns adroitly and succeeded in balancing their fiscal base with their military expenses. They were successful tax collectors and merchants, and they encouraged commerce among the population. It is appropriate that one of the first princes, who ruled from 1328 to 1340, was called Ivan Kalita, or John the Moneybags.

The Moscow princes were also generally successful in avoiding civil war within the princely family. Only once during the two centuries of Moscow's climb to preeminence was there protracted quarreling and strife over the succession to the throne. Finally, they managed to minimize the division of the Muscovite lands among heirs each time a prince died. Although younger sons at times inherited territories of Moscow, every effort was made to ensure that before long these reverted to the larger Moscow state of the senior son, or grand prince.

Diplomatic Skill. The princes of Moscow displayed remarkable ability in dealing with an array of foreign foes. Toward the Mongols they were submissive and helpful at those times, particularly in the fourteenth century, when the Mongols were still strong and could easily crush the fledgling Muscovite state. As a reward for their obedience and cooperation, the princes of Moscow were empowered to serve as tax agents for the Mongols and received Mongol assistance against the rival principality of Tver. Yet, when Mongol power declined in the latter half of the 1300s, the Moscow princes were quick to seize the opportunity to turn against their masters and to lead a virtual crusade against Mongol domination. In 1380 the Moscow prince Dmitrii Donskoi (so called because his victory over the Mongols took place on the Don River) became a hero to many Russians by opposing Mongol rule. Over time the Moscow state emerged as a symbol of resistance to Mongol oppression and marauding, thus giving it a further advantage in its struggle to unify the Russian lands.

The Moscow princes, usually cited for their skill in handling relations with the Mongols, were equally adept in dealing with the Lithuanians, the principality of Tver, and the leaders of Novgorod. On most occasions the Muscovites outmaneuvered their opponents and thus were able to expand their domain at less military cost than would otherwise have resulted.

Identification with the Orthodox Church. An important advantage for the Moscow princes was their close cooperation with the Orthodox religion and Church. In this way Moscow was able to draw directly on the tradition of Kiev and to act as the logical successor of a great and unified Russian state and civilization.

The Orthodox Church played an increasingly important role in the Russian territories at this time. It was, first of all, the primary symbol of unity and continuity for the Russian people. When all else was in confusion and upheaval, the Church served as a refuge for and consoler of the people. The rituals of the Church were familiar and comforting, and its doctrine promised eventual salvation. Moreover, it was a faith and a practice that all Russians, no matter in whose territory they lived, shared.

The Church was also important economically. By the 1500s one quarter of all the land in Russia belonged to the Church and its monasteries, much of it bequeathed by devout parishioners. The monasteries were often active in establishing outposts and havens in the forested wilderness and in colonizing new territory in the north. Many peasants worked on Church land, probably under slightly better conditions than peasants on private or princely estates.

Finally, the Church was the main center of artistic and cultural life throughout this period. Under the Mongol occupation the Church attempted to preserve scholarship and education, but only a few people were literate, and most of the boyars and even many of the clergy could not read or write. Moreover, the emphasis in Russian Orthodoxy was on the church services and rituals, rather than on intellectual training and rational inquiry. The other strand of Church activity, represented in the monasteries and in the work of the revered Russian monk, St. Sergius (1322–92), focused on asceticism and a denial of this world. Consequently, the Orthodox Church did not play the important scholarly, educational, and intellectual role that the Roman Catholic Church did in western Europe during this same period. Nevertheless, it remained the center of the learning and culture that persisted under Mongol rule.

Almost all the written literature of the time was religious: chronicles of events, lives of saints, sermons. It was quite stylized and traditional, and there were few secular writings to match the lyricism and vigor of the earlier *Tale of the Host of Igor*.

The glory of medieval Russian culture was in religious art and architecture. As we saw in Chapter 1, the Kievan Russians had learned icon painting from Byzantium but had already begun to develop it in their own style. Because icons are not familiar to most Westerners (icons were banned in the Latin Church), their importance and beauty are sometimes not fully appreciated. In viewing and understanding an icon, it is important to remember that each icon served two crucial purposes. It was designed both to educate and to inspire the illiterate and bowed-down worshipper who gazed upon it (originally only in churches, later in every Russian home). Thus, it had to be clear and articulate on the one hand, conveying a simple but powerful message about the Bible or the life of Christ or the lives of saints. Yet on the other it had to dazzle and uplift so as to provide an important spiritual experience for the humble churchgoer.

In the 1300s Russian icon painters began to elevate their work to a plane considerably beyond anything that Byzantine masters had achieved, and in the icons of Andrei Rublev, who died in 1430, this art form reached its apogee. Rublev's masterpiece, the *Old Testament Holy Trinity* (see Figure 4), is one of the world's great paintings, combining perfect composition and harmony with warm feeling and exquisite grace. Its rich and soft colors are an important part of the painting, so a black-and-white reproduction unfortunately cannot do it full justice.

A final, significant contribution of the Church to medieval Russian life was in architecture. Some of the finest churches were built in this period. Many of them, particularly the wooden churches in the north Russian style, have not survived, but those that have impress the observer with their clean, utilitarian but graceful lines and with their superb decorations and cupolas. The major stone churches in Moscow, although built under the supervision of imported Italian architects, remain today as complex, impressive monuments to the Russians' creativity in fusing the Byzantine style with indigenous expression. No trip to the Soviet Union makes sense unless you can spend at least a day and a half enjoying at a leisurely pace the four glorious cathedrals and the palace of the Moscow Kremlin (see Figure 5).

As this quick overview has indicated, the Church occupied a central position in medieval Russian civilization. The Moscow princes must have recognized this, for from the beginning they associated themselves closely with the Church and worked with the Orthodox hierarchy continuously in the monumental task of defending and unifying the Russian lands. The political benefits were enormous since the Moscow princes could claim not only the mantle of Kiev and the most glorious Russian traditions but also the blessing of the Church leaders and through them of God Himself. As we shall see shortly, there were also some strains in relations between the princes and the Church, but overall Moscow's identification with Orthodoxy helped it to gain power and set the basic tone of Russian civilization for generations to come.

Other advantages that Moscow enjoyed as it grew and expanded

Figure 4.   *The beautiful* Holy Trinity *icon by Rublev, painted in the early fifteenth century. (Courtesy of Sovfoto/Eastfoto)*

were more fortuitous, having relatively little relation to the policies of the princes.

Moscow's Location. One does not have to accept geographical determinism in history to conclude that Moscow happened to be extremely well situated. The city grew up in the middle of northeastern Russia, almost equidistant in every direction from the borders of the traditional Russian "lands." This site served it well in two ways: the city was strategically placed so it could move easily outward in absorbing the other Russian principalities, yet it was far enough away from its external enemies, such as the Mongols and the Lithuanians, that they could not easily attack Moscow.

Moscow's Commerce. As a corollary to its location, Moscow developed as an important trading center. Two main commercial routes

Figure 5. *Interior of the Church of the Assumption in the Moscow Kremlin, showing the icons painted on the pillars and before the altar.*

crossed in Moscow, one from the northwest to the southeast, that is, from Novgorod to the Black and Caspian Seas via the Don and Volga rivers; and the other from the south up the Dnieper River to the cities northeast of Moscow, such as Rostov and Suzdal. Situated on the Moskva (Moscow) River, the city's merchants had easy access by tributaries to the three main rivers of European Russia: the Dnieper, the Volga, and the Don. Although Soviet historians have stressed the agricultural basis of Moscow's economy, and although the importance of trade had certainly declined since Kievan times, recent evidence suggests that commerce was well developed in Moscow and contributed notably to its success.

Luck. One of the fascinations of history is that time and again the historian comes across a significant incident or factor that can only be ascribed to accident or chance. In this case the princes of Moscow were just plain lucky. They lived much longer than most of their contemporaries and consequently had long reigns. For example, Ivan III (Ivan the Great) ruled for forty-three years from 1462 to 1505, providing remarkable stability and continuity for the state at a crucial period in its development. Between 1389 and 1584, almost two hundred years, the Muscovite state had only five rulers, an incredible record for its time.

This meant that the uncertainty, and often the civil war, that had customarily marked each succession in Kievan times recurred infrequently. Moreover, each prince, beginning with Dmitrii in 1359, ruled long enough to consolidate his position and the power of the state, as well as to carry out a set of consistent policies designed to expand the realm and to strengthen it. Had the throne been in contention every five or ten years, with new princes' struggling to assert their authority, the Muscovite state could hardly have grown and prevailed in the way that it did. Although several of the princes of Moscow took power in their teens, their long reigns are still remarkable in an era when the average life expectancy was thirty-plus years. They may have been hardy but they were also lucky.

The Unification of Russia, 1328–1533

To see concretely how the Muscovite princes overcame their liabilities and took advantage of their assets, we will survey briefly the most important events that marked the "gathering of the Russian lands." Moscow's rise was both rapid and dramatic, with surprisingly few setbacks along the way. In the first one hundred and fifty years, from the early fourteenth century to the middle of the fifteenth century, Moscow grew from a tiny principality smaller than the state of Rhode Island to a major state the size of Connecticut and Massachusetts combined.

Founded in the mid-1100s, Moscow was not at first a significant town in northeast Russia. Its larger neighbors, boasting of princes as colorfully named as George the Long-Arm and Dmitrii Big Eyes, were more powerful and politically influential. In the late 1200s and early 1300s the princes of tiny Moscow took a first step down the road of expansion by incorporating territory along the Moscow River into their principality. They also began what was to be a bitter, almost two-hundred-year-long struggle with the older and better known principality of Tver (today Kalinin) northwest of Moscow.

An important prize in this rivalry was the title of grand prince. Traditionally associated with Kiev, the office of grand prince had been transferred to the northeastern town of Vladimir in 1169, when Kiev was much weakened. In the early 1300s the princes of Moscow and Tver claimed it at various times, but finally around 1330 Ivan I (Ivan Kalita) of Moscow, who also ruled Vladimir, was recognized as grand prince, and the important title was associated with Moscow from then on.

A second significant event at the same time was the move to Moscow of the metropolitan, the highest official of the Orthodox Church in Russia. To some extent chance favored the Muscovites on this occasion. The seat of the metropolitan, originally in Kiev, had been transferred to the northeast in the twelfth century. In 1326 an extremely popular and talented metropolitan, Peter, died while visiting Moscow. He was later canonized, and Saint Peter's name became associated with Moscow. And in 1328 his successor decided to reside in the city. From that time on the metropolitans of the Orthodox Church worked closely with the grand princes of Moscow to oppose the infidel Mongols (converted to Islam in the preceding century) and the heretic Lithuanians (predominantly Roman Catholic after 1386), as well as to bring together the Russian principalities in a unified state (see Map 4).

The reign of Ivan I is important in one other way. An able ruler, he instituted policies that came to be associated with Moscow's success. Ivan made Moscow more secure, managed its resources effectively, and encouraged commerce. He acted as tax collector for the Mongols and minimized Moscow's share of what was paid them. Finally, he bought up territories adjacent to Moscow as one method of extending his domain.

The long reign of Dmitrii Donskoi from 1359 to 1389 was marked by continued expansion and consolidation and by Moscow's recurring struggles with the Lithuanians and the Mongols. From the fourteenth to the sixteenth century the Lithuanian state played an important role in Russian history, and a few words about it are needed. The Lithuanians are a Baltic people with an ancient and distinct language and culture. In medieval times they lived in the forests of northwest Russia and along the southeastern shores of the Baltic Sea. In response to pressure from crusading German knights who occupied much of the Baltic littoral and threatened northwest Russia in the 1200s, the Lithuanians organized their own state. In the 1300s the Lithuanian state expanded rapidly southeast from the Baltic, occupying Russian territories until it encompassed much of western Russia. At its farthest advance the Lithuanian state included such important Russian cities as Kiev, Chernigov, and Smolensk, as well as the territory of Volynia, and reached all the way to the Black Sea.

Because the Lithuanians were few in number, they fused with the local Russian nobility as they expanded. Hence some historians prefer to call their empire a Lithuanian-Russian state. The dominant language was a distinct form of Russian known today as Belorussian. This state could clearly claim to be an heir of Kiev and acted as a formidable rival to Moscow for control of the Russian lands.

In 1386 the Lithuanian ruler married a Polish princess and began to convert his people to Latin Christianity. As a result of this personal union with Poland, Catholic and Polish influences in Lithuania-Russia grew. The union also strengthened the state, and, though checked by Moscow in the east, Lithuania defeated the Germans in the famous Battle of Tannenberg in 1410 and soon extended its suzerainty southwestward toward the Balkans. In 1569 by the Union of Lublin Lithuania and Poland were formally joined. The resulting state was predominantly Polish and continued to contend with Moscow.

Although the most that Dmitrii Donskoi could accomplish against the Lithuanians was to check their expansion eastward into the heart of Russia, he did win an important and famous victory over the Mongols at the Battle of Kulikovo Field in 1380. The *Primary Chronicle* has left us a stirring, colorful, and somewhat exaggerated description of that encounter:

> There never was such a mighty Russian Army, for all forces combined numbered some 200,000. . . . A week later, on September 6, they reached the River Don. Then he [Dmitrii] received a letter from the Reverend Abbot Sergei urging him to fight the Tatars. Dmitrii, however, ordered his troops to put on their native garments while he himself waited for a long time, contemplating. . . . Early Saturday morning, September 8, he told his troops to cross the river and go to the meadow. At first there was a heavy fog but when it later disappeared everyone crossed the Don; there was a real multitude of troops as far as one could see. . . .
>
> At six o'clock in the morning the godless Tatars appeared in the field and faced the Christians . . . and when these two great forces met they covered an area thirteen versts [eight miles] long. And there was a great massacre and bitter warfare and great noise . . . and blood flowed like a heavy rain. . . . At nine o'clock God took mercy on the Christians; many saw an angel and saintly martyrs helping the Christians. . . . Shortly thereafter the godless fled and the Christians pursued them . . . to their camp where they took all of their wealth and their cattle, killing many and trampling others.[1]

This defeat was the beginning of the end for the Mongols, even though two years later they counterattacked and burned Moscow.

Dmitrii's successor, Vasilii I (1389–1425), built up the economic strength of his domain and expanded Moscow's holdings. When he died, a struggle for the throne broke out, and a period of political turmoil ensued. In the fighting the eldest son, Vasilii II (1425–62), was blinded. After finally establishing himself securely in power, he ruled successfully and in 1452 refused to pay any further tribute to the Mongols, although he left it to his son, Ivan III, formally to renounce Mongol suzerainty over Russia in 1480.

[1] From *Medieval Russia: A Source Book, 900–1700* (pp. 134–35) by Basil Dmytryshyn. Copyright © 1967 by Holt, Rinehart and Winston, Inc. Reprinted by permission of CBS College Publishing.

During the reign of Vasilii the Blind, the Russian Orthodox Church took an important step toward becoming an independent institution. With the Byzantine Empire gravely threatened by the Turks, the Greek Orthodox Church had reached a tentative reconciliation with the Roman Catholic Church in the political hope of ensuring European assistance against Turkish attacks. The majority of the clergy in Russia repudiated this agreement and in 1443 established a separate church administration. Moreover, in 1453 the Turks captured Constantinople, and the Russian Church was on its own in any case.

In the course of the long reigns of Ivan III (the Great) and Vasilii III from 1462 to 1533, the Muscovite state and system took nearly final form, and many of the basic institutions that characterized Russian civilization down to the 1700s were firmly established. It was also the period of the maximum expansion of Moscow: it grew from a still relatively small principality in northeastern Russia to a major European power stretching hundreds of miles in every direction from its capital (see Map 4). Ivan the Great (1462–1505) in particular brought to their fullest development the four basic methods used by his predecessors to "gather the Russian lands": inheritance, colonization of unoccupied areas in the north and east, purchase, and conquest.

The defeat by Ivan of the republic of Novgorod in the 1470s brought under Moscow's control Novgorod's vast holdings in the north, as well as its trade contacts through the Baltic with Europe and Scandinavia. Novgorod fell at last, after over one hundred years' opposition to Moscow, because it was a badly divided society. The elite looked to Lithuania for help against Muscovite encroachments, but the majority of the people, resenting the boyars and merchants anyway, objected to allying with Catholics and fought Ivan's forces only halfheartedly. The Novgorodians were defeated first in 1471 and then in 1478, after further resistance, were completely humiliated. The *veche* bell, Novgorod's symbol of freedom, was seized and taken to Moscow, and its lands were annexed to the Muscovite state. In 1485 a similar fate befell Moscow's old competitor, Tver. Thus, Ivan the Great both absorbed Moscow's nearest rivals and formally liberated Russia from the Mongol yoke. Only Lithuania-Russia remained to challenge Moscow for leadership of the lands of the former Kievan state.

Under Vasilii III (1505–33) Moscow further extended its sway, particularly westward against Lithuania, and the important cities of Pskov and Smolensk were annexed. Vasilii also exerted pressure against Moscow's main enemy to the east, the Khanate of Kazan, ruled by descendants of the Mongols.

The extensive expansion under these two important rulers was accompanied by important political and social changes. Although in many respects the Muscovite rulers still ruled the state much as if it were their private domain, state administration became both more complex and

GROWTH OF MOSCOW to 1533

SWEDEN

FINNS

Semidependent

Colonies

White Sea

Lake Ladoga

N. Dvina

Ustiug

Baltic Sea

Reval

Narva

Novgorod

Beloo zero

Yaroslavl

KHANATE

ORDER

Riga

Pskov

Tver

Rostov

Vladimir

Kazan

LIVONIAN

W. Dvina

★ Moscow

OF KAZAN

PRUSSIA

Vilna

Smolensk

Kaluga

Riazan

Dnieper

Oka

Tula

BOUNDARY OF LITHUANIA, 1462

Warsaw

L I T H U A N I A

Orel

Chernigov

Voronezh

Volga

POLAND

Kiev

Belgorod

Don

GOLDEN HORDE

HUNGARY

Dniester

MOLDAVIA

Donets

Sarai

Dnieper

Azov

KHANATE OF ASTRAKHAN

Danube

CRIMEAN

BULGARIA

KHANATE

Caspian Sea

OTTOMAN

B l a c k   S e a

C A U C A S U S

Constantinople (to Turks, 1453)

EMPIRE

0   400
MILES

Corinne Abbazia Hekker Graphics

Moscow, c. 1300

To 1462: Vasili I, Vasili II

To 1389: Ivan I - Dmitrii

To 1533: Ivan III, Vasili III

MAP 4

more institutionalized. At the same time as the power and centralized authority of the rulers increased, grander and more prestigious symbols and trappings were adopted. One reflection of this was the marriage in 1472 of Ivan III to Zoe Paleologus, a niece of the last Byzantine emperor. At about the same time the title of grand prince was superseded by the designation of *autocrat* or *tsar*, both borrowed from Byzantine practice. *Autocrat* in its Russian translation meant literally the self-wielder of power but was increasingly interpreted as the holder of unlimited authority. *Tsar* (derived from the Latin *caesar*) also connoted complete and absolute power. Finally, in 1493, Ivan the Great took for himself the appellation *Gosudar* (ga-sóo-dar), or Sovereign, of All the Russian Lands.

The new grandeur of titles was complemented by adoption of a new symbol, the two-headed eagle used by both the Byzantine emperor and the Holy Roman Emperor in Europe, which lasted down to 1917, and by development of elaborate court ceremonials, including the formal anointing and coronation of the tsar in a Kremlin cathedral. As a reflection of his new status, Tsar Vasilii III opened diplomatic relations with the Holy Roman Emperor and the Pope in Europe and with the Turkish sultan in Constantinople.

The most important political development, however, was the growth of the concept of state service. In the past the majority of the prince's warriors, administrators, and servitors had been boyars. Customarily each boyar had his own hereditary estate, or *votchina*, and on it he exercised almost total authority, without interference from the prince or the state. He contracted with the prince to perform specific duties in return for certain rewards and was free to leave the prince's service at any time (and to sign on with another prince if he wished). In short, the prince had relatively little hold over a boyar, except to offer him money, trade, or protection that he could not obtain on his own. During the course of the rise of the Muscovite state and as the princes of Moscow saw the territory seized by them grow, they naturally tried to set up a system of land tenure and service over which they would have more control.

Increasingly, they took on servitors who were not boyars (or who were sometimes impoverished or landless boyars) and who in return for service received a grant of land to support them. This land was called a *pomestie* (pa-més-tye), and at first it was alloted to the servitor only for the duration of his service. Later, the *pomestie*, like the *votchina*, became hereditary. Clearly, these men of service were much more under the thumb of the prince or tsar, and Vasilii III tried to prevent both boyars and servitors from leaving his service. There was even discussion that such an act was treasonous. In retrospect, it is surprising how quickly the concept of obligatory service to the state emerged in the fifteenth and early-sixteenth centuries. In the next chapter we will see how important it became.

There were obviously significant social implications of this idea of service. One was that it began to be applied to other groups in the population, especially the peasants. An assumption that the peasants too owed an obligation to the state and that this could best be met by service to the landlord, whether prince, monastery, boyar, or servitor, arose. Moreover, as a money economy grew with the expansion of the state, peasants became more indebted to landlords, and the terms of loans and of sharecropping arrangements became increasingly burdensome. As a result, although serfdom (the binding of the peasant to the land) did not develop fully until some decades later, by the early 1500s the peasant's right to move to other land or to the service of a different lord had been restricted to a two-week period in the fall, after the harvest was in.

Commerce remained a significant part of economic life in Muscovy. One of the first European travelers to report his observations of the city, Ambrosio Contarini, an Italian diplomat en route home to Venice from Persia, passed through Moscow in 1476. He described the Moscow market as follows:

> By the end of October the river which passes through the city is frozen over, and shops and bazaars for the sale of all sorts of things are erected on it, scarcely anything being sold in the town. They do this, as the river, from being surrounded on all sides by the city, and so protected from the wind, is less cold than anywhere else. On this frozen river may be seen daily numbers of cows and pigs, great quantities of corn, wood, hay, and every other necessary, nor does the supply fail during the whole winter. . . . [Cows and pigs] are frozen whole, and it is curious to see so many skinned cows standing upright on their feet. . . . Horses run on the river when it is frozen, and a good deal of amusement takes place. Sometimes, also a neck is broken. . . . A great many merchants frequent this city from Germany and Poland during the winter for the sole purpose of buying pelts such as the furs of young goats, foxes, ermines, squirrels, wolves, and other animals. . . .[2]

The tsar engaged actively in trade, and as in other areas of Muscovite society, he did his best to control the commercial life of the city.

Concomitant with the increase in the power of the grand prince and tsar, the authority, wealth, and importance of the Russian Orthodox Church grew. After 1453, when the Turks seized Constantinople, the Russian churchmen concluded that the tasks of defending Orthodox Christianity and ensuring the purity of the faith had fallen to them. This gave rise to the theory of the Third Rome, which, put most simply, declared that the first Rome had fallen because of heresy within the church, that the second Rome (Constantinople) had succumbed to

[2] Ibid., 155–56.

the infidel Turks, and that Moscow was the Third Rome, the new center of true Christian belief—and a fourth Rome there would not be.

This was primarily a religious explanation of secular events and did not produce, as some Russophobes have contended, a Muscovite plan for expansion and for conversion of the non-Orthodox world. But the outlook reflected in the Third Rome idea certainly did make the Russian Orthodox Church (and therefore much of tsarist society) overly defensive and quite intolerant of ideas and influences from outside, including those from the Catholic (and later Protestant) West. To some extent the strong streak of xenophobia that kept surfacing in Russia in subsequent centuries can be traced back to the self-righteous commitment to protect the one true faith inherent in the theory of the Third Rome.

An important issue for the Orthodox Church in medieval Russia, as occurs frequently in organized religions when they expand and become rich, was the proper role and function of the Church in society. In the latter part of the 1400s and the first half of the 1500s, a group of reformers, called the Trans-Volga Elders and led by the monk Nil Sorskii, challenged the Church leadership, urging renunciation of worldly goods and pursuit of a simple monastic life. The reformers wanted the Church to give up its landholdings and other wealth and to emphasize instead contemplation and the striving for moral perfection. In the long run the reformers were defeated. As a result the Russian Church became even more focused on ritual and tradition and less concerned with intellectual innovation and the welfare of the people.

The challenge of the Trans-Volga Elders to established Church policy posed a dilemma for Tsars Ivan III and Vasilii III. In the past relations between the Church and state had seldom been a contentious issue. The metropolitans of Moscow had worked hand in hand with the Muscovite princes to advance their shared interests, the expansion of state and Church. On a few occasions, the metropolitans had virtually ruled the principality when a prince was very young or when there was a succession struggle. By the end of the fifteenth century, however, the tsars began to look greedily upon the vast landholdings of the Church. The tsars could use more land, both to support their court and to parcel out as *pomestie* to their growing body of servitors.

Consequently, when the reformers first called for the Church to give up its estates, Ivan III was sympathetic to their position, apparently hoping that the state would acquire these holdings. On the other hand, the Trans-Volga Elders also insisted on the complete separation of church and state, demanding that the tsar and his government stay completely out of religious affairs. This plank of their platform was clearly less attractive since victory for the reformers would have ended the close, mutually beneficial cooperation between the secular power and the religious authority that had been so instrumental in the rise of Moscow.

The Church leaders, in opposing Nil Sorskii and his followers, argued that the interests of the Orthodox Church and the Muscovite state were closely linked and that the Church should support and obey the tsar. This fitted well the emerging concept of state service, and finally, after some wavering, both Ivan III and Vasilii III backed the church hierarchy in condemning the reformers.

Conclusion

By the mid-1500s, well before the founding of the first colonies in North America, the forerunner of the modern Russian state had been formed and many of its basic policies and institutions established. In the course of its formation several key principles had predominated, and were to continue to do so.

In the first place, the Muscovite state arose out of a need in the forested wilderness of northeastern Russia for security and for unity. The core of the state-building experience was the constant struggle against first the Mongols and other princes and then the Lithuanians, the Novgorodians, and the Mongols' descendants, the Tatars. Because the Moscow princes were talented and long-lived, they were better able to provide protection and to ensure cohesion in their own domains. But in return they demanded service to them and to the emerging state. Assertion of the rights of boyars, or merchants, or peasants could lead to disunity and insecurity. Pluralism was not encouraged, and traditional privileges were slowly eroded and finally were largely abolished.

A second tenet on which unification of the Russian lands rested was a belief in the worth of the community, of the people as a whole. It was not only that group or individual rights were a threat but rather that society valued highly the preservation and cohesion of the community. This view, dating back to Kievan times in the concept of *sobornost'* in the Orthodox Church and in the collectivity of spontaneously formed peasant communes, was now reaffirmed in a new form: the common purpose and significance of the society as a whole as represented in the Muscovite state.

A third important view that predominated in Moscow was a sense of inferiority and of the need to overcome inherent liabilities. To survive and to expand, limited resources had to be husbanded and used efficiently. Surrounded on all sides by powerful enemies, the Moscow rulers were driven to mobilize the people and the society in order to prevail. Everything had to be subordinated to the effort to equalize the balance of forces and to restore the Russian state and civilization.

At the same time the people also benefited from the gathering of
the Russian lands. Christianity and other important elements of Kievan
civilization were preserved and transmitted. A reasonable degree of internal peace was achieved, and economic recovery from the Mongol period began. Russia reestablished extensive relations with the West in the
1400s, and divergent views and patterns still existed in Muscovite society. Yet in the next one hundred and fifty years these options were much
reduced as absolutist, centralized rule was fastened upon Russia.

FURTHER READING

Almedingen, E. M. *The Land of Muscovy: The History of Early Russia.* New York:
    1972.
Fedotov, G. *The Russian Religious Mind.* Cambridge, Mass.: 1966.
Fennell, J. L. *The Emergence of Moscow, 1305–59.* Berkeley: 1968.
———. *The Crisis of Medieval Russia, 1200–1304.* London: 1983.
———. *Ivan the Great of Moscow.* London: 1961.
Florovsky, G. "The Problem of Old Russian Culture." *Slavic Review,* Vol. 21,
    pp. 153–64. 1962.
Kaiser, D. *The Growth of Law in Medieval Russia.* Princeton, N.J.: 1981.
Medlin, W. K. *Moscow and East Rome.* Geneva: 1952.
Thompson, M. W. *Novgorod the Great.* New York: 1967.
Vernadsky, George. *Russia at the Dawn of the Modern Age.* New Haven, Conn.:
    1959.
Voyce, Arthur. *The Art and Architecture of Medieval Russia.* Norman, Okla.: 1964.

4

Ivan the Terrible and the Time of Troubles, 1533–1618

The unification of Russia under Moscow had laid the foundations of state and society, but the events of the next one hundred and fifty years built up and completed the structure, as we shall see in this chapter and the next. Political changes in the eighty years from the death of Vasilii III in 1533 to the election of Michael Romanov as tsar in 1613 marked a major turning point in Russian history, equal in importance to the reign of Peter the Great in the eighteenth century or to the Bolshevik and Stalinist revolutions in the two decades after 1917 (see chart on page 62.

Ivan IV (1533–84) was known as *groznyi* in Russian, a word that is poorly rendered by the English *terrible*. It is more correctly translated as *awesome* or *inspiring reverential dread*. Nevertheless, because it is so well known, we will use the customary term in English-language writing, "Ivan the Terrible," hoping that the reader will bear in mind that Russians of his time and later viewed Ivan with both admiration and fear.

Under Ivan the Terrible the centralizing, absolutist tendencies already prominent in the growth of the power of the grand princes of Moscow and of Ivan III and Vasilii III reached their apogee. At the same time the social conflict and oppression this generated, combined with an economic crisis and the huge cost of major foreign wars, brought state and society to near collapse and temporary anarchy. Russia narrowly missed dissolution again into petty principalities and was nearly conquered by Sweden and Poland. Yet by an extraordinary effort foreign enemies were repulsed, civil war ended, and state and society rebuilt. And making these turbulent times even more dramatic, love, hate, madness, deception, and heroism all figured significantly in the events of this era.

The Personality and Character of Ivan the Terrible

Everyone agrees that Ivan the Terrible was violent and cruel and acted at times in a paranoiac fashion. Some historians go further and

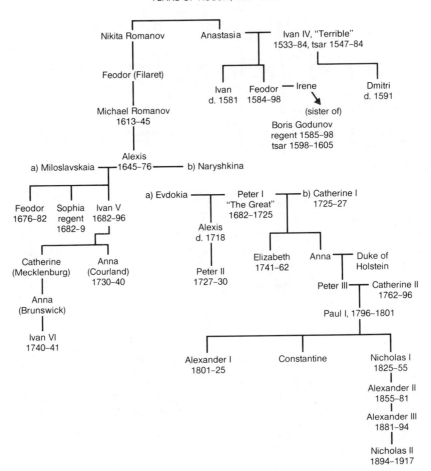

TSARS OF RUSSIA, 1547–1917

believe he had a severe personality disorder bordering on madness. Others argue that although he certainly behaved irrationally on occasion, he displayed considerable method in his "madness" and was most of the time an intelligent, far-sighted ruler driven to extreme measures by scheming and implacable opponents both at home and abroad. One interesting historical-medical analysis, drawing on eyewitness descriptions of the tsar's person and behavior, concludes that Ivan was suffering from syphilis (which spread rapidly through Europe in the sixteenth century). This disease progressively affected his brain as he aged, causing near insanity and finally death. Naturally this cannot be proved, but such a theory explains rather well certain aspects of Ivan's behavior although it fails to account for the extraordinarily long period, over twenty years, that he acted unpredictably and outrageously.

There is some dispute as well about his general level of ability and intelligence. Traditionally, Ivan has been viewed as well educated for his time, widely read, and possessing some skill as a writer and thinker. Recently it has been alleged that letters attributed to him were forgeries and that in fact he was quite unlettered and was altogether a rather crude and uncultured person. In my view, he was certainly literate and whether or not he actually wrote the pieces bearing his name, he was a clever and unusually able leader, though obviously unstable emotionally.

Without getting into a complex Freudian analysis, it is clear that Ivan the Terrible's childhood and upbringing distorted his personality, his values, and his outlook on the world. His father, Vasilii III, died when Ivan was only three. For another five years his life was reasonably normal, with Ivan as a child ruler and his mother serving as regent, in concert with her advisors. Unfortunately, the most powerful boyars resented her position, and when she died (perhaps poisoned) in 1538, a bloody, no-holds-barred struggle for power between two prominent boyar families, the Shuiskiis and the Belskiis, broke out. Ivan, caught in the middle and alternately ignored and abused, witnessed beatings, torture, and murder. Apparently a sensitive boy, Ivan was undoubtedly made suspicious and resentful by the intrigues and violence surrounding him. This atmosphere is melodramatically portrayed in the film *Ivan the Terrible*, made in the 1940s by the great Soviet movie director Sergei Eisenstein.

Ivan also developed at this time a streak of cruelty and suppressed rage and a deep-seated determination to revenge himself on those responsible for his mistreatment and humiliation. Though perhaps exaggerating, Ivan later in life wrote:

> But when I had entered upon my eighth year of life and when thus our subjects had achieved their desire, namely to have the kingdom without a ruler, then they did not deem us, their sovereigns, worthy of any loving care, but themselves ran after wealth and glory. . . . How many boyars and wellwishers of our father . . . did they massacre! And the courts and the villages and the possessions of our uncles did they seize. . . .

But not only the usurpation of power and wealth irked Ivan; petty harassments aroused his indignation as well:

> they began to feed us as though we were foreigners or the most wretched servants. What sufferings did I [not] endure through [lack of] clothing and through hunger! For in all things my will was not my own. . . .[1]

As he entered his teens, Ivan began to assert his rights, and in 1547, when he was sixteen, he had himself crowned tsar and married Anas-

[1] From *The Correspondence Between Prince A. M. Kurbsky and Tsar Ivan IV of Russia, 1564–1579*, trans and ed., J. L. I. Fennell (Cambridge: 1955), 73–75.

tasia, member of the well-liked boyar family, the Romanovs. Even though it was a political marriage, it turned out well, and Ivan lived happily with Anastasia until her death thirteen years later. Many historians believe she was a beneficent influence on the tsar, and it is certainly true that his more unorthodox and violent behavior began after Anastasia died.

The Reforms of Ivan IV

In 1547, the year of Ivan's coronation, extensive rioting occurred in Moscow, and social disorders broke out in other parts of the country. These were symptomatic of major problems that were coming to a head about the time Ivan ascended the throne. The most general was that the Russian state, including by now about nine or ten million people and having expanded too rapidly, possessed an insufficient resource base to support it and too small and antiquated an administration and social system to manage it well. Ivan attempted both to build up the strength of Russia and to rationalize and improve its governance. The first task led him into conflict with aggressive foreign foes—Tatars, Swedes, and Poles—and the second, into a remorseless and violent struggle with the most powerful single group in Russia: the aristocracy of princely families and boyars (see Figure 6).

At first Ivan the Terrible's reforming efforts went well. He surrounded himself with a group of able advisers, including Macarius, metropolitan of the Orthodox Church; Sylvester, a well-educated priest; and Adashev, a talented servitor. These men and Ivan's other close collaborators came to be known as the Chosen Council, although it is unclear whether the council ever existed as a formal body. Ivan did not directly challenge the *boyar duma,* the ancient consultative body to the Russian princes, trying instead to work around it. In 1549 he convened a much broader advisory group, known eventually as the *zemskii sobor* (assembly of the land), representing not only the boyar elite but gentry (servitors), Church officials, townspeople, and on one occasion, a few state peasants (from estates owned by the tsar or the government). Information on the composition and actions of this *zemskii sobor* is lacking, but probably Ivan discussed with it the various reform measures he was about to undertake. Several times in later years he called together and consulted with *zemskii sobors.*

A high priority for Ivan was to improve the fighting capacity of the army. The top commands were held by the highest-ranking boyars, regardless of ability, and this system often created serious leadership deficiencies. Although Ivan could not abolish the boyar-defended system of command by elite birth or rank, he managed to institute rules that permitted exceptions under special circumstances. In this way he was able, for certain campaigns and battles, to advance the best officers to

Figure 6. *Russian boyars in the 1600s; some of their dress reflects Polish stylistic influence. (Courtesy of the British Library)*

top posts. Ivan also regularized the terms of military service: how long a boyar or member of the gentry had to serve, what he received and contributed, and what his responsibilities were. Finally, he formed regiments of regular musketeers (called *streltsy*) under tsarist command.

Second, Ivan supervised collection and codification of the laws and a reform of local government. Both were important to a more orderly and equitable administration of the state, especially when linked to his efforts to build up a core of efficient central administrators in Moscow. Improvement of local government was greatly needed since governors and other local officials were often corrupt and systematically exploited the local population. The new system did not end all abuses but was a step forward at least.

Third, Ivan convened a major council of the Orthodox Church, which came to be known as the Council of the Hundred Chapters (from the number of charges given to it). It clarified a number of issues in internal Church administration, endorsed strongly the close tie between the tsar and the Church, and limited the right of the Church to acquire more land.

Finally, Ivan the Terrible made a strong effort to strengthen Russia's ties with Europe. He invited European specialists to Moscow to help improve the army, to erect new buildings and churches, to introduce new

Figure 7. *St. Basil's Cathedral in Red Square in Moscow. Although built by Ivan the Terrible in the 1500s, today it is still a dazzling sight, with its multicolored cupolas and facades. (Courtesy of the United Nations)*

technology, and to practice medicine. Only a few came, but they were instrumental in introducing new ideas and techniques to Muscovite society. In the 1570s Ivan established a special suburb of Moscow for foreign residents, and by the 1600s many of them were performing important services for Ivan's successors. Ivan also ordered construction of St. Basil's, the wonderfully ornate and colorful cathedral in Red Square. No tourist dares go to Moscow without being photographed in front of this splendid building with its many octagons and shimmering bulbous domes (see Figure 7).

Through good luck Ivan also established friendly and profitable relations with England. In 1553 Richard Chancellor, an English explorer searching for a northern route to the Orient, happened into the White Sea in north Russia. He went on to Moscow, where Ivan cordially welcomed him, and an important trade grew out of this chance encounter. Some English specialists also came to Russia in the latter part of the 1500s.

Ivan versus the Aristocracy: The Establishment of Autocracy in Russia

In none of these early successes of his reign did Ivan confront head-on the basic issue of Muscovite politics: could the tsar exercise unlimited authority, or was his growing power restricted by the customary privileges of princely families and boyars? In this contest the aristocracy had several advantages. First was tradition. From the very founding of Russia they had been the senior warriors and administrators of the state and the closest advisors of the grand princes of both Kiev and Moscow. It was unthinkable that the tsar could act and the state function without their close cooperation and full support. Second, they wielded considerable power: they owned the largest estates, could provide the greatest numbers of armed men for the tsar's army, and had almost total control over the population on their lands. Third, the boyars had institutionalized access to power through the *boyar duma* and through holding most of the top positions in the army and in the government.

At the same time the boyars, particularly when compared to the landed nobility of Europe, were quite weak. They were few in numbers, probably less than two hundred families in the 1500s. They had no corporate identity and indeed could not rely on any extensive body of custom or law that gave them privileges and rights as a class (instead of as individuals). Moreover, they were deeply disunited, quarreling endlessly with each other over precedence and rank and resorting to intrigue and brutality in their internecine struggles, instead of uniting against the tsar. Finally, their position had been gradually undercut by the rise over the preceding century and a half of gentry, or men of service. The latter, originally considered a clearly inferior class, at first held their estates only as long as they served the grand prince, and they were clearly dependent on the tsar; the boyars, however, had hereditary title to their land and in theory could leave the tsar's service at any time. Gradually but steadily in the 1500s the distinctions between boyars and gentry disappeared: Both held their land on a hereditary basis and both owed obligatory service (though some boyars fled to Lithuania to escape this obligation).

The tsar also had certain advantages in an open struggle with the boyars. He had the backing of the Church as an institution, no matter what individual prelates and priests might feel. Second, the theory and aura of autocracy—of unlimited rule—inherited from the Byzantine empire and nurtured under Ivan III and his successors, although not fully accepted in Muscovite society of the mid-1500s, served to strengthen the claim of Ivan the Terrible to absolute authority. Finally, he could count on the support of the gentry, who of course stood to gain much from diminution of the boyars' position. Ivan, however—unlike his contemporary absolute monarchs in the West, such as Henry VIII—did not have a strong merchant class or autonomous towns on which to draw for financial and political backing.

In retrospect, we may view the fierce struggle between Ivan the Terrible and the boyars that broke out in the 1560s as an unnecessary and uneven contest, with the boyars essentially having no chance. But at the time it was far from clear what the outcome would be, and the resulting bloodshed and disruption very nearly brought down the Muscovite state altogether. Had Ivan not won, the nature of Russian society and the subsequent course of Russian history would certainly have been quite different.

Although the evidence is contradictory, two developments seemed to have triggered the bloody showdown between Ivan the Terrible and the boyars. One was an unlucky event, the serious illness of the tsar in 1553. At that time he asked his privileged subjects, including top government officials and boyars, to swear allegiance to his son Dmitrii as heir to the throne. Some did, but many at first refused, apparently because Dmitrii was still a child, and they feared another period of minority rule marked by internal strife and weakness as had occurred in Ivan's boyhood. The incident infuriated and frightened Ivan, who, when he recovered from his illness, apparently marked down for future retribution those boyars whom he believed had wanted to usurp his family's right to the throne.[2]

The second event that brought on domestic discord in Moscow was disagreement over foreign policy. Although the Muscovite state had formally thrown off the Mongol yoke in 1480, the descendants of the Mongols continued to harass Russia from the south and east in the 1500s. Deciding that bold measures were needed, Ivan in 1551 launched a campaign against Moscow's nearest enemy, the Tatar Khanate of Kazan. In 1552 after a long siege Kazan itself, a city on the Volga River east of Moscow, was captured, and by 1557 the Russians had annexed the whole khanate. In 1556 Ivan also succeeded in capturing the Khanate of Astrakhan at the mouth of the Volga and adding it to his domain (see Map 5). Only the Tatars of the Crimean khanate remained, and they, backed by the Ottoman Turks, launched major attacks against Ivan on several occasions throughout his reign and were not finally subdued by the Russians until more than two hundred years later.

In addition to security against the Moslem Tatars, Ivan had an important foreign policy goal in the other direction, toward Europe. Ever since Ivan III's absorption of Lord Novgorod the Great, the Muscovite state had had a toehold on the shore of the Baltic Sea. Ivan the Terrible wanted to increase Russia's territory on the Baltic coast and to expand trade with northern and central Europe. Blocking his way were the Livonian order of Germanic knights, who held what is today Estonia and Latvia, and to their south the Polish-Lithuanian state (see Map 4). In 1558 Ivan launched what came to be known as the Livonian War and at first met with great success. By the early 1560s the Livonian order had been destroyed and some territory captured from Lithuania.

---

[2] A Soviet scholar, R. G. Skrynnikov, contends that this incident was largely a myth concocted later by Ivan himself to justify his policies.

It was, however, a bloody and expensive war, and it meant that Russia was fighting on two fronts at the same time. It required higher taxes and more recruits for the army. Not only was there popular grumbling, but some of Ivan's advisers, including members of the Chosen Council, warned against getting too deeply involved in a costly military struggle in the west.

In 1560 as the policy dispute over the Livonian War was heating up, Ivan's first wife, Anastasia, died suddenly. Whether removal of her loving and calming influence was a factor in Ivan's subsequent irrational behavior is unclear, but in any case Ivan shortly launched an extraordinary vendetta against his friends and against the leading boyar families. Accusing his trusted colleagues, Sylvester and Adashev, of conspiring to poison his wife, Ivan sent Sylvester into remote exile and threw Adashev into prison, where he died. Ivan then turned against their circle of friends and began, mercilessly and without trial, to have them tortured and executed. There seemed no rhyme or reason to his actions, and during this reign of terror a number of prominent officials and boyars fled to Lithuania, including Prince Andrei Kurbsky, with whom the tsar subsequently exchanged a series of letters in which Ivan defended his right to rule despotically. Ivan the Terrible imediately branded these flights as treason and increased the fury of his persecution against those who remained.

One bizarre episode followed another until suddenly and without explanation the tsar left Moscow in late 1564 with the treasury and withdrew to a monastery in a remote area some distance from the city. This action created bafflement and uncertainty, and since no one knew what to do, emissaries from Moscow begged the tsar to return. Finally, several months later, he reappeared, looking haggard and distraught. He agreed to resume his position as tsar only if his authority to punish traitors and evildoers as he saw fit were confirmed and he were allowed to set up a separate and autonomous area within the Muscovite state entirely under his control, conditions that the leading officials accepted.

Thus originated the strange institution called the *oprichnina* (uh-préech-neena), literally, "the area set apart." This area was under Ivan's personal rule and consisted of scattered territories and estates, many of which were seized from the princely families and boyars. The *oprichnina* included some of the best land, as well as districts, of several cities. The rest of the country was left under regular administration. In 1572 Ivan, apparently convinced that he had broken the back of the opposition, ended the *oprichnina* and reunited the Muscovite tsardom.

Because the documents and memoirs from this period are sketchy, it is difficult to evaluate precisely the purpose and significance of the *oprichnina*. There is, however, little doubt that Ivan the Terrible considered it first and foremost as a weapon in his struggle with the boyars and princely families. To administer the *oprichnina,* he appointed ambitious and obedient servitors who did not hesitate to take harsh actions against his enemies and whom he rewarded with land grants and wealth. Ivan ignored or degraded the regular officials and boyars, and he confiscated the estates of many as a means both of punishing them and of undermining their economic and social position. At times the tsar was subject to fits of paranoia and rage against his imagined persecutors. He personally participated—and according to some accounts delighted—in the torture and murder of individuals and groups. On one occasion he killed his favorite son during a furious outburst. At other times he repented of his deeds and sought solace and atonement in contemplation and prayer.

The *oprichnina* as an institution, combined with Ivan's unbridled anger and violent oppression, succeeded in weakening and demoralizing the boyars, and for the last twenty years of his reign Ivan encountered little opposition to his half-mad rule. But the cost was enormous. The division of the state into two parts wrecked the administration and seriously damaged the economy. The aura of terror and suspicion made normal social or political life impossible, and educated Muscovite society became paralyzed and cowed. Ivan the Terrible, with no one to gainsay him, plunged ahead with the draining Livonian War, exhausting the country and sapping its resources. Moreover, the fortunes of war turned against him, and when peace was finally made in 1583, after twenty-five years of wasting struggle, he had lost almost everything originally gained, and Russia was back where it had started. Or perhaps the country was worse off, because in the course of the war the Swedes had entered the fray and were now allied with the Poles as deadly enemies of Moscow.

What did it all mean? Clearly Ivan the Terrible was mentally and emotionally disturbed, at the very least, and we need only look to the recent past in our own "modern" century, to the case of Adolf Hitler, to appreciate how terrible can be the consequences when an intelligent person with a pathological personality wields absolute power, even for a brief time. Yet it would be a mistake to write off Ivan as simply deranged. His struggle with the aristocracy was also a contest for control of the state and, although his opponents were perhaps less serious a threat than he imagined, there is no doubt that Ivan's reign resulted in a victory for the tsar's authority. He established centralized autocratic rule by making sure, in a peculiarly horrible fashion, that no group or institution could oppose the untrammeled will of the tsar. The shape of the full absolutism that was to take final form in the 1600s and 1700s was clearly presaged in the tsardom of Ivan the Terrible.

At the same time the cost was exorbitant. The people were oppressed and squeezed, the economy ravaged, and the society nearly torn apart by civil persecution and unrelenting terror. Although Ivan succeeded in securing Russia's eastern frontier, his grand design for the

Baltic collapsed, and he was unable to subdue the Crimean Tatars in the south. Most significantly, the fears and tensions of his rule, as well as the near ruination of the country, set the stage for one of the most sensational and dramatic periods in Russian history, aptly named the Time of Troubles.

The Time of Troubles, 1598–1613

Three main issues characterized the tumultuous era of the Time of Troubles: a struggle for political power, a widespread social revolution, and a national movement to prevent foreign domination of Russia. These themes were closely intertwined and were often being played out simultaneously. Nevertheless, to make comprehensible the confused events of the Time of Troubles, we will consider each of them in turn.

Struggle for Political Power. The main thread of Muscovite history into the 1500s was the extension of the personal power and authority of the grand prince–tsar from his own estate to the larger principality and finally to the unified Russian lands. This process had culminated in the autocratic rule of Ivan the Terrible, and the position and role of the tsar were what held the Muscovite state together. Moreover, as we saw, Moscow was fortunate in having long-lived rulers and few succession problems. Thus, when Ivan's successor, the weak and sickly Feodor, died in 1598 without an heir, this event not only provoked a major crisis but very nearly led to the complete dissolution of the state that had been laboriously built up in the preceding two hundred and fifty years.

The turmoil that ensued was greatly intensified by the bitterness and resentment still felt by the upper classes as a result of their forcible subjugation by Ivan the Terrible. The great boyar families were determined to recoup their fortunes and recapture their dominant political position in Muscovite society. The gentry, who had benefited from Ivan's *oprichnina* but were suffering economically, were no less determined to advance their own interests by seizing as much political power as possible. The merchants, who had not fared particularly well under Ivan and who were considered second-class citizens by the others, believed a golden opportunity to improve their position was at hand. The stage was set for a maximum amount of political strife.

The prologue was provided by a twenty-one-year period, from 1584 to 1605, during which the talented Boris Godunov dominated the political life of Russia. A minor boyar who participated in the administration of Ivan the Terrible's *oprichnina,* he was the brother-in-law of Tsar

Feodor. Through his sister, Boris Godunov acquired a commanding position in affairs of state early in Feodor's reign. Beginning in 1587, he served as regent and was in fact the ruler of Russia, while Feodor, who was extremely devout, concentrated on religious affairs. Godunov was talented and just, attempting to settle the country down domestically and to patch up the quarrels with Sweden and Poland. He skillfully helped engineer establishment in Moscow of a patriarchate, the highest administrative unit in the Greek Orthodox Church, and had his friend Metropolitan Job named the first patriarch. This arrangement permitted enlargement of the church hierarchy and enhanced Moscow's international prestige because the other patriarchs in the Orthodox Church were located in areas under Turkish rule.

Nonetheless Boris Godunov had two strikes against him. Although he promoted trade and ties with the West, there was little he could do to overcome Moscow's fundamental economic problems: declining agriculture and huge losses caused by Ivan's wars. He also had no legitimate claim to the throne. In 1591, perhaps to improve his chances of becoming tsar, Boris Godunov may have been involved in a conspiracy that resulted in the death of Ivan the Terrible's youngest son, Dmitrii (a story dramatically told in Mussorgsky's great opera, *Boris Godunov*). In any case in 1598, when Feodor died childless, Boris Godunov clearly aspired to be his successor.

In this unprecedented situation a *zemskii sobor* of some five hundred representatives of the boyars, gentry, clergy, and townspeople was convened. This was the first time in the history of Moscow that no natural heir to the throne existed. Moreover, there was no law of succession. Because of the powerful position he had developed over the preceding decade and because he undoubtedly was the most suitable candidate available, Boris Godunov was elected tsar in 1598.

His reign began auspiciously, but before long events over which he had little control undermined his position. First, in 1601–3 Russia suffered a terrible drought and famine. Despite extraordinary efforts by the government to relieve the misery, people were reduced to eating fodder and bark and even, on occasion, to cannibalism, as this contemporary account makes clear:

> But I swear by God that in Moscow I saw, with my own eyes, people who rolled in the streets and, like animals, ate grass during the summer and hay during the winter. . . . Human flesh, finely gound, baked in pies (a kind of pastry), was sold and consumed like beef. . . . Daily, on the Tsar's orders they collected hundreds of corpses and carried them outside the city in wagons—an undertaking which was awesome to observe. Specially appointed people washed the dead, wrapped them in a white cloth, put red shoes on them, and wheeled them to the church to be buried.[3]

[3] From *Medieval Russia: A Source Book, 900–1700* (p. 224) by Basil Dmytryshyn. Copyright © 1967 by Holt, Rinehart and Winston, Inc. Reprinted by permission of CBS College Publishing.

Second, beginning in 1603 rumors began to spread that Ivan's last son, Dmitrii, had not died in 1591; it was whispered that he not only still lived but was preparing to assert his rightful claim to the throne. Despite his best efforts Tsar Boris was unable to squelch these rumors. Moreover, stories also began to circulate that Godunov was a murderer and usurper and that Russia was being punished by God for Godunov's sins. How much Boris's boyar opponents were behind these stories is unclear, but there is no doubt that the boyars fanned the flames of slander, some because they were jealous of Godunov's position, others because they had been slighted or oppressed by his policies.

The upshot was that in the fall of 1604 a major rebellion against Tsar Boris broke out, headed by a pretender to the throne known retrospectively as the first False Dmitrii. It is generally accepted that he was a former monk who apparently deluded himself into believing that he was indeed the lawful heir to the throne. His supporters included a group of Polish nobles, who were patently using him to further their own ends, and a motley collection of discontented Russians, some of whom were convinced he was in fact Dmitrii and others who didn't care about his claims as long as they could channel their grievances against the government through him.

The challenge of this first pretender opened eight years of chaotic and complex maneuvering for political supremacy among the boyars, gentry, and merchants, who backed first one candidate to the throne and then another. At the nadir of this unseemly contest, there was no tsar at all, and it seemed the vaunted Muscovite autocracy would disappear altogether. Greatly complicating the political struggle was the eruption of a major social revolution shortly after the appearance of the first False Dmitrii.

Social Revolution. Although a number of fringe and semicriminal elements participated, the main groups involved in the widespread social revolution that broke out in Russia in 1605–6 were peasants, cossacks, slaves, and runaway serfs. As we will see in the next chapter, by the early 1600s *serfdom*, the binding of peasants to the land, had developed quite far though the process was not yet complete. In the last part of the sixteenth century an agricultural depression and the exactions accompanying Ivan the Terrible's *oprichnina* and his wars had made the situation of the rural population grave, and the drought and famine of 1601–2 made it desperate. As a result, almost all groups in the countryside, particularly in central and southern Russia, whether they were still free peasants, were loosely bound to the landlord by debts, were fully enserfed, or had run away from their obligations and their lords, could unite against the upper classes and the government. And since symbolism and superstition were important in their lives, so much the better if they could believe their rebellious fury was being expended in support of the "true" tsar and the righting of an old dynastic wrong.

The cossacks need a special word of explanation. The name *cossack*, originally derived from a warlike, nomadic group of horsemen in Central Asia, began at this time to be applied to bands of independent frontiersmen who lived on the southern and eastern borderlands of the Russian state. Some cossacks were mainly freebooters and brigands; others were farmers and herders. Cossack bands frequently included escapees from authority, such as tax evaders, runaway serfs, and fugitives from the lord's or the tsar's justice. Proud of their skills as horsemen and fighters, determined to remain free, and fickle in their political loyalties during the Time of Troubles, the cossacks were an effective but volatile force in both the struggle for power and the social revolution. On a number of occasions they switched sides unexpectedly, tipping the balance in favor of one faction or another. As we shall see, they continued to play a significant role in subsequent Russian history.

When the first False Dmitrii invaded Russia in October 1604 with his Polish supporters, the first to rally to his cause were cossacks. But other dissatisfied rural elements soon swelled his ranks, and in the spring of 1605, after the unexpected death of Boris Godunov, Dmitrii's forces captured Moscow, and he was installed as tsar. Ugly and ungainly in appearance, he tried to placate the boyars and the general populace, but his idiosyncratic habits and the haughty conduct of his Polish entourage soon alienated the Muscovites. Having used Dmitrii to dislodge Tsar Boris, the boyars and princely families were now quite prepared to discard the pretender. New rumors, that Dmitrii was an impostor, began to spread. After he had been on the throne less than a year, the first False Dmitrii was unseated and killed in a coup led by the boyar, Prince Vasilii Shuisky, who then arranged to have himself proclaimed tsar. Dmitrii's ashes were supposedly loaded in a cannon and fired back toward Poland.

With Shuisky on the throne, it seemed the boyars had won the political contest. The new tsar was compelled to provide the boyars guarantees against arbitrary treatment and punishment, and his policies reflected their interests. Though his "election" as tsar had been enthusiastically endorsed by the Moscow mobs, who were particularly incensed against the Polish clique that had dominated the city during the brief reign of the first False Dmitrii, Shuisky could offer them little once he was enthroned. As a result, they soon turned against him and joined a countrywide revolt to overthrow the boyar tsar.

With the central authority tarnished and weakened by the dynastic struggle and the successive coups, the country began to dissolve into anarchy. Local governors rebelled, as did non-Russian groups who opposed Muscovite repression. Most important, the lower classes of southern Russia rose in a massive conflagration that raged throughout 1606 and 1607. The rebels' leader was Ivan Bolotnikov, a colorful and extremely able demagogue of obscure origins, who roused and organized the masses to fight for their own interests and needs and to destroy the boyars and landlords. Soviet historians have done valuable research demonstrating the broad scale and the social content of Bolotnikov's rebellion, which they term the first peasant war in Russian history.

During this period various new pretenders emerged, including one who claimed to be the son of Tsar Feodor, even though the record was clear that Feodor had had no sons. Finally, in August 1607, a second False Dmitrii appeared and quickly gathered a considerable following. Nicknamed the "Brigand of Tushino" for the Moscow suburb where he established his headquarters, he soon rallied all the antigovernment forces. Although neither he nor his close advisors took his claim to the throne seriously, many were happy to follow his banner in the hope of seeing order restored and obtaining what they wanted. In two bizarre episodes the mother of the real Dmitrii, now a nun, declared the second False Dmitrii her son, and the Polish wife of the first False Dmitrii recognized him as her husband and bore him a son, the "Baby Brigand." As the social revolution burned itself out during 1608 and with neither the boyar tsar, Vasilii Shuisky, nor the second False Dmitrii able to defeat the other, a stalemate developed.

Movement for National Defense. At this juncture a new theme was introduced: a struggle against foreigners meddling in Russian affairs. This had been presaged in the resentment against the Polish followers of the first False Dmitrii, but it became a major element in the Time of Troubles in early 1609, when Tsar Vasilii, with his back to the wall, turned to Sweden for help. In return for territorial concessions along the Baltic and a promise Russia would ally with Sweden against Poland, the Swedes provided troops who helped Vasilii Shuisky's army put the second False Dmitrii to flight.

To counter this outside assistance for Shuisky, some of the second False Dmitrii's supporters appealed to the king of Poland, Sigismund III, for help. Sigismund, anxious to extend his influence in Russia and to thwart a Russo-Swedish alliance, invaded Russia and agreed to have his son placed on the Russian throne. But, most historians agree, Sigismund really wanted to rule Russia himself, and he apparently saw to it that negotiations over the conditions under which his son would become tsar broke down. Polish forces occupied Moscow, the Swedes attacked in the north because the Russians had allied with the Poles, and the second False Dmitrii reappeared in the southeast to make another try for the throne. In the midst of these disasters, Tsar Vasilii was deposed and sent to a monastery.

This was certainly the low point in the fortunes of the Muscovite state: with no tsar, the capital occupied by Poles and the northwest by Swedes, and a pretender stirring up trouble in the countryside, its chances for survival seemed slim. Yet the very gravity of the situation sparked an upsurge of national (or at least antiforeign) feeling and a determination to restore Russia's independence and some semblance of order. Soviet historians have emphasized the breadth of popular participation in this national movement, but in fact the upper classes seem to have played the dominant role, for good reason. They had the most to lose under Polish domination and continuing civil disorder and the most to gain by resurrection of the Muscovite state of the 1500s, albeit without the arbitrary persecutions of Ivan the Terrible. Moreover, the effort at national regeneration began in the towns of north Russia, which had been least affected by the social revolution and which could still command enough economic resources to support the drive to expel the foreigners.

There was also a strong religious element in the national revival. The Catholic Poles, the main enemy, were considered heretical, and the head of the Russian Orthodox Church, Patriarch Hermogen, played an important role in initiating the national resistance movement. In all likelihood, many illiterate but devout Russians, bewildered by the kaleidoscopic events of the preceding few years, were delighted to be told at last who the true enemy was: the heretical Poles.

In 1612 two remarkable individuals, a butcher named Kuzma Minin, and an experienced general, Prince Dmitrii Pozharsky, combined their organizational, fighting, and inspirational talents to form a national army that liberated Moscow from the Poles by the end of the year. The army was supported by large contributions made by citizens of many towns, and there is little doubt, despite some exaggeration by Soviet historians, that this national movement represented a determined effort by Russians to take their destiny back into their own hands.

It is significant that once the Poles had been driven out, the first step of the leaders of the national resistance was to restore tsarist rule. A *zemskii sobor* was convened in early 1613, and after considerable deliberation it chose Michael Romanov as tsar, establishing a family that was to rule Russia for over three hundred years, down to 1917. Michael was only sixteen and thus had not been compromised in the earlier political machinations of the Time of Troubles. He was a grand-nephew of Anastasia, Ivan the Terrible's "good" wife, and thus indirectly related to the old dynasty. Perhaps most important, the Patriarch Hermogen backed him (although Hermogen died before the actual election), and Michael's father, the Metropolitan Filaret, was a popular and influential churchman and former boyar.

Conclusion

The new government of Tsar Michael was weak, and disorder and civil strife continued until at least 1618, which marks the beginning of firm rule and the end of the Time of Troubles, called by Soviet historians "the Era of the First Peasant War and Foreign Intervention." The most important direct results of this period were that the foreigners and Catholics were driven out, the Muscovite state and the purity of the Orthodox Church saved, and the tsardom restored. But equally significantly, under the surface the upper classes had salvaged their position (even though the boyars' effort to seize power was defeated), the lower classes succeeded only in postponing the day of their final enserfment, and development of the centralized autocracy could be resumed.

The most interesting question is why autocratic tsarist rule first expanded greatly under Ivan the Terrible and then, despite the wracking crisis of the Time of Troubles, survived to become the dominant political institution of modern Russian history? Although any answer must be speculative, four main factors explain this phenomenon, in my view.

In the first place, given the weak economy of Russia, strong centralized authority was needed to mobilize the resources and people for the tasks of unification, growth, and defense. Since centralizing monarchs, fulfilling analogous goals, existed about the same time in western Europe, the Russian experience was hardly unique. But the power of the tsar to command obedience, sanctified by Byzantine tradition and theory and fortified by observation of Mongol practice, was crucial to the further development and expansion of the Muscovite state.

Second, the tsar became a symbol of unity and security in a fragmented and hostile world. This role, enhanced by memories of the glorious days of Kiev under the grand prince, had first taken shape when the prince was simply proprietor of an enlarged private estate turned into a principality; it had been expanded in the struggle to throw off the Mongol yoke and to gather the Russian lands. It is significant that during the Time of Troubles one common thread was the search for the "true" tsar, and again and again the people, both upper and lower classes, rallied around a pretender, no matter how flimsy his claims. Moreover, their first action to reunite the divided society was to elect a new tsar.

Third, the autocracy emerged, flourished, and survived because from the earliest days, first in Kiev and then in the 1300s in Moscow, it was linked with the Orthodox Church. In our secular era it is all too easy to overlook or forget the powerful hold of religion on people. Russians of this period may have understood little of Christian theology or of the ideas and politics of the patriarchs, metropolitans, and archbishops, but they devoutly believed in the rituals and physical presence of the Russian Orthodox Church. Thus, when state and church supported each other and the tsar acted as defender of the true faith as well as ruler of the Muscovite state, this association greatly reinforced his authority and his influence over the population.

Finally, it is important to remember that the tsars prevailed in part because no other group or institution in Muscovite society seemed capable of organizing society and building the state. We will see later how, just when classes and institutions competitive with the king were growing stronger in Europe, they were declining in Russia; in fact once Ivan the Terrible had undercut the power of the boyars, no group existed in Moscow to challenge seriously the growing absolutism of the tsar. The people could resist, individually or in the mass, as they did during Ivan the Terrible's depredations and during the Time of Troubles, but such resistance was either isolated defiance or disorganized rebellion. Even to make revolt coherent it was necessary to raise the standard of a false tsar or a boyar tsar. Group fought group, the masses struck out blindly at the government and their economic oppressors, landlords and merchants, but no alternative basis for organizing society was propounded.

As a result, Russia entered the seventeenth century, the era of the founding of the American colonies, with a battle-scarred but well-entrenched system of tsarist autocracy. What form it would take, how it might be shaped and even restrained in practice, and how the average Russian fared under it are questions to which we will turn in the next few chapters.

FURTHER READING

Barbour, Philip. *Dmitry Called the Pretender, 1605–06*. Boston: 1966.

Fennell, J. L., ed. *The Correspondence between Prince Kurbsky and Tsar Ivan IV of Russia, 1564–1579*. Cambridge, England: 1955.

Keenan, Edward. *The Kurbsky-Groznyi Apocrypha*. Cambridge, Mass.: 1981.

———. "Muscovy and Kazan." *Slavic Review*, Vol. 26, pp. 548–58. December 1967.

Longworth, P. *The Cossacks*. New York: 1970.

Platonov, S. *The Time of Troubles*. Translated by J. T. Alexander. Lawrence, Ks.: 1970.

Skrynnikov, R. G. *Ivan the Terrible*. Translated by Hugh F. Graham. Gulf Breeze, Fla.: 1981.

Vernadsky, George. *The Tsardom of Moscow, 1547–1682* (Part I). New Haven: 1969.

Wipper, R. *Ivan Grozny*. Moscow: 1947.

5

The Molding of
Russian Society, 1613-89

Forenoon prayers had not quite ended when Tsar Alexis heard a great hubbub outside the church. It was a hot summer morning, 25 July 1662, and the tsar, perturbed at this unexpected interruption of his daily devotions, called loudly to attendants in the courtyard beside the church, demanding to know what the commotion was all about. He soon learned that a mob was clamoring to see him, insisting that they be allowed to present their grievances to the tsar in person.

Alexis acted decisively and courageously. Ordering his wife and children, as well as some of the officials against whom the mob was railing, to take refuge in his nearby summer palace, the tsar walked out of the church to deal with the protesters. He was unaware that earlier that morning in Moscow, some ten miles from his summer retreat, riots had broken out over high taxes and allegations of corruption and that the crowds had accused several of his closest advisers of treasonous support of the king of Poland, with whom Russia was at war. A few hotheads had persuaded the mob to march out of the city to find Tsar Alexis himself.

To approach the tsar directly was unprecedented. He was ordinarily a remote and haughty figure, with whom only a few high officials, clergy, and court attendants were permitted to communicate. Nonetheless in this crisis Alexis listened to the rancorous and sometimes profane complaints of the mob's leaders. They demanded a lowering of taxes and the handing over to them of the officials and merchants they had accused. As the American historian, Joseph T. Fuhrmann, has described it, the tsar handled the situation masterfully:

> Alexis spoke to the rioters in a quiet way, hoping to calm them and persuade them to leave. He promised after mass to return to Moscow, to conduct a personal investigation, to right all wrongs. Several of the crowd grabbed Alexis by the buttons of his coat, shouting, "Whom do you believe—the traitors or us?" Alexis swore before God that his faith was in his subjects, and one member of the crowd stepped forward to seal this covenant by shaking the tsar's hand.[1]

[1] Joseph T. Fuhrmann, *Tsar Alexis: His Reign and His Russia* (Gulf Breeze, Fla.: Academic International Press, 1981), 149.

Later that same day the tsar behaved quite differently. When a second mob approached him just as he was setting out for Moscow in accord with the promise he had made earlier, Alexis ordered loyal troops who had rallied round him in the interim to disperse the crowd by force. Over one hundred of the rioters were driven into a nearby river and drowned. Many thousand were captured and flogged on the spot. In the next few days several hundred ringleaders were hanged publicly, and several thousand rioters were exiled to southeast Russia and to Siberia. At the same time the tsar richly rewarded the officers and troops who supported him. Somewhat later he undertook a few of the reforms the Moscow mobs had clamored for.

This major disturbance in Moscow in 1662 was preceded by city-wide riots in the capital in 1648 and by uprisings in other cities and in scattered rural areas. Subsequently in 1667–71 a major rebellion broke out in southeast Russia that mustered an armed force of over twenty thousand men and threatened to topple the government. It was led by Stenka Razin, a colorful and energetic Don cossack, who roused the poorer cossacks and the lower classes in the south against all officials and authority with a vague but appealing cry for freedom and an end to taxes. Much to the relief of Tsar Alexis, who had personally trained the troops to be sent against the rebels, some rich cossacks betrayed Stenka Razin in the spring of 1671 and turned him over to the government. He was tortured and executed in Moscow in June 1671. But Stenka Razin remained a hero for the oppressed masses and passed into folk legend and song as a romantic Robin Hood capable of extraordinary feats in defending the poor from the depredations of the rich.

As melodramatic as some of these instances of popular unrest in the 1600s were, they served merely to underscore the overall helplessness of the people under the dominant institutions of Russian society that took shape in that century. During the reigns of three tsars and a regent—Michael (1613–45), Alexis (1645–76), Feodor (1676–82), and Sophia (1682–89)—a major effort to secure and expand the Russian state and to build a viable military and governmental system was made. It largely succeeded, but because Russia's physical and economic resources were limited, the average subject had to bear most of the burden. By 1690 some fifteen million people were struggling to support a huge state that stretched from the Pacific Ocean into eastern Europe.

In this chapter we will examine three chief pillars of tsarist society: the system of serfdom that lasted to 1861, the institution of the autocracy that was reestablished and refined in the 1600s and persisted until 1906 (and with minor modification to 1917), and the nature and function of the Orthodox Church, which has changed little till the present day, although its role under Soviet rule has been much diminished. In the last two parts of the chapter we will look at the territorial expansion of Russia in its continuing search for security and at the development of closer relations with the West, which had a portentous initial impact on Russian thought and society.

Serfdom

Human bondage is an ancient phenomenon, dating back at least to early recorded history and persisting in some parts of the world until about fifty years ago. Yet it emerged in Russia late, soon took an unusually widespread and oppressive form, and lasted for over two hundred years, down to 1861 (about as long as slavery in the United States). The details of how and why serfdom developed in tsarist society are still being debated among historians, but the overall pattern of its evolution is reasonably clear.

As we saw in Chapter 1, most people who farmed in Kievan times were free. Many were organized in communes or *obshchinas* and possessed their own land. Nevertheless, even then some peasants had begun to incur obligations to others, usually large landholders. In return for assistance—seed, tools, money, use of more land—a peasant would agree to do a certain amount of work for the lord or to pay back a given sum, in cash or in kind. When these debts were paid, the peasant was free once more. Until they were, the peasant could not leave the land and the obligations he had accepted.

In this way some peasants were moving toward being enserfed. During the decline of Kiev, the civil strife that followed, and the invasion of the Mongols, many peasants found making ends meet difficult. Crops were seized, fields and tools destroyed, and villages burned. Moreover, storms, drought, and pests could wipe out any year's harvest. Finally, taxes imposed by the Moscow grand princes, then tsars, made it even more difficult to subsist without falling into debt. For example, scattered evidence indicates that during the last half of the 1500s there was a serious agricultural crisis, probably caused by a combination of bad weather and the exactions resulting from Ivan the Terrible's *oprichnina* and his foreign wars. By 1601 a terrible famine had gripped Russia. Clearly, many peasants were being driven by economic necessity to take on obligations they had little hope of ever repaying. Thus, their bondage was becoming permanent, and serfdom was spreading in Russia.

But it might never have become so extensive had not state policy at this very time acted to bolster and intensify the natural economic trend toward serfdom. To unify and defend Russia the tsars had to finance their armies and reward their servitors. Although they earned some profits from trade in furs and other commodities, the most valuable resource available to the Ivans and Vasiliis of the fifteenth and sixteenth centuries was land: land whose products could be requisitioned or taxed and land that could be given fighting men in return for service. Yet neither sort of land was valuable without peasants to work it. If peasants could run away to the frontier or escape to the cossacks, the land became worthless and the tsars and their state bankrupt.

As a consequence the tsarist government followed several policies that helped fasten serfdom on the Russian countryside. First, they gave many grants of land *(pomestie)* to servitors; most of these grants included peasants with the land, peasants who owed service to the tsar's servitor in return for their continued right to use the land.

Second, the tsars began to interfere in the customary rules that had governed obligations between lord and peasant. Traditionally, peasants who paid their debts (sometimes their debts were paid by another lord, who wanted their labor) were free to leave the land and the lord's service at the end of the harvest season, during the two weeks before and after St. George's Day (usually falling in November). But beginning in the latter part of the 1500s the state now and then decreed a "forbidden" year, that is, abolished in a given year the right to move during the period around St. George's Day. Before long every year was "forbidden" and the peasants were prohibited from leaving at any time. De facto they were bound to the land and after a while, personally to the lord.

Third, the government, at the urging of the major landowners, made it more and more difficult for peasants to run away, to escape their obligations by flight. By long custom if the lord could not recapture a fugitive serf within a certain period of time (in Western Europe it was "a year and a day"), the serf had won his freedom. In Russia the tsars kept extending the length of time in which a lord could recover a fugitive serf, first to three years, then to five, and finally indefinitely. Thus, an individual, even if he escaped, was always subject to reenserfment. As an additional support for the landowner, the government decreed increasingly harsh penalties against those who aided or harbored runaway serfs.

In these ways state policy and economic necessity reinforced each other in transforming most Russian peasants into serfs. The process was a gradual one, over approximately two centuries, but it culminated distinctly in the *Ulozhenie*, or Law Code of 1649. Its provisions forbade serfs to leave at any time and gave landowners unlimited time and rights in reclaiming runaway serfs. From that time on the position of the serf deteriorated. Landlords not only required labor or payments in cash or produce in return for the serfs' right to use the land but also began to exercise judicial and administrative control over their serfs (see Figure 8). By the end of the 1600s the serf had become the personal chattel of the landlord and could be sold apart from the land and separate from his family. In short, the serf was a slave (but, unlike the United States, of the same culture and race as his owner).

Figure 8. *Russian nobles had judicial authority over their serfs, including the right to punish them by flogging. (Courtesy of the British Library)*

What happened to the peasant commune in this process? Interestingly, it was preserved as the peasant passed from free person to serf to slave. The sense of the community was maintained, and decisions in the *obshchina* continued to be taken fairly democratically, that is, by a consensus of the heads of all the households participating. The lord used it as an administrative device, making the commune responsible for the peasants' obligations to him, and later the government also exacted taxes and recruits for the army through the instrumentality of the commune.

Not all peasants became serfs of private landowners, though 60 to 70 percent of the population were in this status by the end of the seventeenth century. The remainder were predominantly state peasants or church peasants. They lived on land holdings of the tsar, the state, or the Orthodox Church, and they owed obligations, usually in kind or in cash, less often in labor, to their respective institutional overseers. Their conditions of work and service were generally less onerous than those of the serfs belonging to private landowners. Finally, a small number of peasants remained entirely free, especially those on the eastern and southern frontiers of the vast country.

Why did serfdom come to Russia so late, and why did it become such an extensive and long-lasting institution? One answer is summed

up in the aphorism "Serfdom is the price paid by Russians for the sake of survival." In other words, the tsars, ruling a poor country but determined to build the Russian state and to defeat Russia's enemies on several fronts, could only mobilize the required resources by demanding service from the whole population. The gentry provided military and administrative service and were paid with land. The peasants, in return for order and protection, served at first by paying taxes and providing recruits for the army. Later, however, they served by supporting the gentry so the latter could in turn serve the tsar and the state. They made the gentry's land valuable either by working a certain number of days per week on it or by paying the lord (usually in produce) to use the land. In essence, Russian society, excluding townspeople, was a simple pyramidal structure, as shown in the chart above.

Yet the question remains: why did serfdom emerge in Russia at the very moment it was disappearing in western Europe? European kings were also trying to unify their territories and set up centralized systems of government, but they did not have to resort to enforced service. The simplest answer is that in attempting similar tasks the Russian tsars and the European kings commanded quite different resources. The latter could draw on the accumulated wealth of towns and merchants who had been engaged in profitable local, regional, and international trade for some time, as well as on an increasing agricultural surplus generated by new farming techniques and technology developed in the High Middle Ages. In Russia, by contrast, agriculture remained at a low subsistence level and there was little commercial surplus concentrated in towns and in the hands of rich merchants. As we saw earlier, the Mongols had appropriated the few resources of the country during their rule, and under the Muscovite tsars trade and towns had grown only slowly. No capital had been amassed on which Russian rulers could draw in their long struggle to consolidate and strengthen the state. Service (and serfdom) had to substitute for capital.

Perhaps if Russia had not been cut off from European technology in the 1200s and 1300s; perhaps if Russia had participated with the Europeans in the overseas discoveries and rich trade with the Americas, Africa, and Asia that occurred in the 1400s and 1500s; perhaps if the early grand princes and tsars had tried more actively to improve agriculture and promote commerce; perhaps if Russia had not been strained by long wars with its neighbors, like Ivan the Terrible's Livonian War, the Russian economy would have flourished without serfdom. But history is not made up of "ifs." None of those things happened, and we will never know whether Russia might have escaped serfdom under different circumstances. Instead we know that serfdom became the dominant social institution of Russia in the 1600s and persisted for over two hundred years.

This system influenced Russia's future development in several important ways. First, it meant that the Russian economy remained predominantly agricultural, that the level of productivity remained low, and that trade, towns, and the merchant class all grew rather slowly. Second, it created a deep and virtually unbridgeable split in Russian society: the great mass of the population (the lower classes, the people, or in Russian the *narod*) who were serfs and second-class citizens of the state, with many obligations and few rights, versus a tiny upper elite who were privileged and mostly conservative. Finally, almost from the beginning serfdom created a great moral dilemma in Russia. How could one justify enslaving millions of one's fellow-Russians? That they were also Christians, also subjects of the tsar, simply made their degradation more stark, the situation more indefensible. These economic, social, and moral dimensions of serfdom became persistent issues throughout the eighteenth and into the nineteenth centuries.

The Autocracy

As we saw in the previous chapter, the autocracy, the unlimited rule of the tsar, nearly disappeared in the turmoil and upheavals of the Time of Troubles. Yet the importance of the tsar as the symbol of the state and the focus of Russian unity was shown in the repeated attempts during those stormy years to put forward a pretender to the throne and in the decision of the *zemskii sobor* of 1613 to elect a new tsar, young Michael Romanov.

For the first part of his reign Michael ruled in concert with boyar advisors and from 1619 together with his father, Metropolitan Filaret. After the latter's death in 1633, Michael ruled alone until he died in 1645, a reign of thirty-two years. Alexis also had a long reign, thirty-one years, to 1676. The very length of the rule of these first two Romanov tsars contributed significantly to restoring stability and authority to the tsardom. Moreover, both Michael and Alexis were moderately capable, if not particularly brilliant or far-sighted.

More important in resurrecting the autocracy, however, was the failure of any alternative system or center of power to develop. Certainly in 1613, at the accession of Michael, it seemed probable that the *zemskii sobor,* or assembly of the land, that had played such a key role in the national resurgence against the Swedes and Poles and that had been ruling the country for some months, would emerge as either an executive body coequal to the tsar or at least as an institutionalized advisory council representing the interests and views of the upper classes in Russian society. And, indeed, in the first years of Michael's rule the *zemskii sobor* was in almost continuous session. It was also convened on the occasion of major foreign policy or domestic crises in the 1630s, 1640s, and 1650s. Yet it met infrequently after midcentury and had died out by the end of the 1600s.

There is no definitive explanation for the demise of the *zemskii sobor,* but we can speculate about two possible reasons. The first is a paradox: its very success in sharing power with the tsar led to its curtailment. When Michael and Alexis were trying to rebuild the tsarist state and in the process faced a series of challenges and problems, they had to rely on the *zemskii sobor* to help them and to marshal support from the upper classes of Muscovite society. But once the autocratic system, with help from the *zemskii sobor,* had recovered from the ravages of the Time of Troubles and the state had begun to grow and expand again, Tsar Alexis hastened to discard any restraints on his authority and gladly let this institution fall into disuse.

Second, unlike the parliaments of western Europe that began to develop about the same time, the *zemskii sobor* had no legal, theoretical, or ideological basis on which to build an ongoing role as a political institution. In an emergency the tsar had convened it to rally support behind him and to give him advice. It was an ad hoc device and never developed an independent position in the Moscow state structure. Consequently, when the tsar no longer needed it and stopped convening it, the *zemskii sobor* disappeared.

In a larger sense the dying out of the *zemskii sobor* reflected the weak political position of the upper classes whose representatives made up the *zemskii sobor.* If the boyars, the high clergy, the gentry, and the rich townsmen had had independent power positions, as separate classes, they might have acted to limit the growing absolutism of the tsar. But the boyars, who during the Time of Troubles had made a remarkable recovery from the setbacks they had suffered at the hands of Ivan the Terrible, were still unable in the 1600s to act together as a class or to assert political rights against the tsar. They continued to squabble over rank and position, they were often venal and narrow-minded, and Tsars Michael and Alexis were able to keep them under control. Moreover, as the historian Robert Crummey has shown, their ranks were swelled greatly in the 1600s by marriage and by appointments of servitors essentially loyal to the tsar. They became an elite of privilege and wealth but posed no threat to the autocracy.

During the Time of Troubles high Church officials had worked closely with other national leaders to save the country, and in the 1620s Metropolitan Filaret had been virtual co-tsar with his son Michael. But the overriding tradition of the Orthodox Church was to support the autocracy and to work closely with it, rather than to challenge it. As we shall see shortly, one churchman later in the seventeenth century did defy the tsar's authority, but his bid to share power was quickly quelled. By the end of the century, the Russian Church, weakened by internal dissension, was politically helpless and wholly dependent on the tsar, a position quite different from that of many Protestant and Catholic Churches in western Europe.

The gentry and the townspeople had even less chance to limit the burgeoning autocratic power. The gentry were essentially the tsar's men. Even though, by the end of the 1600s, they had achieved considerable status and the hereditary rights to their lands, the gentry, like the boyars, did not consider themselves or act as a class, with group interests to be defended or rights to be asserted. Although in the 1700s the gentry did show some political muscle, they were then in a stronger position than they had been in the seventeenth century.

The townspeople of Russia had almost no political influence, partly because they lacked clear status as a class, but most importantly because Russian towns were mainly administrative centers, extensions of the authority of the tsar, whereas in western Europe they were commercial-financial centers with autonomous charters and independent wealth. The tsar himself was the richest merchant, and although some Muscovites became wealthy in commerce and production, there was no autonomous merchant or financial class. There were no guilds, banks, or companies for the accumulation of capital, the protection of economic privilege, and the eventual assertion of political influence.

It is therefore hardly surprising that the autocracy grew and flourished during the seventeenth century to become the overriding political institution of tsarist Russia for almost three hundred more years. To be sure, the tsar's power was limited, but not by individuals, classes or institutions. First, it was limited in spiritual terms: the autocrat was to rule according to God's will, and it would have been impossible for the tsar to act in a way that directly contravened the Orthodox faith and belief of his people. In fact, as we shall shortly see, Tsar Alexis had to face just such a crisis, during which many hundreds of thousands of his subjects rejected his authority over a religious issue.

Second, the tsar's absolutism was tempered by the sheer size of his realm and the magnitude of the task of governing it. No tsar could do everything. Each tsar had to depend to a considerable extent on his military and civilian advisers and officials. Thus, beginning earlier but accelerating in the 1600s, the tsar's army and civil service grew rapidly. The tsar set general policies and even made final decisions on relatively small matters, but obviously the day-to-day business of administration—keeping order, making judgments, collecting taxes—was left to an increasing number of clerks and bureaucrats. The local self-government established under Ivan the Terrible had disappeared during the Time of Troubles, so the first Romanovs relied heavily on military governors to manage local and regional affairs. Corruption and harassment of the people were widespread, and some historians believe that the urban riots in Moscow and other cities in the 1600s and even the great rebellion of Stenka Razin were sparked largely by resentment against the venality and petty oppressions of local officials rather than by any broad rejection of the tsarist system.

Drunkenness and random violence also played a role in these outbursts, as the provincial governor of Khotmyshsk reported in October 1648:

> At prayer gatherings, weddings, christenings and at relatives' homes they drink themselves drunk and fight and struggle in their stupor. Having fought, they make [political] denunciations against [one another].[2]

Before judging Russians of the seventeenth century too harshly, we should bear in mind that their behavior was not outrageous according to the standards of *that time*. We also need to remember that our own "civilized" century has seen the worst violence and killing in human history (in two world wars, Stalin's purges, and the Holocaust).

The Orthodox Church

In the 1600s as the restored autocracy increased its centralized power, so also the might and authority of the Russian Orthodox Church expanded. But two events, occurring about the same time in the third quarter of the century, greatly weakened the Church and prepared the way for its complete subjugation to the state by Peter the Great in the early 1700s. Both events were associated with one imposing, talented, and strong-willed individual, Patriarch Nikon, head of the Church from 1652 to 1667.

Unlike most high clergy, Nikon was not from the upper classes but was of peasant descent. Extremely bright and well educated, Nikon had come to the attention of young Tsar Alexis early in the latter's reign. Nikon's powerful personality and erudition soon exerted considerable

---

[2] Cited in Mark C. Lapham's review of E. V. Chistiakova, "Gorodskie vosstaniia v Rossii v pervoi polovine XVII veka (30-40-e gody) [City rebellions in Russia in the first half of the 17th century (1630s–40s)]," *Kritika*, vol. XII, no. 2 (Spring 1977), p. 87.

influence over the tsar. Nikon, apparently partly through ambition and partly through his interpretation of the role of the Church in the Byzantine system, asserted in the late 1650s that the Church was independent of, or even in some respects superior to, the state. He demanded to share authority with the tsar. This action flew in the face of long-standing Russian tradition and soon provoked a political storm. The tsar finally broke with Nikon, and in 1666–67 a high Church council, including prelates from other parts of the Orthodox world, rejected Nikon's claims, unseated him as patriarch, and exiled him to a remote monastery. That was the last time in Russian history that the spiritual power attempted to challenge the secular authority of the tsar.

Of even more long-lasting consequence, however, was Nikon's other major action: a thoroughgoing reform of Russian Orthodox texts and rituals. What seemed a perfectly reasonable proposition—to correct errors that had crept into liturgical materials and church services over the centuries—soon turned into a major struggle that divided the Russian Orthodox Church irrevocably and sparked social conflict leading to thousands of deaths.

To us the issues may appear obscure, or even ridiculous: for example, whether the sign of the cross should be made with three fingers or with two, the correct spelling of Jesus' name, in which direction around the church the procession that makes up part of the Orthodox Mass should go. But to both sides in the mounting controversy such questions were connected with the fundamental question of what was the true Christian faith. Moreover, each side was led by a powerful, determined, and eloquent individual: the reformers by Patriarch Nikon and the defenders of the old forms by the Archpriest Avvakum, whose autobiographical account of his sufferings is a major work of Russian literature.

The whole affair, known as the Schism (*Raskol* in Russian) because it split the Church, began innocently enough, as a byproduct of the expansion and increasing sophistication of the Russian Church. Early in Nikon's tenure as patriarch, well-educated and scholarly clergy, some of whom came from the Ukraine, which had recently been added to the Church's jurisdiction, called to Nikon's attention that certain parts of the Russian liturgical texts and rituals did not correspond with the Greek versions. The latter were considered more "correct" since they were closer to the original sources, and it was alleged that errors in translating materials into Russian had occurred at various times during the long period since Russia's conversion to Orthodoxy. Nikon, who was anxious to upgrade and improve the Russian Church in various ways, soon accepted this point of view and began an intense campaign to eliminate the errors and to reform the ecclesiastical books and the Mass accordingly.

To his surprise and then anger, a number of high prelates disa-

greed with him and refused to accept the proposed changes. Before long
hundreds of thousands of parishioners had joined the opposition. After
some indecision Tsar Alexis and the government as a whole backed the
reforms and soon began to use force against those who opposed the
changes. Nikon was determined to impose the reforms on the whole
church, but his opponents were equally adamant in rejecting them. As
a consequence the Russian Church was torn apart, and those who opposed the reforms went their own way, known thenceforth as Old Believers. Paradoxically, the same high Church council that deposed Nikon for his political ambitions fully endorsed his reforms in 1667.

Both the Church and the government exerted great moral pressure and even physical coercion in an effort to bring the Old Believers
back into the fold. But few returned. And some, perhaps as many as
twenty thousand, convinced that the changes presaged the end of the
world, burned themselves to death. Others defied the government, and
Old Believers at the Solovetskii Monastery in northern Russia held out
against repeated military assaults for eight years from 1668 to 1676.

The Archpriest Avvakum was imprisoned and then burned at the
stake in 1682 as part of a general persecution of opposition leaders.
Nevertheless the Old Believers survived to become a significant religious and social force in eighteenth- and nineteenth-century Russia. A
few exist today in the Soviet Union, and some Old Believer sects persist
among Russian emigrants in Canada and the United States.

What led the Old Believers to resist so fiercely what were after all
superficial changes, emendations that did not touch basic doctrine and
tenets of faith? In part it was a commendable devoutness, a profound
emotional and intellectual passion to preserve what they believed was
the purity and sanctity of true Christianity, as this appeal of Archpriest
Avvakum makes clear:

> Come, Orthodox people, call upon the name of Christ, stand in the midst
> of Moscow, make the sign of the cross of Christ our Savior holding two
> fingers as we learned it from our Holy Fathers. The Kingdom of God is
> born in this land. . . . Do not falter. I, together with ye, am ready to die
> for Christ. Although I have not much understanding—I am not a learned
> man—yet I know that the church, which we have received from our Holy
> Fathers, is pure and sacred. As it came to me so shall I uphold my faith
> until the end. It was established long before our time, and thus may it re-
> main for evermore.[3]

An innate conservatism, bordering on superstition, was also a factor in the position taken by the Old Believers. Illiterate and insecure
for the most part, they feared change and became convinced that altering the mass or correcting the texts could only be the work of the devil,

[3] In Paul Miliukov, *Outlines of Russian Culture*, Part I, *Religion and the Church* (Philadelphia: University of Pennsylvania Press, 1942), 38.

designed to bring God's wrath down on them. For some schismatics xenophobia may also have played a role: the changes came from Greek-trained or Greek-oriented scholars and threatened true Russian practices. The purity of the faith could only be preserved by rejecting these influences from the outside.

Finally, there may have been an element of sociopolitical protest in the Old Believer movement. Some of the schismatics were extremely poor and may have used the religious issue as a way of expressing their opposition to the government and the existing order. In any case, once the tsar and his administration sided with the church hierarchy, many Old Believers moved willingly to open rebellion against all authority, religious and civil, and waged guerrilla warfare against both the established church and the state. It marked a major crisis in the reign of Tsar Alexis, one that he barely overcame before his death in 1676.

The Schism seriously weakened the Russian Orthodox Church. As the prerevolutionary Russian historian Paul Miliukov argued, the church lost some of its ablest leaders and some of its most devout and vital congregations. Moreover, the triumph of the reformers meant that form won out over content, ritual over feeling and ideas. As a result, Orthodoxy became increasingly formalistic and stultified, with less and less intellectual, social, and political influence in Russian society.

A corollary effect was that Russian life became more secularized. After the Schism the role of religion and the church at the Russian court and among the upper classes was reduced, a change that helped pave the way for Peter the Great's westernization program forty years later.

The Expansion of Russia

The seeker of patterns in Russia's historical development could reasonably argue that before the 1600s the growth of the principality of Moscow and the expansion of the tsarist state were essentially defensive in nature, necessary to consolidate power and territory and to secure Russia's borders against a host of enemies on three sides. But after 1600 it is harder to maintain that the additions to Russia's lands were primarily for self-protection. The tsars now appeared more interested in aggrandizement, power for the sake of power, and territories that would benefit Russia economically. Moreover, prior to the seventeenth century the state annexed lands that were predominantly inhabited by other Russians, except for its conquest of the Tatar khanates of Kazan and Astrakhan. Yet in the 1600s and after, most of the peoples who fell under Russian rule were either distant cousins, like the Ukrainians, or not Russian at all (Balts, Caucasian peoples, Asians). Russia became a multinational state, but Great Russians continued to rule and dominate it.

In the 1600s the two main directions of Russian expansion were eastward and southwestward (see Map 5). The former, a push all across the Eurasian continent to the Pacific Ocean, added an enormous sweep of territory to the Russian state but had little political or strategic significance at the time. The latter, which brought part of the Ukraine, including Kiev, into the tsars' realm, involved only a small amount of land but was very important politically and strategically.

Expansion across the Ural Mountains and into Siberia had begun in the latter part of the previous century but advanced eastward in the 1600s another three thousand miles. By the 1640s Russian explorers reached the Pacific Ocean, and one expedition even sailed through the Bering Strait. The Russian advance was checked only when it ran up against the outposts of the large Chinese empire. By the Treaty of Nerchinsk in 1689 Russia's eastern border was established short of the Amur River.

In some respects the Siberian expansion resembled the westward movement in the United States two centuries later. In both case traders, fur trappers, adventurers, and military officers led the way, motivated by a combination of curiosity, greed, daring, and civic pride. Settlement, government, and taxes soon followed, though in both Siberia and the American West there was for a time a greater degree of freedom and individual initiative on the frontier than in the older, more "civilized" sections of the country. For example, serfdom was never established in Siberia.

At the same time the two movements differed considerably in important respects. The tsarist government played a larger direct role in exploring, colonizing, and reaping the economic benefits (primarily furs) of Siberia than the United States government did in the American West. The Russians treated the indigenous Asian peoples they conquered considerably better than the settlers treated the native Americans. Finally, Siberia remained thinly settled and rather unimportant until recent times, whereas the American West was soon thickly inhabited and rapidly became an important section, politically and economically, of the United States.

For a long time the acquisition of furs was the major advantage of Siberia for the Russian state. But in the past one hundred years extremely valuable mineral resources, including gold, petroleum, and natural gas, have been discovered in Siberia, and today it is of great economic significance for the Soviet Union. Ever since the 1600s migration and colonization in Siberia have developed rather slowly, mainly because of the distances and the harsh climate, but Siberia did offer a chance to escape the oppressive conditions of life in central Russia, and it attracted some peasants and serfs soon after it was opened up. Moreover, on its southeastern borders the Russian state consistently spurred colonization in order to extend its frontiers against Asian nomads and

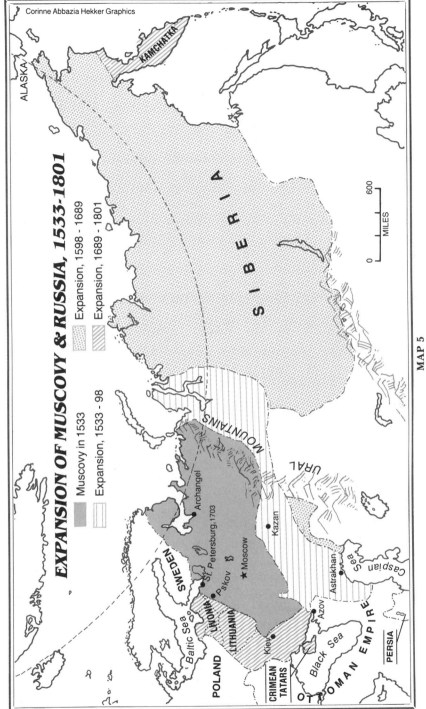

EXPANSION OF MUSCOVY & RUSSIA, 1533-1801

Muscovy in 1533
Expansion, 1533 - 98
Expansion, 1598 - 1689
Expansion, 1689 - 1801

Corinne Abbazia Hekker Graphics

ALASKA

KAMCHATKA

SIBERIA

URAL MOUNTAINS

Archangel
St. Petersburg, 1703
Pskov
Moscow
Kazan
Astrakhan
Caspian Sea
Azov
Kiev
Black Sea

SWEDEN
Baltic Sea
LIVONIA
LITHUANIA
POLAND
CRIMEAN TATARS
OTTOMAN EMPIRE
PERSIA

0   600
MILES

MAP 5

Moslems. Fortified towns and outposts were built farther and farther toward Central Asia, and Russian settlers were given attractive incentives to man them.

Russia's acquisition of the eastern half of the Ukraine between the 1640s and the 1660s was closely connected with the tsars' continuing struggle against Poland, which in the seventeenth century was a more powerful country than Russia. After the Polish effort to conquer Russia during the Time of Troubles had been rebuffed, relations between the two Slavic states remained strained, though a peace treaty was finally signed in 1634 after another inconclusive war. The situation was complicated because the Poles faced increasing difficulty controlling the population on Poland's eastern and southeastern lands, territory that had been part of the Kievan state and that was now known as the Ukraine. Most of the people were peasants and belonged to the Orthodox Church, whereas a majority of the landowners were Polish Catholics. The Ukrainians considered themselves oppressed socially and religiously by their Polish overlords. In the late sixteenth century the Poles had helped establish a special branch of the Catholic Church called the Uniate Church, which acknowledged the authority of the Pope in Rome but had Orthodox liturgy and used Slavic language in the Mass. Although some Orthodox Ukrainians accepted the new church, the majority did not and the religious division in the Ukraine was further exacerbated.

The Poles were also having trouble with a special group living in the Ukraine, the Dnieper cossacks. The Polish government gave them limited support and permitted some continuation of traditional cossack autonomy, but the cossacks could not be won entirely to the Polish cause since they were Orthodox in religion and had close ties with the Ukrainian people as a whole. By dint of ruthless repression and at considerable cost, the Polish government was able to keep a lid on the situation until 1648, when the Ukrainians, led by a great national hero, Bogdan Khmelnitsky, started a broad-scale rebellion against Polish rule.

Although the Ukrainians achieved considerable success against much larger Polish forces, it was clear that in the long run they would need outside help. They turned naturally to their coreligionists in Moscow. At first Tsar Alexis and his advisers were reluctant to aid the Ukrainian rebels, since it certainly would mean war with Poland, an expensive and risky proposition. Finally, in 1653–54, with the approval of a *zemskii sobor*, Alexis responded favorably to the Ukrainians' request for assistance, in return for which the Ukrainians swore allegiance to the Russian tsar. As a result of the ensuing war with Poland, territorial settlements were finally reached in 1667 and 1686, by which all the lands on the left or eastern bank of the Dnieper River, plus the cities of Smolensk and Kiev, became part of Russia. They have remained so to this day.

Ukrainian historians and nationalists have strongly criticized Russia's absorption of the Ukraine, but it is hard to see how an independent Ukraine could have survived, sandwiched as it would have been between Turkey, Poland, and Russia. On the other hand, the Russians, though also Slavic and Orthodox, soon proved stern masters. They failed to respect the autonomy of the Ukraine as stipulated in the arrangements of 1654 and 1667, and before long they imposed serfdom on much of its territory. Later, as we shall see, they also tried to suppress the development of an independent Ukrainian literature and culture.

Relations with the West

Although in the 1300s and 1400s Moscow had some contact with central and western Europe through Novgorod and Poland-Lithuania, the emerging Russian state was largely isolated from the West during the period of its unification and rapid expansion. Increasingly in the 1500s and 1600s relations were reestablished. Not only did trade expand, but ambassadors were exchanged, a few Russians visited the West, and several thousand Westerners traveled or lived in Russia. These contacts stimulated intellectual intercourse, first in religious matters and technology but later in secular knowledge and general culture.

The tsarist state benefited from closer ties with the West in several important ways: First, the trade, though not extensive, was an important source of revenue and brought to Russia a variety of goods and finished products that otherwise would have been unavailable. Second, the Romanov tsars drew on Western military ideas and technology as they built up their army. Finally, Western artisans and entrepreneurs played a significant role in developing early Russian mining and manufacturing enterprises, for example, in glassmaking and iron working.

In the long run the deepest impact of the West on Russia was in the realm of ideas. Part of this intellectual stimulation was a byproduct of religious competition between the Orthodox Church and the Catholic and Uniate Churches. Orthodox leaders recognized that if they were to prevent the influx of Catholicism in the Ukraine and other western borderlands of Russia, they needed better-educated clergy. Spurred by the model of Metropolitan Peter Mogila's educational institution in Kiev, the authorities encouraged schools in Moscow staffed largely by learned monks from the Ukraine. These efforts culminated in the opening in the 1680s of a Slavonic-Greek-Latin Academy, which taught not only those languages but rhetoric, philosophy, grammar, and theology, a curriculum common to most of Europe since the sixteenth century.

At the same time some secular literature modeled on Western forms began to appear, and the first theater was established under the patronage of Tsar Alexis. Not only the tsar himself but the wealthy elite began to take an interest in things Western. European dress, food, tobacco, furniture, and baroque architecture all were in vogue among upper-class Muscovites, and smoking spread rapidly through all levels of the population.

In short, by the third quarter of the seventeenth century, there was a growing receptiveness in Russia to thought, manners, and institutions of the West, an attitude that certainly prepared the ground for Peter the Great and his all-out effort to westernize Russia in the early eighteenth century.

The psychological side effects of this openness to European civilization must not be overlooked, on the other hand. Because the Europeans were richer, thanks to the agricultural and commercial revolutions they were experiencing and to their profitable overseas trade, and because they were more advanced technologically, some Russians felt inferior to the West and were anxious to push Russia to catch up. This led some to criticize their own society as backward and barbaric, a view shared by several Europeans who traveled in Russia and published detailed accounts of this "strange and exotic" land. Yet it is important to remember that in some respects Russians possessed a more advanced society than their Western neighbors; for example, they had a centralized effective state when the Italians and Germans still lived in a motley collection of city-states, tiny principalities, and chopped-up feudal fiefdoms. They enjoyed a common religion and relative peace at a time when Europe was rent with religious strife and recurring warfare. The Russians were certainly different in many respects, but whether they were better or worse off is a moot point.

Conclusion

In many ways the seventeenth century was a transitional period in the development of Russian society. The state, after a long period of growth and after nearly breaking apart in the Time of Troubles, was consolidated and centralized. Nevertheless, despite some reforms and an expansion of the bureaucracy, it had an archaic outlook and administration. The role of the tsar remained highly personalized, and government was not very efficient. At the same time the Russian economy developed only slowly while the western European countries were accumulating wealth and laying the basis for the Industrial Revolution that would begin in the next century. Russia's expansion into the Ukraine added important territory as well as several million fellow Slavs and coreligionists. On the other hand, Russia's expansion eastward brought Asians under tsarist rule and had economic and strategic significance only much later.

In the 1600s class divisions in Russia hardened, and in particular a large proportion of the peasants became permanently enserfed and sank toward the level of slaves. The institution of serfdom widened the gap between a small elite and the bulk of the population and created a major social and moral issue for the next two centuries. The Schism weakened the Russian Orthodox Church, with a large minority of dedicated "outcasts" breaking away from the established religion.

In the largest sense the seventeenth century was a bridge between medieval Russia of the late Kievan, Mongol, and early Muscovite periods and the Russian empire of the 1700s and 1800s that was thrust precipitously into modern times. The 1600s cracked the door to the entry of Western science, technology, and thought, and Russia has been struggling with the impact of modernization ever since.

FURTHER READING

Avvakum, S. *The Life of the Archpriest Avvakum by Himself.* London: 1924, 1968.

Blum, Jerome. *Lord and Peasant in Russia from the Ninth to the Nineteenth Century.* Princeton, N. J.: 1961.

Crummey, Robert O. *The Old Believers and the World of AntiChrist.* Madison, Wisc.: 1970.

———. *Aristocrats and Servitors.* Princeton, N.J.: 1983.

Fuhrmann, Joseph. *Tsar Alexis: His Reign and his Russia.* Gulf Breeze, Fla.: 1981.

Hellie, Richard. *Enserfment and Military Change in Muscovy.* Chicago: 1971.

Keep, John. "The Decline of the Zemsky Sobor," *Slavic and East European Review* (Vol. 36) 100–22, December 1957.

Lantzeff, George. *Siberia in the Seventeenth Century.* Berkeley: 1943.

Longworth, P. *Tsar Alexis.* London: 1984.

Medlin, W. K. *Renaissance Influences and Religious Reforms in Russia.* Geneva: 1971.

Philipp, Werner. "Russia: The Beginning of Westernization." In F. S. Carsten, ed., *New Cambridge Modern History* (Vol. 5). Cambridge: 1961.

Platonov, S. F. *Moscow and the West.* Hattiesburg, Miss.: 1972.

6

Peter the Great and Westernization, 1689–1725

The thud of axes slicing into wood resounded through the walls of the small log house on the riverbank. Peter, tsar of Russia, stirred in his sleep, then sat up quickly. Seeing daylight under the door, he cursed himself and jumped out of bed, throwing on his clothes as he hastened outside. He liked to be first on the job, but already carpenters were perched on top of and around the frames of several large ships nearby. After momentarily warming his hands over a fire alongside several just arisen workmen, Peter picked up his own hammer and axe. Energetically he clambered up the scaffolding surrounding a galley under construction and threw himself into the work. Peter looked supremely happy. As he wrote in a letter at that time, "we are eating our bread in the sweat of our face."

No one seemed surprised to see his tsarist majesty, the autocrat of all the Russias, the "most pious father of his people," laboring as hard as any peasant in the shipyard. Most of his co-workers were already accustomed to the unorthodox ways of the young tsar, and they respected him for his skill as a shipwright and his willingness to tackle the toughest jobs. On this occasion, in March 1696, both Peter's talents and his leadership were being tested to the fullest. Reigning tsar for only two years, he had suffered a serious defeat at the hands of the Turks the previous summer, and there was already considerable grumbling against him in Moscow. In 1695 Peter had tried to capture the fortified town of Azov, which commanded the entrance to the Sea of Azov, at the mouth of the Don River (see Map 5). Peter's army besieged Azov, but because Peter had no support ships on the river, the Turks were able to relieve the garrison with reinforcements and supplies brought in by sea. Peter finally had to retreat.

Undaunted, Peter, as soon as he returned to Moscow in December, decided to resume the attack the following summer, but with a Russian fleet to control the river. That meant he had to build from scratch the armada he needed in only five months: twenty-five sea-going galleys and over a thousand barges for troops and supplies, an almost impossible task even under the best of conditions! Yet Peter had little to work with. It was winter, with numbing cold, ice, and shortened days; there was no shipyard anywhere in south Russia; no one in that region knew how to build large ships; and there was no prepared timber or other supplies for ship construction. As a recent biographer of Peter observed:

> Peter's plan, then, was to build the shipyards, assemble the workmen, teach them to mark, cut and hew the timber, lay the keels, build the hulls, step the masts, shape the oars, weave the ropes, sew the sails, train the crews, and sail the whole massive fleet down the Don River to Azov. All within five winter months![1]

Despite bad weather, delays in the arrival of skilled craftsmen, and the desertion of many conscripted laborers, Peter, to everyone's astonishment, drove the project through to completion. In early May he sailed down the Don at the head of his mininavy, which compared favorably with Turkish and Western ships of the time, and by the end of July he had captured Azov. In the triumphal procession several miles long that entered Moscow the following October to celebrate this important Russian victory, Tsar Peter walked on foot, among other captains of the Russian galleys, wearing a plain black uniform with only a white feather in his hat indicating he had any special status.

As this episode illustrates, Peter the Great was determined to use modern techniques and weapons to strengthen his country and unstintingly applied his considerable energy to this task. Russia had already begun to change under the impact of new ideas and increasing contact with Europe, as we saw in Chapter 5, and doubtless, even without Peter, Russia would have eventually been transformed into a more modern society. What Peter did was to accelerate this transition greatly. At the same time, because he forced the pace of change, he widened the gulf between Westernized and old Russia. In their hearts many Russians refused to accept the reforms Peter insisted on.

Moreover, in some respects Peter the Great failed. On the surface, to be sure, Russian society, or at least the upper classes, appeared to adopt European ideas, technology, and attitudes, but in retrospect the result can be seen as a rough and uneven patchwork of the new and the traditional, with many anomalies and incongruities. Even today, almost 250 years later, it is apparent that Russian society still suffers from a split personality, with part of the national outlook secular, rational, and tolerant and part zealous, emotional, and xenophobic.

Russia, as with all traditional societies that have come in contact with Western science, technology, and power, really had no choice but to modernize. To ignore or reject Europe's influence meant isolation, backwardness, and eventual subjugation. Peter saw this clearly and did

[1] Robert K. Massie, *Peter the Great* (New York: 1980), 142.

everything possible to propel Russia into the modern era. He competed successfully with his nearest and powerful Western neighbors, Sweden and Poland, and he greatly increased Russian security and prestige. He also set in motion far-reaching changes in almost every sector of Russian life. Yet he did not tamper with the institution of serfdom, which meant that societywide modernization could not develop in Russia until after the liberation of the serfs in 1861.

Peter's impact was muted for two related reasons. First, unlike the west European nations, Russia lacked the resources to move quickly to a basic overhaul of its institutions and way of life. It had a relatively small population of about 15 million, and as we have seen, it was at the end of the 1600s still a poor country, with low agricultural productivity, few cities, limited trade, and no substantial surplus. For Peter even to make headway in establishing Russia's place in the European state system and in raising the level of culture in the country required a ruthless mobilization of Russia's available means and heavy exactions on the population.

Second, again differing from the West, Russia lacked many of the institutions and attitudes that could help carry out modernization. In the West a reforming church, an entrepreneurial class, a developed higher educational system, and well-established guilds and other associations all stood ready to assist any king or group of leaders who proposed modernizing techniques and changes. But in Russia Peter and his advisers had to act almost alone: the established church was apathetic and the Old Believers hostile; the merchants weak and the nobles as a group divided, indifferent, and recalcitrant; education almost nonexistent; corporate bodies absent; and the bulk of the population a conservative opposition. It is no wonder that many believed Peter to be the Anti-Christ and that only by compulsion and through his astounding energy and will could progress be made.

Peter's Coming of Age

Peter, like Ivan the Terrible, did not have a happy childhood, punctuated as it was by fights among noble families vying for power and by periods when the boy tsar was isolated and ignored. Peter was born in 1672, the first son of the second wife of Tsar Alexis. His mother, Natalia Naryshkin, a member of a prominent family, was politically ambitious but traditional and conservative. As a young man Peter quickly rejected her position and point of view.

On his death Tsar Alexis was succeeded by Feodor, his eldest surviving son by his first wife, Maria Miloslavsky. After a reign of six years Feodor died in 1682, without an heir. A hundred years earlier a similar succession crisis had opened the door to the Time of Troubles, but this time the Naryshkins quickly had Peter, a boy of ten, proclaimed tsar. Their claim was almost immediately contested, however, by the Milo-slavsky faction, backed by special army regiments known as the *streltsy*, or musketeers. During the subsequent fighting Peter saw some of his mother's supporters murdered. It was finally agreed that Ivan, Peter's elder half-brother, would be senior tsar and Peter junior tsar. An older daughter of Alexis, Peter's half-sister Sophia, ruled as regent, with some effectiveness, until 1689, when a disastrous military campaign in the south against the Crimean Tatars led to her political downfall. Sophia was packed off to a convent, and Peter, who seemed uninterested in exer-cising power, permitted his mother and her family and supporters to manage affairs of state. After five years his mother died, and in 1694, at the age of twenty-two, Peter began to direct policy. In 1696 the sickly co-tsar Ivan died, and Peter assumed full authority.

In the 1680s, when Sophia was in charge, Peter had been shunted off to a village outside Moscow called Preobrazhenskoe, where he was largely left to his own devices. As a result he had little formal education but did a great deal to educate himself, particularly in practical matters about which he was intensely curious. Moreover, he was able to choose his own companions and develop his own interests. He surrounded himself with a motley crew of Russians and a few foreigners. These were selected not because of birth or position but because Peter liked them or because they had talents Peter wanted to tap. As recreation Peter was allowed to form his own "play" army, with which he first displayed his love of organization and his genius at military tactics. These young playmate-soldiers later formed the core of the first guards regiment in Russia, military units that lasted till 1917.

Peter's Personality and Character

Gargantuan is an adjective frequently used to describe Peter the Great, and it is indeed apt. Physically he was huge and very strong. Having read often that Peter was "nearly seven feet tall" and suspecting this was sheer exaggeration, I hastened on one of my first visits to Mos-cow to the military museum in the Kremlin, where I knew a uniform Peter wore was preserved. When no one was looking, I stretched my six-foot five-inch frame alongside the display case holding a dummy of Peter decked out in rather faded but still impressive battle dress. To my surprise Peter towered comfortably above me, certainly not seven feet in height but probably a commanding six feet seven inches. Living in an era when most people were only a little over five feet tall, how Peter must have dominated any meeting or gathering!

His energy; his appetite for food, drink, and work; his enthusiasm and intellectual curiosity were all virtually boundless. He wanted to do everything, know everything, see everything. He drove his officials, soldiers, and people hard, but he drove himself harder. He was determined to make Russia stronger and better; he worked as singlemindedly for education and science as he strove fiercely for victory in battle. He cajoled and goaded his countrymen, and when all else failed, he coerced them, down the path of modernization.

There were also darker sides to his personality and character. He was often rude and inconsiderate. He was frequently ruthless and cruel. He personally participated in the torture and execution of some members of the *streltsy* who had rebelled against his rule, as this eyewitness account makes clear:

> [On 27 October 1698] . . . two rebels, brothers, having had their thighs and other members broken in front of the castle of the Kremlin, were set alive upon the wheel. . . . Their miserable cries had struck the Tsar [Peter] as he was being driven past. He went up to the wheels, and first promised speedy death, and afterward proffered them a free pardon, if they would confess sincerely. But when upon the very wheel he found them more obstinate than ever, and that they would confess nothing . . . the Tsar left them to the agonies of death, and hastened on to the Monastery of the Nuns, in front of which monastery there were thirty gibbets erected in a quadrangular shape, from which there hung two hundred and thirty *streltsi*.[2]

Like so many extremely talented and determined people, Peter tried to do too much. He took on more than he could manage; as a result, some of his actions were haphazard and some of his reforms uncoordinated and incomplete. Nonetheless he accomplished more than a dozen others could have.

Characteristic of his outlook and behavior was the extended trip to western Europe Peter undertook early in his reign. As a youth he had absorbed from specialists residing in the foreigners' quarter of Moscow information and techniques in a wide range of civil and military trades. Peter was particularly fascinated with shipbuilding and navigation. Although he had helped establish shipyards and construct vessels for the first Russian navy in 1694 and 1695, Peter wanted to learn still more and looked naturally to the West. In addition, he hoped that in the course of visiting European nations he might enlist their support in his continuing struggle against the Ottoman Turkish empire.

Consequently he set out in the spring of 1697 as part of a delegation of over two hundred Russians. Peter attempted to travel incognito as simply a member of the group, but his size made him easily identifiable. Moreover, as the first tsar to travel in Europe, he was the center of attention not only among European governments but among the

---

[2] From the published diary of Johann Georg Korb, an Austrian diplomat at Peter's court, cited in Basil Dmytryshyn, ed., *Imperial Russia: A Source Book 1700–1917* (New York: 1967), 11–12.

general public as well. Besides his diplomatic purpose Peter wanted to learn as much as he could about the West, to absorb as much technical knowledge as possible, and to recruit foreigners to serve in Russia. He spent almost a year and a half abroad, visiting Holland, England, and the Hapsburg empire and was about to continue to Italy when political turmoil in Russia compelled him to return home.

His "grand embassy" was largely successful. Peter spent most time in Holland, acquiring a great deal of information about seafaring and boat building and actually working in a shipyard. He hired a number of Dutch specialists to work for him back home. He learned a great deal there and in the other countries about European attitudes, customs, and education, although his own rowdy behavior at times shocked the Europeans. He did not succeed in forging an alliance against the Turks, but he established personal ties with European officials that were useful in his later diplomatic pursuits. Most of all he returned to Moscow with his head crammed with ideas about ways to modernize his tradition-bound homeland.

Peter in War and Diplomacy

Peter greatly changed Russian society but not Russian foreign policy. He consistently pursued objectives abroad that were very like those of his predecessors as far back as the fifteenth century. He viewed Russia's needs and interests as an independent state in a traditional way, in much the same light as earlier tsars had. Of highest priority was securing the vulnerable borders of Russia, particularly in the south and the west. Next came the task of expanding Russia's contacts and territory, especially in ways that would liberate Russia from her long isolation as a land-locked country. Finally, Peter, like Ivan the Terrible and the first Romanov tsars, encouraged exploration and expansion in Asia in a search for new opportunities and trading partners.

The main threat to Russia in the south came from the Crimean Tatars, descendants of the Mongols who periodically attacked the tsarist state from their well-defended khanate based on the Crimean peninsula in the Black Sea. Since the late 1400s the Tatars had been under the protection of the Ottoman Turks, and the Ottoman Empire was therefore the target of Peter's first campaign. In 1695, shortly after assuming full authority as tsar, he attacked Azov, finally subduing it in 1696 with the help of his newly constructed southern fleet, as we saw at the start of the chapter.

Later on, after a second war against the Turks in which Peter narrowly escaped a major defeat, he had to give back Azov and dismantle his Black Sea fleet. Nevertheless a precedent for Russian expansion to the Black Sea had been set, and by the end of the eighteenth century

Russia had established a firm foothold along the northern shore of that important inland waterway.

As we saw in Chapter 3, Ivan the Terrible made a major effort to reach the Baltic Sea but was ultimately defeated. In the Great Northern War, which lasted the greater part of his reign, from 1700 to 1721, Peter renewed this struggle. His two main objectives were to break the power of Sweden, at that time the dominant country in north central Europe and to open trade and contact directly with Europe via the Baltic Sea, his "window to the West." Although partners in the anti-Swedish coalition shifted with the fortunes of war, Poland and Russia were Sweden's main opponents during most of the Great Northern War.

When the war began, Sweden seemed at a disadvantage: not only had most of the states of the region allied against her, but Sweden's new king was a youth not yet twenty, Charles XII. Charles, however, proved to be a formidable adversary, an energetic and talented leader and a military genius. Before his death on the battlefield at the age of thirty-seven, he had conducted some brilliant campaigns and won a number of major victories.

One of his first triumphs was the defeat of Peter and a much larger Russian army at Narva in the Baltic region in late 1700. Dismayed but not discouraged, Peter began at once to rebuild and reorganize his whole military establishment, including training methods, artillery, and supply. As we shall shortly see, civil government was also mobilized completely behind the war effort.

Luckily for Peter, Charles XII, although he probably could have forced Russia's withdrawal from the war had he pursued an offensive toward Moscow, turned his attention southward against Poland, which he considered the main enemy. Peter the Great took maximum advantage of this respite, expanding and reshaping his army and beginning a fleet for use in the Baltic Sea. Beginning in 1701, the Russians captured most of the territories of Estonia and Livonia (present-day Latvia) along the Baltic shore, and in 1703 Peter founded a city strategically located in the northeastern corner of the Baltic Sea at the mouth of the Neva River (see Map 5). It was soon named St. Petersburg (today Leningrad) and served as one of the two capitals of Russia from 1713 until 1918.

Charles XII finally defeated the Poles and thus could focus fully on the Russians. In 1708 he and his army crossed into Russia from Poland, but instead of heading directly for Moscow, the Swedes turned south into the Ukraine, hoping to win over the cossacks and to establish a firm base there. Several thousand cossacks did join forces with Charles XII, but the majority of Ukrainians remained loyal to Peter. After a preliminary battle in which Peter was able to capture some reinforcements and relief supplies intended for Charles XII, the main struggle between the Russians and the Swedish forces was joined in July 1709 at

Poltava. Outnumbered almost two to one, the Swedes fought heroically but finally suffered a crushing defeat:

> At 9 o'clock . . . the Swedish army turned and moved south to get into a position parallel to that of the Russians. . . . Opposite . . . [were] two packed lines of Russian infantry . . . supported by seventy field guns. . . . The Russian first line of twenty-four battalions was 10,000 strong, the second (of eighteen battalions) 8,000. . . . The enemy superiority in numbers was terrifying. So was their superiority in firepower.
>
> The Swedes attacked first to gain a moral advantage. [Swedish General] Lewenhaupt led a charge with *armes blanches* [bared swords] by the Swedish right wing which made the Russians fall back and gave the Swedes some field guns to turn against their enemy. But a gap appeared between the elite regiments of the right and those of the left, which could not keep up the same pace. Russian troops poured into the gap and widened it. Panic gripped men whose colonel was wounded and the Swedish line began to give way. Even Lewenhaupt when he came on the scene could not make the men stand. "I rode up and down in front of them," he later reported, "I begged, threatened, cursed, and hit out. All was in vain, it was as if they neither saw nor heard me."
>
> Within half an hour the battle was over. The Swedes were either casualties of the battle or . . . fled to the safety of the baggage and reserve regiments at Pushkarivka.
>
> Charles XII on his stretcher [from an earlier wound] had been at the head of the right infantry wing. When the panic spread to that sector of the thin line, his cry of "Swedes, Swedes" went unheeded. His stretcher was hit by musket bullets and destroyed. It looked as if the king would become a prisoner of the Russians. . . . Lewenhaupt's call that the king was in danger brought, however, a front of soldiers willing to delay the enemy by laying down their lives for his. Charles forced himself on to a horse, the bandages on his foot came undone, and blood dripped from [his] wound that opened with the unwonted activity. The horse was shot under him and was replaced. . . .
>
> The Russians did not pursue the Swedes. The fight had been one between infantry in the main, and the foot soldiers of Tsar Peter were nearly as shaken as those of Charles. . . . The Swedes had left some 10,000 on the battlefield, 6,901 dead and 2,760 prisoners of the Tsar. Russian losses were relatively light: 1,345 killed and 3,290 wounded.[3]

Charles managed to escape southwest into Turkish territory. But Russia's reconstructed army had acquitted itself well under Peter's personal leadership, and Peter had every reason to be proud of the progress his Europeanizing program had achieved. He quickly followed up the victory at Poltava, capturing the Baltic coast from Riga to southern Finland in 1710, which secured his new city, St. Petersburg.

Shortly thereafter, however, he became embroiled with the Ottoman Empire again, and the war with Sweden, though essentially settled at Poltava, dragged on over a decade longer. Peter made further gains along the Baltic shore and finally by the Peace of Nystadt in 1721 the

[3] R. M. Hatton, *Charles XII of Sweden* (New York: 1968), 299–300.

Great Northern War was concluded. Russia's possession of what are to-day the Soviet republics of Estonia and Latvia and of territory between St. Petersburg and Finland was confirmed. Russia at last had secure access to the Baltic Sea and through it to western Europe. Even more important, Russia replaced Sweden as the dominant power in north central Europe and was able to concentrate its energies during the rest of the century on a contest with Poland for supremacy in eastern Europe. As the British specialist on Russian history, B. H. Sumner, succinctly summed up the outcome: "Peter made Russia a power in Europe and all three knew it." From the Great Northern War to the present, Russia has been a major player in the game of European power politics, and its influence in Europe seems likely to continue into the foreseeable future.

In recognition of his success Peter was given the titles *Great* and *Emperor,* and from that time on the tsarist state was known as the Russian empire. Moreover, by adding Balts and Finns, Peter extended the multinational character of the empire, a feature that has persisted to today. Finally, it can be argued, Russia reached the geographic limits, at least in the west, of any expansion dictated by security considerations. But in fact the expansion of the empire continued steadily into the 1860s.

Although Peter's main concerns in foreign affairs were his wars with Turkey and Sweden, he had a continuing interest in and curiosity about Asia. He maintained relations with China, encouraged explorations and contacts in the Pacific and with Mongolia and Central Asia, and occupied Persian territory along the Caspian Sea (though it was returned shortly after his death). He even planned an expedition to establish ties with India. Peter, a leader of vision, clearly understood that because of Russia's location in Eurasia, she was bound to have increasing intercourse with the Asian peoples and cultures lying to the southeast. Besides, he was curious; he wanted to know more about these other societies, and he encouraged Russians to study them.

Peter's Reforms

In undertaking major changes in Russian society and government, did Peter have a grand design? Or was he driven helter-skelter from one reform to another by necessity, by the need to keep his war machine going? Proponents of the latter view point out that Russia was at peace only a little over two years during the whole period of Peter's reign and that in a society as little developed economically as Russia the major wars Peter waged demanded an all-out effort and overshadowed any other purpose or activity. On the other hand, those who believe Peter had a plan can point to his own justifications for the changes he made and to reforms he undertook that were quite unrelated to the military mobilization of Russia.

As in so many historiographic controversies, the answer seems to lie somewhere between the two positions. Peter certainly had a definite purpose: he intended to introduce into Russia modern ideas, technology, methods, and institutions he had learned about or had observed on his mission to Europe. These, he was convinced, would both make Russia stronger and improve the welfare of his people. On the other hand, Peter certainly did not have a carefully worked out and consciously timed scheme for Europeanizing the country. He often did things impulsively and in an uncoordinated fashion. And certain measures were clearly related directly to the war effort and to the support of his new army and navy.

Though not a philosopher or theoretician, Peter the Great had a practical sense of the sort of state and society he was trying to shape. His models were the European nations of his time: monarchies with effective bureaucracies and commercial economies. Peter accepted completely the concept of autocracy, the idea of centralized absolutism. The governmental reforms he carried through were designed not to limit the tsar's rule but to make it more effective. The one change in the ideology of autocracy he did try to make was to secularize and depersonalize the tsar's role. The tsar was to remain an absolute ruler, but not for his own sake, or even for God's. Instead the tsar-emperor was to serve the state, as everyone else did. Peter wanted the people to obey not the tsar as a person or a patriarch but as a symbol of sovereignty, as the first servant of the state. The bulk of the population, however, continued to see the tsar as both a "father" and a ruler anointed by God.

Consonant with his view of the tsardom was Peter's belief that all should serve the state. Neither religion nor wealth nor birth should exempt one from fulfilling a primary obligation to the state. Civil and military service were the highest callings, and everything should be done to ensure that the army and the bureaucracy were efficient, honest, and just.

So also should economic life benefit the state. Peter accepted the ideas of *mercantilism,* then the dominant economic theory in Europe, that production should be stimulated and trade managed in such a way as to accrue maximum advantage to the state. At the same time the state should encourage and support science, technology, and education, which were needed for effective governance and for expanding the economy.

As already noted, Peter carried out a complete overhaul of the Russian army and founded the Russian navy in order to be better able to wage war against the Ottoman Empire and Sweden. In his military reforms Peter changed almost everything, from *A* to *Z*, from the design, production, and procurement of weapons and ships; through recruitment, training, and supply of enlisted men and officers; to trans-

Figure 9. *A noble's house in Moscow about 1790. (Courtesy of the Board of Trustees of the Victoria and Albert Museum)*

port, deployment, and battlefield tactics. From Peter's time on Russia had a professional army and navy that rivaled those of any European power.

To ensure the manning and command of his armed forces (and his civil service as well) Peter required that everyone serve. To be sure, this was a principle established earlier by the Muscovite tsars, but Peter made it universal and life-long and saw that it was enforced. Nobles served with their units as long as they were fit and peasant recruits were drafted for life (reduced to twenty-five years later in the 1700s). Peter also decreed that appointment and advancement in civil and military service would be according to ability and merit, not through privilege, birth, or "pull." To this end he set up the *Table of Ranks,* fourteen parallel grades in the civil and military service. Peter provided his own best example, working his way up in both the army and navy until he became a general and later an admiral.

Peter encouraged upward social mobility. A person who attained the eighth rank of the civil service, for example, automatically became a noble (see Figure 9). Moreover, Peter chose his own closest advisers not primarily from the old boyar and gentry families but from all classes in society, selecting individuals he thought had special skills or unusual ability. Alexander Menshikov, Peter's most trusted confidant, whom he later made a prince, was of humble origins and reputedly worked as a street vendor in Moscow before becoming the tsar's orderly and rising to prominence. Other high officials in Peter's reign included several Swiss,

Scots, and Germans, a former serf, a shepherd, and a clerk. At the same time one of his ablest generals was a member of an old noble family.

Peter did not, however, alter serfdom. He seemed unaware that it was probably not an efficient system of agricultural production, apart from the moral issues it raised. Yet in other areas of economic life Peter did his best to stimulate activity and output. He established hundreds of small manufacturing enterprises, most, to be sure, primarily to supply the armed forces, and he introduced a number of new products and trades into Russia. He provided subsidies to promote exports and assisted native Russian artisans. Because of the heavy costs of his wars, however, the Russian economy hardly flourished in the Petrine era, and some estimates suggest that Russia was worse off at the end of his reign than at the beginning.

There is certainly no doubt that the average citizen carried a heavy fiscal burden under Peter's rule, the state budget more than doubling between 1700 and 1725. Peter and his advisors were ingenious at devising new taxes, including some intended to discourage traditional practices, such as those on beards and Old Believers. A reform of lasting significance was Peter's decree changing the basis of taxation on the peasantry from the household to the individual. It was suspected, probably correctly, that peasants were crowding together in ever larger households in order to spread the burden of the steadily increasing exactions levied by the central government. In order to prevent this and to make sure everyone paid, Peter's government carried out a crude census and then taxed each adult male. There is some speculation that this led to the setting up of new households and eventually to a marked rise in fertility and population later in the century. In any case, since both serfs and household slaves were counted and taxed, without distinction, Peter's fiscal policies further erased any lingering distinction between serfs and slaves: all became the movable property of their owners.

In a related fashion a reform of Peter designed with another purpose in mind helped eliminate the difference between estates held for service and those that were hereditary without any legal obligation for service. In a decree of 1714 (abrogated after his death) Peter attempted to end the traditional practice of dividing an estate among all the male heirs since it resulted in ever smaller and less efficient landholdings. The new inheritance law required designation of a single son as sole heir, with the eldest son receiving title if no one were named. At the same time the decree made no distinction among estates, assuming that all were hereditary and that all estate owners owed service.

Peter's desire to make the tsarist system work better led to much tinkering with government institutions and procedures. The result was a patchwork of the old, the adapted, and the European. Because he was frequently away campaigning, Peter originally established the Senate, a senior council of about a dozen officials, to rule in his absence. After a while the Senate came to have considerable administrative and judicial power and turned into a permanent institution of the empire. Peter ceased appointing boyars, and the boyar duma and *zemskii sobor* both disappeared. Peter thoroughly reorganized the central bureaucracy, setting up a series of "colleges" to handle such matters as foreign affairs, the army, the navy, justice, finance, mining, and commerce. Modeled on Swedish institutions, the colleges were to be run by a council or collegial group. In theory this system would prevent abuse of power by one individual and would provide a wider range of experience and judgment in making important decisions. In practice the colleges were quite unwieldy but nevertheless lasted for almost a century.

In provincial and municipal government Peter took some bold initiatives, but his reforms were largely unsuccessful. As the Russian empire grew, it became harder and harder to manage and govern, a problem that not only Peter but his successors failed to overcome.

Though Orthodox, Peter engaged at times in drunken and blasphemous parodies of Church rituals and celebrations while relaxing with his friends. As in other fields he called freely on the talents of several educated and able clerics, but he saw little role for the traditional Church in the modernized Russia he was trying to mold. Since the general thrust of his policies was to secularize society, he tried to minimize the role of the Church in Russia. To make sure the Church would be subservient to the state, Peter left the patriarchate vacant when Patriarch Hadrian died in 1700. Later he abolished the post, replacing it with the Holy Synod, a body of high clerics supervised by a lay official, the ober-procurator of the Holy Synod. This arrangement lasted until 1917 and permitted the government to keep tight rein on Church activities and policies. Not yet recovered from the turmoil of the Schism, the Church could do little to resist its subjugation by Peter.

Peter was an enthusiastic supporter of education. Training schools for the armed services naturally received high priority, but Peter also encouraged lay schools. He was particularly eager to advance the sciences and technology and laid plans for a national Academy of Sciences, which came into being shortly after his death. He established the first general hospital and surgical school at Moscow in 1706. Later he reorganized medical affairs under the Medical Chancery headed by a foreign-educated imperial physician.

To make education more accessible to the average citizen he oversaw a simplification of the Old Church Slavonic alphabet. To disseminate culture he sponsored the first newspaper and greatly expanded printing in Russia. The number of titles issued annually rose from six or seven to forty-five, and the content of these books broadened to include scientific and secular as well as religious topics. Peter's efforts in education, though extensive, were in fact only a tiny beginning. As one of the young Russians he sent abroad to study observed, "How can I learn geography without knowing the alphabet?" Russia needed to establish a much broader base of elementary and secondary schools and a better organized system, tasks that were undertaken later in the 1700s under Catherine the Great.

To a considerable extent Peter's most lasting reforms were cultural and psychological. His symbolic gestures, such as cutting off the beards of boyars or forcing them to wear European dress, seem almost silly, but behind them was his relentless determination that the Russian elite change their outlook and attitudes, giving up the parochial, religious, old-fashioned ways and ideas of Muscovy for the worldly, secular, progressive life-style and thought of Europe. Many resisted or ignored him, but in the long run Peter did succeed in orienting Russian society in a different direction, in forcing it to look to the future instead of the past. This wrenching change of direction had two fateful consequences, however. It alienated the educated elite from the mass of the people, and before long it led to a fundamental questioning of Russian society as a whole, and to ideas of revolution.

Resistance to Peter

In attempting to transform Russia Peter was determined and ruthless. As early as 1696 he established permanent political police to persecute his opponents. Nevertheless many Russians openly criticized his reforms, and millions more passively resisted, clinging stubbornly to the old ways. Tragically, in the struggle against Peter's policies, his son Alexis became a symbol of opposition and perished in prison, perhaps by Peter's own hand. For the majority of peasants Peter's reign meant not only new burdens but the introduction of strange and unorthodox customs, both of which they deeply resented. Many believed Peter was the Anti-Christ and feared the end of the world was near.

The most important rebellion against Peter broke out in southeastern Russia, centered on the city of Astrakhan, in 1705. Peter was then heavily engaged in the Great Northern War and could ill afford troops to send against the rebels. Moreover, since the leaders of the uprising espoused a broad range of popular grievances against both central and local government, the insurrection could easily have spread to other parts of southern Russia, the traditional seedbed of rebellion. Peter's opponents in Astrakhan included runaway serfs, Old Believers, and cossacks, but also many conservative Russian citizens who were outraged at the combination of new taxes and iconoclastic policies Peter had imposed on them. In appealing to the Don cossacks for help, the rebels declared:

We wish to inform you of what has happened in Astrakhan on account of our Christian faith, because of beard-shaving. . . . How we, our wives, and our children were not admitted into churches in our old Russian dress. . . . Moreover, in the last year, 1704, they imposed on us, and collected a [new] tax . . . they also took away all our firearms . . . and our bread allowance [for those serving as frontier guards].[4]

The anger of the rebels soon turned to violence, with the killing of the military governor and several hundred officials and nobles. It required a regular army under one of Peter's leading generals to suppress the uprising. Some of its leaders were publicly executed in Red Square as an example to the population.

Nevertheless in 1707–08 a new insurrection erupted, this time in the south, led by a disgruntled Don cossack named Kondratii Bulavin, who exhorted his followers against serfdom and the government. With a motley army of over 50,000 Bulavin occupied several key towns and tried to persuade the Dnieper cossacks to join him but was finally defeated by government troops.

At the same time that these revolts were being suppressed Peter had to contend with sporadic uprisings among the Bashkirs, a Turkic people on the eastern frontier of Russia who resented Russian domination and the taxes of Peter's government.

Those in government circles and among the old boyars and conservative churchmen who opposed Peter's policies hoped to use the heir to the throne, Peter's son Alexis, as the spearhead of their discontent. Intelligent but weak-willed and dissolute, Alexis, under pressure from Peter, renounced his right to the throne. Soon afterward he went into self-imposed exile abroad. He was finally persuaded to return to Russia, but before long his name was linked to plotting against Peter. Relations between father and son had never been good, and now Peter acted willfully against Alexis. In 1718 a broadly composed, extraordinary tribunal sentenced Alexis to death, but shortly thereafter he died or was murdered in prison. Five years later Peter promulgated a new succession law, declaring the tsar had the right to name the heir to the throne, but he died in 1725 without doing so.

Significance of Peter the Great

Within fifty years of Peter's death some writers were arguing that his reign had greatly benefited Russia, and others claimed that it had ruined the country. This controversy became a major issue in the intellectual history of modern Russia, reaching a high point in the 1840s in

---

[4] George Vernadsky, ed., *A Source Book for Russian History From Early Times to 1917* (Vol. 2). (New Haven: 1972), 349.

the polemics between the westernizers, who approved Peter's policies, and the Slavophils, who denounced them (see Chapter 9). In the 1860s the conservative Russian publicist, Michael Katkov, concluded that Peter's rule was "a catastrophe that . . . disrupted the organism of national life and . . . deprived [us] of the instinct and feeling of personal life . . . remaking us into senseless imitators doing everything on order of the government." Soviet historians have generally approved of Peter's reforms (and lavishly so in the period of Stalin's dictatorship) although concluding that they reinforced an absolutist system controlled by the aristocracy and a few rich merchants.

Perhaps Peter's reign can best be summed up as a series of paradoxes (which incidentally help explain why it is so controversial):

- Peter coerced Russia into modernization, but it was coming anyway.
- Peter had a vision of a more efficient, modernized Russia, but his reforms were often haphazard, forced upon him by military necessity and the pressure of events.
- Peter wanted to drive barbarism out of Russia but relied on barbaric methods to achieve that goal.
- Peter wanted to change and improve Russian society but left it with serfdom, an entrenched privileged nobility, and a cumbersome and often corrupt bureaucracy.
- Peter cared about the welfare of his people, but his wars and fiscal demands left them burdened, exhausted, and resentful.
- Peter sought good government and encouraged individual merit, but his reign heightened the arbitrary power of the state.
- Peter saw Russia's distant future but failed to convince most Russians of that destiny.
- Peter set a fast pace and employed coercion to make progress, but this practice alienated most Russians and undercut the changes he was trying to make.
- Peter made Russia a great power in Europe, but he achieved this through aggression against Russia's neighbors and at great cost to Russia.

However one assesses these contradictions in Peter's record, three major conclusions concerning his reign emerge. Peter was clearly one of the most influential personalities in modern history, like Napoleon, Lenin, and Gandhi. Russia undoubtedly would have meandered into modern times at some point, but Peter greatly accelerated the process and in so doing changed Russian society fundamentally.

Second, Peter propelled Russia onto the European stage and made her a great power. Since 1700, Russia has been a major actor in European and world affairs.

Finally, Peter put on the agenda for all Russians fundamental questions with which they are still struggling. How can Russian society react to new ideas and technology and still be true to its own traditions and unique culture? Must the West be imitated, or can Western attitudes and methods be modified and adapted to serve Russian needs and interests? Is it possible to fuse Russian beliefs and Western thought? What is the true essence of Russian civilization?

RECOMMENDED SUPPLEMENTAL READING

Black, C. E. "The Reforms of Peter the Great." In C. E. Black, ed., *Rewriting Russian History*, New York: 1962.

Cracraft, James. *The Church Reform of Peter the Great.* Stanford, Calif.: 1971.

———. "Peter the Great." In *Modern Encyclopedia of Russian and Soviet History.* Vol. 27, pp. 224–235. Gulf Breeze, Fla.: 1981.

Kliuchevsky, V. O. *Peter the Great.* New York: 1961.

Marsden, C. *Palmyra of the North.* London: 1942. (a description of St. Petersburg).

Meehan-Waters, B. *Autocracy and Aristocracy.* New Brunswick: 1982.

O'Brien, C. B. *Russia Under Two Tsars,* 1682–89. Berkeley: 1952.

Peterson, C. *Peter the Great's Administrative and Judicial Reforms.* Stockholm: 1979.

Sumner, B. H. *Peter the Great and the Emergence of Russia.* London: 1951.

Tolstoi, Alexei. *Peter the First.* New York: 1959. (a novel).

7

Change and Continuity, 1725-1801

A large party, in carriages and on horseback, was approaching the lovely summer estate of the Russian tsars, Peterhof. Since it was early summer, the gardens were at their most colorful, and the elaborate system of fountains was playing beautifully. Tsar Peter III, at the head of the group, looked forward pleasurably to the expected festivities that evening in honor of his name day, 9 July 1762. His wife, Catherine, who was staying at Peterhof while he was at another palace, was a renowned hostess, and he could anticipate a good time even though he and Catherine were not on good terms. Recently at a state dinner, he had publicly called her a fool, angering her partisans. Lately, there had even been rumors that she was plotting against him, taking advantage of his unpopularity with many prominent officers, nobles, and clerics who resented his often boorish behavior, his open hostility to the Russian Orthodox Church, and his decision to ally with Frederick the Great of Prussia, Russia's archenemy for the last seven years. As Peter and his companions rode into the courtyard of Peterhof, they were surprised to find no one about to greet and assist them. But when they entered the palace, they were dumbfounded and dismayed. Neither Catherine nor a single person from her retinue was there. All Peter found was her ball gown ready for the party.

What Peter did not know and only found out several hours later was that early that morning Alexei Orlov, one of five brothers, guards officers who were Catherine's closest supporters, had roused the tsarina and hustled her into a waiting carriage for an emergency trip to St. Petersburg, the capital. The conspirators against Peter's rule had planned to wait several more weeks to depose him, but the arrest of one of their number had forced their hand. They were determined to win over key elements in the army before Peter even learned what was afoot. Later on the morning of 9 July,

a travelling carriage drew up outside the barracks of the Izmailov regiment on the outskirts of St. Petersburg. A guards officer descended and disappeared hastily inside. A few moments later, as a drummer alerted the soldiers, a woman of about thirty, dressed in dusty black, with her hair

115

unpowdered, was handed down from the carriage and almost engulfed by a crowd of shouting huzzaing soldiers. Shortly afterwards the crowd parted, and an elderly Orthodox priest advanced bearing aloft the cross. In loud tones officers and men . . . swore allegiance to the newly proclaimed Empress Catherine, Autocrat of all the Russias.[1]

The new empress then proceeded to the barracks of the other guards regiments, all of whom enthusiastically declared their backing for Catherine. By noon she was at the Kazan Cathedral, where the highest Church prelates confirmed her title, and that afternoon the archbishop of Novgorod administered the oath of allegiance to troops drawn up in front of the Winter Palace. All but a few officers, who protested and were promptly arrested, ignored the point that only six months previously they had sworn loyalty to Peter.

The deposed tsar, after learning of the coup d' état, awaited his fate. Catherine herself rode out to arrest him, and a few days later, while in custody, he was strangled by Alexei Orlov and others, allegedly in a fight. Catherine, determined to keep the throne, overlooked the murder, declaring Peter had died of "a hemorrhoidal" colic and rewarding the conspirators lavishly.

Catherine the Great knew where she was headed: to sit on the Russian throne and to make her mark in modern European history. But where was Russia headed? Catherine herself, in my view, was not quite sure. If Russia were moving in the direction of becoming an "enlightened" society, then something would have to be done about serfdom, a reform that might unravel the whole social system and would certainly arouse the bitter opposition of the serf-owning nobility, the state's chief supporters. If Russia were to evolve toward a society based on law and institutions, or even on classes, then the arbitrary authority of the autocracy would have to be curbed and alternate centers of power created almost from scratch. Although Catherine nodded a few times in this direction, she had no intention of surrendering her autocratic prerogative. If Russia were to proceed down the path toward industrialization, as England was just starting to do, the role of the state in economic life would have to be greatly reduced, private entrepreneurs encouraged, markets found, and techniques learned. This course was beyond the resources available to Catherine. In all cases she had to work with what Peter and his successors had left her.

In two important ways Peter's efforts survived him and shaped the future course of his country: Russia remained a major European power, and Europeanization continued to develop and take root in Russia. Nevertheless in other significant ways the eighteenth century saw fundamental divergences from Peter's program of service to the state and of modernization. First, during the 1700s obligatory service for the no-

[1] Isabel de Madariaga, *Russia in the Age of Catherine the Great* (New Haven, Ct.: 1981), 1.

bility was abolished though many nobles continued to serve. But because the nobles did not succeed in establishing an institutional basis for themselves as a class, they were unable to turn their freedom into a regularized device for limiting the autocracy. Moreover, since the nobles no longer owed service to the state, the political and moral justification for their role as serf owners was weakened. Criticism and self-criticism of their position mounted.

Second, the political system of Russia became inherently unstable. The tsars ruled, not on any legal, institutional, or consensual basis, but through custom, the fickle support of the nobility, popular apathy (except for a major rebellion in the 1770s), and the absence of competing sources of power. Though seemingly splendid, the tsarist empire turned into a facade that masked the political weakness behind it. The autocracy survived because of its powerful army and bureaucracy, for lack of alternatives, and because the people were generally too dispirited or confused to push it over.

Third, Russia continued to develop economically, largely under state encouragement, intervention, and control, but it did not possess the requisites to participate in the Industrial Revolution that began at the end of the century in Europe. Thus, by 1800 Russia's rate of economic growth had begun to fall markedly behind that of the west European nations, and its agricultural productivity remained low.

Fourth, Russia's continuing expansion brought new non-Russian peoples under tsarist rule. Their mistreatment by the government sowed the seeds of later conflicts between a Russian majority and non-Russian minorities in the Russian empire.

Fifth, by the end of the 1700s Russia had begun to develop a national consciousness and literature, as well as a small number of radical critics of the regime, forerunners of the revolutionary movement of the nineteenth century.

In this chapter we will examine these five themes, beginning with a concise sketch of political developments from the death of Peter in 1725 through the end of Catherine's reign in 1796, then analyzing throughout the eighteenth century Russia's expansion and colonization, its economic and social development, the changing role of the nobility, and the spread of education and culture. We will conclude with a brief description of the rule of Paul I (1796–1801), Catherine's successor.

Peter's Successors, 1725–62

For one hundred years, beginning with Peter's death and ending with the Decembrist Revolt of 1825, the question of who was to sit on the tsarist throne created political turmoil and imperial insecurity in

Russia. This seems puzzling, when one considers the dominant position that Peter, the tsar-emperor, occupied, but several factors help explain the uncertainties that followed his reign. Peter himself muddied the succession issue by treating the tsardom as private property. In 1722 he declared that he alone would name his successor, but he then failed to do so. Moreover, the nobles, who wanted to exert more political influence, could achieve their goals only through control of the tsar, whom Peter had made the embodiment of the supremacy of the state in Russian society. The locus of power was in the tsar; there was no other way to affect the government. There were no well-defined estates, no autonomous church, no municipalities, no middle class, and not even an independent bureaucracy. Control of the throne itself was the key to political success. Finally, until Catherine the Great, Peter's successors were neither capable individuals nor strong rulers.

In the thirty-seven years after Peter's death Russia was ruled by three women, a boy of twelve, an infant, and a mentally unstable person. Under the empresses, though each possessed a strong personality and had her own ideas, lovers, courtiers, and advisers largely set and executed policy. The sequence of rulers in the eighteenth century was as follows:

Catherine I	1725–27
Peter II (a boy)	1727–30
Anna	1730–40
Ivan VI (an infant)	1740–41
Elizabeth	1741–62
Peter III	1762
Catherine II (the Great)	1762–96
Paul I	1796–1801

Catherine I, the second wife of Peter the Great, was of humble Latvian origins but had the backing of Peter's colleagues and friends, although Peter's grandson, another Peter, was the logical heir. Pressure from the guards regiments, set up originally by Peter and manned in all ranks mainly by nobles, finally settled the issue in Catherine's favor. On four more occasions in the 1700s the guards, who directly represented noble interests, intervened to determine who should be tsar. In this way the nobility played a significant political role, but they never found a way to institutionalize this influence.

Moreover, the nobles were not a unified and coherent group, and the one attempt they made to formalize their participation in the government foundered on divisions among them. On Catherine's death, Peter II, Peter the Great's young grandson, succeeded her, but he died of smallpox in 1730, leaving no male Romanov in line of succession. A small clique of upper-crust nobility, including members of the Supreme Privy Council, a kind of executive body on which Catherine had relied, decided to offer the throne to Anna, a daughter of Peter's step-brother,

Ivan V. In so doing they asked Anna to accept a number of conditions sharply limiting her autocratic power: she was in effect to rule jointly with the council. Anna, eager to ascend the throne, agreed. However, less privileged members of the nobility, jealous of the ploy effected by the council, demanded their share of the political pie, and when Anna arrived to be crowned, the guards demonstrated in her favor. Taking advantage of this turmoil, Anna tore up the conditions and dissolved the Supreme Privy Council.

She ruled for the next ten years as an empress-autocrat but relied heavily on a group of advisors who were predominantly Germans from the Baltic region. One of them, her favorite, Count Biron, was particularly corrupt and cruel, and his persecutions of Old Believers and others aroused bitter enmity among Russians of all classes.

Before dying in 1740 Anna appointed her grand-nephew, Ivan VI, as tsar, but he was only an infant when he ascended the throne, and the so-called German party continued to rule Russia. Again the guards staged a coup d' état, putting Peter the Great's daughter, Elizabeth, in power in 1741. Though quite capable and well-meaning, Empress Elizabeth was also vain, lazy, and extravagant. She, too, ruled through favorites, though now they were Ukrainians and Russians. During her reign the influence of French culture spread in Russia, but almost nothing was done to tackle the basic social, economic, and administrative backwardness of Russia.

In 1762, when Elizabeth died, Peter III, Peter the Great's grandson by his oldest daughter and a German princeling, succeeded to the throne. Brought up in a German household, Peter moved to Russia when he was a teenager to prepare himself to become tsar, but he never lost his suspicion of his new surroundings and his admiration for things German, including the leading German sovereign, Frederick the Great of Prussia. In several areas Peter's policies as tsar were quite forward-looking, but his attacks on the Orthodox Church, his attempt to prussianize the army, and his radical volte-face in the Seven Years' War, making peace with Russia's traditional enemy Prussia on the verge of the latter's defeat, alienated broad circles in Russian society. Moreover, his crude, adolescent, and unpredictable behavior gave people little hope for improvement in his rule. The result was yet another palace revolution, as we saw at the start of the chapter, carried out by elements of the guards regiments, with Catherine's connivance. The unfortunate Peter was soon killed, perhaps accidentally, probably deliberately.

Catherine the Great, 1762–96

Although Catherine the Great did not have so abrupt and marked an impact on Russian and European history as Peter the Great, she was a powerful and effective ruler for over three decades. She was both extremely able and a charmer, as the British ambassador to Russia made clear in a 1762 dispatch to London:

> Her Imperial Majesty is neither short nor tall. . . . Her features were far from being so delicately and exactly formed as to compose what might pretend to regular beauty, but a fine complexion, an animated and intelligent eye, a mouth agreeably turned, and a profusion of glossy chestnut hair produce that sort of countenance which, a very few years ago, a man must have been either prejudiced or insensible to have beheld with indifference. . . . Her eyes are blue, their vivacity tempered by a languor in which there is much sensibility and no insipidity. . . . She expresses herself with elegance in French, and I am assured that she speaks Russian with as much precision as German, which is her native language. . . . She speaks and reasons with fluency and precision. . . .[2]

Outgoing, intelligent, hardworking, ambitious, and self-confident, Catherine poured all her considerable energy and skill into the task first of ascending the throne and then of advancing the cause of Russia, her adopted land, and of herself as its "enlightened"ruler. Her love life has often been sensationalized, but in fact there is no evidence that it ever interfered with her judgment or effectiveness as empress or that any of her acknowledged twenty-one lovers exerted influence on state policy solely on the basis of a liaison with her, rather than on their own merits.

In almost every respect Catherine was a self-made woman. Born Sophie of Anhalt-Zerbst, a small German principality, she lived as a child in modest circumstances and without great expectations. It was assumed that at best she might be married to some minor German princeling or nobleman, and it was only a stroke of great good fortune that, through complicated family connections, at age fifteen Sophie was selected by Empress Elizabeth as the fiancee of the heir to the Russian throne, the future Peter III. She and her mother were commanded to go to St. Petersburg to live at Elizabeth's court. Before long her mother was evicted as an agent of the Prussian king, and Sophie realized that her betrothed was no bargain, being coarse, poorly educated, and emotionally underdeveloped.

With spunk and determination, she nevertheless set about preparing herself for her future role as a tsar's wife. She converted to the Orthodox faith, was rebaptized Catherine, learned Russian, and plunged assiduously into finding out all she could about her new country and about the larger world. She read widely, particularly in the works of the French writers of the Enlightenment, and studied politics and human nature close up, first observing the maneuvering and intrigues at Elizabeth's court and then taking part in them. Caught out on one oc-

---

[2]Warren B. Walsh, comp. and ed., *Readings in Russian History* (4th ed., vol. 1). (Syracuse, N.Y.: 1963), 225–26.

Figure 10. *A portrait of Empress Catherine the Great that suggests her forceful personality. (Courtesy of Sovfoto/Eastfoto)*

casion, Catherine shrewdly threw herself on the mercy of Empress Elizabeth, protesting her devotion to Russia and the monarch. Elizabeth forgave her, and by the time Peter III ascended the throne Catherine, in sharp contrast to her husband, had thoroughly russianized herself and had developed a wide circle of powerful friends among the elite of Russian society.

Through self-education and by character and inclination Catherine the Great was indeed an "enlightened despot," comparable to other European monarchs accorded that designation in the eighteenth century. She believed in natural law, the rule of reason, religious toleration, and the orderly functioning of government for the good of society (see Figure 10). Although Catherine was happy to use her acquaintance and correspondence with Voltaire and other leaders of the European Enlightenment to boost her own ego, to build support for her regime, and to spread her fame abroad, she was also genuinely stimulated and inspired by their ideas and advice.

Regarding Russia her intentions were good, but her hell was that, having usurped the throne, she never felt entirely secure on it and thus hesitated to undertake basic social reforms, such as the abolition or amelioration of serfdom, for fear of destabilizing the system and alienating her chief political supporters, the nobility. Moreover, she was dealing with a vast country that had huge problems, and on some practical matters she simply felt she could make little headway. She remained dedicated to the ideals of the Enlightenment and to improving Russian society, but as she wrote Diderot, the French philosopher: "You only write on paper, but I have to write on human skin, which is incomparably more irritable and ticklish."

Though adhering to principles of the Enlightenment, Catherine strengthened rather than curtailed the autocracy and opposed the French Revolution. This was not hypocritical as some have charged. In both the concept of enlightened despotism and the Russian political tradition, beneficial change was to be directed from above, and the monarch was not to give up authority but to use it wisely. Moreover, Catherine never espoused radical eighteenth-century ideas such as representative government and liberty. She wanted a more efficient, more humane autocracy but nevertheless an autocracy.

She was particularly sensitive about her authority because despite her repeated proclamations after the deposition of her husband that she was acting in the interests of all the people and for the good of the whole country, she was in fact an outsider, a German upstart, who had seized the throne by force and who had no legal claim to it. To make her even more jittery, two legitimate heirs to the throne existed and several pretenders arose. Ivan VI, deposed in 1741, was now a young man though still imprisoned. In 1764, however, he was killed by his guards during a failed attempt to rescue him and use him against Catherine. A second threat was her son Paul, born in 1754. Although recognized as Peter's son and therefore heir to the throne, Paul was almost certainly sired by a lover of Catherine, Sergei Saltykov. As Paul grew to adulthood, he posed the continuing danger that he might become a rallying point for opposition to Catherine.

Among the pretenders, the most important was Emelian Pugachov, a Don cossack, who in 1773–74 led the last major peasant revolt, or *jacquerie*, in a series that dated back at least to Bolotnikov in 1607. Although this widespread uprising was directed more against the system than against Catherine personally, it was a frightening affair since it dramatically revealed to Catherine deep-seated weaknesses in Russia's central and provincial administration, as well as the extent of the country's social inequities. The spectrum of those who joined Pugachov reflected the diversity of groups with major grievances against the regime: cossacks whose privileges and autonomy were being undercut, Bashkirs and Tatars whose culture and ethnic rights were being trampled upon, Old Believers persecuted by the Orthodox Church and the government, factory serfs condemned to work in the mines and manufacturing enterprises of the Ural region in inhuman conditions, agricultural serfs ground down by increased taxes and recurring army conscription, and fugitives of every kind from army deserters to runaway serfs and criminals.

Claiming to be Peter III, Pugachov declared an end to serfdom, taxes, and the draft and a war on landlords and the government. Molding his motley supporters into a surprisingly effective force, Pugachov ranged along the Ural and Volga rivers and briefly captured a number of important towns. Because Russia was then engaged in a major war with Turkey, the government nearly panicked, fearing at one time that Pugachov might march on Moscow. Repeatedly defeated by regular troops, he was finally captured and as one account put it, "drawn and quartered but not tortured"! The Pugachov revolt strengthened Catherine's political alliance with the nobility, virtually the only group that supported the government in the disaffected regions. It also bolstered her resolve to undertake fundamental reforms of Russia's administration.

Aware when she came to power in 1762 that governance in Russia was chaotic, Catherine, with her usual determination and acumen, set about putting state affairs back into order. She reformed the Senate to make it more efficient as an administrative overseer, she improved tax collection, and she revamped the budget and fiscal policy. At the same time she was interested in a broader and more deep-rooted approach to Russian problems and decided to convene a representative body of leading officials and citizens to initiate a codification of the laws (the last had been in 1649) and to study what basic reforms should be undertaken. Known as the Legislative or Grand Commission, it included delegates from the nobles, townspeople, the government, state peasants, and non-Russian groups but no serfs and only one cleric. Opening its sessions in 1767, Catherine presented the commission with a long set of "instructions" that she had labored over for many preceding months. Drawing heavily on thinkers of the Enlightenment, Catherine had personally written many sections of her charge to the commission, which was quickly translated into all the main European languages.

After almost two years of deliberations the commission adjourned. It had served quite effectively as a broadly constituted consultative body. It did not reach definite conclusions partly because of its unwieldy size (almost six hundred members) and because few delegates had the education, experience, and judgment to turn Catherine's theoretical considerations into practical law or policy. But it also gave no specific policy direction because it mirrored differences within Russian society, particularly between nobles and merchants, as well as the general reluctance of any group to attack the root institution of serfdom. The

Grand Commission, however, did have several positive results: it educated Catherine concerning the basic problems of the society she presided over and in the limits of what she could alter; it provided concrete information and opinion that were later incorporated in her
administrative reforms; and its subcommittees, which met for several
more years, drew up a number of useful proposals.

Partly spurred by the Pugachov revolt, Catherine in 1775 instituted a major reorganization of the countrywide administration of Russia, changes that lasted in some cases till the 1860s and in others till
1917. The most important reform was to divide the nation into provinces *(guberniia)* equal in population—fifty by the end of Catherine's
reign—with equal districts within each province. The provincial governors were responsible for coordinating government policy and for
overseeing the operations of functionally separate judicial, legislative,
and administrative departments in each province. Although not ideal,
this was a marked improvement over previous patterns of governance.

In 1785 Catherine undertook two other major reforms, granting a
charter of rights and obligations to both the nobility and the towns. The
former was more important because it confirmed the liberation of the
nobility from compulsory service, first decreed under Peter III in 1762,
and because it established noble organizations in the provinces and districts of the reorganized empire. A few historians have argued that the
Charter of the Nobility was the first step toward formation of independent interest groups in Russian politics and that it might have opened
the door to eventual representative government. But this interpretation
is off the mark. Indeed Catherine wanted to establish the nobility as a
separate and privileged order in Russian society, but mainly so that they
could serve the government more effectively. She certainly did not intend for them to develop into an alternate center of power. The nobles
themselves, for reasons to be discussed, did not attempt to turn their
charter into a weapon against the autocracy. The complicated and limited system of governance set up for the towns in 1785 did not entirely
work, and municipal administration remained a problem for Catherine's successors.

Catherine was of course active in many other areas—social policy,
education and culture, economic development, minority affairs, and
foreign policy—and her role in these matters will be discussed as part
of our review of long-term trends in Russia during the whole period
from Peter's death to the end of the eighteenth century.

Russian Expansion and Colonization

Throughout the 1700s but particularly during Catherine's reign
Russia continued to expand its frontiers in all directions and to settle

new areas. In many respects this trend marked a continuation of earlier policies and movement, but in the eighteenth century much of the new territory acquired had never been under Kievan or Russian rule, and most of the peoples absorbed were not Great Russians. By 1800 the Russian state was an enormous, multinational empire, prominent in both Europe and Asia, as it has been ever since.

After Peter's death Russia maintained the influential position in European politics he had claimed for it, and the government also continued his interest in exploring and colonizing in Asia. Russian foreign policy in Europe was directed in large part toward weakening Russia's two major western neighbors, Poland and the Ottoman Empire. Since Austria was also concerned about the same countries, Russia and Austria were allied for much of the century. Russia also tried to stay on good terms with Britain, its largest trading partner.

As we saw in the previous chapter, it is hard to evaluate Russia's foreign policies in the past few centuries, and today. Are Russia's leaders motivated primarily by considerations of defense and national security? Are they trying to protect Russia's borders and forestall possible attacks by enemies? Or are they mainly interested in extending Russia's rule and influence over other countries? Are they imperialistic, seeking widened power and profit in Europe and Asia (and perhaps the world)? Unfortunately, the record of the 1700s provides no clear answers to these questions.

On the one hand it can be argued that the Turks, and particularly their protégés the Crimean Tatars, posed a constant threat to the southwestern flank of European Russia. Similarly, the Poles, historically inhabiting a larger and more developed kingdom, could be viewed as a danger. But in fact the Tatars were more of a nuisance than a threat, and the Ottoman Empire was already in that period of decline that was to lead to its collapse in World War I. Moreover, Poland, economically weak and wracked by internal problems, was in no position to menace the Russians. And in Asia no power posed any possible danger to the Russian empire. On balance, then, Russian foreign policy in the 1700s appears more aggressive than defensive, even though Russia's expansion to the Black Sea under Catherine fulfilled a long-cherished goal dating back to Kievan times and extended Russia's southern border to a natural geographic limit.

The chief loser in the game of European politics in the eighteenth century was Poland, which was swallowed up by its neighbors before the end of the century (see Map 5). Details of the diplomatic maneuvering and of the three partitions of the Polish state that led to this result are beyond our scope. At the same time the general circumstances of Poland's annexation are important, not least because they shed light on the strong antipathy most Poles have today for the Russians. To be sure, the Poles were to some extent their own worst enemies, but essentially Poland was victimized by stronger neighbors coveting its land.

Although Poland recovered from its defeat by Charles XII of Sweden during the Great Northern War, increasingly in the 1700s it was weakened, partly because it could command fewer resources than most of its neighbors and partly because it was being torn apart by social, religious, and political conflict. Polish peasants struggled against their landlords, Catholics persecuted those of other faiths, and the Polish nobility steadily undermined the power of the king. Finally, by the 1760s civil war erupted in Poland, an irresistible temptation for the major countries surrounding Poland to interfere in its affairs. This led in 1772 to the first partition, under which Russia, Austria, and Prussia each took Polish territory adjoining their states, the whole totaling about one third of Poland. Although most of the land annexed by Catherine was inhabited by Russians, Belorussians, and Ukrainians, the predominance of these nationalities hardly justifies the action. The humiliation of the first partition led to a national revival in Poland, which greatly strengthened the country but also alarmed its neighbors.

After some maneuvering the powers joined in two more partitions, in 1793 and 1795, that eliminated Poland from the map of Europe. In these Russia, Prussia, and Austria annexed lands inhabited primarily by Poles, who became an important and hostile minority within each empire. Although reasons of prestige, economic benefit, and security were advanced for this bare-faced dismemberment of an independent state, greed, opportunism, and a determination to share in the spoils seem to have been the basic motivations. As one contemporary noted about Maria Theresa, the empress of Austria: "She wept but she kept on taking." The Poles of course were bitterly resentful, rebelling against their Russian masters three times in the 1800s before resurrecting their country in 1918, as an outcome of World War I.

Russia's other major territorial gains were in the southwest as the result of several wars against the Ottoman Empire, the most important of which occurred under Catherine in 1768–74. By the end of the century Russia had acquired all the territory north of the Black Sea from the Dniester River eastward, including the mouths of the Don and Dnieper rivers; had annexed the Crimea, the home of the Crimean Tatars; had obtained commercial rights in the Black Sea and through the Straits at Constantinople; and was vaguely authorized to act as protector of Orthodox Christians under Turkish rule. Strategically, economically, and politically Russia gained a great deal, securing her southern border, opening up profitable trade through the Black Sea, obtaining rich agricultural lands, and weakening one of Russia's main enemies. Nevertheless, the Turkish problem remained a major issue in Russian foreign policy throughout the next century.

Russian colonization of Siberia and the fringes of Central Asia had begun in the 1600s but was stepped up in the 1700s. In addition to encouraging Russians to move out to the frontier regions, the government induced a large group of Catholic and, later, Mennonite Germans to settle along the Volga River. And after acquisition of territory north of the Black Sea, Russians and Ukrainians were settled there in large numbers. Although in earlier times Jews had been prohibited from living in the Muscovite state, Catherine surreptitiously encouraged the immigration of Jews, both into western Russia and into the new lands in the south. Incorporation of the Polish territories also added numbers of Jews to the empire's population. At first they were granted equal rights as citizens, but in the 1790s, for reasons that are unclear, an imperial decree assessed double taxation on Jews of all classes.

As the empire expanded by conquest and colonization, administration of this vast state became more and more difficult. Catherine, although making the reforms noted earlier, essentially followed the policies of her predecessors; that is, she treated the new territories and peoples as integral parts of Russia. This meant that with a few exceptions, centralized rule was established, local rights were ignored, and efforts were made to russify the non-Russian population. For example, the Ukrainians lost the last vestiges of their autonomy and were fully absorbed into the empire. Serfdom was also permitted in the western Ukraine and selectively in the new lands north of the Black Sea, although not in Siberia and the Asian borderlands.

Economic and Social Development

Russia, like much of Europe, experienced a remarkable population boom in the eighteenth century. The reasons for this growth are not clear, but improved public order and public health, a feeling of greater security and stability, and an increase in the acreage farmed may all have contributed. In any case the population more than doubled in about four generations, from roughly thirteen million in 1722 to twenty-nine million in 1796. To the latter figure were added another seven million people living in the recently acquired Polish and southwestern lands. The result was a much larger work force and potential market, but it also produced more mouths to feed while agricultural productivity had increased little. The overwhelming majority of the population remained serfs and state peasants living at a bare subsistence level.

Although towns grew with the increasing population, the urban-rural ratio changed slowly: In the early 1700s about 97 percent of the people lived in the countryside and 3 percent in towns, and by 1800 the figures were 92 to 94 percent and 6 to 8 percent. The upper nobility remained a tiny fraction of the population, numbering in the tens of thousands, and the whole noble class reached only the hundreds of thousands, barely 1 percent of the population at most. Over 90 percent of the population were peasants, and the proportion of those who were privately owned serfs grew slowly in the 1700s, reaching an estimated 55 percent by the end of the century, when serfdom was at its height. This meant that by 1800 between fifteen and twenty million Russians were virtual slaves. Another ten to fifteen million were state peasants of various categories who owed heavy obligations in money or kind but were slightly better off than the private serfs.

During the 1700s while the percentage and total number of serfs increased, their situation deteriorated. Not only did the eighteenth-century tsars give to favorites, military heroes, high nobles, and other worthies land containing hundreds of thousands of peasants (often from non-Russian areas in the Ukraine and eastern Poland), thereby making the inhabitants serfs, but they also gave all serf owners greatly increased power over their serfs. For example, owners could now interfere in serf marriages, could send recalcitrant serfs into the army, and could administer judicial and physical punishment to serfs, including banishment to Siberia.

Advertisements offering serfs for purchase are reminiscent of the American South: "For Sale: two plump coachmen, two barbers, one knows how to play musical instruments. . . ." But unlike slavery in the United States, serfdom in Russia was not limited to one region of the country but existed almost everywhere, except in the far north, Siberia, and parts of Russian Asia. Finally, data are insufficient to determine how much state taxes on the peasants increased in the eighteenth century, but a reasonable estimate is that they doubled. In short, the 1700s marked the apogee of the institution of serfdom in every respect: numbers, extent, conditions, and oppressiveness. Catherine, though concerned in principle, apparently believed, particularly after the Pugachov revolt, that tampering with serfdom would threaten the whole social system. Consequently, she attempted only minor reforms, encouraging voluntary emancipation of serfs and limiting the use of serf labor in industry.

The inefficiencies and lack of incentives to produce associated with serfdom help explain why the Russian economy in the eighteenth century advanced only slowly. Serfdom held back development of a national market, slowed capital accumulation, and hindered technological innovation and entrepreneurship. But the economic policies of the state were also at fault. Catherine, for example, offered inducements for nobles to found industries and enter trade, but this policy also discouraged merchants and townsmen. Serf artisans and producers, though making a substantial contribution to the economy, were not encouraged. As a result, although Russian nonagricultural output grew in the course of the century, the ground was not prepared for a major takeoff into industrialization, like that occurring in western Europe. At the end of the century Russia was a leading producer of iron and copper, her output of pig iron in 1790 equaling that of England, but in the first decades of the nineteenth century Russia fell far behind.

The Changing Role of the Nobility

As we saw in the last chapter, the nobility began the century tightly harnessed to the service of the state by Peter. Their sons were expected to be ready for education or duty in their teens and were to serve for life. By the end of the century nobles owed no service in peacetime, though they could be summoned in time of need. The nobles had become a dominant and privileged elite in Russian society, far and away the best educated and wealthiest element in the state. The steps along their path to liberation were many, and we need note only a few major ones here. In 1731 the first school for military cadets was opened. Nobles' sons could enroll there and graduate with an officer's commission, thus avoiding the Petrine system of being required to enter the guards regiments as enlisted men and work their way up to officer rank. In 1736 the term of service for nobles was reduced to twenty-five years. In the 1740s one son in each noble family was exempted from service so he could stay home to manage the family's land and affairs. Another decree stipulated that only nobles had the right to own serfs. Finally, in 1762 under Peter III nobles were exempted from state service in peacetime altogether, a privilege confirmed in Catherine's Charter of the Nobility issued in 1785.

Although service was no longer obligatory, the crown of course strongly encouraged it, and in fact most nobles continued to serve in some military or bureaucratic capacity. It was expected that those who did not would be running their estates in the countryside and would be active in local affairs, including the provincial and district assemblies of nobles established in the 1785 charter. But few had any altruistic interest in improving production of their lands, and there was little incentive to do so as long as they did not go too far into debt. From boredom or a sense of responsibility some did participate in local administration, but many frittered away their time or simply vegetated.

In any case, the nobility were not a homogeneous group, as we saw when they split over the conditions the Supreme Privy Council tried to impose on Anna. In addition to differences along lines of rank, wealth, and political influence, the nobility was divided by location and education. At the top of the social pyramid stood the nobles of the two capitals, St. Petersburg and Moscow. These were individuals who either held important state posts or were wealthy enough to keep a town house in one of the two major cities. They would spend part of the year on their rural estates and part in urban social life. Beneath this elite were the provincial nobility, that is, nobles who either resided or kept town houses in the other major cities of the Russian empire. At the bottom of the scale were the rural nobility, probably half of all nobles, who lived on small estates, often with ten or fewer serfs, and seldom if ever went to the towns. They were generally poor, some little better off than their peasants, and usually poorly educated. There were also "personal" nobles who owned neither land nor serfs.

In fact, education became in the eighteenth century a major dividing line among the nobility and in Russian society generally. Before 1700 only the high clergy and a few of the elite were educated at all; even parish priests were generally illiterate or had the most rudimentary education. During the eighteenth century the nobility, as part of their dominance, became much better educated, either through schools or through private tutors. Those nobles who lacked either the money or the opportunity for education soon found that the top jobs in the tsarist administration were out of their reach and that they were slipping into an inferior social status.

At the same time education affected the outlook of the elite nobles in two ways. Since their education was primarily Western in orientation, they found themselves increasingly isolated from their fellow citizens, whether they were poorer, uneducated nobles or humble serfs. The sophisticated elite increasingly adopted European manners, customs, dress, and even language, thereby opening a huge and unbridgeable chasm between them and their fellow Russians. For example, many educated Russians customarily spoke French and read only foreign literature. The noted Russian publicist of the nineteenth century, Alexander Herzen, characterized the alienation that resulted as follows: "Foreigners at home and foreigners abroad, idle onlookers—spoiled for Russia by their Western prejudices and spoiled for the West by their Russian habits—they constituted a strange kind of intelligent superfluity, and lost themselves in their artificial life, in sensual pleasures and in an intolerable egoism."

A small minority who found themselves adrift between two cultures but who were determined to do something about it became radical critics of the situation in Russia. They concluded that Russian society as a whole, and particularly the institution of serfdom, needed fundamental change if it were to measure up to the standards that Enlightenment thinkers had postulated as the natural and inalienable rights of all peoples. These critics became the forerunners of the Russian revolutionary intelligentsia of the nineteenth century.

Whatever the differences in education, rank, and wealth among the nobility, the question remains: Why didn't they become an independent political force in Russian society, once they were liberated from obligatory state service? Two related factors were decisive, in my view. First, the tsar controlled entry into and placement within the noble class, a practice begun under the Muscovite tsars and confirmed in the bitter, bloody struggle between Ivan the Terrible and the boyars. Peter's Table of Ranks institutionalized the dependence of the nobility on state service, and the tsar, at least indirectly, controlled who was appointed and who became a noble. To be sure, there were hereditary nobles, and old families persisted in positions of influence and wealth. But the basic structure of the system was that status and power depended on service, and the tsar ultimately controlled who would serve and therefore who would be important. This was true whether service was obligatory or voluntary.

Second, and a natural corollary, the nobility had no separate or autonomous institutional base outside the government. They were not organized as a class; they had no corporate rights except petitioning the tsar, but only rights as individual nobles; and they had no mechanism, since the end of the *boyar duma* and the *zemskii sobor,* to be represented as a group before the tsar. Although Catherine's provincial and district assemblies of nobles could be viewed as the embryo of an independent organization, they were in fact creations of the state, serving mainly state administrative purposes. Only on a few rare occasions in the nineteenth century were they turned to the purpose of representing the independent interests and views of the nobility.

Education and Culture

As an enlightened despot, Catherine worked hard to broaden and improve education in Russia. Theoretically, a well-run state required an educated populace; practically, Catherine desperately needed trained individuals to staff her administration and help her govern an immense country. More sensibly than Peter, who tried to build an educational system from the top down, Catherine strove to develop an integrated system at all levels. She had some previous developments to work with, but not many.

Some of the state schools Peter had founded failed for lack of funds, teachers, or students, but a few survived and during the middle of the eighteenth century were complemented by the opening of a number of private schools. Moscow University was founded in 1755, although it enrolled barely one hundred students in its first few decades. Catherine began with an idealistic plan for a network of state boarding schools that would produce an enlightened elite. This plan proved impractical, although it did encourage the founding of the first school for women, the Smolny Institute in St. Petersburg (which in the Revolution of 1917 became the headquarters of Lenin's Bolshevik party). Finally in the 1780s a system of general public and free education was instituted; schools were opened in provincial cities and district towns but not in the countryside. At the same time the first teachers' training institute was founded.

By 1796 over twenty thousand pupils were enrolled in the recently created elementary and secondary schools, a paltry number in a country
Russia's size, but a start and an authentic triumph for Catherine, who
had to overcome lack of interest and funds to create the system.

Catherine, as one would expect, vigorously promoted cultural activities in the empire, beginning with her own court, where plays, readings, and musical soirées intermingled with games, balls, and other light
entertainment. The number of books published in Russia more than
tripled in Catherine's reign as compared with the total output up to that
time. The empress also encouraged periodicals and newspapers, and as
education spread among the nobility and townspeople, an informed and
interested, if tiny, reading public developed. Catherine also encouraged the arts, and the Russian theater flourished, producing mainly
European plays but also the first plays by Russian authors.

As with much of the cultural development of the 1700s, painting,
architecture, and music largely imitated Western models. But to a considerable extent this schooling in European styles and values was the
indispensable preparation for the astounding outburst of independent
artistic creativity in nineteenth-century Russia that has so enriched world
culture. Literature of the 1700s already foreshadowed the cultural ef-
florescence to come, with development of the first modern Russian poets,
playwrights, and authors, including Antiokh Kantemir, Michael Lomonosov, Denis Fonvizin, and Nicholas Karamzin. Lomonosov was also
a gifted scientist and a leader of the Russian Academy of Sciences
founded just after Peter's death. By the end of the century Russian
writers had developed a distinct style and an independent identity,
characterized by one historian as the beginnings of a definite national
consciousness.

Intellectual debate and social criticism, both important aspects of
the European Enlightenment, developed in Russia as well. In Catherine's time one of the leading critics was Nicholas Novikov, who was also
a freemason and publisher of several of the country's most widely read
journals. But the boldest commentator on Russian society was Alexander Radishchev (1749–1802). He was an outstanding example of a type
of Russian intellectual that became prominent and troublesome to the
government in the next century. Radishchev, of noble birth and well
educated in Germany and Russia, entered state service and performed
creditably as a middle-level administrator in Catherine's regime. At the
same time under the influence of Enlightenment thought, particularly
the writings of Rousseau, he became increasingly disturbed over what
he observed about him in Russian society. He was particularly appalled
by the moral and social implications of the serf system; employing a
typical eighteenth-century literary device, the travelogue, Radishchev
poured out devastating criticism of serfdom in his *Journey from Petersburg to Moscow* published privately in 1790. Catherine, already alarmed

at what she considered the excesses of the French Revolution, which had begun the year before, banned Radishchev's book and had him arrested and imprisoned in Siberia. Thus at the end of Catherine's reign the state, which had fostered the spread of culture and of "enlightened" ideas, turned to censorship and repression against theories and individuals considered harmful to state interests, a policy followed, with rare respites, by Russian governments ever since.

The Reign of Paul I, 1796–1801

The brief rule of Catherine's son, Paul, supplied a disturbing coda to eighteenth-century Russian history. Bubbling to the surface in Paul's reign appeared harsh manifestations of Russian civilization that had been suppressed or minimized under Catherine. Paul was a militarist above all; his mother emphasized civil administration and civic development. The son was irrational and quixotic; Catherine emphasized reason and considered policies and behavior. Paul gave orders without explanation; his mother tried to encourage and lead her people, or at least her officials and the educated public, into accomplishing what had to be done in their and the state's interest.

In Paul's defense, his background may partly account for his instability and failure as a ruler. As noted earlier, he was undoubtedly a bastard son, though accepted by all as the legitimate heir. Catherine, a strong-willed mother, found it difficult to mold Paul as she would have liked. In addition, as we saw, she continually feared him since he had a stronger claim to the throne than she and could always serve as a rallying point for opposition, should it develop. Consequently, fairly early in her reign, when Paul was still a young man, she shunted him aside. He was kept out of state affairs and encouraged to busy himself with military training, which he loved, on his own estates, near St. Petersburg (today one of them is a lovely public park, Pavlosk, near Leningrad).

Moreover, because Catherine lived well into her sixties and reigned for over thirty years, Paul had to wait a long time for the throne and had plenty of opportunity to build up resentment against his mother, her advisers, and their policies. Finally, near the end of her reign Catherine indicated fairly clearly that she would probably name her grandson, Alexander, as her successor; he was a handsome and intelligent young man, who with his brother Constantine had been taken away from Paul and his wife at an early age and reared by grandmother Catherine with suffocating tenderness and in accord with "enlightened" principles. In short, Paul had a good deal to be disgruntled about when his mother died unexpectedly in late 1796. Since she had not yet named a successor, Paul ascended to the throne at the age of forty-two.

Not unlike his father, Peter III, Paul instituted some progressive measures in his short reign, encouraging religious toleration and education and attempting to have the obligations of serfs defined and limited. He also finally settled the succession issue that had created such political turmoil throughout the century, decreeing that the throne was to pass to the eldest male heir. But both his policies and his style upset the nobility and the bureaucracy, on whom after all the administration and welfare of the state mainly depended. He was high-handed, which was bad enough, but also inconsistent and unpredictable. As one critic put it, his reign could be characterized as "Order, Counter-order, Disorder." Paul tried to enforce Prussian-style discipline on the army and conducted endless parades and drills, all of which antagonized both officers and enlisted men. Moreover, he seemed completely insensitive to the feelings of either individuals or the citizenry as a whole. This was perhaps because he was wholly self-centered and made a bit giddy by the assumption of despotic power after waiting so long. He reportedly told a senior official on one occasion: "The only person in Russia who is important is the person I am speaking to, and only as long as I am speaking to him."

Paul was thoroughly conservative, probably little understanding the ideas of the Enlightenment or the aspirations of his mother. He tightened censorship, relied on political repression, and joined the European coalition against revolutionary France. But as in other matters his foreign policy was contradictory and unpredictable. In 1800, disgusted with his allies, Paul switched sides, joined Napoleon, and ordered some Don cossacks to set off to oust the British from India.

The alliance with France may have been the final straw in the developing resistance to Paul's rule, and in early 1801 he was deposed and killed in yet another coup d' état, which we will discuss at the start of the next chapter.

Conclusion

By the end of the eighteenth century Russia was largely what Peter and Catherine had made of her. In many respects Catherine completed what Peter had begun, adding, however, a more reasoned and humane touch to the changes affecting Russian society. The result was an almost schizophrenic society: Europeanized in elite culture and thought, military affairs, and even technology, but deeply Russian and traditional in popular culture, religion, social system, and agriculture; a leading power of Europe politically and economically but with an arbitrary and repressive autocracy and a relatively backward economy; a modern educational system and an ordered and even "enlightened" administration that supervised a degrading and inefficient social system and relied heavily on censorship and coercion.

Russia's historical experience differed from that of western Europe, and she obviously could not be like the West. But neither could she turn her back on Europe and the onrush of new ideas and inventive technology. Russia had to live in a European-dominated world and had to adjust. Neither Peter nor Catherine had found a magic formula to blend the best of Europe with the best of Russia, but probably one did not exist, and none of their successors has fared any better.

To Catherine's great credit she demilitarized the society, tried to improve governance, promoted education, helped found a national culture, and confirmed the nobility in their rights while trying to inspire them to higher ideals of rationality and service. On the other side of the ledger, however, she was unable to cope with the problem of serfdom, she enhanced autocratic power without removing its inherent arbitrariness, and she expanded Russian rule over Poles and other non-Russians with little moral or other justification. On balance, one has to conclude about the fascinating Catherine that she did what she could, which may not have been enough for Russia's needs but was far more than her immediate predecessors and most of her successors accomplished.

FURTHER READING

Alexander, John T. *Emperor of the Cossacks; Pugachov and the Frontier Jacquerie of 1773–75.* Lawrence, Ks.: 1973.

———. *Bubonic Plague in Early Modern Russia.* Baltimore: 1980.

Catherine II. *The Memoirs of Catherine the Great.* New York: 1957.

Dukes, Paul. *Catherine the Great and the Russian Nobility.* Cambridge, England: 1967.

Freeze, Gregory. *The Russian Levites.* Cambridge, Mass.: 1979.

Garrard, John, ed. *The Eighteenth Century in Russia.* Oxford: 1973.

de Madariaga, Isabel. *Russia in the Age of Catherine the Great.* New Haven, Conn.: 1982.

Raeff, Marc. *Origins of the Russian Intelligentsia: The Eighteenth Century Nobility.* New York: 1966.

———. *Understanding Imperial Russia.* New York: 1984.

Ragsdale, Hugh, ed. *Paul I.* Pittsburgh: 1979.

Ransel, David. *The Politics of Catherinian Russia.* New Haven, Conn.: 1975.

Rogger, Hans. *National Consciousness in Eighteenth Century Russia.* Cambridge, Mass.: 1960.

8

Power, Backwardness, and Creativity, 1801–55

An icy gust of wind from the Neva River swept across St. Petersburg's Senate Square, causing the soldiers drawn up in ragged ranks to hunch down into their tunics. Eyes watering from the cold, they looked about vainly for a sign from their officers. Some units had been there since early that wintry morning, 26 December 1825. For two weeks there had been confusion over who would succeed the deceased tsar, Alexander I. His oldest brother Constantine had renounced the throne in favor of a younger brother Nicholas, in accord with a secret memorandum approved by Alexander several years earlier. But when Alexander died, Nicholas, reluctant to appear a usurper, had hesitated, providing an opportunity for a group of revolutionary army officers to attempt to seize power. They called out elements of four regiments, some three thousand troops in all, to demand that Constantine be made tsar. The Decembrists, as the dissident officers came to be called, wanted a number of liberal reforms in Russia, but the soldiers understood little of this, as is illustrated by the apocryphal story that they clamored for "Constantine and Constitution," believing the latter (a feminine noun in Russian) to be Constantine's wife.

Earlier that morning the soldiers had shot and fatally wounded their commanding general when he had appeared to persuade them to surrender. A high Church official, the Metropolitan Seraphim, had fared better when he appeared in full vestments and bearing a cross to appeal to them to give up: the soldiers had merely shouted at him to retire to the cathedral and pray for their souls. The tsar-to-be Nicholas had himself barely escaped when he met a company of disheveled and disgruntled soldiers in the nearby Palace Square in midmorning. Intending to put the men in formation, Nicholas without identifying himself, called, "Halt!" to which the troops replied, "We're for Constantine." To avoid a confrontation, Nicholas simply told the unit it should go to the Senate Square to join their comrades already there.

By afternoon the impasse between the rebels ranged in front of the Senate Building, and some twelve thousand loyal troops confronting them across the square remained unbroken. The two top leaders of the Decembrists were nowhere to be found at this crucial moment, and junior

136

conspirators were uncertain what to do. A sullen group of laborers who had been constructing St. Isaac's Cathedral at the end of the square expressed sympathy for the soldiers by tossing stones and pieces of lumber at the government forces.

Because of its northern latitude, in mid-December dusk comes to St. Petersburg as early as three in the afternoon. Fearing that the rebellion might spread under cover of darkness, Nicholas finally ordered his artillery to fire grapeshot at the mutineers. Some sixty or seventy were killed, more wounded, and the rest fled. One hundred and twenty-one leaders of the Decembrist movement were arrested, of whom five were put to death after an official investigation and trial. Decisive action might have carried the day for the revolutionaries, but since their goals and motives were vague and unpublicized, it seems unlikely they could have succeeded in the long run.[1]

What sort of society were the Decembrists rebelling against? By the early 1800s Russia was a large but economically underdeveloped country, profoundly conservative yet with the first stirrings of revolutionary ferment, powerful militarily but inherently weaker than its Western rivals, and socially repressive despite spreading education and bursting cultural creativity. In this chapter we will explore these paradoxes, focusing in turn on Russia's serf economy, political stagnation punctuated by efforts at reform under tsars Alexander I (1801–25) and Nicholas I (1825–55), the flowering of literature and the arts, the development of revolutionary ideas, and Russia's dominant role in Europe and Asia. We will sketch the picture of what was in many respects a faltering giant: a great empire with endemic structural weaknesses, a socially divided citizenry, and uncertain and conflicting values. In spite of the foundations laid by Peter the Great and built upon by Catherine, Russia in the 1800s was unable to keep pace with the rapid economic modernization and political transformation that the West was experiencing in the nineteenth century.

By the early 1800s the Russian empire included forty-one million people, as compared with twenty-six million in France, only eighteen million in Great Britain, and eight million in the United States. In extent it stretched from central Europe to the Pacific Ocean, and from the Arctic to the Black Sea. Although Slavs were the dominant nationality, many other ethnic groups lived in Russia, including Germans, Finns, Jews, Tatars, Baltic peoples, and Asians of various nationalities. The people were overwhelmingly Orthodox in religion, but there were also Catholics, Lutherans, Jews, and Muslims. Official policy increasingly advanced russification, that is, the imposition on all citizens of Russian language, culture, and administration. The government also encour-

[1] This vignette of the Decembrist uprising is based largely on material in George Vernadsky, ed., *A Source Book for Russian History from Early Times to 1917*, Vol. II: *Peter the Great to Nicholas I* (New Haven: 1971), 524–30.

aged Orthodoxy as the preferred faith. Fewer than two million people lived permanently in towns and cities. St. Petersburg had the largest population, 308,000 inhabitants, with Moscow next at 270,000.

An authoritarian government headed by the autocratic tsar and run by an extensive bureaucracy managed this huge and diverse empire. Administration was cumbersome, inefficient, and often venal. Civil liberties were limited, and censorship, arbitrary actions, and repression were common. Some eight hundred thousand people were nobles of various levels, and another eight hundred thousand were clerics, merchants, artisans, and other town dwellers. All the rest, almost forty million people, were privately owned serfs and state peasants. State and society were richer than they had been in the eighteenth century but were already falling behind the wealth and progress of western Europe.

Most Russians were formalistically religious, little educated, vaguely loyal to the tsar, and increasingly resentful of the harsh life they endured and of the privileged elite who appeared to reap the benefits of their sacrifices. Within Russian culture as a whole and particularly among the educated elite a deep-seated and divisive clash of values was developing. On the one side were ranged secular, rational, worldly ideas and attitudes associated with the European Enlightenment. Opposed to them were religious, emotional, traditional views and feelings derived from old Russian culture. Eloquent spokesmen for both positions and philosophies arose, and a lively debate ensued throughout the 1800s.

The Serf Economy

Since so much of the social and economic life of the country was built upon the peasantry and the system of serfdom, we need to take a closer look at rural Russia and its institutions. The primary social unit was the extended peasant family. It customarily included grandparents, parents, and children, with a son's wife moving into the household of her husband's family. The dominant authority in the family was normally the senior male, but in the absence or incapacitation of such an individual, a grandmother or mother could fill the role. The family unit shared work and property, as well as being jointly responsible for taxes and other obligations.

American farms are single homesteads with surrounding land. But Russian villages, like European villages, are (and were) clusters of dwellings, usually laid out side by side along one or two muddy streets, averaging forty to fifty houses and several hundred to a thousand in population. Each small dwelling had space within it for animals, such as a few cows, pigs, geese, or chickens, as well as a tiny orchard and vegetable garden in the back. In most villages the surrounding lands were divided into grazing, timber cutting, and tillable fields (and similarly for the lord's acreage). Each household had the right to farm strips of land in the crop fields. A collective village institution, the *obshchina* or commune, whose forerunner arose in Kievan times, allocated these farming strips among households, usually every ten years, on the basis of the size and needs of the household. The *obshchina*, composed of heads of all the households in the village, made general agricultural decisions, such as what and when to plant, but each household worked its strips individually. The *obshchina* was also responsible as a whole for the general obligations of the village: work or payments to the lord, taxes and conscripts for the tsarist government.

In central southwestern Russia the serfs worked the lord's land as well as their own; in other parts of the country the serfs and state peasants owed payments in produce or money, in lieu of labor on the lord's fields. Depending on the size of his landholdings, his financial situation, and his inclinations, a noble landowner might closely supervise farming on his estate or show little or no interest in it, leaving agricultural decisions almost entirely to overseers and managers. During the nineteenth century the financial position of most noble landholders declined markedly, and by midcentury well over half of them were in debt.

From even this cursory description of the agricultural system its inefficiency and low productivity emerge. Serfs and state peasants had little incentive to produce since a good part of the fruits of their labor went to the lord or to the state in the form of taxes. Moreover, even an ambitious peasant was restrained by having to tailor his farming to the pattern set by common *obshchina* decisions on sowing, tilling, and harvesting. Nobles had little incentive to invest in agriculture or to introduce new farming techniques. As long as their estates produced enough for them to live comfortably, they were content to follow traditional practices. As a result the Russian land as a whole produced only a modest surplus, enough to feed the cities and to export a bit to western Europe, but not enough to accumulate rapidly the capital needed for large-scale industrialization.

Nevertheless, even if there had been general recognition that the serf economy was not very efficient or productive, it would have been difficult to change it. For, as an institution serfdom was still a useful administrative and social mechanism. It permitted the nobles and the government to control the bulk of the population, maintaining the peasants at a bare subsistence level. The nexus of lord, commune, and household helped keep order, collect taxes, and man the army. Moreover, because the system was so widespread and because so much of privileged Russia appeared to depend on serfdom, most officials feared the social disruption its abolition would cause; in particular they were afraid that the nobility would turn against the government. Only a major military defeat and rapidly changing attitudes finally permitted, in 1861, dismantling of this antiquated socioeconomic system.

The rest of the Russian economy in the first half of the nineteenth century suffered from the same drawbacks that it had in the 1700s, in particular a limited internal market, insufficient capital for investment, state restrictions and interference in the economy, and a small and timid entrepreneurial class. At the same time it did begin to grow, laying the foundations for its remarkable development in the latter part of the century. The number of manufacturing enterprises doubled while the number of workers increased fourfold. Particularly significant was the increasing use of free hired labor, which led some to conclude that Russia would be better off without serfdom. New branches of production were established, and a major cotton textile industry was developed. Transport and communications were greatly expanded, with the building of canals and railroads and the use of steamships on Russian rivers and seas. Trade and a money economy grew, and Russia became an exporter of grain and other raw materials to western Europe. The number and size of towns increased, and the urban population had almost doubled by midcentury.

Despite nascent industrialization and slowly improving productivity, Russia remained essentially an underdeveloped country, with an economy linked too heavily to an inefficient agricultural system. In terms of both economic growth and economic strength Russia began to fall markedly behind western and even central Europe. This trend had two significant results: Russia became increasingly dependent economically on Europe and, though still playing the role of a great power, was relatively weak politically and militarily.

Russia Unchanged

At the time few people were aware of this erosion of Russia's position. Reforms were discussed in the reigns of both Alexander I and Nicholas I, but no fundamental changes in the political and social system were made, despite an abundance of new ideas and the first emergence of a revolutionary movement. In part this stagnation can be explained by the fact that Russia continued to enjoy great success as a participant, often even an arbiter, in European affairs. Defeat was needed to force change, as we shall see in the next chapter. But in part the "frozenness" of Russian life in this era stemmed from the fact that under the autocracy only the tsar could initiate peaceful change, and neither Alexander I nor Nicholas I was prepared to undertake radical reform, though they were quite willing to tinker with the system.

Alexander in particular was a disappointment to those who looked for new directions for Russian society. A favorite grandson of Catherine, he had enjoyed a privileged childhood and an exemplary education under the supervision of a private tutor committed to the ideals of the Enlightenment. He seemed both born and trained to rule brilliantly. Moreover, he was a striking and charming individual. Tall, blond, gracious, and having a lively imagination, Alexander commanded admiration and respect from friends and enemies alike. But he also had an enigmatic personality and character, restless, vague, inconsistent, and in the end quite mystical. He had difficulty putting his ideas into practice, he vacillated on important issues of state policy, and he finally came down much more clearly on the side of absolutism than on that of enlightened change.

Some historians have suggested that the uncertainties and vagaries in Alexander's behavior resulted from his rather tortured upbringing, torn as he was between his father Paul and his grandmother Catherine while trying to please both, and from guilt over his father's murder during the coup d' état that brought Alexander to the throne. Although these are plausible suppositions, it is important to note that flights of mysticism and erratic action occurred more often in Alexander's later years and that as a young tsar—twenty-three years old at the time of his accession in 1801—he was quite decisive and seemingly well balanced.

In fact Alexander's reign had a promising start. He annulled some of Paul's most unpopular measures and amnestied people Paul had disgraced, exiled, or imprisoned. Alexander then began regular meetings with a small group of young and liberally minded advisers to plan improvements in Russia society. This coterie, which came to be known as the Intimate or Unofficial Committee, discussed frankly what changes should be made in the autocratic system and whether serfdom should be abolished. All the participants, including Alexander, soon confronted the great complexity and delicacy necessarily involved in reforming the two major institutions of Russian society. No comprehensive plan was propounded, but out of the discussions of the Unofficial Committee did come useful administrative changes, including strengthening the Senate established at the time of Peter the Great and establishing ministries to run various departments of government. Regulations for the personal manumission of serfs were decreed, and serfs in the Baltic provinces were emancipated, though without land. A number of new universities and schools were founded, and the educational system was both extended and improved.

Alexander's concern with domestic issues was interrupted in 1805 by Russia's joining in a European war against Napoleonic France, but Alexander returned to a consideration of reform between 1807 and 1812. The most radical proposal came from Michael Speransky (1772–1839), a remarkably able and far-sighted official, who on the basis of his talent, education, and effectiveness rose from humble origins to become a close adviser of both Alexander and Nicholas. In 1809 Speransky drew up an elaborate system of governance for Russia, which in fact amounted to a constitution. It provided for separation of the administrative and judicial functions of the state, as well as for legislative bodies at four levels and the specification and protection of certain rights for citizens. It was a bold plan, and if it had been adopted, it would have moved Russia much closer to the patterns of political development then unfolding in western Europe. But Alexander put into effect only a small part of Speransky's project, and later, in 1820, he also failed to implement a constitutional proposal submitted by another adviser. At the same time Alexander strongly supported constitutions for France after Napoleon's defeat and for the kingdom of Poland set up under Russian control after the Napoleonic wars. This anomaly in Alexander's political policies is one of the enigmas about him that have never been fully explained. In my view, Alexander retained the basic attributes of the autocratic system in Russia proper in part because he enjoyed the power and authority he wielded and in part because his exploration of radical reform in the deliberations of the Unofficial Committee had convinced him that giving the average Russian a say in government might undermine the whole system and lead to revolution.

In the latter part of his reign Alexander continued to approve some minor reforms but also adopted strongly conservative policies in education and social affairs, including a scheme proposed by the reactionary General Alexis Arakcheyev for military settlements: estates and villages inhabited by enlisted soldiers who between military assignments farmed the land under strict discipline and harsh conditons. Moreover, as we shall see shortly, Alexander pursued antiliberal policies abroad and spearheaded efforts to suppress revolutionary movements in Europe. The tsar also maintained a large army and navy, with over 40 percent of the state budget in 1825 allotted to military expenditures.

Alexander's unwillingness to introduce basic reforms in Russia's social system and political order evoked disillusionment, frustration, and despair among those of the educated elite who opposed serfdom and autocracy and who favored institution in Russia of civil rights and some form of representative government. Particularly disaffected were numbers of younger military officers, most of whom had served in the campaigns in Europe against Napoleon and had been exposed there, and in their education and reading, to the liberal ideas of the Enlightenment. Largely of noble background, these young men, after their return to Russia, formed secret societies to discuss their hopes and ideas for reform and to plot a course of action. Proud of their country's victory over Napoleon and its role in European affairs, they found themselves ashamed and distressed at Russia's economic backwardness, social oppression, and political obscurantism, and as men of action, they determined to do something about the situation. By the early 1820s these idealists had coalesced into two main groups, the Northern Society, whose moderate leaders espoused a limited constitutional monarchy for Russia, and the Southern Society, whose more radical thinkers urged overthrow of the tsar, establishment of a republic, and possibly the abolition of serfdom.

Reports of these dissident activities reached Tsar Alexander, but he seemed little concerned, probably because he was aware that only a small group was involved and that they had no following among the people as a whole. As we saw at the start of the chapter, when Alexander's unexpected death (he was only forty-eight years old) was followed by confusion over the succession, the conspirators seized this opportunity to move against the government. Their plans were not well laid, there was confusion and timidity in executing them, and the Decembrist rebellion was a fiasco, as we saw.

Although many of the Decembrists were noble officers in guards regiments like their forebears who had participated in seizures of power in the eighteenth century, the Decembrist revolt was not a palace revolution of the traditional type: the Decembrists did not simply want to change tsars but to change government and society. In that sense and even though they acted in splendid isolation from the masses, the Decembrists were the first modern Russian revolutionaries. Perhaps their goals were idealistic and their methods hopelessly impractical, but the Decembrists had a vision of a better Russia and a determination to realize that dream. Consequently, they were soon idolized as revolutionary pioneers, and their tradition inspired the Russian revolutionary movement throughout the nineteenth century. Even Lenin and the Bolsheviks acknowledged the Decembrists as their progenitors.

Alexander's youngest brother, Nicholas, who at age twenty-nine came to the throne in late 1825 during the tumult of the Decembrist rising and reigned for almost thirty years, was militaristic in outlook and deportment. Half-Prussian through his mother and tutored by a general, he had felt most comfortable as a youth in military drill and routine. He wanted Russia to be well ordered, efficient, and strong, and he applied his considerable determination and capacity for hard work to that end. Meticulous about detail, he personally supervised the investigation and trial of the Decembrists, clearly convinced that such dangerous and hare-brained activities as theirs should never be allowed in a properly run autocracy.

Although reserved, suspicious, and characterized by an almost fanatical sense of duty, Nicholas was by no means stupid, and he was well aware that Russia faced serious problems. In 1842 Nicholas stated candidly:

> There is no question that serfdom in its present state in our country is an evil palpable and obvious to everyone. However, to attack it now would be, of course, an even more disastrous evil.[2]

[2] Ibid, 552.

He nevertheless took several steps to mitigate the harshness of serf-dom, including decrees that serf families could not be broken up and that serfs could not be sold apart from the land. He also implemented the recommendations of one of the many bureaucratic commissions he established, regularizing and ameliorating the obligations of state peasants. At the same time Nicholas carried out a number of administrative and bureaucratic reforms designed to make the existing system work better. Among the most significant were a massive codification of Russian laws in 1838 overseen by Speransky and a series of financial improvements supervised by his minister of finance Egor Kankrin.

The government's slogan of "Autocracy, Orthodoxy, and Nationality" summed up the ideology of Nicholas's conservative regime. He reinforced the tradition of the authoritarian state and is reputed to have said, "I regard the whole of human life as service." Defending the prerogatives of the autocracy, Nicholas did not hesitate to resort to arbitrary action, censorship, and police surveillance and harassment to hector the government's critics and suppress dissent. Although the notorious Third Section of His Majesty's Own Chancery, established by Nicholas, was a forerunner of the political police set up by twentiety-century dictatorships, it was quite inefficient and unwieldy and achieved rather minuscule results despite enormous efforts.

Nicholas strongly supported the Orthodox faith and espoused Russian nationality as a supreme good. He applied russification measures to the western provinces of the empire, and after the Poles revolted against Russian rule in 1830, Nicholas suppressed the rebellion bloodily and abolished the Polish constitution, replacing it with new regulations that greatly restricted Polish autonomy and repressed Polish culture.

There is no doubt that despite minor improvements under his rule Nicholas essentially preserved and defended the old system and the traditional outlook of Russia. The ideal of service to the state, together with the authority of the government, was maintained and extended. The autocracy and serfdom remained basically unchanged, while the bureaucratic civil service grew to oversee almost every aspect of life. Russian society was still divided into classes, or *estates,* with the upper nobility retaining extensive privileges of status, wealth, and influence. Although there were merchants, artisans, and other free townspeople, almost no middle class or bourgeoisie comparable to that in western Europe developed. This was because Russia had a predominantly agrarian economy and because the government dominated all activity: its bureaucrats outnumbered all other nonlaboring and nonagricultural workers, it controlled education and the professions, and it played a leading role in finance, production, and trade. Even the towns were, or had until recently been, predominantly administrative centers. In such a centralized, hierarchical structure there was no place for independent interest groups or for pluralistic inputs to policy and operations. Finally, except among those who espoused the ideals of the French Enlightenment, the rights and aspirations of the individual were largely ignored in Russian society. State, church, army, and village commune all stressed the good of the whole community over that of the individual person.

Creativity and Dissent

What causes sudden surges of human creativity, such as the Renaissance? How can one explain a flurry of brilliant artistic activity, as occurred in midnineteenth-century Russia? In the space of not more than thirty or forty years, a dozen Russians produced some of the greatest works in world literature and Western music. It was an astounding, and largely inexplicable, performance. It was also paradoxical that these creative heights were reached at the very moment when Russian society, under Nicholas I, was culturally repressed. The government was trying to block new ideas with censorship and persecution, and the atmosphere was one of stagnation and disillusionment. Moreover, the official and widely held values were mystical and religious, related to the traditional tenets of Orthodox Christianity and the conservative principles of autocracy and privilege. Under such circumstances how could magnificent secular works of literature and music be written and composed?

It is tempting to answer that the coincident movement of dissent and criticism stimulated this creative flowering, but it is almost impossible to support such a causal connection. Most of the literature was about life not revolution, and the writers represented a broad spectrum of political and social views. All one can say is that artists and revolutionaries existed side by side and that to some extent both combined what Russia had learned from Western culture with Russian traditions and ideals to create brilliant new art and thought. It is also true that both writers and critics of the system moved in the same circles, a special group in Russian society known as "the intelligentsia."

This subclass was composed of individuals well educated in both Russian and Western culture whose main focus was intellectual life and discussion and who were deeply concerned about the nature of their own society and the future of Russia. The intelligentsia, although predominately from the upper classes, included sons and daughters of the poorer clergy, of lower-ranked civil servants, and of service and professional townspeople. They worked at all sorts of jobs, from tutoring and teaching to serving in the tsarist army and bureaucracy. Most felt alienated from the government and "official" society; on the other side, though they did not always acknowledge it, the intelligentsia were almost completely cut off from the mass of the Russian people: the peasants and the small but growing number of workers. They had varying criticisms of the existing situation and system, while propounding a wide range of solutions, from conservative to revolutionary. A common mistake of American students is to equate the intelligentsia with revolutionaries, whereas in fact a majority of intelligentsia preferred peaceful change in Russian society.

The remarkable outpouring of outstanding literature from writers among the intelligentsia began in the 1820s and 1830s with the poetry and prose of Alexander Pushkin, perhaps the most versatile and lyrical of all Russian writers. His long poem, *Eugene Onegin,* describes "the superfluous man," the individual who, restlessly but in vain, seeks a place and purpose in life and society, a story that became the basis of a magnificent opera by Tchaikovsky. Unfortunately Pushkin's brilliant career was cut short at the age of thirty-eight, when he was killed in a duel. His place as the premier Russian poet was taken by Michael Lermontov, who composed moving romantic poems and also wrote a superb realistic novel, *A Hero of Our Times.* He, too, died in a duel, when only twenty-six years old.

Nicholas Gogol, often considered the founder of Russian romantic realism, wrote about everyday life. His rollicking comedy, *The Inspector General,* and highly enjoyable novel, *Dead Souls,* satirized rural Russian society and its petty landlords and officials. In such short stories as "The Overcoat" and "The Nose," Gogol, with macabre humor but considerable empathy for his protagonists, depicted the dreary life and outlook of the "common man," the downtrodden bureaucrat or citizen struggling to exist in a society filled with pomposity and privilege. Although Gogol was politically conservative, his work was hailed by the radical critics among the intelligentsia who urged that literature be used as a weapon against the evils of government and society.

From the 1850s to the 1870s three giants dominated Russian literature. Ivan Turgenev's most influential book, *Fathers and Sons,* incisively portrayed the conflict between a more moderate older generation and a new breed of radicals personified by Bazarov, a "nihilist" who rejects all old values and mores in the name of materialistic science. Fyodor Dostoyevsky, perhaps the greatest of psychological novelists, depicted Russian life realistically, in such works as *Crime and Punishment* and *The Brothers Karamazov.* Yet the essence of his books was the conflict of emotions and ideas. He was thoroughly critical of Western materialism and values while seeing true salvation in a refinement of selfless love attained only through suffering.

Dostoyevsky's contemporary, Leo Tolstoy, remains a favorite epic novelist, best known for the broad sweep and riveting detail exemplified in his lengthy depiction of Russia's struggle against Napoleon, *War and Peace.* Tolstoy had the knack of making scenes and characters seem more vital and absorbing than reality itself. In the late 1870s Tolstoy underwent a religious "rebirth" and became an influential advocate of nonviolence and a devastating critic of the artificiality and immorality of modern life. His estate, Yasnaya Polyana, on which he tried to put into practice his teachings, has been preserved and may be visited today by bus from Moscow.

Russian artists of the midnineteenth century excelled in music as well as in literature. The first great Russian composer was Michael Glinka, who lived from 1804 to 1857. His operas, and those of other composers later in the century, effectively joined classical musical forms from Europe with Russian folk melodies, songs, and stories. This tradition was followed in the 1860s through 1880s in the works of a group of outstanding composers known as the "Mighty Bunch" or "The Five": Modest Mussorgsky, Nicholay Rimsky-Korsakov, Milii Balakirev, Cesar Cui, and Aleksandr Borodin. Working separately at about the same time was Pyotr Ilich Tchaikovsky. Together, these six composers produced romantic ballets, operas, symphonies, and other pieces that have enchanted lovers of classical music in Russia and abroad ever since.

While Russian writers and musicians were producing impressive masterpieces, essayists and social critics were engaged in a lively debate over philosophical and political issues. Much of the discussion focused on the nature of Russian society and the direction it ought to follow. Although almost all the debaters were schooled in a common body of European philosophy, especially German idealism, they reached diverse and often conflicting conclusions. Most were optimistic about Russia's future, rejecting the gloomy assessment of Peter Chaadayev in 1836 that because "we are not Western or Eastern and have the traditions of neither," Russia had contributed nothing to world culture.

The two main schools of thought that developed were the westernizers and the Slavophiles, small informal groups of noblemen intellectuals in Moscow. The former, as the name indicates, believed that Russia should adapt essential values and institutions developed in the West to the needs of Russian society. The westernizers stressed secular and rational thought and were voluntarists; that is, they believed that individuals and groups could act to change and improve society. Looking with favor on Peter the Great, they urged the expansion of education and the reform of Russian institutions. Although some later became revolutionaries, most westernizers urged the introduction into Russia of civil freedom and constitutional government through peaceful, evolutionary change. Two prominent westernizers, Alexander Herzen and Michael Bakunin, became increasingly critical of the government and went into exile in Europe in the mid-1840s. Herzen became a prominent journalist and mild revolutionary, while Bakunin moved in a sharply radical direction to become a leading anarchist.

The Slavophiles were romantic nationalists who idealized the Russian past, rejected Western civilization as a model for Russian development, and espoused a future good society in Russia based on the spiritual values of Orthodoxy and the social values of the people, especially as expressed in the peasant commune. At the same time they were critical of the government and the tsar, arguing that the mystical bond between ruler and people that had existed in old Russia had been broken by the interference of the bureaucracy and by the changes introduced by Peter. It was therefore necessary to restore a simpler, purer form of rule that would both protect the rights of Russians and give the tsar freedom to rule. The Slavophiles also criticized the established Church and urged its purification and the widespread propagation of basic Orthodox ideals. With these changes, the Slavophiles concluded, Russia could build a unique civilization that would be far superior to Western soceieties and that would contribute constructively to world culture. This visionary future would be based on brotherly love, peace, and harmony.

These contrasting attitudes toward the West and differing views of Russia's mission and future remained important issues of intellectual discourse in Russia in the nineteenth and early twentieth centuries and still today affect Soviet ideology and policy. Some writers have even classed Stalin as a Slavophile and have blamed outbursts of xenophobia in the Soviet Union on Slavophile influences.

Russia, Arbiter of Europe, Colonizer of Asia and America

For several decades in the first half of the 1800s Russia was considered the most powerful country in Europe and played a prominent, if not dominant, role in European affairs. This position was a result of Russia's major contribution to the defeat of Napoleon and to the peace settlement that followed. At the same time Russia was busy extending its borders, primarily in Asia, where tsars Alexander and Nicholas annexed most of the Caucasus and expanded Russian colonies in North America. Finally, throughout this period the Russian government was deeply involved with Turkey, an imbroglio that culminated in the Crimean War, 1854–56.

Tsar Alexander had come to the throne determined to keep his country at peace, but in the first ten years of his rule he waged war with Persia, Turkey, Sweden, and France. The struggle with Persia grew out of a request for protection from the small Christian state of Georgia in the Caucasus. The Russians assisted the Georgians against both Persian and Turkish incursions and pressures, and by 1810 Alexander had incorporated Georgia and several small neighboring areas into the Russian empire (see Map 6). Conflict with Turkey that lasted from 1806 to 1812 and with Sweden in 1808–9 resulted in Russia's acquiring two strategically important territories on its western border, Bessarabia and Finland.

But the main foe during Alexander's reign was revolutionary France led by Napoleon. Alexander opposed France because of Russia's political ties to Austria, Prussia, and Great Britain; its close economic relations with Great Britain; and Alexander's personal opposition to Napoleon's plans for dominating and transforming Europe. Alexander considered Napoleon a parvenu and usurper. Armed conflict broke out first in 1805–7 but Napoleon soundly defeated the Russians at the battles of Austerlitz, Eylau, and Friedland. In July 1807 a famous peace between Napoleon and Alexander was signed at Tilsit, and for the next four years the two major powers on the continent of Europe were uneasy allies eying each other warily.

The Tilsit agreement finally broke down over several issues. First, Napoleon wanted the Russians to adhere strictly to his "continental system," which was essentially a Europe-wide economic blockade against Great Britain, France's major remaining foe. Not only did many Russians ignore the restrictions and continue to trade with Britain, but to the extent the blockade was observed, this harmed the Russian export economy, the English having been the Russians' major trading partner over the preceding decades. Moreover, the Russians resented their defeat at the hands of the French and the growing French domination of Europe. The French in turn considered the Russians an unreliable ally and the only important obstacle to complete French hegemony on the continent. Finally, the two governments differed over policy in the Near East, in the Balkans, and in Poland and northern Europe, and there were other minor irritants in the relationship.

At last in June 1812, without declaring war, Napoleon invaded Russia, with the largest military force ever assembled in Europe, the so-called Grand Army, which at its height included six hundred thousand troops. However, less than half were French, with the rest supplied reluctantly by Napoleon's allies. The Russians were outnumbered more than two to one and were forced to fall back steadily before Napoleon's advance. Eventually, in September 1812 the Russians, under a newly appointed and popular commander, Prince Michael Kutuzov, made a stand at Borodino, a village just west of Moscow. In one of the bloodiest battles in history the Russians lost over a third of their force, some forty thousand men, while Napoleon's army suffered proportionate losses, over fifty thousand casualties, all in one day's fighting. Though forced to retreat, the Russians lost few prisoners and Napoleon could not destroy the remnant of the Russian army. He entered Moscow unopposed a few days later, believing the capture of Russia's traditional mother city would compel Alexander to surrender. But to Napoleon's indirect overtures for peace the tsar responded "at this moment no proposition of the enemy can induce me to terminate the war, and by that to weaken the sacred duty that I have to perform in avenging my injured country."[3]

Russians of all classes rallied patriotically around Alexander and the army, and Napoleon soon found himself in an untenable position. Harassed by Kutuzov's forces; with greatly extended lines of communication and supply; unable to draw much support from Moscow itself, which had been first evacuated and then partially destroyed by mysterious fires; and with the harsh Russian winter approaching, Napoleon withdrew in mid-October. In one of the great disasters of military history Napoleon's forces, weakened by disease, dwindling military and food supplies, and the raids of guerrilla bands and half-frozen to death by the bitter cold, staggered out of Russia. Only fifty thousand men out of the original six hundred thousand escaped death or capture. In the succeeding months the victorious Russian armies carried the war to Europe and played a major role in the ultimate defeat of Napoleon. The campaign concluded with Alexander's marching into Paris at the head of his victorious troops.

The triumph of 1812–13 had several important consequences. It was then, and has always been since, both a source of national pride and a reminder of Russia's vulnerability to attack from the West. It greatly increased Russian prestige in Europe and ensured major Russian influence in European affairs for several decades to come. At the same time it may have led Russian leaders to consider their country more powerful than it in fact was, and it may thus have reduced the pressure for basic reforms.

Alexander was a leader at the Congress of Vienna, which worked out a peace settlement for post-Napoleonic Europe. Under pressure from the other powers Russia had to settle for a smaller kingdom of Poland under Russian rule than Alexander had sought, but the tsar did obtain approval for his formulation of the Holy Alliance: a high-flown proclamation by the leading monarchs that they would band together to promote peace and Christian brotherhood in the world. Its practical manifestation was the Quadruple Alliance (Russia, Austria, Prussia, and Great Britain, with France joining in 1818), a powerful political coalition that acted to regulate the affairs of Europe for over a decade. In particular, the alliance, under Russian and Austrian prodding, moved firmly to suppress revolutionary movements in various parts of the continent. Although an internationalist in outlook, Alexander saw collective action primarily as a means of safeguarding the restored order in Europe and forestalling revolution.

Nicholas I pursued the same goals, but with such added vigor that he earned the unfortunate sobriquet of "the gendarme of Europe." In 1830, when revolutions broke out in France and Belgium, Nicholas would gladly have intervened against them, but the Poles also rose in revolt

---

[3] Cited in W. G. F. Jackson, *Seven Roads to Moscow* (New York: 1958), 160.

against their Russian masters, and the Russian army had to be employed to restore order there. However, in 1848, when revolution again swept across Europe, Nicholas sent Russian troops to help quell the uprising in Hungary, an intervention that was repeated a little over one hundred years later when the Soviet army put down the popular revolution of 1956 in Hungary.

Nicholas also extended the gains his predecessor had made in the Caucasus, acquiring part of Armenia in 1818 and waging a long war against Caucasian mountaineers led by the brilliant and tenacious Moslem warrior Shamil. In the Pacific Nicholas encouraged the development of Russian Alaska, but in 1867 under his successor, Alexander II, it was sold to the United States.

Although Russia had been in conflict with the Moslem Turks of the Ottoman Empire since the sixteenth century, only in the first half of the nineteenth century did relations with Turkey, the so-called "Eastern Question," become a major issue in tsarist foreign policy. The Russians and the Turks were at loggerheads in the 1800s—four major wars—for several reasons. Religious differences created one set of problems. The Orthodox Russians asserted the right to protect Christian minorities in the Ottoman Empire, particularly Christian groups in Turkish-ruled lands in the Balkans who were closest to Russia, some of whom were fellow Slavs. The Russians also claimed they should be allowed to manage and safeguard Christian holy places in the Near East, preserving them not only against Moslem but also Catholic interference.

A second set of issues centered on economic and strategic control of the Black Sea and of the Straits, the passage between the Black Sea and the Mediterranean. In the 1800s the tsars struggled to obtain the right of free passage through the Straits first for merchantmen and later for warships.

Finally, relations between Russia and Turkey were strained because the Ottoman Empire was rapidly weakening; in fact it became known as "the sick man of Europe." As Turkish power declined, Russia expanded in the Caucasus on the eastern border of the Ottoman Empire. Even more important was what would happen to territories under Turkish rule in Europe itself—in the Balkans and therefore on Russia's southwestern border. The Balkan peoples themselves rebelled against the Turks in a series of nationalist uprisings, but in addition the great powers, and particularly Austria, strove to exert influence in the Balkans. Consequently, while the Russians tried to reduce or eliminate Turkish control over the Balkans, they had also to contend with the intrusion of Austrian and later German power there. At the same time France and Great Britain were eager to prevent a Turkish collapse, from which the Russians would reap enormous gains, and as Ottoman power eroded, they strove to block any excessive accretion of influence to the tsars.

Beginning in the 1820s when the Greeks rebelled successfully against their Turkish overlords, recurring crises developed in the Near East and the Balkans over these issues. On almost every occasion the Russians and most of the other European great powers were drawn in, yet for three decades a major war among them was somehow averted. In the late 1840s and early 1850s, however, Tsar Nicholas I, who had until then managed Russian policy quite skillfully, made two major miscalculations. After extended conversations in England in 1844 Nicholas believed that he had reached an understanding with Great Britain to consult in advance and to act together on all issues relating to Turkey. In retrospect it appears that he assumed this gave Russia more scope in the Balkans than in fact the British leaders intended. In addition, Nicholas—or at least his emissary in Constantinople, the capital of the Ottoman Empire—underestimated the resistance of the Turks to Russian pressure and demands.

Although the details of the negotiations and the particular issues at hand need not concern us, the result was that the Turkish sultan appealed for support to the European powers, and when war broke out between Russia and Turkey in 1853, France and Great Britain soon sided with the Turks. Austria, although not participating, kept a threatening pressure on the Russian flank, and Nicholas found himself isolated and outnumbered. In September 1854 an Anglo-French expeditionary force landed on the Crimean peninsula and after a grueling campaign, marred by gross incompetence of the generals on both sides (which prompted Tennyson's famous poem "The Charge of the Light Brigade") and heavy sacrifices and casualties all around, the Russians were defeated and in 1856 had to sign the humiliating Treaty of Paris.

The Crimean War burst the bubble of Russia's superpower status in Europe, revealing to the West its military weakness and social and political backwardness. Although Russia, as we shall see in Chapter 10, continued for the next sixty years to play a significant role in European affairs, her position was now that of a junior player struggling to keep up with the varsity. Even more importantly the war displayed in glaring fashion to the new tsar, Alexander II (Nicholas had died near the end of the war), and to the Russian educated elite the serious internal problems of Russia and the urgent need to reform its archaic socioeconomic system and its cumbersome and inefficient government.

Conclusion

In several respects the history of Russia in the first half of the nineteenth century represents a golden opportunity missed. With a burgeoning population and a slowly rising level of education, the Russian government, drawing on the experience of neighboring Europe, might have bent every effort to accelerate the country's economic growth and to initiate processes of industrialization and modernization. Instead Russia, although developing slowly, fell markedly behind the booming European economy, which left the empire considerably weaker than its great power rivals for the rest of the 1800s and into the 1900s.

To be sure, to be able to surge ahead economically the tsars would have had to abolish serfdom and greatly reduce the overweening and stultifying intervention of the government in all aspects of social, ecomomic, and political life. To contemporaries it seemed that Alexander, favorite of Catherine, child of the Enlightenment, and a man of imagination and ability, might be the perfect tsar to undertake these necessary changes. Yet his complex personality and his enjoyment of power prevented him from grasping the nettle of reform, even after his glorious triumph over Napoleon. Constitutional projects languished and serfdom continued. Out of frustration with the lack of progress came the Decembrist uprising in 1825 and in the 1840s the beginning of a revolutionary movement among the intelligentsia.

Under Nicholas hopes for reform dimmed, given his character and outlook, with the result that Russia marked time, its social problems festering and its political climate frozen. Nicholas could wield a "big stick" in Europe and Russia's international prestige was high, but even this bubble was burst by Russia's humiliating defeat in the Crimean War.

By 1856 Russian society was in a fairly desperate situation. Much of its educated elite, although creative participants in European culture and bringing renown to their country in such fields as literature and music, were alienated from the government and out of touch with 90 percent of the population, who remained uneducated, burdened, and a potential "dark force." Underdeveloped economically, repressed politically, divided socially, Russia nevertheless continued to absorb European values and modernizing influences and tried valiantly to compete with Western societies that were already stronger and were moving rapidly in quite a different direction. It was urgent that Russia seek its own salvation, find its own path, and move into the modern world on its own terms. The task facing the new tsar, Alexander II, was monumental, to say the least.

FURTHER READING

Blackwell, W. *The Beginnings of Russian Industrialization, 1800–1860*. Princeton, N.J.: 1967.

Bolkhovitinov, N. N. *The Beginnings of Russian-American Relations, 1775–1815*. translated by E. Levine. Cambridge, Mass.: 1976.

Curtiss, John S. *The Russian Army under Nicholas I, 1825–55*. Durham, N.C.: 1965.

Grimsted, Patricia. *The Foreign Ministers of Alexander I*. Berkeley: 1969.

Lincoln, W. B. *Nicholas I*. Bloomington, Ind.: 1978.

McConnell, Allen. *Tsar Alexander I: Paternalistic Reformer*. New York: 1970.

Malia, Martin. *Alexander Herzen and the Birth of Russian Socialism.* Cambridge, Mass.: 1961.

Monas, Sidney. *The Third Section.* Cambridge, Mass.: 1961.

Raeff, Marc. *Michael Speransky.* The Hague: 1957.

Ragsdale, Hugh. *Bonaparte and the Russians.* Lawrence, Ks.: 1980.

Riasanovsky, N. *Nicholas I and Official Nationality.* Berkeley: 1959.

Simmons, Ernest J. *Pushkin.* Cambridge, Mass.: 1937.

9

Reform, Reaction, and Modernization, 1855-1904

In nineteenth-century Russia the people, proud of the country's armed might, loved to watch parades and other military ceremonies. The tsar, the first soldier of the Russian empire, often presided at these occasions. In that respect Sunday, 13 March 1881, was like many other holidays. Tsar Alexander II, known to many as the "tsar-liberator" for his freeing of the serfs, planned to review a parade around noon, and then visit a royal cousin on his way back to the Winter Palace in the heart of St. Petersburg. But unknown to Alexander, twenty-seven determined revolutionary terrorists, members of a radical fringe group called the "People's Will," had fixed that Sunday as his date of execution.

After four unsuccessful attempts to assassinate the tsar, the terrorists had recently rented a small basement shop on one of St. Petersburg's main streets, from which they halfheartedly sold cheese to disguise their main activity: burrowing a tunnel under the street with the aim of blowing up the emperor's carriage should it pass that way. On 13 March, just before Alexander left for the parade, his mistress had persuaded him not to return by his usual route, which would indeed have taken him along the street in front of the cheese shop. But the terrorists, aware that as a precaution the tsar often took alternate ways home, not only had a large cache of dynamite in their tunnel under the street but had posted five of their number along other streets and squares of the capital. Four of them were armed with a primitive, near-suicidal bomb of nitroglycerin that had to be tossed at extremely close range; the fifth, Sophia Perovskaia, a young woman of twenty-six from a noble family, was the lookout and supervisor.

As soon as Sophia saw that Alexander intended to take a different route back to the palace, she signaled by hand for the bomb throwers to take up new positions. A short while later when the imperial entourage started down a street called the Catherine Canal Embankment, Nicholas Rysakov stepped close to the carriage and hurled his weapon (see Figure 11). The explosion wrecked the wheels of Alexander's carriage

Figure 11.   *A painting showing a bomb exploding under Alexander II's carriage during his assassination by terrorists, March 1881.*

and wounded several onlookers, but the tsar himself was unhurt. Fool-hardily but overcome by curiosity and by concern for the wounded, Alexander dismounted from the carriage and approached Rysakov, whom the police had instantly seized.

At that moment a second assassin moved out of the crowd to within a few yards of Alexander and threw his bomb at the tsar's feet. Both Alexander and his assailant were mortally wounded, dying several hours later. Twenty others were also wounded, and blood was spattered across the snow banked on both sides of the street. Later the Church of the Savior's Blood was built on the spot where Alexander was killed.

Five terrorists were executed, but one of their leaders declared triumphantly: "An overwhelming weight has fallen from our shoulders. Reaction must end in order to make way for the rebirth of Russia." That did not happen, making the terrible events of that gray late winter afternoon in St. Petersburg only an episode in a continuing pattern of violence, reform, and reaction that marked the last half of the 1800s in the tsarist empire.[1]

The terrorists were right: change was needed. And in an impressive burst of reform in the 1860s and early 1870s the old order was considerably altered. With these reforms and under the impact of the rapid economic development and social transformation of the country,

[1] This account of the assassination is based on information in W. Bruce Lincoln, *The Romanovs: Autocrats of All the Russias.* (New York: 1981), 443–47.

Russia moved belatedly down the path of modernization. At the same time, however, retrograde forces—from individual tsars and officials through most of the landed nobility down to proto-fascist elements in the cities—strongly opposed reform and tried to bind Russia in a traditional framework. They insisted on long-established values and fought bitterly to preserve privilege and autocratic rule. This reactionary attitude and its reflection in state policy, together with the dislocation and discontent caused by the massive socioeconomic changes taking place, led to conflict and finally to the Revolution of 1905.

The Era of the Great Reforms, 1855–81

In three important respects Russia at the time of the accession of Alexander II in 1855 differed markedly from the country his uncle, Alexander I, had inherited half a century earlier. First, Russia was a good deal bigger, both in territory and in population. Finland, Bessarabia, and the Caucasus had been added, but even within its old boundaries, the number of inhabitants of the Russian empire had increased dramatically, from about thirty-seven million to fifty-nine million people. This meant that the agricultural economy, with little or no increase in productivity, had more people to support and less land per person. The result was widespread peasant unrest.

Second, the Russian economy as a whole was changing, and was falling further behind that of western Europe. The first signs of nascent industrialization appeared, the number of free workers grew, and trade and a money economy expanded, while the position of the nobility deteriorated. In these circumstances continuing the system of serfdom made less and less sense to a number of contemporary observers.

Finally, after its defeat in the Crimean War, Russia was considerably weaker vis-à-vis its rivals in Europe than it had been in 1801.

Alexander II, the eldest son of Nicholas I, ascended the throne at the age of thirty-seven, having been prepared for his responsibilities both through tutorial education and through occasional participation in state affairs. Conservative in outlook and upbringing, he seemed an unlikely candidate for the role of "tsar-liberator." Yet several factors worked to turn Alexander into an effective reformer. Since he was realistic and hard-headed, he concluded early in his reign that serfdom would have to be eliminated and other changes made if more serious difficulties were to be avoided. He was also patriotic, deciding that if Russia were to be powerful again, its government and social system would have to be brought up to date. Moreover, Alexander, respecting the ability of the senior civil servants charged with implementing change, steadfastly supported them, even in the face of strong noble opposition. Like his predecessors, Alexander had no intention of destroying the autocracy, but, unlike them, he became convinced of the need for basic reform if it were to be saved.

This last point is well illustrated by his famous remark to the Moscow nobility in 1856: "It is better to begin to abolish serfdom from above than to wait until it begins to abolish itself from below. I ask you, gentlemen, to think over how all this can be carried out." Thus, starting with the elimination of serfdom, Alexander launched a series of "Great Reforms" that transformed Russian society but by no means solved all its problems. Affecting some 52 million people, over 85 percent of the entire population, ending serfdom was at the time the most extensive and influential government-directed social change undertaken in human history. Extremely difficult and complex, the reform was carried out remarkably smoothly and quite effectively.

There was of course opposition, particularly among the nobility and some bureaucrats. But the majority of articulate society strongly favored the emancipation, for three main reasons, in my view. In the first place, the serf system was increasingly indefensible on moral grounds; hardly anyone could support the practice of Russians' owning other Russians. As education spread in the 1800s, serfdom became increasingly repugnant to the Russian elite, including many nobles. Second, defeat in the Crimean War convinced most Russians that a thorough overhaul of the country's antiquated social system was needed. Serf soldiers had not fought particularly well, and Russia's serf army had no trained reserves. Finally, many Russians were beginning to realize that for Russia to move ahead, free labor and an expanding industry were needed.

Soviet historians have argued that fear of revolution, or at least of massive peasant *jacqueries* like that of Pugachov eighty years earlier, also motivated the reformers, both inside and outside the government. Although Soviet scholars have effectively shown the rising incidence of peasant unrest, most of the contemporary comment about emancipation does not allude to the danger of peasant rebellion. It may, however, have affected many people subconsciously as Tsar Alexander's remark to the Moscow gentry suggests.

Much oversimplified, the main issue in the reform was who would get how much land. The more conservative nobles suggested freeing the serfs without land but having the nobles compensated for the loss of serf labor or dues. The most radical position was to provide the peasants with all the land, not only the fields they had traditionally worked but also the lord's tillable acres, with compensation to the lord for the land but not for the lost services. The peasants apparently expected to get most of the land, as their proverb suggests: "O lord, we are yours but the land is ours."

For four years beginning in 1857 the terms of the emancipation were discussed in provincial committees of the nobility and in the Main

Committee, the government's supervising body for the reform. Details were worked out in editing commissions, and on 15 March 1861, the emancipation manifesto was proclaimed, the same year Lincoln freed the American slaves. The compromise reached was quite reasonable under the circumstances. It favored the nobility but not so greatly as one might have expected, given their long role as a privileged elite and the tremendous pressure they exerted on the tsar and the government during discussion of the reform. The peasantry did not get as much land as they wanted, but their situation might have been tolerable had they not undergone a population explosion that doubled their numbers in the next fifty years and created a desperate need for land. The provisions of the reform let the lord keep most of his land and in principle gave the liberated peasants what they had traditionally farmed. In practice, and particularly in central Russia, where land was most valuable, the peasants finally received some 10 to 20 percent less land than they had previously tilled. Moreover, the government compensated the lord for the lost services of his serfs and collected this amount from the peasants in so-called redemption dues spread out over forty-nine years. This was a heavy burden, which in the long run the peasants could not pay.

Because it was a useful social and administrative device, the *obshchina* (peasant commune) was retained by the reformers, with two unfortunate effects. It meant the peasant was still bound to the village and its collective assembly, which determined when and how he would farm, as well as his share of taxes to the government. As some cynics observed, the peasant, far from being emancipated, exchanged one master (the lord) for another (the *obshchina*). However, he had always been part of the commune so this undoubtedly rankled less than his failure to obtain all the land. But keeping the *obshchina* also meant the peasant remained a second-class citizen, with special status and institutions and without the same standing as other subjects of the tsar. In fact, the government, concurrent with the emancipation, introduced new peasant courts and local organs of government (the *volost* system).

However much the terms of the emancipation favored the interests of the nobles, this arrangement did them little good since few were able to manage their estates profitably, and noble indebtedness steadily climbed in succeeding decades. As noted, the situation of the peasants also deteriorated because of the population explosion among them and the scarcity of land. In addition, having to stay in the commune dampened individual incentive, and the productivity of peasant farmers, even as freemen, remained low.

Nevertheless the emancipation had two important positive results: it removed a moral and economic millstone from around Russian society's neck, and it provided a supply of free labor for the development of capitalist agriculture and industry. Available for hire were household serfs who were freed without land and serfs who took "beggars' allotments," quarter shares of land in exchange for no redemption dues, which proved too small to support them. In addition, some landed peasants left the village temporarily for off-season work in factories.

Most of the other "Great Reforms" followed the pattern of changes that had occurred earlier in Western society, but they stopped short of providing Russians with full civil liberties or a national representative government. Instead the reforms in Russia made the governance of the country more orderly, efficient, and just, but within the framework of autocracy. The judicial reform of 1864 was a good case in point: it provided for trained and independent judges, open and sensible judicial procedures, and equality before the law. It gave Russia one of the most advanced and fair judicial systems in Europe. At the same time, because there was no political or constitutional reform accompanying it, the tsarist government was later able to carry out a number of extralegal actions, through imperial decrees, administrative regulations, and so-called extraordinary measures (which amounted to a form of martial law).

Other important reforms established partial self-government at two local levels. A series of municipal institutions were created in 1870, and new district and provincial organs called *zemstvos* were set up in 1864. The latter were assemblies whose members were elected by all classes: nobles, townsmen, and peasants. Although the nobles predominated and although the *zemstvos* had limited budgets and were restricted to managing only such local issues as education, public works, health, and welfare, they provided excellent training in politics and governance for future liberal opponents of the autocracy and served local needs quite well, certainly far better than the centralized bureaucratic government had in the past. The central ministries in St. Petersburg continued to control and administer most fiscal, police, and economic activity at the local level, and governors and other bureaucrats did not hesitate to pressure or interfere with *zemstvos*. Nevertheless the success of these unusual institutions belies the common adage that Russians have no experience with representative government and prefer authoritarian rule.

Another reform of Alexander's reign was an extensive reorganization of military affairs that helped modernize the army by introducing universal conscription, reducing the term of military service to six years, and creating a reserve. Also, education was expanded and improved, journalism and book printing were encouraged, and censorship was eased.

Taken together, the "Great Reforms" produced a significant transformation of Russian society, though the core of the political system, the autocracy, remained largely untouched. The reforms served as a significant safety valve, releasing long pent-up resentments and offering many the promise of a better future. At the same time the reform era aroused false hopes, leading some to believe that more had changed than in fact had and encouraging others to dream of a constitutional system and the establishment of full civil freedoms.

For the long run the most influential impact of the reforms was to open the door to rapid social and economic change and to permit the accelerated industrialization and modernization of the country. This was an important step in restoring Russia's strength, but it may have been too little, too late, as its rivals in the West—and even Japan to the East—accelerated at about the same time the pace of their social and economic development, making it even harder for Russia to catch up with them.

Terror and Reaction

Although in 1880 and 1881 Alexander had not turned his back on reform, considering at that time a constitutional project prepared by a liberal adviser, Count Michael Loris-Melikov, he had disappointed many in the intelligentsia who believed his reforms had not gone far enough and who were appalled at his appointment on occasion of avowedly conservative ministers and his lapses into reactionary policy. Moreover, a series of untoward events in the 1860s strengthened the hand of those who were urging the tsar to hold back. There were outbreaks of student rioting; a revolution in Poland in 1863, which aroused nationalist and conservative feeling in Russia; and an attempt to assassinate the tsar in 1866. Moreover, in some areas such as religion and education (after the appointment of a reactionary minister of education in 1866) the conservatives were given virtually a free hand. Religions other than Orthodoxy were repressed, and measures to squelch national movements in Poland and the Ukraine were taken. Romantic supporters of the government also began to develop an idealized kind of Slavic nationalism that came to be known as Pan-Slavism. Vague and abstract, it argued that all Slavs in Russia and eastern Europe were true brothers and should be united in common purpose and in interacting cultures under the general and benevolent leadership of the Russian state, the largest Slavic country.

A combination of dismay at apparent slips into reactionary policy under Alexander and of disillusionment with the limited nature of his reforms produced in the 1860s a new, more radical opposition among the intelligentsia. The "generation of the sixties" voiced more fundamental criticisms of Russian society and espoused more revolutionary solutions than their forerunners of the 1840s. Many were nihilists, who on principle rejected old values, institutions, and policies and who, according to their detractors, stood for nothing (hence their name). In fact, they did believe in science and rationality, and some, like Nicholas

Chernyshevsky, went on to propound utopian societies of socialist harmony and plenty. In rejecting traditional authority and conventions they sought a freer, simpler life for all, as well as personal liberation. Among their ranks were a number of able and courageous women who brought to the revolutionary movement a special emotional intensity and moral fervor.

The majority of the revolutionaries of the 1860s favored radical change but urged peaceful means and popular education to bring it about. Their views, broadly categorized as populism, motivated several thousand of them to "go to the people" in the early 1870s. Young radicals went to the countryside to work among the peasantry, whom they idealized as a fount of moral purity and untainted simplicity. The peasants, bewildered and suspicious, did not know what to make of these well-meaning city folk who wanted to help them. In the end the "people" either ignored the populists or turned them over to the police as dangerous troublemakers.

When it was clear that this and other efforts to promote radical change by education, example, and propaganda were having no effect, a small group of revolutionaries, the People's Will, broke off from the mainstream of populism and turned to terrorism. Although numbering probably fewer than one hundred persons, these intelligent and zealous revolutionaries succeeded in killing more than a dozen prominent officials and frightening much of society. Their rationale was explained by Andrew Zhelyabov, speaking in his own defense at his trial for complicity in the assassination of Alexander II in 1881:

> This temporary movement to the people showed our ideas to be impracticable and doctrinaire. . . . From dreamers we became workers. We took to deeds, not words. Action meant some use of force. . . . Circumstances were forcing me, among others, to declare war against the existing political structure.[2]

The program of the People's Will adopted a year earlier had defended violence:

> The purpose of terroristic activities . . . is to break the spell of governmental power, to give constant proof of the possibility of fighting against the government, to strengthen in this way the revolutionary spirit of the people and its faith in the success of its cause, and, finally, to create cadres suited and accustomed to combat.[3]

But in practice terrorism and assassination only repelled much of educated society, puzzled the peasants, and strengthened the position and

[2] Cited in Thomas Riha, ed., *Readings in Russian Civilization*, vol. 2, *Imperial Russia, 1700–1917*. (2d ed., Chicago, 1969), 375.

[3] In George Vernadsky, ed., *A Source Book for Russian History from Early Times to 1917* vol. 3, *Alexander II to the February Revolution*. (New Haven: 1972), 664.

determination of conservatives. The result was that the era of the Great Reforms ended not only in the murder of the tsar-liberator but in a period of reaction and counterreform that immobilized political life in Russia for twenty-five years.

Since Alexander III (1881–94), who succeeded to the throne at the age of thirty-six, greatly admired his grandfather, Nicholas I, it is perhaps no accident that there were striking parallels between the two reigns. Both tsars came to the throne after periods of change and reform that had ended in tragedy: a revolt and an assassination. Both were determined to restore law and order; both wanted a well-regulated and efficient state; both believed in the sanctity and power of the autocracy; and both were ardent Russian nationalists. To some extent both also reacted against their predecessors' policies. Alexander III had never been close to his father, and in the last years of Alexander II's reign the son had deeply resented the father's open flaunting of a mistress, who in 1880 was even moved into the imperial palace with her bastard children by Alexander II.

Whatever personal and psychological reasons might have influenced Alexander III to reject the reform policy of his father, it is also clear that he did not believe further change would be good for Russia. From the late 1860s, long before he came to power, he had increasingly adopted a traditional and religious outlook consonant with the philosophy of his former tutor, Constantine Pobedonostsev, a conservative intellectual who served after 1880 as head of the Holy Synod, the council that managed the affairs of the Orthodox Church. Pobedonostsev was highly critical of the Great Reforms and believed wholeheartedly in defending and buttressing the autocratic power of the tsar. He stressed moral values while sharply criticizing science, materialism, and the growing industrialization of Russia.

Austere, not especially bright, and somewhat self-righteous, Alexander III did his best to turn back the clock in Russia. Such an effort was singularly inappropriate because Russia's society and economy were at that very moment changing rapidly and fundamentally. Consequently, political retrenchment resulted in substantial incongruencies and asymmetries in the system and made subsequent efforts to readjust that much more difficult. The only areas in which Alexander III's administration acted to take account of the new realities were fiscal policy and labor legislation designed to ameliorate slightly the dreadful conditions under which Russia's new working class toiled.

Otherwise a stern repression and systematic reaction ruled. For example, in the countryside, although they could not undo the emancipation of the serfs, Alexander and his conservative advisers created a new instrument of control that bypassed both the existing administrative framework and the reform-era institutions of *volosts* and *zemstvos:* the post of *land captain,* an official charged with supervision of all rural affairs, who combined both judicial and administrative authority, in direct violation of the separation of functions sought by the reformers of the 1860s. Alexander III and his counterreformers also limited the jurisdiction and effectiveness of the self-governing *zemstvos* and the municipal institutions set up under Alexander II.

At the level of the central government nothing was done to modify autocracy in any way, but in fact the complexity of governing a slowly modernizing society meant that Alexander III had to rely, more than any of his predecessors, on the state bureaucracy, which on occasion blocked some of his reactionary measures. But most were passed, including tight restrictions on the press and universities, and Alexander III did not hesitate to resort to extralegal steps, such as sending opponents into exile in Siberia and decreeing areas of the empire subject to stringent "temporary regulations."

Alexander III was a dedicated nationalist, favoring, as one observer put it, "Russian principles, Russian strength, Russian people." He disliked Germans and detested Poles and Jews. In his reign anti-Semitism flourished. Admission quotas for Jews in secondary schools and universities were established, and restrictions were enforced to limit Jewish habitation to the so-called Pale of Settlement, an arc of territory in western Russia were Jews had traditionally lived. The first pogroms, or riots, directed against Jewish property and Jewish individuals occurred, if not with government encouragement at least with government indifference. In the non-Russian territories of the empire russification policies begun earlier in the century were greatly intensified, provoking a nationalistic resistance among the minorities.

In 1894 Alexander III died unexpectedly of a stroke, and his son Nicholas II ascended the throne at the age of twenty-six. More intelligent than his father but not broadly educated, Nicholas was weak-willed and irresolute, perhaps because his father had tyrannized him. Although a devoted family man and quite charming when he wished to be, Nicholas was also suspicious and narrow-minded. He had few qualities necessary to lead a complex society in turbulent times. He did not really understand the swift changes taking place in Russia and remained committed to preserving the autocracy and traditional values. Early in his reign he called the aspirations of a group of liberal aristocrats for limited representative government "senseless dreams," and he proceeded in the first decade of his rule to continue the reactionary policies of his father. He also supported russification, extending it even to Finland, which had enjoyed some autonomy since it had come under Russian rule in 1809.

Nicholas, however, could be influenced by powerful personalities, and he supported for a time the program for economic modernization advanced by his minister of finance, Sergei Witte. Witte was typical of the new bureaucrats emerging in the latter half of the nineteenth century, an individual from non-noble origins who worked his way up in government service by talent, hard work, and imagination. Witte believed fervently that if Russia were to remain competitive with European nations, it would have to modernize, particularly by exploiting its natural resources and building up its economy. He supervised what has been called "the Witte system": this included subsidies and tariffs to promote heavy industry and Russian exports; extensive borrowing from abroad to accelerate Russian industrialization; stabilization of the fiscal system, including adoption of the gold standard; building of railroads; and accumulation of capital for these purposes by taxing the peasantry and by selling Russian grain in European markets. Witte was astonishingly successful, but the cost to the peasantry was heavy, contributing to widespread agricultural disorders that began in 1902 and lasted off and on through 1907.

Economic and Social Modernization, 1861–1905

Witte's efforts were part of a larger process of economic and social development that swept over Russia in the forty-odd years from the emancipation of the serfs in 1861 to the Revolution of 1905. The newly freed peasants were perhaps least affected by these sweeping changes in Russian society, but even they felt the impact of Russia's rapid modernization. In the first place new factories and workshops drew heavily on peasant labor. At first peasants worked in industry primarily on a seasonal basis, returning to their villages for key agricultural tasks such as sowing and harvesting. But later they resided permanently in the cities, perhaps leaving their families in the countryside until they could earn enough to support them in town. Under either arrangement part of their wages went to pay their share of village and communal taxes. Second, improved transportation and communication meant that new ideas, including appeals for revolution, spread across much of Russia. If not fully aware politically, peasants at least began to think about joint action against the landowners and the government.

At the same time their economic position deteriorated. The peasant population grew in this period on an average of eight hundred thousand persons a year, reaching almost one hundred million by 1905. Although some peasants emigrated to Siberia and to Russian Asia, they were far fewer than the natural increase of people. Demographers have not been able fully to explain this population boom. In part it resulted from improved conditions of health and public order in the villages. Peasants may also have had a more positive attitude about the future as a result of emancipation and so have risked ever larger families. But to a considerable degree this phenomenal growth remains a mystery.

Its consequences were clear, however: from 1861 to 1905 the av-

Figure 12. *A meeting of village elders, 1910. (Courtesy of the Board of Trustees of the Victoria and Albert Museum)*

erage size of a peasant's share of the communal land decreased by one third; the price of land doubled; the peasants' redemption dues were 119 percent in arrears by 1900; a serious famine occurred in 1891; and extensive peasant disorders broke out in 1902–3. A substantial increase in agricultural productivity might have compensated for the population explosion, but in fact the yield per acre increased only slightly in this period, primarily because the *obshchina* system of collective ownership and farming provided little incentive to improve farming methods or to work harder (see Figure 12).

To the difficulties created for the peasants by growing numbers, insufficient land, and low productivity must be added the heavy exactions imposed on them by the government. Quite deliberately, successive tsarist administrations from the 1870s on squeezed the peasantry to support the state budget and to help finance industrialization. Three methods were used: direct taxes levied through the commune, indirect taxes on such widely used items as vodka and kerosene, and buying of grain relatively cheaply and then exporting it abroad at higher prices. Given the peasants' overall situation it is hardly surprising to find them playing a major role in the Revolution of 1905.

The nobility, both as an economic force and a social class, declined in the postemancipation era. Noble landholding fell by almost 30 percent, and much of the land the nobles retained was mortgaged. Only a small minority ran their farms well or developed large capitalist-style agricultural enterprises. Another small group went into industry, banking, or professional work, but the majority remained civil servants or barely subsisted on their estates. Still influential at court and in the bureaucracy, they were nevertheless increasingly challenged by upstarts from lower echelons in society, like Witte.

While agriculture lagged, with the peasantry struggling to survive and the aristocracy slipping, Russian industry was growing by leaps and bounds. To some extent its expansion was made possible by extraction of capital from the agricultural sector, but several other factors promoted an industrial boom. To begin with, Russia, like the United States and Japan, was able to benefit from the earlier European experience with industrialization by installing the latest technology and machinery and by drawing heavily on European capital for investment. Second, the Great Reforms not only furnished a pool of peasant labor for the new factories but created an atmosphere of legality and stability that encouraged both Russian entrepreneurs and foreign investors. Finally, the tsarist government actively supported industrialization through subsidies, tariffs, large government orders, and outright ownership of key sectors, such as railroads.

Between 1861 and the 1880s Russian industry grew at a moderate pace, the number of factories increasing from about ten thousand to twenty thousand and the value of their output from about 200 million rubles to 1 billion rubles. By 1905 the number of factories passed forty thousand, and total output soared to over 4 billion rubles. Railroad trackage grew from about one thousand to over twenty-five thousand miles between 1860 and 1905. Russia became a major producer of coal, iron, and petroleum and began to export manufactured goods to Asia and parts of Europe. Russia's rate of industrial growth in the two decades before the Revolution of 1905 was 8 percent, equaling that of the United States at a comparable period in its development.

This first surge of Russian industrialization had certain distinguishing characteristics. Production was highly concentrated, both in a few major cities and regions—such as Moscow, the Urals, the Ukraine, St. Petersburg—and in large factories, such as the Putilov works, which gathered thousands of workers in one place. This concentration resulted in some economies of scale but also produced large clusters of workers, giving them greater solidarity and later facilitating the spread of revolutionary ideas among them.

Another special feature of the growth of Russian industry was the dominant role played by the state, both directly by state investment, management, and purchases, and indirectly through favorable economic and fiscal policies. The other major bloc of capital for Russian industrialization came from abroad, from European and American investors. Foreign investment in Russia grew from 100 million rubles in 1880 to 900 million rubles in 1900, and by 1914 one third of all Russian industry was foreign-owned.

The dominance of state and foreign capital in the Russian economy had several important effects. It meant that revolutionaries could charge that the country and especially its working class were being exploited by a privileged few around the tsar and by foreigners. In addition, Russian loans from France helped tie Russia to France diplomatically and militarily. Moreover, because the government and foreign investors played such a prominent role, the development of a Russian capitalist class was stunted. Russian businessmen never had the economic strength and political clout of their counterparts in Europe and the United States. They were never powerful enough to force needed political changes, and even when they worked together with Russia's professional classes, as during World War I, they succeeded only in harassing the autocracy rather than reforming it.

The social impact of industrialization on Russia was much like its effects in western Europe a half century earlier. Cities expanded in size and number, and the urban population of Russia doubled. The number of workers shot up, reaching over 2.25 million by 1905. Most of the proletariat worked and lived under deplorable conditions, as these excerpts from reports of government factory inspectors in the 1880s show:

> Sanitary conditions in the workers' settlement of Yuzovka are highly conducive to the contraction and spread of disease. The market place and streets are full of filth. The air is rotten with the stench from factory smoke, coal and lime dust, and the filth in gutters and organic wastes on streets and squares. . . . The majority of workers lived in so-called "cabins" built in the outskirts of the settlement. . . . These cabins are simply low, ugly mud huts. The roofs are made of earth and rubbish. Some of them are so close to the ground that at first sight they are nearly unnoticeable. The walls are covered with wood planks or overlaid with stones which easily let in the dampness. The floors are made of earth. These huts are entered by going down into the ground along earthen stairs. The interiors are dark and close, and the air is damp, still, and foul-smelling. . . . The furnishings are completely unhygienic, although frequently the workers live here with their families and infant children. . . .
>
> The very worst, most unhealthy conditions I saw were in tobacco factories. . . . The shops where tobacco is chopped and dried are so filled with caustic dust and nicotine fumes that each time I entered one of these rooms I had spasms in my throat and my eyes watered. If I stayed there very long I even became dizzy, though I am a smoker myself. Yet even women sometimes work in this atmosphere. . . . Children work in these tobacco factories as wrappers, baggers and packers. There were even children under twelve working there. . . .[4]

In addition, wages were low, hours long, and the workers were at the mercy of arbitrary regulations and fines imposed by management.

[4]Riha, *Readings*, 410, 413.

Forming unions and striking were prohibited, although as early as 1878–79 the first illegal strikes occurred.

Almost as important as their physical situation in creating a revolutionary frame of mind was that most workers found adjusting to factory discipline and city life difficult. Away from the traditional routine and values of family, village, and church, they sought some new purpose and anchor for their lives. Some fell into drunkenness and petty crime; others readily joined social or discussion groups. Open to new ideas, such workers' circles debated Marxism and other revolutionary creeds, under leaders who were usually intellectuals, not workers.

Competing Ideologies

As the pace of economic and social change in Russia quickened in the last quarter of the nineteenth century, intellectual ferment accelerated as well. Most educated Russians sought solutions to Russia's problems in two schools of political philosophy that had developed earlier in Europe: socialism and liberalism. Among the Russian intelligentsia two main categories of socialism emerged in the 1880s and 1890s: Marxism and peasant socialism. A bit later, just after the start of the twentieth century, an organized liberal movement developed. Since all three ideologies played important roles in the revolutionary events of the 1900s, we need briefly to examine each of them.

Karl Marx developed his theories in the midst of the Industrial Revolution in Europe. He was outraged at the misery and exploitation he saw all about him, concluding that the promise of freedom and equality trumpeted by the leaders of the French Revolution had not been fulfilled. Marx explained the injustice of contemporary life by arguing that the material world—and in society this meant the economic factor—was the basic reality; under industrialization therefore the productive forces (the factories) and the relations of production (who owned the factories) determined social, political, and intellectual life. Applying this *materialist,* or economic, interpretation to history, Marx argued that, powered by conflict between positive and negative forces (the *dialectic method),* human development would pass, according to immutable laws, through five stages: primitive communal or clan society, slave-holding society, feudalism, capitalism, and socialism. When society reached the final phase of the socialist stage of history, known as communism, the dialectic contradictions within it would cease and a future good society for all mankind would be established.

From this set of ideas, known as *dialectical* and *historical materialism,* Marx drew certain conclusions about the society around him. Europe, he believed, had passed from feudalism to capitalism in the upheaval of the French Revolution, and another great revolution would be needed to complete the passage from capitalism to socialism. This revolution, Marx was convinced, was inevitable and in fact was being prepared by the capitalists themselves. Driven by economic necessity, they were exploiting the workers so unmercifully that the capitalist system would be forced into a crisis of diminishing profits and overproduction and would collapse. Confronted with their imminent demise, the capitalists would resist, only to be overthrown by an organized and class-conscious proletariat. By this time workers would be the overwhelming majority of the population, and they would establish a dictatorship of the majority as a transition to a one-class society in which the state as a coercive mechanism would wither away. In the new socialist society all its citizens would own the productive forces, thereby liberating them from the artificial constraints on production imposed by the capitalists. This would produce a superabundance of goods, and each individual could then receive under socialism enough to meet basic needs. At the same time each new-type socialist citizen, eager to help the whole society, would work and contribute to the full extent of his or her talents. According to Marx, the socialist or proletarian revolution needed to bring all this about had not yet occurred anywhere in Europe, but the crisis of capitalism was deepening all the time.

At this point you may well be wondering how on earth could these theories of Marx, so closely tied to European experience and to the advanced industrialization of the West, have any relevance for underdeveloped, predominantly agricultural Russia? Marx himself never satisfactorily answered this question, although on several occasions he talked optimistically about the possibility that Russia might be able to develop a unique brand of socialism, building on the collective tradition of the peasant commune. But even before his death in 1883, Marx's writings had been translated into Russian (the censor thought they were too ponderous to be dangerous), and a few Russian revolutionaries, eying the rapid industrialization of their country, had begun to speculate that Marxism might be a useful political program, if it could be adapted to Russian conditions. Before long, wretchedness and desperation made Russian workers quite willing to listen to any theory that promised to improve their lot and put them in charge, no matter whether its fine points really applied to Russia or not.

In the 1880s a few Russian populists, who were in exile in Europe, converted to Marxism, and by the 1890s several dozen Marxist revolutionaries were active within Russia, leading workers' discussion circles. One of those early Marxists was Vladimir Ilich Ulianov, who later adopted the revolutionary pseudonym Lenin. Lenin's father was a provincial civil servant at the middle level, his mother the daughter of a doctor. Lenin grew up in moderate circumstances and excelled at school. Not unhappy or deprived, he turned to revolution mainly from idealism but partly also because his older brother was executed for complicity in a plot to assassinate the tsar. Expelled from university for participation in student agitation, Lenin read widely in European political philosophy and in the history of the Russian revolutionary movement and became a dedicated Marxist. In the 1890s Lenin was exiled to Siberia for his propagandizing and organizing efforts among the workers of St. Petersburg. He used his time there to study and write, and he soon became an acknowledged leader of the Russian Marxists. They had founded an embryo party, known as the Russian Social Democratic Labor party, in 1898, but most of its members were almost immediately arrested by the police.

In this period Lenin and his colleagues engaged in extensive polemics against two competing sets of ideas, which they were convinced would undercut the development of a strong Marxist revolutionary movement in Russia. One was *economism*, the view of some workers and intellectuals that the main goal was to improve the economic and social conditions of the Russian proletariat. They sought shorter hours, higher wages, improved factory safety, and decent housing. The Marxists argued that such a program only deceived the workers. As long as the capitalists owned the factories and used their economic power to control the government (although in Russia they in fact did not), concessions wrung from the capitalists would be only temporary and inadequate. The only correct course of action was political: organizing the workers for the eventual socialist revolution. The Marxists made some headway in their arguments, though in practice they often had to lump the workers' economic demands with the Marxist political platform.

The other ideology against which the Marxists struggled was peasant socialism. It grew directly out of the earlier populist movement, but its proponents argued that instead of education or "going to the people," organization and revolutionary activity were the correct weapons for effecting radical change in Russia. The leaders of peasant socialism believed that Russia could avoid some of the worst evils of capitalism as it had developed in Europe by moving directly from its present agricultural, semifeudal system to socialism, drawing heavily on the peasantry and their socialist experience with the peasant commune. In the 1890s and the first decade of the 1900s the peasant socialist movement spread rapidly, and its followers were soon organized as the Socialist Revolutionary (SR) party, a main rival of the Marxists from then on. The SRs, though counting heavily on the peasants, also courted workers, establishing cells at factories and workers' settlements and enjoying considerable success.

Although both Marxists and peasant socialists favored revolution to bring about the changes they desired, large numbers of Russians in the professions, among the nobility, and in the civil service opposed using violence and espoused peaceful, evolutionary reform. They were just as strongly hostile to the tsarist government, but their vision of the future was not socialism but *liberalism*. This was a rather loose set of social and political principles that had evolved in Europe in the nineteenth century, building on the ideas of the Enlightenment and the experiences of the French and American revolutions. Unlike socialists, liberals had no strict doctrine, but they generally believed in full civil freedoms in Russia; equality for all citizens, including the peasantry; benevolent social and economic reforms, with no infringement of private property; free trade and laissez-faire economic policies; and some form of representative government, through a constitution or some other mechanism. A few believed in a *republic,* that is, in abolishing the tsardom, but most would have been content to see Russia reformed under a constitutional monarchy over which the tsar could still preside. The liberals also began to organize in the early years of the twentieth century, forming the Constitutional Democratic party in 1905 (known as the Kadets from its Russian initials, K. D.).

At about the same time that the socialist and liberal movements were getting established in Russia, nationalism increasingly affected some of the non-Russian groups within the empire. Polish demands for reestablishment of an independent Poland, or at the very least for greater Polish autonomy, had recurred throughout the nineteenth century, culminating in the rebellions of 1830 and 1863 and reviving again in the 1890s. The Finns, particularly after the repression practiced under Nicholas II at the turn of the century, clamored for a separate or an autonomous Finland. To a lesser degree they were joined by the Baltic peoples—Estonians, Latvians, and Lithuanians—and by Armenians and Georgians in the Caucasus. Even more threatening to the centralized structure and policies of the Russian empire was the emergence of a nationalist movement among the Ukrainians. Growing out of a literary renaissance and an interest in Ukrainian history, Ukrainian nationalism was beginning by 1900 to press social and political demands against the dominance in the empire of Great Russians.

These threads of disaffection within the Russian state—socialism, liberalism, and nationalism—began to come together in the first years of the twentieth century to threaten the tsardom. Their impact was greatly intensified when Russian society suffered, in short order, an economic and then a foreign policy crisis. The economic emergency was created by a severe depression in the first years of the twentieth century and by sporadic peasant disorders across a number of provinces in 1902 and 1903. How serious these economic disruptions would have become is unclear because in 1904 they were overshadowed by Russia's involvement in a losing war with Japan that helped spark the Revolution of 1905.

Before looking at that dramatic revolution, we need to review quickly the way in which developments in Russian foreign policy ended in Russia's going to war. As you recall, the Crimean War reduced Russian in-

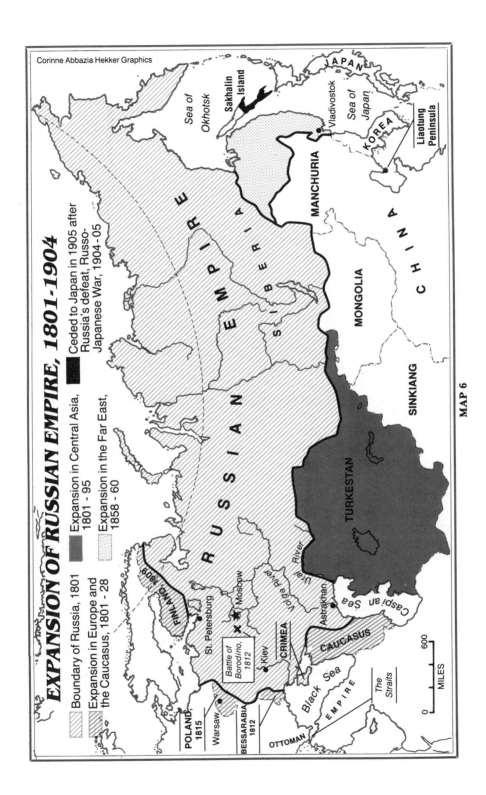

EXPANSION OF RUSSIAN EMPIRE, 1801-1904

Corinne Abbazia Hekker Graphics

Legend:
- Boundary of Russia, 1801
- Expansion in Europe and the Caucasus, 1801 - 28
- Expansion in Central Asia, 1801 - 95
- Expansion in the Far East, 1858 - 60
- Ceded to Japan in 1905 after Russia's defeat, Russo-Japanese War, 1904-05

JAPAN

Sea of Okhotsk

Sakhalin Island

Vladivostok

Sea of Japan

KOREA

Liaotung Peninsula

MANCHURIA

RUSSIAN EMPIRE

SIBERIA

MONGOLIA

CHINA

SINKIANG

TURKESTAN

Caspian Sea

Astrakhan

Ural River

Volga River

CAUCASUS

FINLAND 1809

St. Petersburg

Moscow

✕ Battle of Borodino, 1812

Kiev

CRIMEA

Black Sea

OTTOMAN EMPIRE

The Straits

POLAND 1815

Warsaw

BESSARABIA 1812

MILES

0   600

MAP 6

fluence in Europe and checked Russian expansion into the Balkans. But this was only a temporary setback. Before long Russia joined Germany and Austria-Hungary in an informal alliance system, called the Three Emperors' League, that lasted for most of the period between 1873 and 1887. This meant the Russian empire was once again an active participant in European politics and in the European balance of power.

Moreover, Russia was soon embroiled with the Ottoman Empire again. New crises arose when the subject peoples of the Turks in the Balkans tried to fulfill their nationalist aspirations by rebelling, and when the European powers, who had lent the Turkish sultan large amounts of money, were dissatisfied with his fiscal policies and plans for repayment. The Russians would probably have been dragged in anyway, but the sudden upsurge among educated Russian opinion of vociferous feelings of Pan-Slavism brought great pressure on the government to assist Russia's Slavic and Orthodox brethren in the Balkans.

Between 1875 and 1877 occurred a string of events, any one of which might have been resolved peaceably, but the cumulative effect of which was to bring Russia and Turkey to the brink of war. The Turks, rejected by Western public opinion after their bloody suppression of a Bulgarian revolt, were prepared to make substantial concessions, but Alexander II, pushed by inflamed nationalist feeling in Russia, took his country into war against the Ottoman Empire. After an early defeat the Russians' superior numbers brought them a considerable victory, which was reflected in a preliminary peace treaty signed in March 1878 that gave the Russians substantial gains in the Balkans. At the Congress of Berlin, a subsequent conclave of all the European powers, Russia's spoils were somewhat reduced; after 1885, when the Bulgarians repudiated Russian tutelage, Russian influence in the Balkans was minimal for the next twenty years. But this issue was only dormant, and when new crises erupted in that region after 1908, great power entanglement there led eventually to World War I, as we shall see in Chapter 10.

After the Congress of Berlin European statesmen encouraged Russia to look in other directions. Otto von Bismarck, the architect of the unification of Germany, who had claimed for himself the role of "honest broker" at the Congress of Berlin, declared: "Russia has nothing to do in the West. She only contracts nihilism and other diseases. Her mission is in Asia. There she . . . stands for civilization." Whatever Russia really stood for in Asia, the empire did expand notably in that direction from the 1840s on (see Map 6). At first the push was into Central Asia, an area of steppe, desert, and high plateaus inhabited by warlike, nomadic Muslim tribes. To forestall their constant raids the Russians established control over much of the region in the 1860s and 1870s. The British were alarmed, fearing a Russian threat to Afghanistan and even to British India, but by the end of the century the main focus of Russian interest in Asia had shifted to the Far East.

Under aggressive administrators in that region the Russians moved into the basin of the Amur River in the 1850s, occupied the southern half of Sakhalin Island, and in 1860 founded the important Pacific port of Vladivostok, meaning "ruler of the east." In the 1890s the Trans-Siberian Railroad was built, linking European Russia and the Far East, and in the early twentieth century the Russians were extending their influence into Manchuria and Korea. Here, however, they confronted not the enfeebled resistance of a declining Chinese empire but the vigorous expansionism of a newly modernized and ascendant Japan. The clash of interests led to war in 1904, and to a major crisis in Russian society.

Conclusion

Not since the days of Peter the Great had Russian society been in such ferment as it was in the second half of the nineteenth century. The decision to emancipate the serfs transformed a socioeconomic system that had predominated for at least 250 years. Together with the other Great Reforms and growing economic ties with Europe, the abolition of serfdom helped launch an accelerating modernization of Russia's society and economy. By 1900 Russia was partly industrialized and, with its rich natural resources, had the basis to become a powerful modern nation.

Yet substantial problems remained unsolved. Backward and inefficient agriculture acted as a brake on the economy. Overpopulation and government taxation created a land-desperate and impoverished peasantry ripe for revolution. In the cities an uprooted and exploited proletariat listened attentively to calls for action from a spectrum of revolutionary agitators. In the borderlands of the empire non-Russian minorities, resentful of the government's russification policies and fired by nationalist enthusiasm, struggled for autonomy or independence.

These issues, however, might have been worked out if only Russia had changed as much politically as it had socially and economically. But sporadically under Alexander II and blatantly and forcefully under Alexander III and Nicholas II, the government acted to preserve the autocratic system virtually unaltered. The tsar was still an absolute sovereign, and no national policies could be carried out without his sanction. Nor were the people as a whole, not even interest groups among them, to have any say in national governance, whatever small measure of self-government existed at the local level. The tsar needed the bureaucracy to rule, to be sure, but the bureaucracy could do nothing without the tsar's approval.

As a result, the ruling elite became increasingly isolated from the rest of society, and both sides girded for a decisive struggle over what

Russia's future should be. As the country changed and as the political crisis matured, Russia continued to play a major role in European and world politics. But if it could not resolve its domestic schism, it was hardly strong enough to survive a major showdown on the international stage.

FURTHER READING

Black, C. E., ed. *The Transformation of Russian Society: Aspects of Social Change Since 1861*. Cambridge, Mass.: 1960.

———, ed. *The Modernization of Japan and Russia*. New York: 1975.

Byrnes, Robert F. *Pobedonostsev: His Life and Thought*. Bloomington, Ind.: 1969.

Carew Hunt, R. N. *The Theory and Practice of Communism*. New York: 1957.

Curtiss, John S. *Church and State in Russia*. New York: 1940.

Emmons, Terence, ed. *The Emancipation of the Russian Serfs*. New York: 1970.

Figner, Vera. *Memoirs of a Revolutionist*. New York: 1927.

Fischer, George. *Russian Liberalism*. Cambridge, Mass.: 1958.

Freeze, Gregory. *The Parish Clergy in Nineteenth Century Russia*. Princeton: 1983.

Keep, John. *The Rise of Social Democracy in Russia*. Oxford: 1963.

Maynard, Sir John. *The Russian Peasant and Other Studies*. London: 1942.

Miller, Forrest. *Dmitrii Miliutin and the Reform Era*. Nashville, Tenn.: 1968.

Mosse, W. E. *Alexander II and the Modernization of Russia*. New York: 1958.

Pierce, Richard. *Russian Central Asia, 1867–1917*. Berkeley: 1960.

Robinson, Geroid T. *Rural Russia Under the Old Regime*. New York: 1932, 1949.

Stites, Richard. *The Women's Liberation Movement in Russia*. Princeton, N.J.:1978.

Treadgold, Donald. *The Great Siberian Migration*. Princeton, N.J.: 1957.

Venturi, Franco. *Roots of Revolution*. New York: 1960.

Von Laue, T. *Sergei Witte and the Industrialization of Russia*. New York: 1963.

Vucinich, W., ed., *The Peasant in Nineteenth Century Russia*. Stanford, Calif.: 1968.

10

Revolution, Reform, and War, 1904-17

The small steamer rolled from side to side, but the three men inside the cabin seemed oblivious to this motion as they bent their heads over several sheets of paper on the table in front of them. There was animated discussion, and from time to time one of them corrected the Russian script of the document. In less than an hour they arrived at their destination, disembarking at Peterhof, the country palace of the Emperor of all the Russias, Nicholas II. While two of the men waited in an anteroom, the third, Sergei Witte, met with Nicholas and his advisers, including the tsar's uncle, Grand Duke Nikolai Nikolaevich. There was a sense of urgency in the discussions, for St. Petersburg, the capital, was largely paralyzed by a general strike, and riots and disorders were spreading throughout Russia. It was clear to everyone that decisive action would have to be taken promptly.

Witte, who had returned to Russia only a few weeks previously as something of a popular hero because of his successful negotiation of a peace treaty with Japan at Portsmouth, New Hampshire, had presented a report to Nicholas II the day before urging reform as the best means of choking off the growing revolution. He now summarized that report and concluded by iterating his view that the tsar had only two alternatives. Either he could move along a path of reform, or he must choose a dictator to suppress the civil unrest by force. The meeting adjourned without a decision but was reconvened after lunch, when Witte presented a draft imperial manifesto promising reform, the document that he and his colleagues had been working on during the boat trip to Peterhof that morning. No one raised objections during the meeting, but the next day the tsar asked other senior officials to make recommendations. Witte, learning this, sent word to Nicholas that he would be willing to head a government committed to restoring order and initiating reform but only on the basis of the report they had just discussed, without modifications.

The following morning, 30 October 1905, Baron Vladimir B. Fredericks, the secretary of the imperial court, explained to Grand Duke Nikolai Nikolaevich that since Witte would be available only on his own terms, the tsar would have to establish a dictatorship after all and that the grand duke was the logical person to be appointed dictator. Hearing this, the grand duke pulled a revolver from his pocket and exclaimed, "Do you see this revolver? I am now going to the tsar and will ask him to sign Count Witte's program and manifesto. Either he will do this or I shall shoot myself in the head!" Whether Nikolai Nikolaevich repeated his dramatic threat to the tsar is unknown, but returning a short while later after seeing Nicholas, the grand duke reported that the tsar would accept Witte's program and manifesto.

After meeting with Witte again that afternoon, Nicholas II signed the manifesto, which was immediately promulgated and became known as the October Manifesto. It was only partially successful in quelling the revolutionary movement, but it did establish civil freedoms and a limited form of constitutional government in Russia, a system that lasted, with some modifications, until the collapse of the tsardom in the Revolution of 1917. That Nicholas was not entirely happy with his decision is shown by what he confided to his diary that night: "After such a day my head began to hurt and my thoughts were confused. God help us and comfort Russia." [1]

Nicholas's "headache" over granting extensive reforms is understandable. He had come to the throne determined to preserve the autocratic legacy of his predecessors. Yet Russian society was changing rapidly, and when the tide of unrest and revolution threatened to sweep away the traditional system, Nicholas decided his only course was to give ground a little. But he remained committed to the absolutist principle and resented the concessions he had been forced to make. As a result, the period between the Revolution of 1905 and the outbreak of war in 1914 saw a changing society, but one whose top leadership still clung to an outmoded past. As economic development and social transformation altered Russian life irrevocably, the tsar and his conservative supporters were able to block evolution of the political system, preserving many old ways of governance. Russia on the eve of World War I was markedly asymmetrical: an antiquated state structure ruled a modernizing society. Whether the former would eventually have changed enough to synchronize with the latter remains a fascinating but unanswerable question, since the war cut off whatever line of development Russia was embarked on.

The Revolution of 1905

The early twentieth-century popular uprising against the tsarist government is known as the Revolution of 1905 because the peak of revolutionary activity occurred in that year. In fact, however, its first

---

[1] Based on the account in Howard D. Mehlinger and John M. Thompson, *Count Witte and the Tsarist Government in the 1905 Revolution* (Bloomington, Ind.: 1972), 40–45.

manifestations date to 1904, and the revolutionary movement in the countryside and in the army continued into 1907. During these years the tsarist regime faced a major challenge to its authority, the breadth and intensity of the opposition reflecting in part the enormous socio-economic changes that had taken place in Russian society in recent decades. Comparing the Revolution of 1905 to the Decembrist Revolt only eighty years earlier, one is struck by how isolated from and unrepresentative of the whole society the Decembrists were and how by contrast almost every social group participated in the 1905 revolution.

Some of the participants came from totally new classes: industrial workers and people from the professions and business. Others, such as the national minorities, were newly aroused, whereas the peasants had a long tradition of rebellion but had never acted countrywide and en masse before. Finally, mutinies in the army and navy marked the first time that military rank and file had risen against authority. The very breadth of the revolutionary forces in 1905 was also of course an element of weakness. Each group had somewhat different aims and favored different methods of struggle. Yet the wide range of revolutionary cadres—middle-class liberals, workers, peasants, non-Russian minorities, soldiers, and sailors—and the spontaneous nature of much of their antigovernment activity clearly foreshadowed the Revolution of 1917, and for these and other reasons Lenin called 1905 a "dress-rehearsal" for the more decisive uprising twelve years later.

Russia's war with Japan in 1904–5 triggered the Revolution of 1905 but did not cause it. The revolution grew out of long-standing grievances, social injustices, and political frustrations in Russian society; the strain and sacrifice of war, coupled with the humiliation of Russian losses and the country's final defeat by Japan, provided the immediate pretext to attack the government.

During Russia's expansion into the Far East and well into the war itself members of the tsarist administration consistently underestimated the strength and skill of the Japanese government. The minister of the interior even went so far as to observe that "a little victorious war" might not be a bad thing since it would dampen the growing popular unrest. Yet the Russian army suffered a series of defeats on land in the Far East, as well as a naval disaster at the Straits of Tsushima between Korea and Japan, where a major Russian fleet that had sailed halfway around the world from the Baltic Sea was almost totally destroyed by the Japanese. Only because Japan was feeling the financial burden of the war and thanks to the diplomatic skill of Witte was Russia able to salvage a reasonable peace, the Treaty of Portsmouth signed in August 1905. The Russo-Japanese War was significant in two major respects: it marked the first defeat in modern times of a European power by an Asian nation, and it added fuel to the burgeoning revolutionary movement in Russia.

In the first years of the twentieth century, grain prices in Russia dropped and agricultural wages declined, making the plight of the already desperate peasantry worse and seeming to confirm the peasant saying, "The shortage will be divided among the peasants." As the following description shows, most peasants lived at the margin of existence:

> [In] a village eighty miles from Moscow, . . . the people lived in wooden huts . . . thatched with straw. . . . The stoves were great erections of clay, upon which some of the family slept. Many had no chimney. There was a little opening over the door near the roof, which let out the smoke after it had warmed, and blackened both walls and people. . . . Clay was the material for cooking vessels, and clay or wood for plates and dishes. China was a rarity for holidays. Splinters of wood supplied the function of forks. The general sleeping place was the floor, on straw, which was brought in each night and taken out in the morning. All clothes were home spun. . . . The usual footgear was birchbark sandals; leather boots only on holidays, and to church, and a pair lasted more than ten years. . . . For a long time there was only one cloth coat in the village: it was borrowed by friends for festive occasions. . . . Meat was a rarity. The rye-bread was supplemented by cabbage-soup and barley-porridge. . . .[2]

Under such conditions it is hardly surprising that beginning in 1902 the peasants began to protest, particularly in the areas of greatest land hunger in south central Russia. A wave of peasant disorders started in 1904 and expanded considerably in 1905.

At about the same time strikes were spreading through a number of industrial centers, and by 1905 hundreds of thousands of workers were on strike. A number of these strikes included demands for political reform, as well as insistence on higher wages and shorter hours. There was also a renewal of terrorist activity, and several tsarist officials were assassinated.

But it was the liberals who took the political initiative in challenging the tsarist government. In November 1904 a meeting of representatives of *zemstvo* organizations called for equal status for the peasantry, civil freedoms, and a representative legislative assembly. In March 1905 the Union of Unions was formed to bring together over twenty professional associations of lawyers, doctors, engineers, and other occupations, and it sought similar reforms.

In early 1905 the first dramatic clash between the government and the people took place in an incident on 22 January 1905, a day subsequently known as "Bloody Sunday." In hopes of diverting radical workers from direct antigovernment activity the ministry of interior had begun in 1904 to support associations of workers organized and supervised by the police. In St. Petersburg an ambitious, idealistic, and slightly muddled priest, Father George Gapon, headed such a group. On Bloody Sunday he led a crowd of peaceful working-class petitioners, men,

[2] Sir John Maynard, *Russia in Flux* (London: 1941), 42–43.

women, and children carrying icons and pictures of the tsar, to the imperial palace. Unaware that Nicholas II was away, they intended to present him with an address that was couched in the high-flown rhetoric customary in such petitions to the throne but that also proved to be ominously prophetic. It said in part:

> Lord, we workers, our children, our wives and our old helpless parents have come to seek justice and protection from you. We are impoverished and oppressed, unbearable work is imposed on us, we are despised and not recognized as human beings. . . . We are pressed ever deeper into the abyss of poverty, ignorance and lack of rights. . . . We have no strength left, O Lord. . . . If thou wilt not respond to our plea, we shall die here on the square before thy palace.[3]

And die they did. In a tragic display of incompetence, security officials in St. Petersburg, without the knowledge of the tsar or higher authorities, chose to disperse the unarmed crowd by force, firing into several columns of protesters. More than a hundred people were killed and many more wounded. Public opinion reacted strongly against the government, and Bloody Sunday marked an important turning point in the development of the Russian revolutionary movement generally, destroying the myth of a mystical bond between the people and a gentle and caring father-tsar.

From January 1905 on the government found itself increasingly powerless as a series of parallel protest activities by liberals, workers, peasants, national minorities, and soldiers and sailors engulfed Russia. It was an impressively broad national movement for change, manifesting itself in speeches, meetings, proclamations, mutinies, strikes, riots, assassinations, land seizures, and demonstrations. A popular rejection of the tsarist administration, the revolution was largely leaderless and spontaneous.

There was little the government could do. In August the unpopular war with Japan was finally ended. That month the tsar issued a decree establishing a consultative legislative assembly to be elected by a restricted franchise. But this was clearly too little too late. By October the strike movement culminated in a general strike that shut down almost all activity in St. Petersburg and produced the urgent conference between Nicholas II and Witte described at the opening of the chapter.

The October Manifesto that Witte proposed and the tsar signed, albeit reluctantly, promised the people a broadly representative legislative assembly to be called the Duma, as well as full civil liberties, that is, freedom of press, assembly, and speech. A short time later the tsar made further concessions, legalizing trade unions, cancelling the remaining redemption dues owed by the peasants, and relaxing restric-

[3] Adapted from the version in Basil Dmytryshyn, ed., *Imperial Russia: A Source Book, 1700–1917* (New York: 1967), 309–13.

tions against minority nationalities. Although disorders continued, these reforms divided the opposition and thus marked the first step in the government's regaining control of the situation. To be sure, the extreme parties, the Marxist Social Democrats and the peasant Socialist Revolutionaries, together with most workers rejected Nicholas's package of concessions as totally inadequate and continued to clamor for a constituent assembly and radical economic changes. The peasants, who wanted land, were hardly mollified. But much of the educated public, especially the middle and professional classes, was satisfied. The Kadets, the leading liberal party, which had only recently been formed, decided that the reforms did not go far enough but that they would press for further change within the system granted, and they condemned continuing violence. The Octobrists, a newly established party of businessmen and moderately conservative landowners, concluded, as their name indicates, that the October concessions were sufficient and no further reforms were needed. By December 1905, although underneath Russian society was still seething, at the top, articulate elements had opted for peaceful evolution and had begun to rally around the government in its efforts to restore order.

Two developments in the fall of 1905 had particularly frightened educated and propertied circles in Russian society: the continuing violence and illegal land seizures perpetrated by the peasantry and the political radicalization of the workers, especially in St. Petersburg and Moscow. During the October strikes the workers of the capital had spontaneously formed a coordinating committee of elected representatives from many of the main factories to supervise and direct the strike movement. Modeled on similar committees formed that summer in several small industrial towns, which in turn may have been adaptations to the city and the workers' situation of the traditional communal assembly in the village, the St. Petersburg committee took the name *Soviet,* or *Council, of Workers' Deputies.* This body soon began to exercise a number of welfare, administrative, economic, and political functions and was the forerunner of the soviets that, after being reestablished in the revolution of 1917, became the basic institutions of the new revolutionary state.

Although the St. Petersburg Soviet and the soviets that soon sprang up in a number of other cities were formed by and for the workers and most remained worker-dominated, the radical parties did their best to use the soviets as platforms for revolutionary agitation and as political weapons against the factory owners and the government. They had some success, and in particular Leon Trotsky, a talented speaker and writer for the Social Democrats and a leader of the Bolsheviks in 1917, gained considerable renown as chairman of the St. Petersburg Soviet and a forthright champion of the rights of the masses. But the continuous upheavals and constant strikes began to take their toll among the tired and poverty-stricken workers, and in mid-December 1905, when the

Soviet tried to organize a massive strike to win the eight-hour day for workers, the movement collapsed and the government arrested the leaders of the St. Petersburg Soviet. In protest the Moscow Soviet took to the barricades, and for eleven days workers in Moscow battled government troops and artillery in a herioc but futile struggle.

Emboldened by its success against the soviets, the government, with support of much of public opinion, enlarged its efforts to restore order. It attacked the peasant revolution directly by sending punitive military expeditions into the most disaffected provinces to put down peasant unrest by force. It dispatched similar repressive units to the Baltic provinces to quell nationalist disorders there and along several main railway lines to restore lines of communication throughout the country.

Several factors worked in the government's favor, in addition to the shift of public attitudes against further violence and the exhaustion of the workers. With the war over in the Far East the government was able to bring back to European Russia reliable units to be used in suppressing civil disorder (though mutinies and unrest in the armed forces continued sporadically through 1906). In addition, the government's financial position, badly weakened by the war with Japan and the revolutionary disruption of the Russian economy, was salvaged when Witte managed to secure a major loan from France. Finally, conservative forces began to organize and soon were actively supporting the government's repressive policies. A proto-fascist organization, the Union of the Russian People, was formed, with a reactionary political, religious, and Russian nationalist platform. Furthermore, conservative gangs, the Black Hundreds, were tolerated by the police. Spurred by primitive anti-Semitism, they were involved in pogroms against the Jews that broke out all too often in 1905 and 1906. On a few occasions honest government officials or military officers intervened to protect the Jews and Jewish property, but more frequently the authorities stood by and let the mobs wreak havoc on the Jewish community.

By spring of 1906, when the first Duma convened, the government had clearly mastered the revolution, although peasant and military disorders continued throughout the year and into 1907. The Revolution of 1905 had succeeded in forcing the tsarist regime to make significant changes, but it had failed in its larger purpose of toppling the old structure entirely.

The Duma Period, 1906–14

Between the Revolution of 1905 and the outbreak of war in 1914 Russia had a brief period of "normal" development, marked by a limited constitutionalism, renewed economic growth, rapid social evolution, basic changes in agriculture, and a remarkable spurt of cultural creativity. Some historians see this period as the beginning of the peaceful emergence in Russia of a modernized, democratic society, quite similar to Western societies. Others, however, including Soviet writers, see these few years as a desperate, last-ditch effort by reactionary forces to paper over some of Russia's most fundamental flaws, a ploy that was doomed to fail, whether the war had come or not. In their view the changes of the Duma era succeeded only in temporarily staving off an inevitable and sweeping social revolution, the first portents of which appeared in 1913 and early 1914.

In December 1905, when the government was still feeling threatened, the tsar had approved a broad franchise for elections to the Duma, the legislative body promised in the October Manifesto. Virtually all adult Russian males could vote, although voters did not elect representatives directly but through assemblies of electors. By April 1906, when Nicholas II issued the Fundamental Laws, the constitution that set forth the specifics of the new system, the government felt strong enough to water down in several ways the power of the Duma. A reorganized State Council (an advisory body set up by Alexander I) was designated a co-equal legislative chamber, alongside the Duma, with its members chosen to ensure that it would be very conservative: half were appointed by the tsar, and half were chosen by several elite groups and institutions. In addition, the Fundamental Laws contained a provision that allowed the tsar to issue legislation when the Duma was not in session, although such laws were to be approved or rejected by the Duma when it reconvened. Finally, the first section of Article I of the Fundamental Laws reaffirmed the theoretical basis of autocracy in the following terms:

> The All-Russian Emperor possesses Supreme and Autocratic Power. To obey His authority not only from fear but also from conscience is ordered by God Himself.[4]

Other sections reserved to the tsar and his ministers authority over foreign and military affairs and over certain parts of the state budget.

The elections to the First Duma evoked some lively campaigning. Although most members of the radical parties boycotted the election, the opponents of the government still won a comfortable majority of the seats. This was no small shock to the government, which had expected the peasants to be a conservative political force. Some of the electors chosen by peasant voters supported nonparty Duma deputies, but a large number backed Kadet or other antigovernment candidates.

The scene when Tsar Nicholas II convened the Duma reflected some of the basic divisions of Russian society, with the Orthodox clergy on his right hand, and higher nobility on his left, and the rest of the pop-

---

[4]Mehlinger and Thompson, *Count Witte and the Tsarist Government in the 1905 Revolution*, 336.

ulation (the Duma deputies) in front of him. In the Duma sessions the opposition, emboldened by its electoral success, pressed vigorously for additional concessions. They wanted to exert greater control over the state budget and to make the tsar's ministers responsible to the Duma, and they particularly urged sweeping land reform. When the government resisted staunchly on these issues, an impasse resulted. Only three months after the Duma was convened, the tsar dissolved it. Some two hundred Duma deputies challenged the government by calling on Russian citizens not to pay taxes or serve in the army until the government made further concessions, but there was little popular response, and the deputies were arrested. At the same time the government continued its policy of forcibly restoring order, not hesitating to use such extralegal measures as military courts-martial, which condemned several thousand people to death in 1906–7, and administrative banishment, which sent over twenty thousand individuals into exile in Siberia.

The extreme left parties decided to participate in the election for the Second Duma, and peasant electors, angered over the government's recalcitrance on the land issue, supported radical candidates, with the result that the Kadets lost ground to the leftists while government and conservative parties gained seats but remained in a minority. The Second Duma therefore proved even less tractable than the first, from the government's point of view, and after three months of wrangling it too was dissolved.

The government, now led by a resolute prime minister, Peter Stolypin, acted illegally to change the electoral law, issuing in July 1907 new regulations that greatly reduced representation of peasants and of national minorities and provided that the gentry would choose one half of the electors. Or, put another way, under the revised franchise one elector represented each 250 landowners, 1,000 large urban property holders, 15,000 small property holders, 60,000 peasants, and 125,000 workers. This weighting of the elections had the desired result, as the Third Duma consisted of 270 conservative deputies, 114 Kadets, 30 leftists, and 17 nonparty deputies, giving the government a comfortable working majority.

The Third Duma deputies served their full terms of five years, and the Fourth Duma, elected in 1912, lasted almost to its prescribed end, before the 1917 revolution interrupted its work. Although the tsarist government controlled both the Third and Fourth Dumas, the evolutionary impact of these two bodies is important in two ways. First, the Dumas provided useful political experience, not just for the deputies and party members themselves but for the articulate public as a whole, who followed Duma debates closely and who, in newspapers and journals, expressed opinions on a wide range of issues that the Dumas considered. In other words, educated Russians not only had a little taste of political democracy but obviously savored it. Second, the Dumas did accomplish a good deal in noncontroversial areas. For example, they pushed the government to begin improving and modernizing the Russian armed forces. Duma committees helped work out important legislation related to public education, labor safety, and social insurance. The Dumas also encouraged more effective economic and fiscal policies by the government.

Finally, the Dumas played some role in the most significant legislation of the prewar period, the *Stolypin reforms* in agriculture. The general features of these changes in Russian rural life had been developed during Witte's premiership in 1905–6. A major goal was to make agriculture more productive so that it would be less of a brake on the economy as a whole. Another objective was to give peasants a sense of proprietorship, thereby encouraging them not to seize land illegally as they had in 1905 and not to follow the enticements of revolutionary parties that promised to expropriate land in the peasants' behalf. Witte believed that to accomplish these aims it would be necessary to break up the village commune, making each peasant an individual owner, and to eliminate the old strip system of farming, giving each peasant instead a consolidated plot of land. Since the individual peasant would then control his own land, crops, and profits (after government taxes), he would have an incentive to work harder and to use newer farming techniques, thereby notably raising yield per acre throughout the country.

Stolypin took over this program, and between 1906 and 1911 it was initiated in a series of laws and administrative regulations. Since the war cut short its implementation, it is difficult to assess how successful the Stolypin land reform might have been, but one has to respect Lenin's judgment that if completed, it would have significantly reduced the potential for revolution among the peasantry. Like the emancipation of the serfs, it was a major social revolution, and it would have turned some 100 million Russian peasants into small landowners. By 1915, it is estimated, only a little over a million peasant families, having withdrawn from the commune, had both acquired ownership of their land and consolidated their strips into a single plot. On the other hand, almost a quarter of all peasant families had left the commune and owned their own land, though it was still scattered among the various communal fields. The remaining peasants were only in the preliminary stages of the reform process.

How did the peasants feel about the Stolypin program? No one is entirely sure because most of our evidence is filtered through the government agencies responsible for administering the reform at the grassroots level. It is significant, however, that although the commune continued to exist until its replacement by the collective farm in 1928–29, many peasants during the revolution of 1917 seized land and used it as if they owned it individually. On the other hand, since the Stolypin policies provided only limited opportunities for the peasants to acquire *more* land and since the peasant population continued to multiply, one wonders whether even the most successful promotion of private ownership and land consolidation could have blunted the peasants' desperate hunger for additional land or could have solved the problem of the growing numbers of landless and nearly destitute peasants.

In the Duma years the Russian economy resumed the rapid industrial growth that had characterized it in the 1890s. Between 1906 and 1914, industry increased at about 6 percent a year, and enough miles of railroads were added to make the Russian empire second only to the United States in total trackage. New manufacturing sectors developed, banking and service enterprises expanded, and mining and other extractive industries grew rapidly as the richness of Russia's natural resources began to be tapped. The pre-1900 pattern of heavy concentration in large factories and a few places continued, and foreign capital retained its major role in many sectors of the Russian economy. The labor force increased to about 3.5 million workers. Just before the outbreak of World War I labor unrest revived notably, and in the spring and summer of 1914, on the eve of the war, the strike movement reached its highest peak since 1906. Clearly this restiveness reflected basic divisions and unresolved tensions in Russian society. Moreover, despite its impressive economic growth, Russia remained substantially less developed and modernized than the European nations with which it was competing in foreign affairs.

Were Russians better off in 1914 than before the Revolution of 1905? Unfortunately data to permit a clear answer to that question are not available. Probably the average real income of both peasants and workers was slightly higher, although some of the poorest individuals were in desperate straits. Yet even if the standard of living was rising in prewar Russia, so were the expectations of the people. Many certainly wanted far more than they were getting. And the masses' resentment of privileged Russia, a hostility that had simmered just below the surface for centuries with only occasional eruptions like the Pugachov Revolt, was perhaps nearing the boiling point. After the Revolution of 1905 the people felt less powerless, and for the first time they began consciously to heed the appeals of the revolutionary intelligentsia. Convinced they were being deprived of basic equity and increasingly desperate over the conditions in which they lived, the bulk of Russia's workers and peasants were attuned to revolution.

Another factor helping to create a revolutionary situation on the eve of the war was the rigid and unyielding nature of the tsarist regime. The tsar, his closest advisers, and the conservative elite in Russian society were determined to resist change, and the bureaucracy was so structured that major reform of the political system could come only from the top. Since there was no established mechanism for innovation, only occasional powerful personalities, such as Witte and Stolypin, could develop new approaches. And though both were politically conservative, their fate was hardly encouraging to potential reformers: Nicholas

II, pressed by reactionary circles, dismissed Witte as premier in April 1906, and Stolypin was assassinated in 1911. After that no strong, reform-minded individual appeared inside the government. There was no further opportunity for the system to modify itself before it was blown away by the revolutionary storm of 1917.

Does all this mean that Russia was moving steadily and inexorably toward revolution? Not necessarily, argue many historians, pointing to a number of signs of peaceful progress during the Duma era. Not only were peasants being encouraged to become stable individual proprietors, but the economy was booming, and the benefits of that boom were just beginning to reach the workers. Higher education was spreading, and the government and the Duma, working together, initiated a broad educational program designed to put all Russian children into elementary school within fifteen to twenty years. There were a dramatic increase in cooperatives, continuing improvement in communications and transportation, slow but steady progress in public health, beginnings of an intellectual and social renaissance among a few Orthodox religious thinkers, and rapidly growing advanced science and technology. But these evolutionary trends needed time to make their impact felt, and that time was not vouchsafed them. In any case, the changes of the Duma years may have been too late, after centuries of social oppression, political absolutism, religious obscurantism, and personal exploitation. Perhaps too many grievances and too much resentment had accumulated for Russian society to avert the violent explosion that the country's disastrous involvement in World War I made almost certain.

The Silver Age: Russian Culture, 1890–1917

In the years immediately preceding the war Russia experienced not only economic and social change but also a surge of artistic and intellectual creativity. Perhaps not so dazzling as the cultural outpouring in literature and music that marked the mid-1800s, this new outburst nevertheless made major contributions to world culture in such fields as poetry, theater, ballet, music, design, and painting. Russians participated significantly in the twentieth-century modernist movement, and today we are still enjoying and benefiting from the pioneering works of Russian artists active in the period from the 1890s to the revolution of 1917.

Russian culture in this era could draw on its own rich past, as well as being stimulated by the ferment and excitement of such European artistic movements as realism and impressionism. Moreover, after 1905 the intellectual climate in Russia was freer, with little censorship and a growing appreciative public. On the other hand the achievements of the outstanding artists of this Silver Age are all the more remarkable when set against the relatively low cultural level of the country as a whole.

Although the number of graduates of schools and universities was shooting up, on the eve of the war 50 percent of Russia's population was illiterate, and the overwhelming majority of the population was acquainted only with folk culture and the emotional religious experience of the village church.

Russian theater developed remarkably in the last part of the nineteenth century and the first years of the twentieth. Particularly prominent were a famous director, Konstantin Stanislavsky, whose "Stanislavsky method" has influenced actors ever since; an outstanding theater company, the Moscow Art Theater; and a subtly powerful playwright, Anton Chekhov. Chekhov also wrote wonderful short stories, but beginning in 1895 until his death in 1904 he produced a string of successful plays that, though set in Russia of his times, deal with such modern and timeless themes as loneliness, boredom, alienation, and frustrated dreams. Among the classics Chekhov bequeathed to playgoers the best known are *Three Sisters* and *The Cherry Orchard.*

Emerging early in the 1900s, Russia's first major revolutionary author, Maxim Gorky, drew on his experiences drifting about Russia as a youth for such realistic works as the play *The Lower Depths,* and the novel, *Mother.* Gorky was bitterly critical of Russian society and eloquently argued the need for radical change. Embracing the Revolution of 1917, he remained the dean of Soviet writers, despite disagreements with Lenin and Stalin, until his death in the 1930s.

In sharp contrast to the psychological probing of Chekhov or the revolutionary realism of Gorky were the symbolist writers, primarily poets, who came to the fore after 1905. They espoused aestheticism, beauty, "art for art's sake," and individual lyricism, exploring and expanding language in new and dramatic ways. The most talented was Alexander Blok, famed for his mystical poem about the revolution, *The Twelve,* but the most active politically was Vladimir Mayakovsky. He threw himself into propaganda work after 1917 and in the 1920s helped develop an avant-garde revolutionary theater, but, disillusioned and depressed, committed suicide in 1930. A few lines from his poem "The Cloud in Trousers" suggest the imagination and brashness of Mayakovsky, even though they are less powerful in translation:

But it seems,
before they can launch a song,
poets must tramp for days with callused feet,
and the sluggish fish of the imagination
flounders softly in the slush of the heart.
And while, with twittering rhymes, they boil a broth
of loves and nightingales,
the tongueless street merely writhes
for lack of something to shout or say.[5]

[5] Vladimir Mayakovsky, *The Bedbug and Selected Poetry,* ed., Patricia Blake (Cleveland: 1960), 75.

In the early 1900s Russian artists excelled in bringing together various art forms in a single presentation that was markedly more than the sum of its parts, what today we might call a "multimedia" work. This approach was pioneered by a group of young artists who published a daring journal, *The World of Art,* which combined content (prose, poetry, criticism) with beautiful typography, layout, and illustration. The *World of Art* movement soon spread to the ballet and theater, where the artist Alexander Benois and the impressario Serge Diaghilev brought together the best dancers, such as Anna Pavlova and Vaslav Nijinsky, with the music of the most daring new composers, such as Igor Stravinsky, and mounted the performance against sets, costumes, and lighting designed by outstanding modern artists. The result was integrated and stunning presentations that were the sensation first of Russia, and then, when Diaghilev took his Ballet Russes company abroad, of all Europe.

At about the same time a brilliant group of avant-garde artists was developing in Russia, who were influenced by postimpressionism in Europe and contributed importantly to modern art in the West after World War I. For example, Vladimir Tatlin was an important leader in the constructivist movement, N. J. Goncharova and M. F. Larionov developed rayonism, Kazimir Malevich initiated suprematism and was a forerunner of minimal art, and Marc Chagall and Vasily Kandinsky, both of whom emigrated to the West after the 1917 revolution, were important abstract artists.

Finally, Russian intellectuals contributed significantly to modern science and scholarship in this period. Russians built on earlier achievements in such fields as mathematics, chemistry, and engineering. At the same time they made new contributions in physics, biology, physiology, psychology, and history. Russian scholars and scientists were supported by an expanding system of higher education, including new universities and research institutes, additional specialized technical and professional institutions, and a growing array of scholarly and scientific libraries and journals.

Put briefly, the quality and output of Russian intellectual and cultural life on the eve of the war were remarkably high, especially in relation to the general level of education and culture in the country. Whatever its deficiencies in social and political terms, Russian society could be proud of its artistic and creative contributions, an area in which Russia was not only not "backward" but was instead a leader of world culture.

Russian Involvement in World War I, 1914–17

As the American scholar and diplomat, George Kennan, has persuasively contended in a recent book, the origins of Russia's involvement in World War I are to be found in the fateful decision, taken in the early 1890s, to ally with France. This flew in the face of Russia's recent diplomatic tradition, which had stressed the ideological and power advantages of Russia's remaining closely linked with the German and Austro-Hungarian empires, since they dominated both central Europe and Russia's western borders. The tie with France also seemed to defy common sense, for France was not only far away, antiautocratic in ideology, and a potential rival in the Near East, but also isolated, vengeful, and therefore a potential troublemaker on the European scene. Nevertheless, a number of factors worked to bring Russia and France together. The Russians wanted support against their chief rival in the Balkans, Austria-Hungary, and they also feared the increasingly aggressive and militaristic German empire. Russia, like France, seemed to be alone and vulnerable in the lions' pit of European power struggles, once the Three Emperors' League with Germany and the Austrian empire had dissolved in the 1880s. Finally, the French were Russia's chief creditor, and they suggested that a political-military alliance could only strengthen the economic connection.

After the first formal ties were established in 1893–94, the French over the years cleverly drew the Russians into their military embrace, ensuring that the vast numbers of Russia's peasant army would be thrown against the Germans, should the French ever have the chance they had sought for so long to avenge their defeat at the hands of the Germans in 1871 and to recover the lost territories of Alsace and Lorraine. Following Russia's defeat by Japan, the French alliance seemed even more important to Russia's leaders. When it was supplemented in 1907 by an understanding with Great Britain, they felt secure in a powerful system, soon known as the Triple Entente. The difficulty, however, was that the opposing system, the Triple Alliance of Germany, Austria-Hungary, and Italy, emboldened the Russians' archenemy in the Balkans, the Austrians, to be more aggressive in that region.

Beyond our scope are the details of the militarism, diplomatic maneuvering, and imperialistic rivalry that marked international relations in Europe in the decade before 1914. The most important point for Russia was that in 1908 during the crisis over Bosnia and, to a lesser extent, in 1912–13 during the Balkan Wars the Russians believed they had been forced to back down diplomatically under pressure from the Austrians, supported by Germany. Therefore, when in 1914, as restitution for the assassination of the Austrian heir to the throne by a Serbian nationalist, the Austrian government tried to force humiliating concessions from Serbia, Russia's ally in the Balkans, the Russian leaders were in no mood to compromise, believing their status as a great power was at stake.

The crisis was exacerbated in all countries by intense nationalist feeling, and Russia was no exception. Although some government officials knew that Russia was no match for German economic and military power and one predicted that Russia's defeat would result in "hopeless anarchy, the outcome of which cannot be foreseen," others feared that a Russian concession might mean the eventual domination of the country by its central European rivals, and publicists and orators beat the drums for Russian patriotism and Slavic unity. Consequently, when the crisis turned into war between the Entente nations, Russia, France, and England, and the Central Powers, Germany and Austria-Hungary, Russian public opinion welcomed the conflict, and all parties and groups except the Social Democrats rallied around the throne and vowed enthusiastically to support the war effort.

In the beginning Russia's war aims were simply to check German and Austrian ambitions, to fulfill its treaty obligations to France, and to defend Russian territory. After Turkey entered the war at the end of 1914, Russia's principal goal became obtaining the Turkish Straits and Constantinople. In a secret treaty signed in 1915 France and England agreed to support Russia in this imperialistic acquisition after the war.

On the fighting front against Germany the Russians fared poorly. Their opponents had a fivefold advantage in artillery, and three times as many rifles and machine guns as the Russian soldiers. The latter fought bravely but were poorly led and supplied. Mismanagement and inefficiency plagued the government's conduct of the war. As the French had hoped, the masses of Russian troops managed to tie up many German divisions in 1914 and helped to save France from being overrun, but by 1915 the Central Powers had crossed Poland and advanced into Russia proper. Refugees from the occupied western regions poured into the central cities, adding to the already existing problems of food, housing, and fuel supply.

The Russian army remained intact, but its defeats and losses mounted. By the end of the fighting in late 1917 the Russians had mobilized over fifteen million men and had lost six to eight million killed, wounded, and taken prisoner, with perhaps another two million deserters. The mobilization of such large numbers of men both weakened the domestic economy and changed the character of the army. Its largely untrained peasant recruits, uprooted from their traditional routines and circumstances, became radicalized under conditions of defeat and harsh discipline into a potentially revolutionary force.

On the home front the strain of the war led, by 1916, to a gradual breakdown of the economy and a sharp decline in civilian morale. A number of Russia's educated elite had thrown themselves into the war effort, attempting in several public and voluntary organizations to make up the deficiencies of the government in medical and hospital services, war production, food distribution, and other areas. But the transport system could not meet the enormous demands placed on it, and supplies to the cities began to dwindle. Resulting shortages worsened the plight of urban workers who were already suffering as the cost of living rose faster than their wages. In the countryside the peasants, short of labor because of the army mobilization and facing low prices for grain and high prices for the few manufactured products that were available, began to produce less, mainly feeding themselves, a course that naturally intensified the food supply problems in the cities.

Even the economic hardships, coupled with the military defeats and sacrifices, might have been bearable if the Russian masses had some sense of what they were fighting for and if they had had inspired leadership at the top. Instead, the tsar and his advisers refused to promise reforms after the war while furnishing only incompetent and aimless direction of the war effort. The disintegration of the Russian government at its highest levels was symbolized by the notorious influence of Gregory Rasputin, a self-proclaimed holy man who was able to affect government appointments, if not policies, because Nicholas's wife Alexandra believed "Our Friend," as she called Rasputin, was able to stop the bleeding of their hemophilic son, the heir to the throne (see Figure 13). Realizing that his presence in court circles was only discrediting the monarchy, a group of conservative conspirators murdered Rasputin, who to their horror seemed impervious at first to the poison they had given him, but finally succumbed when shot and pushed into the river.

Figure 13. *Nicholas II and his family, with members of the court. Uniforms and military ceremonials played an important role in court life. (Courtesy of the Library of Congress)*

The government refused to accept proposals for reform and co-operation made by a large majority of deputies to the Fourth Duma, and the tsar continued to endorse the appointment to ministerial posts of second-raters and incompetents. Even the tsar's cousin commented, "The Government itself is the organ that is preparing the revolution." In 1916 and early 1917, as economic and living conditions worsened and the military situation deteriorated, talk that a change was needed grew, and rumors of a coup d' état circulated in the capital, now called Petrograd because St. Petersburg had too Germanic a sound in Russian. Many predicted revolution, yet when it actually occurred, it happened suddenly and with no immediate forewarning.

Conclusion

It is hard to see how Russia, once involved in massive, draining war, could have avoided some sort of violent upheaval. In four important ways World War I brought on a revolutionary crisis. First, the war accelerated the disorientation of Russian society that the processes of modernization, industrialization, and urbanization had launched in the preceding decades. Tens of millions of Russians were physically displaced, some by mobilization into the army, others as refugees from the war zone, and many more who moved voluntarily to undertake war work in factories and in various war-related organizations. This great migration of individuals within the country meant that old ties, habits, and attitudes were disrupted and people were exposed to new ideas and experiences. The result was to weaken the fabric of the old society, leaving many people and groups searching for new roots and increasing the potential for radical social and political change.

Second, the war intensified the sense of injustice and resentment that had been building among the Russian masses in the previous decades. Although at first there was a surge of patriotic support for the war, people became both exhausted and bitter as the war dragged on. Russian losses in people and territory were enormous; many families suffered personally and directly, and almost everyone was affected indirectly. The harsh conditions under which the workers and peasants labored and lived seemed increasingly intolerable, and the sacrifices of the soldiers at the front, pointless. As a historian of the Russian army has recently concluded, "The soldiers felt they were being used and recklessly expended by the rich and powerful, of whom their officers were the most visible, immediate representatives."[6] War-weariness, despair, and hatred of the old system became dominant at all levels of

---

[6] Allan K. Wildman, *The End of the Russian Imperial Army: The Old Army and the Soldiers' Revolt, March–April 1917* (Princeton: 1979), 89.

Russian society. The people's only hope seemed to lie in victory, which seemed increasingly distant and illusory, or in radical change, some sudden liberation from their bonds and burdens.

A third immediate effect of the war was to bring about a partial collapse of the Russian economy, with a resultant deterioration of conditions in the major cities. As the real income of both workers and peasants declined, as the transportation and distribution systems ceased to function effectively for civilian needs, and as food and fuel shortages in the cities worsened, people's attitudes toward the government and the war hardened until finally they simply refused to tolerate the situation any longer.

Finally, Russia's participation in the war completely discredited Nicholas II and his already weak regime. People were therefore able to discard the tsar and his government entirely, with almost no one coming forward to defend them. For centuries the Russian masses had retained faith in the divinely inspired tutelage of the benevolent "father-tsar." But in the twentieth century this faith dissipated, as workers and peasants wondered why the tsar did nothing to ameliorate their lot. During the war many held Nicholas responsible for the grief, suffering, and fear the war brought: "If the tsar were a good tsar, why couldn't he save Russia and its people?"

Nicholas's own actions did not help matters. He associated himself personally with the war effort, finally making himself commander-in-chief of the Russian army and moving to general headquarters at the front to oversee operations. In this way he became linked to the continuing defeat, loss of life, and sacrifices. He did nothing to correct the incompetence and moral corruption of the government. People despised the tsarist ministers and bitterly criticized their mismanagement of the war effort. It was bad enough to suffer and to lose, but to do so in part because the country was being run by a clique of misfits and sycophants, some of them selected by Rasputin, was intolerable.

By 1917 Russia was a society twice changed, first by the economic, social, and political developments of the late-nineteenth and early-twentieth century and then by the devastating impact of World War I with its disruptions, sacrifices, and despair. That the old government and system could not go on was clear to all—except perhaps the tsarist leaders themselves—but what was to replace it? The answer lay both in Russia' past and in the circumstances of Russia's dramatic revolution.

FURTHER READING

Charques, Richard. *The Twilight of Imperial Russia*. London: 1974.

Florinsky, Michael. *The End of the Russian Empire*. New York: 1961.

Gray, Camilla. *The Great Experiment: Russian Art, 1863–1922*. London: 1962.

Haimson, Leopold. "The Problem of Social Stability in Urban Russia, 1905–17." *Slavic Review*, 23, 4 (1964), 620–42, 24, 1 (1965), 1–22.

Harcave Sidney. *The Russian Revolution of 1905*. London: 1970.

Hosking, Geoffrey. *The Russian Constitutional Experiment . . . 1907–1914*. New York: 1973.

Kennan, George F. *The Fateful Alliance: France, Russia and the Coming of the First World War*. New York: 1984.

Lincoln, W. B. *In War's Dark Shadow: The Russians Before the Great War*. New York: 1983.

Massie, Robert K. *Nicholas and Alexandra*. New York: 1967.

Mehlinger, H. and Thompson, J. *Count Witte and the Tsarist Government in the Revolution of 1905*. Bloomington, Ind.: 1975.

Oberlander, E., *et al. Russia Enters the Twentieth Century*. New York: 1971.

Smith, C. Jay. *The Russian Struggle for Power, 1914–17*. New York: 1956.

Stavrou, T. G., ed. *Russia Under the Last Tsar*. Minneapolis: 1969.

Wallace, D. M. *Russia on the Eve of War and Revolution*. New York: 1962.

11

Revolution, Civil War, and the Founding of Soviet Society, 1917–28

Everyone was glad it was warmer. During the street demonstrations the past two days people had shivered and nearly frozen, but despite the bitter cold they had continued their protests against the shortage of bread and against the war. Now by midmorning, Saturday, 10 March 1917, the thermometer had climbed to twenty degrees Fahrenheit and crowds of strikers, unemployed workers, students, and housewives were again on the streets, heading for the center of Petrograd, the Russian capital. The mood of the demonstrators on the previous two days had been amiable, almost jolly, as if they were on holiday. On Saturday, however, more clashes with the police occurred, as more and more workers left work to join the protest marches. By noon three hundred thousand people, or about one fifth of the total population of the city, were milling about. Some, besides demanding bread, shouted "Down with the Tsar," and a few even called out a truly revolutionary slogan, "Down with tsarism!" Nevertheless, Tsarina Alexandra, who despite her involvement in government affairs during the war understood almost nothing about popular attitudes, wrote to Nicholas about the throngs on the streets of Petrograd: "If the weather were very cold, they would all probably stay at home."

In Znamenskaia Square, at the end of Nevsky Prospect, the main street of the city, a revolutionary orator was haranguing a large crowd when mounted police arrived to break up the demonstration. The speaker urged the throng not to move on, as ordered. The detachment commander then raised his pistol and took aim. Before he could fire, a cossack, a member of the capital's security forces, rode forward and cut the commander down with his saber. Although cossacks and army troops had been tolerant toward the demonstrators previously, this was the first time that anybody from the government's side supported the protesters. The next day soldiers from the Pavlovskii guards regiment attacked a police unit, and that night members of the Volynskii regiment, who, under orders, had fired on unarmed demonstrators in the morning, vowed not to do so again. The next morning when their com-

manding officer again ordered them out against the crowds, the soldiers mutinied and killed him.[1]

These incidents marked the turning point of the revolution that
overthrew the tsardom. Once the cossacks and the troops stationed in
Petrograd sided with the revolutionaries, the government was helpless.
The police were too few to restore order if military force could no longer
be relied on. The subsequent arrest of the tsarist ministers and the ab-
dication of Nicholas II were anticlimactic.

The February Revolution: The Collapse of the Tsarist System

The popular uprising that led to the disappearance of tsarist rule
after three hundred years of the Romanov dynasty took place 24–28
February 1917, according to the old-style (Julian) calender then in use
in Russia and is known in Soviet and most Western historiography as
the February Revolution. According to the new-style (Gregorian) calendar used in the West and adopted in Russia in 1918, the tsar's down-
fall occurred 8–12 March, and so it is sometimes referred to as the March
Revolution. Under either name this revolution was the first of two that
took place in 1917 and that together are usually designated the Russian
Revolution. Since the second upheaval, which brought Lenin and the
Bolsheviks to power, happened 24–26 October 1917, old style, or 6–8
November new style, it is called the October Revolution (or the Great
October Socialist Revolution by Soviet historians) but is celebrated in
the Soviet Union, with a huge parade reviewed by Soviet bigwigs in
Moscow's Red Square, on 7 November.

The February Revolution and the October Revolution were two separate events, but many writers argue they were simply stages in one
continuous radical transformation of Russian society in 1917: a people's rebellion sparked by the oppression and injustice of tsarist rule that
culminated in the founding of an entirely new social and political system, Soviet socialism. Others, minimizing the shifts of political power
reflected in the two revolutions, stress the more fundamental and long-
range modernization of Russian society in its economic, social, and intellectual aspects, a process that began in modern times with the emancipation of the serfs in 1861, that was accelerated in the massive Soviet
industrialization drive after 1928, and that is only now being completed
in the 1960s–1980s. In our account we will try to include both perspec-
tives on the Russian Revolution: its specific features and its long-run
impact on both Russia and the rest of the world.

---

[1] This description of events on 10 and 11 March is based on W. Bruce Lincoln, *The
Romanovs: Autocrats of All the Russias* (New York: 1981), 717–22, and on other accounts.

The protests over bread, the strikes, and the street demonstrations in Petrograd that led to the collapse of the tsardom occurred spontaneously, without particular leaders or heroes. It was truly a mass popular revolution in which the bulk of the citizens expressed, quite peacefully, their refusal to tolerate the existing situation and government any longer. Once the soldiers joined the crowds, the old regime simply disappeared, and this deliquescence of authority was repeated throughout the country. Nicholas II soon abdicated, without protest, and no one came forward to defend the autocratic system.

The nature of the February Revolution raises an important question about Russian society: How could the old order be discarded so easily? The answer lies in part in the discrediting of the tsarist regime at the top and in the terrible burdens and discouragement of the war, for which people blamed the tsarist government, as we saw in the last chapter. But the tsardom vanished in a moment because of longer-range weaknesses as well. In the latter part of the nineteenth and the beginning of the twentieth centuries the traditional belief system and norms that had bolstered the autocracy for so long began to erode rapidly. The tsar had counted on ingrained obedience and on gratitude for his benign rule, on the rituals and divine support of the Orthodox Church, on a system of classes in which each group knew its place and acknowledged its obligation to serve the state, and on a mystical sense of the rightness and goodness of Slavic peasant life. By the 1900s these values had become vitiated or outmoded, and no new conservative tenets had emerged to replace them. The old order rested on custom and inertia; once these weakened it was easily toppled.

Tsar Nicholas abdicated in favor if his brother, but the latter refused the throne. It soon became clear in any case that there was no support for continuation of the monarchy, even if it were reformed. Nicholas and his family met a tragic fate. After spending some fairly pleasant months under mild "house arrest" in Siberia, the deposed tsar, his wife, and their five children were brutally murdered in July 1918 by local authorities to prevent their possible capture by anti-Bolshevik forces involved in the Russian civil war then raging. The Bolshevik leaders in Moscow, though they did not order this execution, were indifferent when informed of what had happened.

Even before the tsar abdicated, a group of liberal leaders had formed a committee of Duma members, which soon appointed a provisional government. Its ministers were mainly members of the Octobrist and Kadet parties, plus a few other moderates. From the start the Provisional government labored under several handicaps. Its own members as well as the populace at large considered it temporary and transitional until a constituent assembly democratically elected by all the Russian people could convene and decide on Russia's permanent future government. In addition, the Provisional government represented a considerable range of political views, particularly after May 1917, when moderate socialists joined the cabinet. As a result, it could not agree on even temporary solutions for some of Russia's most urgent problems. Finally, the Provisional government tried to govern in an atmosphere of unrealistic popular expectations, revolutionary euphoria, and widespread feelings of liberation that impelled people to reject all authority.

In practical terms, moreover, the Provisional government almost immediately found itself sharing power in the country with a grass-roots organization, the Soviet. On 12 March, in the same Petrograd building in which Duma members were meeting to form the Provisional government, assembled a group of revolutionary activists: representatives of the workers, a few socialist and radical politicians, and some soldiers. They soon decided to reconstitute the soviet that had played such a dramatic role in the Revolution of 1905. In recognition of the contribution troops of the Petrograd garrison had made in the recent revolution, the resurrected organization was called the Soviet of Workers' *and* Soldiers' Deputies. It chose an executive committee dominated by moderate socialist politicians.

The Petrograd Soviet soon exercised considerable authority because workers in such key sectors as transport, communications, and supply looked to it for guidance and because it had influence over troops stationed in Petrograd and other major cities, particularly after 14 March, when the Soviet issued Order Number 1, a call for sweeping reforms in the army and the election of soldiers' committees in each unit. As it became established, the Soviet acted as a check, or watchdog, on the formal administration of the country, the Provisional government, creating a situation of "dual power" that lasted until the October Revolution seven months later.

The February Revolution spread quickly throughout the Russian empire. As in Petrograd, tsarist authorities were replaced, usually without bloodshed, by public committees, and before long soviets were formed, first in the cities and then more slowly in district towns and villages. Outside Russia, the Central Powers welcomed the revolution because they thought it might lead to an unraveling of Russian society and a collapse of Russia's fighting capacity. The Allies and the United States were also delighted, first on ideological grounds since they could now fight side by side with another democracy instead of an autocracy, and second, because they hoped the new government would invigorate the Russian war effort and strengthen Russia's contribution to the Western cause.

But what did the Russian people think about the down-fall of the tsar? Most of them were overjoyed, embracing the revolution as a panacea for all of the country's and their own problems. Exhilarated and optimistic, they exercised their new freedom to the fullest, attending meetings, founding parties, sending petitions and telegrams to Petrograd, and talking, always talking. At the same time, except for a common belief in the glory and value of "The Revolution," all had their own ideas about the future: workers expected higher wages, the eight-hour day, and better working conditions; peasants counted on more land and higher grain prices; the national minorities dreamed of autonomy, local rights, and, in a few cases, independence; soldiers and sailors wanted fairer treatment, civil and political rights, and their own committees. Moreover, most individuals believed their dreams would come true, if not right away, at least in the near future.

The reality of course was far different. The Provisional government had to struggle with the same problems that the tsarist regime had confronted, most prominently the war and its effects. In retrospect we can see that the war was destroying orderly society in Russia and that at heart people were sick of the war. But at the same time inertia, the lingering effects of patriotism, fear of the Germans, and, among educated classes, a sense of duty to Russia's allies, all combined to make it unthinkable that Russia should pull out of the war. The Provisional government announced it would continue to fight and to support the Allied cause. The Petrograd Soviet also endorsed the war, although at the same time calling for a redefinition of Allied war aims to eliminate annexations of others' territory and indemnities against the losers.

The Provisional government promised independence to the Poles and full autonomy to the Finns but could not agree on policy toward the other national minorities. Both the Provisional government and the Soviet backed expanded civil liberties, immediate elections to the Constituent Assembly, and lifting of restrictions against religious minorities and Jews. But they were far apart on what social and economic policies should be followed. Nevertheless the Soviet decided to tolerate the Provisional government as long as "it fulfills its promise and effectively combats the old regime."

A month after the February Revolution a new element was introduced into the situation, when on 16 April V. I. Lenin (see Figure 14), who had been in exile in Europe for ten years, arrived back in Petrograd. Although the German government helped Lenin return by letting him pass across German territory and although the Bolsheviks later secretly accepted money from the Germans, neither Lenin nor his party were German agents, as has sometimes been charged. They took money from whatever source was available and used it for their own purposes. In this case, Lenin intended to stir up a radical revolution in Russia, for which the Germans assisted him, but he counted on that revolution's spreading to Europe and to Germany itself.

Lenin was now leader of the Bolsheviks, an important faction of the Russian Social Democratic Party. Lenin and his followers had established a separate identity within the party beginning in 1903 at the party's Second Congress, where they had argued that the party should be

Figure 14. *V. I. Lenin, 1870–1924. (Courtesy of the Library of Congress)*

a small, elite, highly disciplined band of professional revolutionaries. His opponents, soon known as Mensheviks, favored a larger, broadly based, more open party. After 1914 the two factions also disagreed over World War I. Lenin interpreted the war as the result of struggles among the capitalists over colonial empires and over trade, and he concluded that capitalism was in a final phase of decline, which Lenin dubbed "imperialism." Most Bolsheviks followed Lenin in denouncing all sides to the struggle and urging the workers to turn the imperialist war into a civil war against the capitalists; most Mensheviks approved defensive military action to protect Russia but also called for a peace of justice and brotherhood.

The Mensheviks welcomed the February Revolution and accepted the Provisional government in part because they clung to orthodox Marxist theory, which taught that all societies, including Russia, had to pass through a capitalist phase of development, however brief, before they could undergo a proletarian revolution and enter the final stage of history, socialism. For the Mensheviks the February Revolution represented the overthrow of the old feudal order in Russia's equivalent of the French Revolution, and Russian society was now in its capitalist, or "bourgeois-democratic," phase. It was doctrinally correct to support the bourgeois-democratic Provisional government and to use the freedoms it granted to proselytize the workers for the forthcoming proletarian or socialist revolution. In a set of statements known as the April Theses, Lenin attacked this view. He called on the Russian people to struggle against, rather than support, the Provisional government; to begin at once to prepare the transfer of all power to the Soviet; and to end the war immediately. This radical program shocked even his fellow Bolsheviks and was ignored by moderate socialist and liberal politicians as extremist nonsense.

Undaunted, Lenin continued to espouse his ideas, reflecting two of his most dominant traits as a revolutionary leader: his tenacious will that often wore down and overpowered the resistance of doubting comrades and his devout conviction of both the necessity and the possibility of a socialist revolution in Russia. As the spring wore on, the tide of events began to move in a direction that favored Lenin's view of the situation. The war dragged on, and the Provisional government was weakened by a crisis over its alleged retention of the imperialist war aim of acquiring Constantinople and the Straits. Social and economic conditions worsened instead of improving after the February Revolution. The government made no progress on two key issues, land reform and rights for minorities, partly because its liberal leaders stuck resolutely to democratic principles. They insisted that such fundamental questions as redistribution of land, which the peasants were vociferously demanding, and whether the future Russian state should be a federal system, as the non-Russian nationalities insisted, could only be settled by the free vote of all Russian citizens through their representatives in the soon-to-be elected Constituent Assembly. Yet they did not do enough to speed up preparations for the elections, and they could not agree on how to meet the most immediate social and economic problems.

More important than the government's ineffectiveness, however, was the growing disillusionment of the masses with the results of the February Revolution. Not only had it not solved everyone's problems, but most individuals were worse off. When it seemed they were no nearer achieving their cherished goals, many people grew frustrated and bitter, blaming privileged Russia—the educated leaders of the Provisional government—for the dashing of their hopes. War-weariness was spreading rapidly, and even front-line troops became restive. The government nevertheless pushed forward with its plans to mount a major military offensive designed to relieve pressure on the Allies on the Western Front. Workers became embroiled in sharp disputes with factory owners, and peasants began to seize private and state land illegally. As mass attitudes and actions became increasingly radical, authority and order began to dissipate in the country and tensions mounted. Clearly a new crisis was imminent.

The Bolsheviks Come to Power

Two climactic events of the summer of 1917 paved the way for the Bolsheviks to take power with relative ease in the fall. The first was the July Days, a spontaneous mass uprising in Petrograd on 16 and 17 July. People poured into the streets of the capital with no specific purpose in mind except to show their dislike of the Provisional government and their disgust with the existing situation. Some may have also vaguely wanted the Soviet to replace the government. During the demonstrations Victor Chernov, a Socialist Revolutionary leader and a member of the Soviet, was trying to persuade a crowd to disperse when an outraged worker interrupted, shaking his fist at Chernov and bawling, "Take power, you son-of-a-bitch, when they give it to you." But Chernov and other moderate leaders of the Soviet did not believe they should assume power at a time not yet ripe for a socialist revolution. The riots in Petrograd died down, and the Provisional government regained control of the situation for a time, but the July Days had shown how revolutionary the masses were and how, with proper direction, they might easily overturn the government.

The second event was a bungled attempt by an army general, Lavr Kornilov, to seize power and establish a military dictatorship in the country. After the major offensive planned by the Provisional government had failed, in part because some military units proved unreliable, the prime minister, a socialist liberal named Alexander Kerensky, had supported a movement within the top command to restore discipline in the army and to put down unrest on the home front. Kerensky thought he was using General Kornilov to strengthen the government, but Kornilov believed Kerensky was giving him a free hand. The result of this tragicomic misunderstanding was that Kornilov, encouraged by conservative elements in Petrograd, rashly ordered troops to move against the capital. Kerensky, fearing that Kornilov intended to take over the government, appealed to the Soviet and the masses for support, thereby alienating himself from conservative circles and making him dependent on radical elements. Railway and communications workers prevented the movement of Kornilov's troops, while revolutionary agitators persuaded many of his soldiers to give up. As a result, the attempted coup was a fiasco, and the position of the radicals was strengthened. Even more importantly, most Russians were now frightened of the possibility that reactionary forces, however vaguely defined, might attempt a counterrevolution, threatening whatever gains "the Revolution" had provided. Throughout the fall of 1917 the Bolsheviks effectively used the bogey of counterrevolution in their bid for power.

By September 1917 the Bolsheviks' slogan "Peace, Land, and Bread" was winning over large numbers of workers, soldiers, and peasants. The Bolsheviks also promised the non-Russian minorities the right of self-determination. Their program fitted well the goals of many Russian citizens, and the Bolsheviks soon obtained a majority in the Petrograd and Moscow soviets. In the meantime the war continued to go badly, and the Provisional government under Kerensky seemed paralyzed, despite several attempts to rally democratic elements around it.

The vulnerability of the liberal-moderate socialist coalition that was trying to govern Russia arose from several factors. It lacked strong leadership, Kerensky in particular being a vain, mercurial, often impractical person who between bouts of apathy and despair rushed around giving speeches and exhorting his fellow countrymen without accomplishing much. Moreover, as noted earlier, the moderate socialists were reluctant partners in the coalition cabinet since according to Marxist theory the government should have been a capitalist one. They were not willing to assume power themselves because it was the wrong historical age for a socialist government, yet they were stalemated by the liberals from taking immediate steps to alleviate the socioeconomic ills of Russia. Finally, the circumstances were such that even a united government with strong leadership could not have survived so long as it continued an unpopular war and refused to grant the people's most urgent demands. On the very eve of the Bolsheviks' assumption of power, several moderate socialists proposed a program of peace and land reform to Kerensky, but by then it was too late.

As the Mensheviks and the Socialist Revolutionaries, tainted by their association with the war and with the Provisional government, lost influence with the masses, the Bolsheviks gained strength. In an amazing turnabout the Bolsheviks had grown from a tiny fringe group of around twenty thousand at the time of the February Revolution to a huge party of about two hundred sixty thousand with substantial influence in the army and among the urban masses. Within the party a sharp debate erupted in September–October 1917 over whether to attempt an armed revolution. Lenin, with his brilliant political acumen, argued vigorously that now was the moment to strike while the Provisional government was weak and while a majority of articulate opinion favored the Bolsheviks. Others urged caution and a longer period of preparing the masses for action. It was finally decided to move toward revolution.

The Bolsheviks' success in the October Revolution, during which they took power as it slipped from the hands of the Provisional government, was facilitated by two events occurring on the eve of the revolution. One was formation of the Military Revolutionary Committee (MRC) of the Petrograd Soviet in the third week of October. Although it was charged with preparing defensive measures in the event of a German attack on Petrograd and with coordinating the movement of troops in the capital, it soon became, under the forceful leadership of Leon Trotsky, a planning committee for the Bolshevik uprising. Several days before the revolution the MRC posted its own commissars with most military units in the capital and announced that no military orders were valid unless countersigned by the MRC. This meant that the government had lost control of the troops in Petrograd, and although only a few of them joined in the Bolshevik uprising, the rest declined to defend the Provisional government.

Second, Trotsky, who did an excellent job organizing and directing the revolution, cleverly managed affairs so the Kerensky was provoked to move against the Bolsheviks on 5 November. This permitted them to appear not as illegal subverters of a democratic government but as righteous defenders of freedom and "the Revolution" against the dark forces of reaction.

On 6–7 November the Bolsheviks took control of key locations in the capital—banks, post offices, railroad stations, and government buildings—most often without a struggle. On the night of 7 November they also captured the Winter Palace, former seat of the tsars (see Figure 15), arresting the ministers of the Provisional government, who had retreated there. Only a few military units tried half-heartedly to defend the palace, and Kerensky, after slipping out of the city, could not rally a sufficient military force from the regular army to recapture Petrograd from the Bolsheviks. Casualties during the October Revolution in the capital were only a few hundred, and most of the citizenry passively accepted the new order with a wait-and-see attitude.

On 8 November Lenin formed a Soviet government called the Council of People's Commissars, and presented to the Second Congress of Soviets, made up of deputies from soviets throughout Russia, decrees calling for immediate peace and for nationalization of all land and its transfer to the peasantry for their use. He also decided to proceed with elections to the Constituent Assembly late in November.

Outside Petrograd the October Revolution proceeded unevenly. In some cities power passed quickly to Bolshevik-dominated Soviets, but in others fighting erupted, and it was days or even weeks before the Bolsheviks established their authority. The peasants, happy with the decree on land, generally acquiesced in the Bolshevik takeover, and most of the army, except a number of officers, supported the new Soviet government after Lenin pushed through an armistice with the Germans pending peace negotiations.

Figure 15. *A popular demonstration in front of the Winter Palace, former residence of the tsars in Petrograd, during the early days of the Russian Revolution of 1917.*

During his first weeks in power Lenin had to deal with a serious political crisis. Most of the delegates to the Second Congress of Soviets, including many of the Bolsheviks, had been sent to the congress with instructions from local soviets to support formation of a new government that included all the socialist parties, including the Mensheviks and Socialist Revolutionaries (SRs). But since the moderate socialists opposed the Bolshevik assumption of power and their delegates had walked out of the Second Congress on that issue, Lenin had formed an all-Bolshevik government. Not wishing to share power, Lenin would have preferred to continue that arrangement, but pressure not only from Soviet representatives but from within the Bolshevik party and from key trade unions, including the railway workers, forced him to enter negotiations with the Mensheviks and SRs for creation of an all-socialist cabinet. By the end of November the talks collapsed, the pressure dissipated, and Lenin reorganized the Council of People's Commissars to include a few individuals from the Left Socialist Revolutionaries, a radical faction of the party. In this way Lenin established what was essentially a one-party government, a practice that became a central feature of the Soviet system from then on.

A couple of months later Lenin made it clear that the Bolsheviks intended to dominate not only the government but also the general political life of the country. Lenin had permitted elections to the Constituent Assembly, as promised in the Bolshevik platform, but since the majority of voters were peasants and the Socialist Revolutionary Party was closest to the peasants, the SRs won a majority of seats in the new Assembly. When it convened in January 1918 and it became evident the Bolshevik minority could not control the Assembly, Lenin forcibly dissolved it. Although the moderate socialist parties occasionally contested local Soviet elections during the next few years, for all practical purposes the Bolsheviks, by that act, created a one-party dictatorship over the country, which has existed ever since.

As a result of the October Revolution in a few days, or weeks at most, power in the largest country in Eurpoe had been transferred into the hands of a radical socialist minority bent on entirely restructuring Russian society and on carrying their proletarian revolution to the advanced countries of the West and eventually to the whole world. Lenin justified the socialist revolution in less industrialized Russia by saying that special circumstances, such as the war and the revolutionary actions of the Russian peasantry, had permitted it and that the October Revolution would fulfill the capitalist stage of history in Russia as it proceeded. It was a rather vague formulation, but Lenin counted on the socialist revolution's spreading to highly industrialized Western Europe; once the proletariat had come to power there, they could give Russia the assistance it needed to develop an advanced economy and support true socialism. As Lenin often put it, the Bolsheviks needed to hold on to power in Russia until their ally, the workers of the West, came to their aid.

We know that the October Revolution had fateful consequences for modern world history, but what sort of a revolution was it? It was certainly not an evil conspiracy designed to fasten a new form of human bondage on the Russian people, as some extreme anti-communists have argued. On the other hand it was not a great libertarian revolution opening the way to freedom and plenty for all of Russia, as Soviet historians claim. Neither vilifying the Bolsheviks nor glorifying the masses is a convincing way to interpret the revolution. Rather the Bolsheviks were able to build upon deep popular feelings—resentment of the injustice and oppression associated with old privileged Russia, fear of counterrevolution, revulsion against the war and the sacrifices it entailed, and dreams of a better, securer, more just future—to come to power and have the chance to construct a new order. That many of the aspirations of the masses were unfilfilled and that the Bolsheviks built a revolutionary society quite unlike that which their early members envisaged are key elements of the story that will unfold in the remaining pages of this book. But it is important to remember that the vision, the dream, the yearning for a future good society that animated so many

Russians in 1917—not the reality of what actually happened after-ward—have had, and still have, a powerful impact on the rest of the world.

Civil War and Foreign Intervention, 1918–21

Within six months of their coming to power the Bolsheviks had to confront major internal and external challenges to their authority that led to a bitter, no-holds-barred conflict lasting almost three years. An intriguing question is to what extent this desperate struggle for survival determined the contours of Soviet society. How much of the harshness, intolerance, and authoritarianism of the Soviet system can be traced to its birthpangs in civil strife and economic stringency? Or, put another way, if the Bolsheviks had been allowed—nay, even assisted—to put their ideas into effect without outside interference and without the necessity of improvising to stay alive, what sort of socialist society might have emerged? There are no precise answers to these questions, but several factors need to be borne in mind when considering them. Russia was not an advanced country in 1914, and regardless of the further devas-tation caused by the civil war, Russia's three-year involvement in World War I had nearly wrecked the economy. So the Bolsheviks would not have had extensive resources to work with, in any case.

Second, as we have seen, Lenin and his party made clear, well be-fore major armed attacks against them began, that they would brook no interference with their rule and that they would not share authority with other parties or interest groups, nor with the people. This was partly because Lenin and the Bolsheviks believed the party should not only lead, but act on behalf of, the people and partly because Lenin was con-vinced that the Bolsheviks must hold power in Russia until the Russian Revolution could spark a revolution in Europe and the advanced pro-letariat of the West could come to the Bolsheviks' assistance. Conse-quently, Bolshevik Russia, even at peace, was not likely to a democratic, participatory society. At the same time it seems fair to conclude that the rigors and exigencies of the civil war and foreign invasion intensified authoritarian trends within Bolshevism and reinforced attitudes and policies that emphasized control, centralization, and suppression of dis-sent.

The issue that touched off the civil war and intervention was not dissolution of the Constituent Assembly or the Bolsheviks' radical eco-nomic measures, such as repudiation of Russia's foreign debt and na-tionalization of property—though these acts hardly pleased many peo-ple at home and abroad—but rather Lenin's policy toward the war. By making peace with the Central Powers, as he eventually did in March

1918, Lenin alienated millions of patriotic Russians, who concluded that the Bolsheviks had sold the country down the river, as well as the Allied powers, whose leaders believed the Russians had betrayed their cause and were forcing the Western democracies to make even greater sacrifices to defeat Germany and Austria-Hungary. To be sure, neither the anti-Bolsheviks nor the Allied statesmen were delighted with the Bolsheviks' revolutionary policies and with their appeals to workers throughout the world to revolt, but the primary reason they took up arms against the new Soviet regime was because it had made peace with the German enemy.

Ironically Lenin was faced with a no-win situation. He had promised the Russian people peace; if he didn't deliver, his government would not last long. Yet he also knew that peace meant not only humiliating concessions to the Germans but probably stirring up widespread opposition against the Bolsheviks. Faced with this dilemma, Lenin risked the potential of attacks from foes within and without against the certainty of German occupation and popular rebellion if he tried to continue the war. Yet even within his own party he had a major struggle before convincing a slim majority of Bolsheviks to accept the Peace of Brest-Litovsk, under which Russia lost a quarter of its territory and population, a third of its industry, and three quarters of its coal mines to Germany and Austria-Hungary. Lenin believed that the peace treaty was a temporary surrender, a scrap of paper to be torn up when the proletarian revolution broke out in Germany, as he was convinced it would. In fact, the treaty lapsed eight months after it was ratified in March 1918, not because of a revolution in Germany but because the Allies won the war despite Russia's defection.

In December 1917, at the time armistice negotiations with the Germans began, the first anti-Bolshevik forces were formed in south Russia, primarily from high officers in the army and cossack soldiers. Major hostilities did not begin, however, until May–June 1918, when a military front against the Bolsheviks was set up in Siberia, supported by Czechoslovak troops who had formed part of the Russian army and were being evacuated to the Western Front when they clashed with the Bolsheviks. Other fronts were established in north Russia, supported by British and American troops, and before long in northwest Russia, with assistance from the British. Later, anti-Bolshevik, or White, armies were also active in southwestern Russia, supported by the French, and in the trans-Caspian area, supported by the British. The military history of the civil war is both extremely complex and beyond our scope, but as a glance at Map 7 shows, at one time Soviet Russia, the Bolshevik state, was surrounded on all sides by anti-Bolshevik forces and was compressed into a relatively small area in central Russia.

The civil war was greatly complicated by the participation of non-Russian minorities, who often were at odds with the Russian Whites,

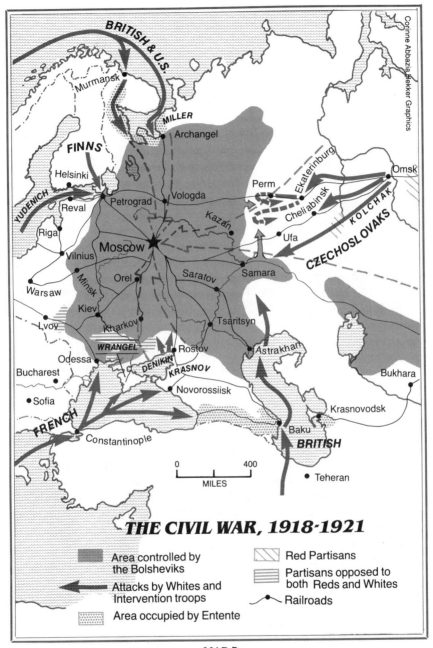

THE CIVIL WAR, 1918-1921

Area controlled by the Bolsheviks

Attacks by Whites and Intervention troops

Area occupied by Entente

Red Partisans

Partisans opposed to both Reds and Whites

Railroads

MAP 7

since the latter favored a centralized Russia and were generally unwilling to make concessions to the nationalities. At various times in the period 1918–21 a majority of the Finns, the Baltic peoples, the Poles, the Armenians, the Georgians, the Ukrainians, and the Moslem peoples of

Central Asia were fighting the Bolsheviks. To confuse the picture even further, some members of these national groups were Bolsheviks and supported Lenin and the Soviet government in their efforts to incorporate the minority areas into Soviet Russia. When the struggle finally ended in the early 1920s, the Poles, the Finns, and the Baltic peoples had established their independence, and the others had been absorbed in the Soviet state.

The third important element in this drawn-out and fierce struggle were the foreign powers who intervened in the Russian civil war. In the summer of 1918 the Central Powers, worried that the Bolsheviks were not completing the economic payments required under the Treaty of Brest-Litovsk, occupied western territory of the Soviet state. At about the same time Britain, France, the United States, and Japan decided to intervene in Russia, mainly in hopes of restoring a military front against the Germans and partly for anti-Bolshevik or imperialistic reasons. Although the American president, Woodrow Wilson, disapproved of this action, he went along with his allies as a gesture of wartime unity. Allied troops, mainly Japanese but including seven thousand Americans, were landed in the Russian Far East, British and American troops in north Russia, and, later in 1918, French troops at Odessa in south Russia. The greatest Western contribution to the anti-Bolshevik cause, however, was not direct military support, most of which was withdrawn in 1919 after the victory over Germany, but military equipment and financial assistance for the White forces. This aid unquestionably helped the anti-Bolshevik armies fight on considerably longer than they otherwise could have and was therefore a source of much Soviet resentment against the Western powers, as the memory of it still is today.

After the defeat of Germany, the Western intervention took on a definitely anti-Bolshevik character, but public opinion in the democracies was unwilling to support a major effort to bring down the Bolshevik regime, and the whole enterprise petered out by 1920 (although Japan, did not remove its troops until 1922). The legacy of intervention was suspicion and mistrust between the Soviet government and the West, which has lasted down to the present day.

At the same time that the Bolsheviks were desperately defending the Soviet state against White armies and foreign interventionists, they were also on the offensive, trying to stir up revolution in the West. When the German radical leader, Karl Liebknecht, was let out of jail in the fall of 1918, Lenin announced in a burst of optimism: "The release from prison of the representative of the revolutionary workers of Germany is a sign of new epoch, the epoch of victorious socialism which is now beginning for Germany and for the whole world."[2] For a time Lenin convinced himself that the proletarian revolution predicted in Marxist

[2] Warren B. Walsh, ed., *Readings in Russian History*, (Syracuse: 1963), 3, 727.

theory was about to erupt in Europe, partly because of the Russian example and partly because of disillusionment and economic hardship in Germany and Austria following their defeat. To distinguish his movement of revolutionary socialism from the moderate or evolutionary socialists in Russia and Europe, Lenin had his party renamed the Russian Communist Party (Bolshevik). He sent propaganda, agents, and a little money to spur the revolutionary cause in Europe, and short-lived Communist uprisings in Hungary and in southern Germany momentarily raised Lenin's hopes. In March 1919 Lenin founded the Communist International (Comintern), a league of revolutionary socialist parties dominated by the Bolsheviks that was dedicated to promoting world revolution.

Although revolution did not spread to the West, neither were the Western powers able to snuff out the revolution in Russia. Consequently, some observers have viewed relations between Soviet Russia and the West in these years as a stand-off, with neither side able to achieve its maximum goals. And although many in Europe and the United States were terrified of "the Red menace" and the potential spread of communism, many others were swayed by Soviet appeals for peace and an end to intervention and by Soviet calls for a new postwar order based on social justice and economic equality.

In the all-out struggle to survive the Russian Communists adopted stringent policies at home. As early as December 1917 they established the Cheka (from its Russian initials), the forerunner of the Soviet secret police, and by the summer of 1918, when a political opponent shot and wounded Lenin, both the Bolsheviks and the Whites were resorting to terror and extensive political coercion. Lenin and Trotsky defended such repressive policies as necessary to make sure the revolution and the Soviet state survived, but a leading European Communist, Rosa Luxemburg, sharply criticized these actions.

The social and economic policies the Bolsheviks adopted between 1918 and 1921 are sometimes called war communism, and indeed demands of the war effort dictated many of these measures. But they might also be called militant communism because some policies were ideologically motivated and were designed to introduce socialist concepts in Russia. Industry was nationalized and tightly controlled; private enterprise and trade were reduced to a minimum; the state provided all public and social services, including education and culture; and the Orthodox Church and other faiths were persecuted.

Soviet policy toward the peasants was ambiguous. They were allowed to keep the land they had seized in 1917, and additional public land was given them. At the same time, since the Soviet government needed grain to feed workers in the cities and troops of the growing Red Army, it resorted to requisitioning of peasant surpluses. This policy greatly angered the more prosperous peasants and one reason the civil war lasted so long was that peasants kept switching back and forth between the Reds and the Whites. At last, when they realized that the anti-Bolshevik forces were determined to take the land back and to restore many aspects of the old order, the majority of peasants passively sided with the Bolsheviks.

The Soviet government survived as much because of the deficiencies of its opponents as its own strengths. To be sure, the Soviet forces had interior lines of communication, and the Red Army, built up to a force of several million men and effectively organized and led by Trotsky, often with assistance from former tsarist officers, fought bravely for the most part. Yet the disorganization, disunity, and reactionary attitudes and policies that characterized the Whites made them far less formidable opponents than they might have been. Moreover, as we saw earlier, they failed to reach an agreement with the national minorities, thereby losing valuable support. The Allied powers, in the face of a public opinion weary of war and partially sympathetic to the Bolsheviks, could not provide decisive assistance.

The last episode of the civil war and intervention was an attack on Soviet Russia by Poland that led to a bloody summer of fighting in 1920. With the military situation stalemated in the fall, peace was agreed to on the basis of a compromise boundary line between the two countries.

The New Economic Policy and Co-existence, 1921–28

By the winter of 1920–21, when it was clear that Soviet Russia had survived, the major question became, What next? Lenin's hoped-for revolution in Europe had not materialized and did not seem imminent. Little help could be expected from that quarter, although Lenin hastened to restore diplomatic and commercial relations with the Western capitalist countries (except the United States, which refused to recognize the Soviet state until 1933), and he was quite happy to grant economic concessions to capitalists willing to invest in Russia. But few were interested, and it was soon apparent that Soviet Russia would basically have to go it alone.

At the same time the Bolsheviks faced a disastrous situation at home. The civil war and intervention had completed the wrecking of the Russian economy begun in 1914. By 1920 industrial production was at only 20 percent of its 1913 level, and even agricultural production was only two thirds of what it had been. The country was virtually a wasteland, with some regions facing famine and serious epidemics of typhus and smallpox. Some 15 to 20 million people had been killed or had died of disease and starvation between 1914 and 1921. Moscow and Petrograd had shrunk to less than half their prerevolutionary size. Workers in the cities were dissatisfied, and there were several million Red Army veterans to be employed and resettled. The peasants were violently resisting further requisitioning of their grain and were demanding nonexistent manufactured goods before they would sell their produce. Peasant uprisings reminiscent of 1905 and 1917 broke out in a number of regions, and in March 1921 a major revolt erupted in Kronstadt, an industrial town and navel base not far from Petrograd. The Kronstadt rebellion was particularly alarming because all through 1917 and much of the civil war the Kronstadters had been among the most loyal and spirited supporters of the Soviet government. Significantly, what they now demanded went to the heart of the political dilemma the Bolsheviks faced:

> immediate re-election of the soviets by secret ballot and upon the basis of free political agitation, "in view of the fact that the existing soviets do not express the will of the workers and peasants," freedom of speech and press for "workers, peasants, and for the Anarchists and the left socialist parties"; freedom of meeting, and free trade unions and the formation of peasants' unions; liberation of all socialist political prisoners, . . . abolition of all special political departments (in the army, navy, and transport) "since no one party can enjoy privileges for the propaganda of its ideas and receive money from the state for this purpose"; equal rations for all, except those engaged in work detrimental to health; . . . full rights for the peasants to "do as they please with all the land" and to keep their own cattle, "provided that they use no hired labour"; and the right of individual small-scale manufacture, again without the employment of hired labour.[3]

Lenin had no intention of meeting the democratic political demands of the Kronstadt rebels and ordered the uprising suppressed by force. But he fully recognized that economic concessions would have to be made to save the revolution and Bolshevik rule. At the Tenth Party Congress in March 1921 he set forth his reform program, the New Economic Policy (NEP). It was not a retreat to capitalism, as some anti-Bolsheviks believed, but rather an example of Lenin's tactical flexibility as expressed in his dictum "one step backward, two steps forward." Lenin knew that changes were needed to restore the economy of Russia before a forward movement toward socialism could be contemplated.

NEP had three main features, all designed to stimulate economic recovery. Peasants were allowed to pay the government a fixed tax in money or in kind and could sell anything they produced beyond that in the open market; this was an effective incentive for them to grow and distribute more. Second, much of industry was denationalized, with the government retaining ownership of only "the commanding heights," that is, the largest factories, transportation, and the banks, with the rest reverting to private ownership. Finally, most retail trade and much of the

---

[3] Leonard Schapiro, *The Origins of the Communist Autocracy: Political Opposition in the Soviet State, First Phase, 1917–1922* (Cambridge, Mass.: 1956), 301.

labor market were freed from government control and allowed to operate privately and for profit.

NEP worked exceedingly well, despite the famine of 1921–22, which private relief assistance from the United States did much to alleviate. Industry surpassed its prewar output levels by 1926–27, and agriculture nearly reached its 1913 production total the following year. Moreover, with peace at hand life settled into a normal routine, and many older Soviet citizens look back on the NEP years as a happy and relatively prosperous time. Some outside observers have argued that the seminationalized, semiprivate structure of the Soviet economy under NEP could have provided a continuing mechanism of economic and social development for Russia, even though it was not fully socialist. It is clear though that Lenin never envisaged NEP as anything but a temporary measure. Before Lenin was able to work out how Soviet Russia, still an underindustrialized country, could advance toward socialism in the absence of revolution in the West, he suffered a stroke in May 1922 and died twenty months later in January 1924.

The March 1921 Party Congress was important not only because it launched NEP but also because key decisions concerning the party and concerning the state structure were taken there. Throughout its history the Bolshevik (Communist) Party had been regulated internally according to the rules of democratic centralism. Under those rules ideas and policies could be freely debated at various levels of the party before a decision was made. Once the decision was taken, however, it was binding on all party members and units. In practice, however, party members had been free to continue discussion of controversial questions and had on occasion even formed groups within the party to oppose various policies. At the Tenth Congress, Lenin insisted on adoption of a rule against "factionalism," which stated that once a decision had been made, no organized group could continue to agitate against it. Although Lenin did not enforce this new provision rigidly, it gave Joseph Stalin, Lenin's successor, a powerful weapon against internal opposition and helped him establish a dictatorship within the party.

The March 1921 party conclave also encouraged the movement already developing to make Soviet Russia a federal state, giving the national minorities some cultural and structural autonomy as long as the Communist party retained power in each region and ensured political subjugation to the national government. The result was the emergence between 1922 and 1924 of the Union of Soviet Socialist Republics (USSR), still the basic constitutional structure of the country. Each of today's fifteen autonomous republics is run by governments controlled by the Communist party, and although each republic has the theoretical right to secede from the Union, it is understood that such a step would never be taken since it would be inimical to the welfare of the larger state, the Soviet Union, the first socialist nation in the world.

During the NEP period the Soviet government continued the ambiguous foreign policy it had initiated at the time of the October Revolution. On the one hand, the government called for peace, for normal relations between itself and all other nations regardless of their ideology, and for active trade and commercial intercourse between socialist Russia and the capitalist West; on the other, the Communist party, which ran the Soviet government, agitated vigorously for immediate world revolution, the overthrow of capitalist governments in the West, and destruction of the traditional international order. Moreover, through the Comintern and its ties with Communist parties abroad the Russian Communists sought actively to promote these revolutionary objectives. No wonder Western politicians and diplomats were perplexed.

Nevertheless, with the exception of the United States, the Western nations, because they too wanted trade, peace, and normal relations, established ties with the Soviet state and even invited the Soviet leaders to such Europe-wide meetings as the Genoa Conference of 1922. This respectability reflected nicely Lenin's doctrine of peaceful coexistence, his view that socialist states and capitalist states could live quietly side by side interacting on matters of mutual interest. What Lenin did not stress in the 1920s was another aspect of the theory of coexistence, that the socialist society should try to gain all the advantage it could from such a relationship, and that eventually—after a period of time Lenin did not specify—coexistence would disappear in a "frightful collision" between the socialist and capitalist systems, from which socialism would emerge triumphant on a worldwide scale. As we shall see in Chapter 14, the "frightful collisions" idea had to be revised in the 1950s after the advent of nuclear weapons.

The Struggle for Power

While Lenin lived he dominated the Communist party and the Soviet state by virtue of his experience, his intellect, and his strong will. Although other comrades did not hesitate to disagree with him, he was widely admired and respected, and his views generally carried the day. In the early 1920s Lenin, even before his first stroke in May 1922, began to lose his grip on the party and state. In the first place he was unsure, as we have seen, about how socialism could best be built in Russia, and so he could not provide clear direction and ideological guidance. Moreover, since the party and the state were larger and more complex than they had been in the immediate aftermath of the October Revolution, it was much harder for Lenin to be on top of everything. One of the younger party members on whom Lenin came to rely for administrative and organizational detail was Joseph V. Stalin, who became general secretary, or chief administrator, of the party in 1922.

Stalin, meaning "steel," was a revolutionary pseudonym. His real name was Dzhugashvili, and he was born in the Caucasus in Georgia in 1879, the son of a poor shoemaker. Rebellious as a youth, Stalin was expelled from the theological seminary to which his devoted mother had sent him for a pious education and was soon involved in daring revolutionary activity, probably including robberies to raise money for the cause. Stalin rose in the ranks of the Bolshevik party by determination, hard work, thoroughness, and, perhaps most important, by being self-effacing. How much the later abnormality of his personality can be traced to resentment over his humble origins and over the subsidiary role in which his better educated and more brilliant comrades cast him is unclear, but at the time Stalin swallowed his pride and reliably and uncomplainingly did what he was told. Extremely ambitious, he realized the importance of ingratiating himself with Lenin and before World War I had become the latter's assistant on issues affecting national minorities and the right of socialist self-determination.

Returning from exile in Siberia right after the February Revolu-

Figure 16. *Joseph V. Stalin 1879–1953. (Courtesy of Sovfoto/Eastfoto)*

tion, Stalin was an industrious and loyal comrade in the years of the revolution and civil war, although he had his first disagreement with Trotsky at that time. Stalin was always willing to take on boring tasks that had to be done, yet as early as 1921 when he helped arrange the forcible incorporation of his native Georgia into the new Union of Soviet Socialist Republics, he showed he could be ruthless and decisive. Partly because of Stalin's methods and attitudes in that case, Lenin became increasingly critical of Stalin in 1922 and 1923. After his first stroke Lenin returned to work and planned to present to the Twelfth Party Congress in the spring of 1923 a major criticism of Stalin, recommending his demotion. Luckily for Stalin, just before the congress convened, Lenin had a further paralyzing stroke, which incapacitated him until his death in January 1924.

He had earlier written down, however, some of his growing doubts about Stalin, a document that came to be known as Lenin's Testament: "Comrade Stalin, having become *gensek* [general secretary of the party], has concentrated boundless power in his hands, and I am not sure that he will always manage to use this power with sufficient caution. . . . Stalin is too rude, and this fault . . . becomes intolerable in the office of general secretary. Therefore I propose to the comrades that they devise a way of shifting Stalin from this position. . . ."[4]

After Lenin's incapacitation Stalin allied with two other party leaders, Lev Kamenev and Gregory Zinoviev, in an effort to isolate Trotsky and reduce his power. When Lenin died, Stalin delivered the funeral oration; for reasons that are still unclear, Trotsky failed to attend the funeral and did not publish Lenin's Testament (which also contained some milder criticism of Trotsky), even though Trotsky was the best-known Bolshevik after Lenin, and was Lenin's logical successor. By early 1925 Trotsky had been replaced as Commissar for War; in 1926 he was removed from the Politburo, the party's ruling executive committee, and then expelled from the party; in 1928 he was exiled; and finally, in 1940, an agent of Stalin's police murdered him while he was in exile in Mexico.

Beginning in 1925 Stalin turned against Zinoviev and what was known as the Left Opposition, allying himself with more moderate leaders in the party, such as Nicholas Bukharin. In 1928, however, following his triumph over Trotsky and the Left Opposition, Stalin reversed himself again. Now he attacked his erstwhile supporters, dubbing them the Right Opposition and reducing their role in the party to insignificance. As a result, Stalin emerged from the power struggle to succeed Lenin as undisputed leader of the party and dictator of the Soviet Union. He triumphed in part because his opponents consistently

---

[4] Quoted in Robert C. Tucker, *Stalin as Revolutionary, 1879–1929* (New York: 1973), 270–71.

underrated him, in part through skill and ruthless ambition, in part because he cleverly controlled and manipulated the party from his position as general secretary, and in part because he espoused a persuasive ideological platform. The last point we will examine at the start of the next chapter, but Stalin's methods and his mastery of the party boded ill for the future of the Soviet people.

Conclusion

Indeed their recent past had been difficult enough, full of stress and high drama. During the decade from 1917 to 1927 a centuries-old social and political system was jettisoned, a disastrous and brutal war was ended only to be followed by three more years of bitter fratricidal struggle, a new society struggling to find its identity and to set fresh goals was born, and an unheralded yet powerful leader emerged to dominate the country and extend the revolution. It was little wonder that some Russians thought of it as a new "Time of Troubles."

In retrospect we can see that those years had several distinguishing characteristics. In the first place, the Russian Revolution saved Marxian socialism, which had been nearly destroyed as an influential movement by nationalist feelings aroused at the outbreak of World War I. Lenin and the Bolsheviks, even though they came to power in a backward country, rescued the socialist ideal and ensured that it would survive in the twentieth century as an alternative way of organizing modern society.

Second, the Russian Revolution fulfilled some aspirations of the people and dashed others. From it the Bolshevik or Communist party emerged as the strongest force in the new society, yet the events of 1917 intensified the Leninists' distrust of mass organizations and other parties. The course of the revolution reinforced their belief that they knew what was best for the people and that their way was the correct way. The Bolshevik leaders had no intention of letting the masses decide important issues, and the result was that even though the people wanted an all-socialist government responsive to the popularly elected soviets, what they were given was a one-party dictatorship over the government and country with the Bolsheviks dominating and using the soviets for the party's own purposes.

On the other hand, the Boslheviks did meet popular demands in a number of areas: they gave the peasants land; they brought peace, at least temporarily; they tried to provide greater equity; and they gave many Russians a sense of dignity and self-worth that they had never had before. In short, the people had gained and they had lost, as so often happens at major turning points in human history.

Finally, the revolutionary years provided remarkable evidence that a single individual can affect the course of history. It is hard to conceive of the Russian Revolution without Lenin. He returned to Russia to galvanize his party, he insisted stubbornly on bidding for power at the only moment when the Bolsheviks could probably have succeeded, and he forced through the peace with Germany, without which the revolution could not have survived. If there is such a thing as a "hero in history," Lenin fits the bill.

FURTHER READING

Carr, E. H. *The Bolshevik Revolution* (3 vols.). New York: 1951–53.

Chamberlin, W.H. *The Russian Revolution, 1917–21* (2 vols.). New York: 1965.

Clements, Barbara. *Bolshevik Feminist*. Bloomington, Ind.: 1979.

Cohen, Stephen. *Bukharin: A Political Biography*. New York: 1974.

Daniels, Robert V. *The Conscience of the Revolution: Communist Opposition in Soviet Russia*. Cambridge, Mass.: 1960.

Hasegawa, T. *The February Revolution: Petrograd 1917*. Seattle: 1981.

Howe, Irving. *Leon Trotsky*. New York: 1978.

Katkov, G. *Russia 1917: The February Revolution*. New York: 1967.

Kennan, George F. *Soviet-American Relations, 1917–20* (2 vols.). New York: 1967.

Lewin, Moshe. *Lenin's Last Struggle*. New York: 1968.

Pipes, Richard. *The Formation of the Soviet Union*. Cambridge, Mass.: 1954.

Rabinowitch, A. *The Bolsheviks Come to Power*. New York: 1976.

Reed, John. *Ten Days That Shook the World*. New York: 1935 [eyewitness account of the October Revolution].

Schapiro, Leonard. *The Origin of the Communist Autocracy, 1917–22*. Cambridge, Mass.: 1955.

Sholokhov, M. *And Quiet Flows the Don*. New York: 1966 [novel about the Russian civil war].

Tucker, Robert. *Stalin as a Revolutionary, 1879–1929*. New York: 1973.

Von Laue, T. *Why Lenin? Why Stalin? A Reappraisal of the Russian Revolution, 1900–1930*. Philadelphia: 1964.

Wildman, Allan K. *The End of the Russian Imperial Army . . . March–April 1917*. Princeton, N.J.: 1979.

12

The Second Revolution, the Stalinist System, and World War II, 1928–46

Who broke the chains that bound our feet, now dancing,
Who opened lips that sing a joyous song,
Who made the mourners change their tears for laughter,
Brought back the dead to life's rejoicing throng.
Who is in heart, in every thought and action,
Most loving, true and wise of Lenin's sons—
Such is the great Stalin.[1]

This excerpt from "The Song of Stalin" illustrates the extent of the official adulation of Stalin at the height of his power. Yet this individual was responsible for launching a virtual civil war against the peasants in which millions died and for instituting purges and repression against the general population in which millions more perished. At the same time he oversaw the industrialization of Russia, the survival of the Soviet Union in World War II, and the establishment of Soviet dominance in Eastern Europe. Because he was a suspicious, secretive person presiding over a xenophobic, terror-ridden system, we know little about Stalin's later years, and he remains in many respects an enigma. Was he a cruel, paranoic despot, or a determined, far-sighted leader? In either case, he left a powerful and lasting imprint on Soviet society, and its contours today cannot be understood without careful consideration of Stalin and the Stalinist system he created.

The Revolution from Above: Industrialization and Collectivization

In 1917 the Bolsheviks seized political power in Russia but, despite sporadic experiments under war communism, they did not radically

[1] Quoted in Warren B. Walsh, ed., *Readings in Russian History*, Vol. 3, 4th ed. rev. (Syracuse: 1963), 761.

transform Russia's social and economic system in their first decade of rule. Beginning in 1928–29, however, Stalin and the Communist party carried out a second major revolution, one that completely changed the configuration of Soviet society. Until the Chinese Communist revolution some twenty years later, it was the most sudden and thoroughgoing alteration in a people's way of life in history, even surpassing in its sweep and in the numbers of people affected the French Revolution of 1789.

Stalin and a few party leaders, not the people as a whole, decided on this revolution and then drove it through in the succeeding decade. The dislocation, suffering and outright loss of life were enormous, but the achievements were also considerable. As a Soviet citizen once shouted at me, when I questioned the costs of this second revolution, "Yes, yes, it was a frightful price to pay, but it was all worth it—it made us strong and respected!" The goal of making the Soviet Union powerful enough to withstand any external threat was certainly a primary reason for the decision of Stalin and his comrades to force through rapid industrialization. In a speech he made in 1931 Stalin, in his usual blunt, didactic fashion, summed up this line of argument, dismissing complaints that the pace of industrialization was too fast:

> To slacken the tempo would mean falling behind. And those who fall behind will get beaten. But we do not want to be beaten. No, we refuse to be beaten! One feature of the history of old Russia was the continual beating she suffered because of her backwardness. She was beaten by the Mongol Khans. She was beaten by the Turkish beys. She was beaten by the Swedish feudal lords. She was beaten by the Polish and Lithuanian gentry. She was beaten by the British and French capitalists. She was beaten by the Japanese barons. All beat her—because of her backwardness, because of her military backwardness, cultural backwardness, industrial backwardness, agricultural backwardness. They beat her because to do so was profitable and could be done with impunity. . . . That is why we must no longer lag behind. . . .
>
> We are fifty or a hundred years behind the advanced countries. We must make good this distance in ten years. Either we do it, or we shall go under.[2]

Just ten years and three months later Hitler's Nazi armies invaded Russia!

There were other reasons for the industrialization decision. Ideologically, Marxist theory ordained that a socialist society must be highly industrialized, must have an overwhelming preponderance of workers. Yet the Soviet Union under NEP was only partly industrialized, with fewer workers than peasants. Politically, Communist rule was to be on behalf of the proletariat. How long could the party continue to govern

[2]Joseph V. Stalin, *Works,* Vol. 13, *July 1930–January 1934.* (Moscow: 1955), 40–1.

confronted by increasingly prosperous peasants, small businessmen, and private traders, whose class interest and actions were distinctly petty bourgeois? Economically, something had to be done. The post-1921 recovery had been dramatic, but it had been based on earlier capital investment and by 1927 it was slowing down. If Russia were to move ahead, new investments and production were needed.

All in the party agreed on the necessity to industrialize; the difficult question was how to do this, in the absence of revolutions in the highly industrialized countries of the West. At the very end of his life Lenin talked vaguely about using cooperatives or about the importance of stimulating revolutions in Asia, but he patently had no answer. How to industrialize, because it was such an urgent question for the Communist party, became an important issue in the debates that accompanied the struggle for power after Lenin died. The position of the Right Opposition, led by Nicholas Bukharin, was to industrialize through intensified NEP, very much as the western European countries had originally done it. This would mean encouraging a productive agriculture, the surplus of which could be accumulated to invest in industry and to trade abroad in exchange for advanced technology. In other words the Soviet Union would benefit from the normal exchange between city and countryside, the former making larger numbers of manufactured goods to trade for the latter's increasing crop yields, with government taxation of this process providing capital with which to build new factories.

Opponents criticized the Right's plan on three main grounds: it was a slow process, as the Right leaders readily admitted, whereas the Soviet Union needed to build its strength and its socialist base quickly for both national security and ideological reasons. Second, it permitted politically unreliable peasants and traders to play a dangerously key role in the process. Finally, and most damningly, the urban-rural economic nexus, instead of improving, began to break down in 1927–28, when peasants withheld grain from the market because they believed prices of manufactured articles were rising faster than the price of grain. Faced by unfavorable terms of trade, peasants ate more, hoarded grain, and made it into illicit vodka.

The Left Opposition, headed first by Trotsky and later by Zinoviev, argued that only high-tempo industrialization could produce the rapid economic growth socialist Russia required. Consequently, the peasantry must be taxed and squeezed in order to provide "primitive socialist accumulation" of capital, which could then be quickly infused into the rapidly expanding industrial sector. The Right denigrated this scheme as visionary, concluding "You can't build today's factories with tomorrow's bricks."

But another aspect of Trotsky's views, part of his theory of permanent or uninterrupted revolution, was that the Bolsheviks must carry the proletarian revolution into Europe and Asia as quickly as possible because the building of socialism in Russia depended on the triumph of the world revolution abroad. Or, put another way, the Soviet Union could and should launch the process of rapid development but could complete it only with the help of outside revolution, which the Communist party should work vigorously to promote.

Between 1924 and 1928 Stalin occupied a middle position, not accepting high-tempo industrialization but criticizing the proposal of the Right as too slow and dangerous. Most importantly Stalin vigorously attacked Trotsky's view that Russia had to depend on revolutions abroad, propounding instead a doctrine that came to be known as "socialism in one country." He based his case on a single quotation from Lenin, taken out of context. In a 1916 article Lenin had speculated that in exceptional circumstances it might be possible for a country that experienced a proletarian revolution to build socialism alone, in its own borders, without help from the international socialist revolution that both Marx and Lenin had previously considered integral to the process. Lenin, however, made it clear that this could happen *only* in an advanced industrialized country. Stalin nevertheless applied the idea to Russia, and it was naturally immensely popular. In essence what Stalin told his fellow citizens was that we Soviet comrades, by our own effort, sweat, and ingenuity, can build the glorious socialist future in our homeland without having to rely on help from outside. It was an appealing nationalistic vision and helped him to secure support from within the Communist party in his struggle against Trotsky and his other rivals.

After he had defeated the Left Opposition and as he was emerging in 1928 as the undisputed head of the party and leader of the country, Stalin adopted the Left's high-tempo plan as his own and determined to carry through a radical transformation of Soviet society. According to Robert C. Tucker, one of Stalin's best biographers, Stalin may have wanted to emulate his hero, Lenin: to make his own revolution to match the one Lenin had led in 1917, and to make his mark in Soviet and Communist history as Lenin had. The program Stalin espoused initially had three major components: complete nationalization and socialization of all nonfarming activity, from large industry to small service establishments; central state planning, under which economic decisions were made at the top and transmitted down to all enterprises; and extensive expansion of mechanization and new technology in every branch of economic activity. The State Planning Commission, known as Gosplan, drew up the first Five-Year Plan for the Soviet Union in August 1928, with the substantial but not unthinkable goal of increasing industrial output by 120 percent by 1934. In the following year Stalin decided to up the pace of industrialization and doubled the goal. This required herculean efforts and seemed an unattainable objective.

Another aspect of Stalin's economic revolution was *collectivization:* transferring all peasant land, whether managed by the commune or by individuals, into new agricultural units called collective farms, which all peasants had to join. They were also required to contribute most of their livestock and tools to the collective farm. As you might expect, poor peasants were delighted and richer peasants were outraged. The party labeled the latter *kulaks* and during collectivization directed its main attacks against them.

Collective farms operate today, with minor modification, much as they did in 1929. Members of the farm share the work and the profits, according to the number of workday units an individual has contributed. But before profits the farm must provide a certain share of its produce to the state: in 1929 a fixed amount to be delivered, and today, most commonly, a certain percentage of the output to be sold to state agencies. From the party's point of view an obvious advantage of the collective farm system is that it gives party planners and state administrators greater control over agricultural production and particularly makes more predictable how much the state-run economy will obtain from agriculture. When peasants were individual proprietors and could trade on the open market, it was difficult for the government to know what was going to be produced and how much of it would enter the marketplace.

In my view this degree of control was the main reason Stalin and his advisers finally opted for collectivization and pushed it so hard, but there is widespread disagreement among Western specialists in Soviet affairs on the circumstances of and motivations for the decision to collectivize. Some writers argue that the planners never intended it to be the main method of organizing agriculture but that when the peasants started to withhold grain from the market and thus threatened the industrialization drive, overzealous party officials at the national and local levels began to push collectivization as a way of intimidating the peasants, and it soon acquired a momentum of its own. In any case at the end of 1929 and the beginning of 1930 collectivization was pursued so vigorously that Stalin had to make a speech, "Dizzy with Success," urging restraint on party cadres and offering peasants a chance to withdraw from the collective farms. Many did so, but in subsequent months pressure to form such farms was slowly but steadily increased until by 1936, 90 percent of all farming in the Soviet Union was collectivized, with most of the rest organized in farms run directly by the state.

Many collective farms were organized by pressure and, if required, by force. A Soviet friend of mine, then a young student, recalled being sent to the countryside to assist in the collectivization drive. She and her comrades went door to door trying to persuade the peasants to join. If they were not won over, the army would be called in, the village surrounded, the most recalcitrant peasants loaded on trucks to be sent to Siberia or Central Asia, and the remainder required to sign up, virtually at gunpoint. In some areas there was violence as peasants physically resisted, and in 1933 there was a major famine, which some critics believe the Soviet government did nothing to alleviate, in which several million peasants died. In addition, many peasants, rather than give up their livestock, slaughtered them. As a result, Soviet livestock herds were on the average reduced by as much as one half and had not recovered their pre-1929 numbers when they were decimated again by World War II.

Whatever the debates on the origins of collectivization, almost all Western analysts agree that the program was an economic disaster. Peasant disruption and resistance meant that under the First Five-Year Plan agricultural output increased only 65 percent of its planned target, creating the necessity to ration food in the Soviet Union. Moreover, in the long run, collective farm agriculture has not proved to be efficient, and as we will see in Chapter 13, it remains a major problem in the Soviet Union today.

Industrialization under the First Five-Year Plan enjoyed a greater success. The plan was declared completed at the end of 1932, after four years and three months. Although there were many difficulties and its goals were not fully met, the astonishing fact is how much progress had been made. The planners had counted on good weather, large crop yields, and substantial increases in agricultural productivity; in fact, there were two years of bad weather and crop failures, plus the disastrous collectivization already discussed. The planners had also assumed reduced defense costs and expanding trade with the outside world. Instead, because of Japanese expansion in Manchuria, the Soviet Union spent more on defense, and the great world depression that began in 1929 meant that Soviet foreign trade fell off, with the Soviet Union therefore unable to buy as much Western technology as it needed.

The Second Five-Year Plan was completed in 1933–37, and the Third Plan was two thirds over when Hitler attacked the Soviet Union in June, 1941. During the twelve years of intensive industrialization, from 1928 to 1940, Soviet industry grew fitfully but at an average pace of 12–14 percent a year, an impressive performance surpassed only by the Japanese in the 1950s and 1960s. The urban population doubled, as did the number of workers. The plans emphasized heavy industry, which showed the greatest gains. For example, steel production increased fourfold, coal production fivefold, and generation of electric power ninefold. Plan goals were set in terms of quantity output, so that generally quality was slighted. Improving the quality of goods in the Soviet economy remains today a major objective of Soviet planners.

Outside heavy industry the Five-Year Plans achieved much less success. Production goals for light industry and for consumer goods and services were consistently underfulfilled, and agriculture lagged even further behind. As with raising quality, increasing agricultural output and production of consumer goods is a continuing concern of the Soviet regime today.

No one can doubt that the massive effort to industrialize the Soviet

Union in the 1930s produced a substantial economic base for the society and paved the way for the nation to become the second largest industrial power in the world (after the United States) after World War II. The more difficult questions are, How was it done and what did it cost? In the decades since, Soviet leaders have encouraged developing nations in the Third World to follow the Soviet pattern of industrialization and with it the Soviet ideology of Marxism–Leninism. For some in Asia, Africa, and Latin America this has been a tempting idea, in the light of apparent Soviet successes. Although only a few countries have chosen to take this route, the potential appeal remains: the Communist model seems to promise a quick build-up of industry and strength and rapid emergence as a power in world affairs.

In analyzing the Soviet performance one feature stands out. Soviet industrialization required total mobilization of all resources, material and human, of the country. In turn, this demanded prescriptive centralized planning of the economy and maximum control over every institution and individual member of the society. High-tempo growth under Soviet conditions left no room for the operation of autonomous interest groups or the enterprise and wishes of private individuals. Party and state set the goals, chose the methods, managed the effort, and ensured that each Soviet citizen made the contribution that the plan required. In this way industrialization greatly reinforced the authoritarian trends already present in Bolshevism, with which Stalin was enamored. As a result, the Stalinist system can best be summed up as a blend of Bolshevism (one-party rule), industrialization (mobilization and total control), and Stalinism (paranoia and the use of terror).

Stalin and the party used three basic instruments to ensure all-out participation by the Soviet people in industrialization and in the Stalinist system: persuasion, incentives, and coercion. All three still play a role in Soviet society today. Western critics sometimes overlook the genuine enthusiasm with which many Soviet citizens supported the industrialization effort, despite the heavy sacrifices it required. Several appeals the party stressed were particularly enticing. First, there was the vision of the future. The hard work, low pay, and wretched conditions of the present were simply a down payment on the better life for all socialism promised. "Perhaps you, but certainly your children, will enjoy prosperity and happiness in the decades ahead," exhorted party members and government propaganda.

Second, there were appeals to patriotism, both the ideological variety calling for diligence and devotion to defend the socialist revolution and the first workers' state and the nationalistic sort that urged people to sacrifice so that Mother Russia could become strong enough to repulse external enemies. Chauvinism became increasingly prominent as the threat from Nazi Germany grew.

Finally, there was the subtle call to commit oneself to this great crusade, to find personal satisfaction in working shoulder to shoulder with one's fellow-comrades for the good of all. Some of these themes can be identified in the following passage from a Soviet novel about the heroic construction of a new factory:

> On the landing of the steel-trellised tower stood Gleb, Shidky, and Badin, the members of the Factory Committee. . . . Right and Left in long rows red flags blazoned like beacon-fires. . . .
>
> In the distance a band was playing a march, and from the depths came the thunderous clamor of the people mingled with the roar of the Diesel engines and the clanging of metal. It was impossible to distinguish the roar of the crowd from the roar of machinery. Brynza was right: machines and people are one. . . .
>
> The factory! What strength had been put into it, and what struggle! But here it was—a giant, a beauty! Not long ago it had been a corpse, a devil's mud-heap, a ruin, a warren. And now the Diesels roared. The cables vibrated with electricity, and the pulleys of the ropeway sang. Tomorrow the first giant cylinder of the rotary furnaces would begin to revolve, and from this huge smokestack grey clouds of steam and dust would roll. . . .
>
> And he, Gleb, no longer existed; there was only an unbearable rapture in his heart which was almost bursting from the flooding blood. The working class, the Soviet, the great life they were constructing! God damn it, we understand how to suffer, but we also know the grandeur of our strength. . . .[3]

As a second mode of mobilizing the citizenry for industrialization, Stalin and the party provided two kinds of incentives. The first was material, primarily higher pay for producing more or for working in dangerous conditions or in a remote area. Under war communism some ideologues had wanted to move toward equal pay for all, but Stalin made clear in the early 1930s that in building socialism the motto would be "to each according to his work" and that the slogan "to each according to his needs" would come into effect only when socialism had triumphed completely, on a world-wide scale. Engineers, technicians, and skilled workers were paid more than laborers and unskilled workers, and almost everyone was paid on a piecework basis. Norms or goals of output were set for different categories of work, and those who overfulfilled their norms were rewarded financially, as well as being lionized. In fact, the Soviet government encouraged a whole movement to stimulate record-breaking output, called Stakhanovism after Alexis Stakhanov, a Soviet coal miner who consistently produced amounts of coal way beyond his production quotas. Another, more subtle incentive was the chance to move ahead in society, to achieve quickly higher status and more prestige. Those who were loyal to the party and worked hard could expect to be promoted rapidly, and Stalin created a whole new gener-

---

[3] F. V. Gladkov, *Cement* (London: 1929), 302–4.

ation of upwardly mobile administrators and technicians to staff the party and the government.

Finally, persuasion and incentives were backed up by coercion. Labor discipline in the factories was tightened, and those who worked poorly faced not just peer pressure, ridicule, and ostracization but loss of their job, cancellation of their work card (needed for employment anywhere), and even sentencing to a correctional labor camp as a "wrecker" or "saboteur" of the industrial effort. We now know that many of those sent to the camps were put to hard labor, undertaking especially dangerous or heavy construction tasks or carrying out routine jobs, such as timbering or mining, but in unbearable climatic conditions. Millions died in the forced labor camps. Moreover, coercion was used against the peasants, as we saw, and in general anyone who resisted party policy, or just tried to stand aside, was subject to harassment, intimidation, and eventually arbitrary arrest, imprisonment, and dispatch to the camps.

These methods of ensuring total immersion of the whole population in the industrialization drive were applied in all areas of Soviet life. No area could escape being harnessed to the overall effort. The arts, science, education, sports, what was left of the Orthodox and other churches in Russia, and even the writing and teaching of history—all were expected to orient their goals and activities to promote industrialization. It was a countrywide, across-the-board struggle.

What was the cost? Much of the price the Soviet people paid has already been alluded to: millions dead, millions more in labor camps, and the party and state intruding into every aspect of a person's life. Moreover, in the 1930s Soviet wage earners suffered a decline in their standard of living from its level in the 1920s, and because of the influx of new workers into the cities housing conditions deteriorated and for several years food was rationed. Most peasants were clearly worse off, although many who moved to work in the new factories eventually improved their lot. Was industrialization worth the cost? Some Soviet citizens believe it was, as we saw at the start of the chapter. Others do not, and it is a question that can only be answered in the long run in terms of an individual's own values and principles. Nevertheless, in assessing the outcome of industrialization it is important to consider whether there was perhaps another way, a plan and a set of methods that might have achieved comparable results but at a lower cost. For Third World leaders deciding how to proceed in developing their own countries, this consideration must loom large.

The Stalinist System

We noted earlier that the Stalinist system grew out of an agglomeration of three elements: the authoritarian traditions of Bolshevism, the total mobilization and control demanded by industrialization, and the suspicions and resort to terror of Stalin himself. Before turning to this last point, we need to summarize the formal structure of Soviet society in the 1930s.

The country was a federation of Soviet socialist republics, as Stalin's new constitution of 1936 confirmed. The various republics and smaller national units operated under the slogan "national in form, socialist in content." This meant that although some measure of autonomy in cultural matters and local government was encouraged, ideology and political control were to be unswervingly communist. It is unclear just how the national minorities fared (and still fare) under this arrangement. Some observers believe they have been better off than under tsarist russification, with a flowering of their own culture, educational opportunities, economic development, and a chance to exercise local rights. Others conclude that non-Russians have been exploited and oppressed under Communist, predominantly Great Russian, domination, with strict centralized control by the party, heavy migration of Russians into the non-Russian republics, limited opportunities for social and political advancement for minorities, and economic and cultural discrimination against local regions. Although information is scanty, it seems reasonable to conclude that there have been both continuing Russian domination and considerable social, economic, and cultural progress for the minorities.

Federal, republic, and local governments were (and are) all based on soviets, councils of deputies at various levels elected directly by all Soviet citizens. The population is expected, exhorted, and pressured to vote, and turnouts of 99 percent of the electorate are regularly achieved. There is no political contest since only a single slate of candidates is presented to the voter (a few defiant voters cross out the list or otherwise mar their ballots, but they are exceptional). The Communist party arranges the nomination of the candidates (not all are party members) and controls the actions of the soviets. The highest representative body is the Supreme Soviet, which confirms the official government, the USSR Council of Ministers.

Only about 7 percent of the population are party members, but the party sets and revises both ideology and policy, manages and oversees the government, and directs and controls judicial, social, economic, and cultural life. It does this through party units in every institution and at every level of the system. For example, if this were the Soviet Union, your college or university (or whatever institution you are associated with) would have a party committee that would advise the administration, organize meetings of students and employees to explain national policy and to encourage everyone to work harder, and would keep a weather eye on the general conduct and progress of the institution and its members. Each party unit elects representatives to the next highest party body, and the topmost group is the Central Committee, several hundred leading party officials who elect the Politburo, or executive committee, usually consisting of ten to fifteen members, which in effect runs the country. Party members are expected to be exemplars of rectitude and diligence, and their conduct and activity are constantly being scrutinized by party officials and by the secret police. Consequently, some individuals choose not to enter the party, although it remains the chief avenue for advancement to the highest positions in almost all fields of endeavor.

A huge bureaucracy and managerial class run day-to-day life in the Soviet Union. When the 1936 Constitution was adopted, the USSR officially became a one-class proletarian society, although subgroups of workers, collective and state farmers, and the toiling intelligentsia were recognized. In principle the whole society owns the means of production: all significant economic enterprise. In fact, the state, directed by the party, runs the economy, and the average citizen has no say in its operation. Collective farmers are permitted a small plot of private land and a few animals, and all citizens own personal property, including, for the few that can afford it, an automobile. Public housing provides cramped quarters for a very low rent; education and medical care are free. By 1940 almost all Soviet citizens under age fifty were literate, and today there are universal seven-year education and almost no illiteracy.

These basic features of Soviet life were established or consolidated under the Stalinist system. Because of the system of incentive pay and the superior economic and political position of high state and party officials, the 1930s saw increasing social differentiation. The Yugoslav Marxist critic Milovan Djilas has even argued that the elite of the government and the party form a "new class" of rulers determined to defend their privileges against the mass of the population.

A puzzling aspect of the Stalinist system was its increasing reliance on terror. Historians have advanced various explanations of this phenomenon, but none seems entirely satisfactory. Lenin and the early Bolsheviks had resorted to terror in the desperate days of the civil war and had not hesitated to use force to suppress bloodily the peasant uprisings and the Kronstadt rebellion in 1921. Yet it was never a regularized part of the early Soviet system. Political opponents were encouraged to emigrate or to drop out of politics; the secret police existed but had limited jurisdiction and authority; and there was no extensive system of forced labor camps. Even Stalin in the late 1920s did not eliminate the rivals he defeated, sending a few such as Trotsky into exile and demoting others, such as Bukharin and Zinoviev. Between 1934 and 1938, however, all this changed in an escalating series of purges, arrests, banishments to labor camps, and finally mass terror against a large part of the population.

Attempts to explain this nightmarish period as the consolidation and reshaping of power by Stalin, as an evolving component of the Stalinist system—the cleansing of the party—that somehow ran amok, or as a coldly calculating effort by Stalin to ready the country for war and to ensure that he would have a free hand in foreign policy are, singly, or even taken together, simply not convincing. Since Stalin destroyed both the records and most of the high officials involved, we will probably never know precisely what led to the purges and terror. Rational and policy considerations there undoubtedly were, but any persuasive explanation of this era must take account of Stalin's warped personality and outlook. Much of what occurred only makes sense if it stemmed in part from the disturbed mentality, pathological cruelty, and extreme paranoia of Stalin himself. Insecure despite having established a dictatorship over the party and the country, hostile and defensive when confronted by criticism of the excesses of collectivization and of the sacrifices required by high-tempo industrialization, and deeply suspicious that past, present, and even yet unknown future opponents were plotting against him, Stalin began in 1934 to act as a person beleaguered. He soon struck back wildly at enemies, real or imaginary. The atmosphere of uncertainty, fear, and denunciation spread rapidly through the Soviet system and soon began to feed on itself. Petty tyrants sprang up at all levels of the party and the bureaucracy, and soon almost the whole society was engulfed by recriminations, irrational punishments, and paralyzing terror.

Our account can only touch on what happened at the highest levels of the party and government, but readers are reminded that the terror reached into almost every Soviet family and that its victims suffered terribly in both psychological and physical terms (an unforgettable account is *Journey into the Whirlwind* by Evgenia Ginzburg). During 1933–34, shortly after the Second Five-Year Plan started, there was considerable grumbling across the Soviet Union about the continuing rapid pace and intense pressure of the industrialization drive. This was reflected within the party, and at the Seventeenth Party Congress opposition to Stalin surfaced, which undoubtedly frightened him. In any case, for reasons that are unclear, on 1 December 1934, Sergei Kirov, a popular party leader and head of the party organization in Leningrad (Petrograd renamed after Lenin's death) was murdered by an operative of the secret police. There is some evidence that Stalin ordered the killing. If so, he may have wished to eliminate a potential rival or perhaps he needed a pretext to undertake a broader attack on possible opposition within the party.

In any case the investigation of Kirov's murder touched off a widening offensive aimed at first at such 1920s opponents of Stalin as Kamenev, Zinoviev, and several other "Old Bolsheviks" of Lenin's generation. In January 1935 this group was arrested and imprisoned, and a few months later they were accused of complicity in Kirov's murder. In the summer of 1936 Zinoviev, Kamenev, and fourteen others were publicly tried, the charges now including not only subversion of the party but treason to the Soviet state on the grounds that some of the alleged conspirators had connived with Trotsky, who was still in exile in Europe, and with agents of the Nazis. Further trials took place in 1937 and 1938. In these "show" trials most of the defendants confessed to crimes they had not committed, probably as a consequence of intimidation (perhaps torture), drugs, and psychological brainwashing. The last technique became the basis of Arthur Koestler's famous novel *Darkness at Noon*. Those not prepared to confess were generally shot without trial. Nicholas Bukharin, however, may have outwitted his persecutors as the following excerpt from his initial plea and final statement at his trial reveals:

> I plead guilty to . . . the sum total of crimes committed by this counter-revolutionary organization, irrespective of whether or not I knew of, whether or not I took a direct part in, any particular act [his denial of guilt]. . . .
> For when you ask yourself: "If you must die, what are you dying for?"— an absolutely black vacuity suddenly arises before you with startling vividness. There was nothing to die for, if one wanted to die unrepented. And, on the contrary, everything positive that glistens in the Soviet Union acquires new dimensions in a man's mind.[4] [his rejection of Stalinism]

Stalin had him shot.

The terror reached its climax in 1936–38. Its dimensions are hard to believe. Seven to eight million people were arrested, of whom some three million were shot or died in prison. Millions more were sent to forced labor camps, where many of them died. A major target was the Communist party itself, with 40 percent of its members arrested and the top leadership destroyed. Almost 70 percent of the delegates to the Seventeenth Party Congress in 1934 were arrested, most of whom were shot. One hundred ten of the 139 members of the 1934 Central Committee were killed or driven to suicide. The generation that had made the October Revolution and built the Soviet state was eliminated, with few exceptions. Their places were quickly filled by a rough, less educated, ambitious new generation willing to knuckle under to Stalin, among whom were future leaders of the Soviet Union, Nikita Khrushchev and Leonid Brezhnev.

The army was decimated, as well. Only a few years before Hitler's attack on the Soviet Union, the Red Army lost to the purges three of the five highest-ranking officers (called marshals of the Soviet Union), thirteen of fifteen commanders of army groups, 90 percent of all generals, and 80 percent of all colonels. Other elites in Soviet society—the professions, economic managers, and writers and artists—were similarly destroyed. Even the secret police fell victim, several of its chiefs

---

[4] Bukharin's inital plea is found in Stephen F. Cohen, *Bukharin and the Bolshevik Revolution: A Political Biography, 1888–1938* (New York: 1973), 377; his final statement is in Walsh, *Readings in Russian History*, vol. 3, 770–71.

being accused and executed. Finally, in early 1939 the purge wound down, perhaps because Stalin recognized that conflict with Germany was an imminent possibility. Throughout and after the purges the official cult of Stalin continued to grow unabashedly. The monstrous crimes associated with the terror did nothing to temper the fulsome praise and repetitive flattery the Soviet press heaped on Stalin, tributes that he apparently craved and accepted as his due.

Soviet Culture, 1917–53

An area greatly affected by the conservatism, rigidity, and authoritarianism of the Stalinist system was the arts. For a decade after the October Revolution experimentation and daring marked much of the work in Soviet literature, theater, and the visual arts. Some of this was a continuation of the modernism and avant-garde trends that we saw characterized Russian culture in the first years of the twentieth century. But this artistic boldness was now linked to a sense of responsibility to society and to the glorious new order the revolution was to bring. Mayakovsky, among many others, placed his talents at the service of the new Soviet state, designing posters, writing propaganda poems, and staging pageants and plays with revolutionary themes. A few artists, like Marc Chagall, felt uncomfortable bearing this burden of social commitment and moved to the West. But many others, like Vsevolod Meyerhold, the innovative theater producer, and Sergei Prokofiev, the composer, while keeping in touch with artistic movements in the West, continued to develop bold new forms and themes within Soviet Russia. As a result, the 1920s were years of great artistic ferment and of considerable achievement, with Soviet artists making major contributions to world culture in such fields as music and the cinema. For example, Sergei Eisenstein, the creative film producer and director, helped to pioneer new techniques, and his major films remain classics today.

Much of this modernist art and experimental creativity was quite incomprehensible to the masses of Soviet society, many of them illiterate or barely educated. Consequently, some critics, within the arts and within the party, began to insist that Soviet culture should strive to achieve greater simplicity and directness, and that it should instruct and uplift the average Soviet citizen. This point of view received a decisve boost when the "second revolution" began in 1928. Every aspect of Soviet life was to be conscripted to help drive the engine of industrialization, and the arts were soon assigned the role of instilling enthusiasm, patriotism, and a dedication to higher production goals among the Soviet public. Artists were called upon to serve as "engineers of the soul." This new trend was officially confirmed in 1934, with promulgation of the doctrine of "socialist realism," which still remains the guiding principle of the arts in the Soviet Union.

The principle of socialist realism is that the artist or writer is enjoined to portray life not as it really is but as it ought to be. Individuals are to act positively, and events are expected to develop in ways that accord with the policies and goals of the party. The heroes must be clearly delineated, and the villains appropriately characterized. Happy endings are common, and although the charge that too often the farm boy meets girl but marries tractor is exaggerated, many socialist realist stories and plays have a predictability and sameness that make them tedious, if not downright boring. Socialist realist art, for example, does not intend to portray a "real" worker or peasant but rather a romanticized version of what they ought to look like.

Although a few creative artists, like the composer Dmitri Shostakovich and the poets Anna Akhmatova and Boris Pasternak, were able to continue to produce fine pieces, even when criticized for not adhering to the guidelines of socialist realism, most Soviet literary and artistic works of the 1930s and 1940s were banal and uninteresting. How much they served their purpose of inculcating uplifting values and attitudes among the bulk of the population is difficult to tell, but certainly the vitality of Soviet intellectual and cultural life declined in this period. Science and technology, which had been given an influential role to play in industrialization, continued to advance, although even there, in certain fields, party orthodoxy intruded, as for example when Stalin endorsed the erroneous views of the geneticist Trofim Lysenko, mandating that all scientists adhere to them.

Stalin and the World, 1928–46

During the late 1920s the Soviet Union continued the two-track foreign policy it had begun as soon as the Soviet state was established: promotion of proletarian revolutions abroad, and accommodation and trade with other nations. As had happened earlier, pursuit of the former goal made the latter more difficult at various times, and in 1927 there was even a "war scare" in the Soviet Union, a fear that Great Britain, perhaps assisted by France, might attack the USSR, partly as a result of revelations of Soviet-sponsored subversive activity in England.

Stalin and Trotsky had clashed over the degree of emphasis to give to inciting socialist revolutions in other countries, with Trotsky urging a more aggressive policy in this regard. But whatever line the Soviet Union took seemed to backfire. In China, for example, Stalin, after Trotsky's expulsion from the party, pressured the small Chinese Communist movement to ally temporarily with the larger Nationalist forces, led by Chiang Kai-shek. In 1927, however, Chiang turned on his Communist collaborators and destroyed all but a remnant of the Chinese Communist party. On the other hand, in Germany Stalin advised the German Communists not to make common cause with the moderate Marxist party, the Social Democrats, against the nascent Hitlerite movement. Again, the result was disaster: The Communists fought the Social Democrats tooth and nail, thus making it easier for Hitler and the Nazis to come to power. Once firmly in control, Hitler crushed both the Communists and the Social Democrats.

With Mussolini's Fascists in power in Italy and Hitler's Nazis gaining strength in Germany in the early 1930s, and since both Fascism and Nazism made Communism their chief foe, the Russian Communists agitated vigorously in international meetings for general disarmament and for the signing of nonaggression pacts. This effort met a fairly limited response, although the Soviet Union succeeded in completing nonaggression and mutual defense treaties with Poland in 1934 and with France and Czechoslovakia in 1935.

Beginning in 1933–36 Stalin and his foreign policy advisers took a new tack. On the diplomatic front they urged strengthening the League of Nations, to which the USSR was admitted in 1934, and they espoused the doctrine of collective security. The latter was a call for the nonfascist states, including both the Soviet Union and the Western democracies plus the latter's allies in Eastern Europe, to band together against the menace of Mussolini and Hitler, who were in the process of forming the Rome-Berlin Axis (later joined by militaristic Japan). Meanwhile in the domestic politics of the nonfascist European countries Communist parties were instructed by Moscow to seek political alliances and coalitions with democratic (and occasionally even conservative) parties to ensure that local fascist elements would not seize power. This new policy was called "the united front," or, in the case of France, where such a Communist-democratic coalition came to power temporarily, the Popular Front.

In 1935 and early 1936 the strategy of collective security suffered two serious setbacks. Mussolini conquered Ethiopia, for which the League of Nations administered a slap on the wrist, and Hitler remilitarized the Rhineland area of Germany in defiance of the Versailles peace treaty after World War I, while Britain and France did nothing. In the middle of 1936 General Francisco Franco led a conservative rebellion in Spain against the leftist antifascist government there. The resulting Spanish Civil War provided a major test of the collective security and united front policies, a test failed by both, which revealed fundamental weaknesses in each.

During the Spanish Civil War Fascist Italy and Nazi Germany supplied financing, weapons, and even some troops to the Franco forces. The Soviet Union eventually aided the existing government, the Loyalists, in the same fashion. But Great Britain and France adopted a stance of neutrality, arguing that it would be illegal to assist the Loyalists. Since collective security depended on the major antifascist powers' acting together, the Anglo-French position undercut the possibility of preventing or punishing Axis intervention in Spain and raised grave doubts in Stalin's mind about the reliability of the Western democracies as partners in the struggle against Hitler. Moreover, within Spain mutual suspicion and mistrust between the democratic parties and the Communists weakened the Loyalist war effort, and in the end the Communists used the situation to destroy some of their political enemies on the left. This outcome naturally alarmed democratic elements in the rest of Europe about the real purposes of the Communists in a united front.

By 1938, after Hitler had swallowed up Austria and German ambitions seemed boundless, it was clear that Europe was moving toward war. It became a three-sided game, almost like a love triangle:

Great Britain France	Germany Italy	USSR

The question was which two would ally against the third. At the time the most likely and natural alignment appeared to be the Soviet Union and the Western democracies against the Axis. But since strong conservative and profascist forces existed in France and, to a lesser extent, in Britain, a combination of Germany-Italy with the Western countries against the Communist menace, so detested in fascist and Nazi propaganda, was certainly a possibility, one that Stalin and his advisers greatly feared, given their Marxist distrust of capitalism. Least likely seemed a match between the USSR and the Axis, separated as they were by an immense ideological gulf. Yet it happened.

Two developments in 1938 apparently led Stalin to decide to cast his lot with Hitler, as incredible as this tie seemed. The first was the outbreak in 1937–38 of substantial armed clashes with Japan along the border between the Soviet Union and Japanese-occupied Manchuria. The Red Army acquitted itself well, but Stalin was concerned that if he became involved in war with Hitler, Japan might seize the opportunity to attack Siberia, catching the USSR in the vise of a two-front war.

Second was the crisis over Czechoslovakia, details of which are still being debated by historians and in any case lie beyond our scope. The essential point for Stalin, however, was that when Hitler brazenly threatened an important ally of both the Soviet Union and the Western powers, the latter reneged on their treaty obligations, backed down, and meekly handed Czechoslovakia on a silver platter to Hitler at the Munich Conference in September 1938. What sort of collective security was this? What did this say about the reliability of the Western powers as allies against Hitler? Did it not suggest that they hoped to get the Soviet Union embroiled with Germany and then stand aside?

The USSR was also pledged to aid Czechoslovakia, but we will probably never know whether the Soviet Union would have made good on this commitment. The Soviet government said that it was prepared to, but since its promise was contingent on French support of the Czechs, which did not materialize, the Soviet Union never had to act.

Regardless of what Soviet intentions actually were, the lesson Stalin drew from the whole affair was plain. In early 1939 the Soviet foreign minister who had been the architect of the policy of collective security, Maxim Litvinov, resigned, and in a speech of 10 March Stalin subtly suggested the possibility of negotiations to the Germans.

Secret talks got under way a few months later. Although concurrently Soviet diplomats continued to negotiate with the Western democracies about a possible alliance, neither side trusted the other, and those talks languished. On 23 August 1939, the conclusion of a non-aggression treaty between the Soviet Union and Nazi Germany was announced to an astonished world. Hitler achieved his immediate aim, the neutralization of the Red Army, and within ten days he launched an invasion of Poland. This prompted Britain and France to declare war on Germany, and World War II had begun.

Tens of thousands of loyal Communists around the world resigned from their parties because of this bizarre about-face, in which the Soviet Union joined hands with Communism's worst enemy. Stalin seems to have been unconcerned; he had achieved his objectives by this diplomatic coup. First, he had avoided getting entangled in a war with Hitler, especially at a time when the Red Army and Soviet industry were not fully prepared for such a major conflict. Second, he hoped that the Germans, once Britain and France came into the war, would be checked by the Western powers and that the two sides would exhaust themselves in a long struggle. Finally, he had made the Soviet Union far more secure; a by-product of the pact with Hitler was Soviet acquisition of eastern Poland under a secret protocol (still unpublished and unacknowledged officially in the Soviet Union today) and Soviet domination of the Baltic states and of Bessarabia on the USSR's southwestern border (all of these were annexed to the Soviet Union in the summer of 1940). This meant that Stalin had gained considerable territory as a buffer between the Soviet Union and the West, distance that in fact proved valuable when the Nazis invaded the USSR in 1941. In addition, there is some evidence that Stalin, shrewd as he usually was, genuinely believed he had made a deal with Hitler that might last for some time. In *Mein Kampf* and in numerous speeches Hitler had made clear that eventually he intended to conquer Communist Russia. Perhaps Stalin thought it was just brave talk and that because Hitler must be a realist, as Stalin was, Hitler would be content with the division of territory and influence in Eastern Europe that the Nazi-Soviet pact provided for.

Whatever the reasons, Stalin and his advisers acted as if it were a long-term arrangement. The Soviet government soon provoked a quarrel leading to war with Finland, but the Finns fought courageously, though far outnumbered, and retained their independence, although they had to cede some territory to the USSR. The Soviet side assumed that they had a free hand in the Balkans and even revived the old question of Russian interest in the Straits, pressing the Turkish government for bases there. Hitler and his advisers resented this Soviet "pushiness," and in December 1940 Hitler decided to invade Russia the following year.

When the Nazi armies rolled into Russia on 22 June 1941, having earlier in 1940 and 1941 defeated Norway, the Low Countries, and France and having occupied much of the Balkans and Greece, no one was surprised, except perhaps Stalin. For reasons that are still unclear, Stalin right up to the last minute refused to believe that Hitler would attack him, even though British intelligence, his own military authorities, and others had warned the Soviet government for some months that Hitler was preparing the invasion. A Soviet friend of mine who at the time was in an army unit not far behind the front line told me that only some forty-eight hours before the attack were they put on alert.

Caught unaware, the Red Army fell back, sometimes in good order, sometimes in disarray, with heavy losses and with large numbers of prisoners taken (see Figure 17). For the first few days the party and Soviet government made no response, leading to speculation that Stalin panicked at that moment. He finally made a radio address to the Soviet

Figure 17. Russian prisoners captured during the German invasion in the summer of 1941.

people exhorting them to a patriotic defense of their socialist home-land, and he soon created a five-man Defense Committee to organize and direct the war effort. The British, who had been standing alone against Hitler for the past year, rallied to the Soviet cause, and an Anglo-Soviet treaty was signed in July 1941. After the United States entered the war in December 1941 following Japan's attack on Pearl Harbor, the so-called Grand Alliance of the Soviet Union, Great Britain, and the United States (later joined by Free France) was formed to fight Hitler and Mussolini.

In July 1941 the Germans made a decisive breakthrough on the center front but decided not to throw all their strength at Moscow, turning instead to the south with its agricultural and mineral riches, as well as the oil fields of the Caucasus. Nevertheless, by November–December 1941 the Nazi forces had besieged Leningrad and were only a few miles from Moscow, where winter weather and Soviet resistance halted them. Leningrad held out for two and one-half years under in-credibly difficult conditions, and the pressure on Moscow was relieved the following summer by a Soviet counterattack. During the summer of 1942 the Germans renewed their advance, making large gains in the south. At the end of 1942 in a brutal and devastating battle at the city of Stalingrad (formerly Tsaritsyn, today renamed Volgograd), the Red Army in house-to-house and sometimes hand-to-hand fighting checked the German advance. Moreover, because Hitler refused to order a re-treat, most of the German Seventh Army was captured there. The So-viet forces, however, failed to follow up their advantage, and a second major turning point in the military history of the war occurred at the Battle of Kursk in July 1943. Soviet units led by tanks badly defeated and routed a strong German force, starting a German retreat back across Russia that ended only with the occupation of Berlin by the Red Army in April 1945 (see Map 8).

In addition to military mistakes in Russia the Germans made a ma-jor political mistake. When the Nazi forces first entered Russia, many people, particularly Ukranians, welcomed the Germans because they resented Communist rule and exactions. If the Germans had treated the occupied population decently and had met their most basic de-mands, such as breaking up the collective farms and reestablishing religion, they would have greatly weakened the Soviet people's will to resist and perhaps have won the war. But in part because Nazi ideology considered Slavic peoples as "subhuman" and in part because the Ger-mans wanted to exploit the occupied territories economically, they in-stituted a reign of terror. Before long the local population began to re-sist and partisan bands that formed did much to harass the Germans throughout the war. Moreover, word of what German rule was like spread behind the Soviet lines and stiffened the resistance of the Soviet population.

Relations between the Soviet Union and its Western allies were far

THE EASTERN FRONT WORLD WAR II 1939-1945

ALLIED SUPPLY LINE FROM U.S. & BRITAIN

Corinne Abbazia Hekker Graphics

0   400
MILES

Murmansk

White Sea

Archangel

N. Dvina

FINLAND

(War with Russia 1939 - 1940)
·
Joined Germans in attack on Russia, 1941

NORWAY

SWEDEN

Leningrad

U.   S.   S.   R.

Tikhvin

Dec. '41

Volga

Kalinin

Kazan

DENMARK

Baltic Sea

ESTONIA

Riga

Moscow

Gorky

"Polish Corridor"

Danzig

LATVIA

LITHUANIA

Vilnius

Oka

Kuibyshev

EAST PRUSSIA

Smolensk

July '43

Tula

Berlin

Elbe

Oder

GERMANY

Russia

Warsaw

Brest-Litovsk

FARTHEST GERMAN ADVANCE, 1941 - 1942

Allies, April 26, '45

Torgau

POLAND

June '41

Kursk

Voronezh

Danube

CZECHOSLOVAKIA

Lvov

Kiev

Kharkov

Dec. '41

Stalingrad

1939

U   K   R   A   I   N   E

AUSTRIA

Vienna

Budapest

1941

HUNGARY

1940

Bessarabia

Don

Rostov

Volga

ROMANIA

Dnieper

Kuban

1941

(Taken by Germans in 1941)

Belgrade

Bucharest

YUGOSLAVIA

1940

Yalta

Novorossiisk

Mozdok

ITALY

Sofia

CAUCASUS MTS.

Batum

Tbilisi

BULGARIA

Black   Sea

GREECE

Istanbul

Erevan

ALBANIA
(to Italy, 1939)

Izmir

Athens

Ankara

T   U   R   K   E   Y

ALLIED SUPPLY LINE FROM PERSIAN GULF

IRAN

CRETE

(Taken by the Germans, 1941)

	1938 Boundaries	Front lines in Russia	✳ ✳ ✳ ✳ ✳ Russian boundary, 1941
	Axis and occupied areas June 22, 1941	⊣⊢⊣⊢⊣⊢ 1941	
		∿∿∿∿∿∿∿ 1942	
		⋈⋈⋈⋈⋈⋈ 1943	◀ Russian and Allied drives, 1941 - 1945
		✛✛✛✛✛✛ 1944	

MAP 8

from smooth during the war. The latter provided $11 billion in Lend-Lease aid to the USSR, and both sides were committed to the total defeat of Hitler, but prewar suspicions and mistrust lingered. The major bone of contention was how soon the Western powers would open a second front against the Germans, thus relieving pressure on the Russian front. The Allies insisted they needed time to prepare it, that it would be disastrous to launch an invasion of Nazi-occupied Europe prematurely, and that diversionary efforts, such as the campaigns in North Africa and the Allied landing in Italy, did in fact weaken the Nazis and draw forces away from the German-Soviet front. The Soviet leaders kept pressing for an early invasion of Western Europe (it finally took place June 6, 1944), and subsequent Soviet comment has underscored Soviet suspicions that the Allies were deliberately holding back, hoping the Germans and the Russians would exhaust each other, thereby reducing Western casualties and preserving Allied strength as a way of assuring Western domination of the postwar world.

Specific incidents also fueled the bad feeling among the members of the Grand Alliance. For example, Western leaders allied with those Poles who had escaped from Poland and were still fighting Hitler were appalled at the Soviet attitude toward the discovery in eastern Poland of a mass grave of several hundred Polish officers who had been brutally murdered. Despite strong evidence that the perpetrators of this Katyn Forest massacre were Soviet forces, the Soviet government refused to permit an independent investigation and blamed the Germans. There were also difficult diplomatic issues connected with the shape of the postwar world, but we will take those up in Chapter 14.

Conclusion

In May 1945 the Nazis surrendered, and three months later, after a belated Soviet entry into the war against Japan and a token invasion of Manchuria, the Japanese gave up as well. The Soviet Union suffered the greatest loss of life, 20 million military and civilian dead, of any participant in World War II, as well as extensive destruction of almost one third of the country. Yet the Great Fatherland War, as World War II is called in the Soviet Union, acted as a psychological purge, removing the suspicion, tension, and uncertainty of the 1930s. The people and the party eventually banded together in an all-out struggle to defend the country and repulse the German aggressors. By the end of the war Soviet morale and prestige were high, and Soviet writers were heralding the Soviet people as saviors of Western civilization from Nazism, just as the Russians had saved Europe from the Mongols in the thirteenth century and from Napoleon in 1812. Although again the vastness of Russia, assisted by General Winter, General Hunger, and General Mud, had helped the nation survive, Soviet patriotism could

justifiably boast of the triumphs of the Red Army and of the total mobilization of the people for the war effort. As a result, the Soviet Union
emerged from World War II as one of two superpowers, along with the
United States. These two large countries would dominate world affairs
in the decades ahead.

At the same time the Soviet Union was a scarred and exhausted
society. Within a period of seventeen years the Soviet population had
experienced forced industrialization and modernization, the brutal reorganization of rural life in the country, a chilling and inexplicable terror that killed millions of people, and a wearing, savage, and devastating modern war that lasted almost four years. People were shell-shocked
and bewildered. What had their sacrifices meant? Where were they
headed? Would Stalin, whom, after some doubts, they had loyally followed in the fight for survival, at last turn out to be a benevolent leader,
a "good tsar"? For Soviet society in 1945–46 the future was open, and
great hopes could be cherished.

FURTHER READING

Adams, Arthur. *Stalin and His Times.* New York: 1972.

Bialer, S. *Stalin and His Generals.* New York: 1969.

Brown, Edward J. *Russian Literature Since the Revolution.* Cambridge, Mass.: 1982.

Clark, Alan. *Barbarossa: The Russo-German Conflict, 1941–45.* New York: 1965.

Conquest, Robert. *The Great Terror.* New York: 1968.

Curtiss, John S. *The Russian Church and the Soviet State.* Boston: 1953.

Dallin, Alexander. *German Rule in Russia, 1941–45.* New York: 1957.

Deutscher, Isaac. *Stalin, a Political Biography.* New York: 1967.

Erickson, John. *The Soviet High Command . . . 1918–41.* New York: 1962.

Gerschenkron, A. *Economic Backwardness in Historical Perspective.* Cambridge, Mass.:
1962.

Ginzburg, Evgeniia. *Journey Into the Whirlwind.* New York: 1975 [unforgettable
memoir of a victim of the purges].

Kennan, George. *Russia and the West Under Lenin and Stalin.* Boston: 1960.

Koestler, Arthur. *Darkness at Noon.* New York: 1970 [novel about the purges].

McCagg, William. *Stalin Embattled, 1943–48.* Detroit: 1978.

Medvedev, Roy. *Let History Judge: The Origins and Consequences of Stalinism.* New
York: 1973.

Mosely, P.E. *The Kremlin and World Politics.* New York: 1961.

Ulam, Adam. *Expansion and Coexistence . . . 1917–73.* New York: 1973 [a history of Soviet foreign policy].

13

"Mature Socialism": The Soviet Union Since World War II, 1946–85

In the forty years since the end of World War II the Soviet Union has become a major world power, as we shall see in the next chapter, and has continued to modernize socially and economically at a moderate pace. Yet its performance has been disappointing, not just to its own citizens and to outsiders who looked to it as a model for socialist development, but, it seems likely, even to Soviet leaders themselves. The Soviet population is somewhat better off, almost everyone is better educated, and the pressure and terror of Stalinist days are only a distant memory. But the atmosphere is one of stagnation, of indifference, of cynicism. Few Soviet citizens have any enthusiasm for "the Revolution," for socialism, or for a better future of any kind. They seem resigned to more of the same stifling mediocrity.

In politics Stalinism was discarded in the 1950s, only to be replaced by a deadening authoritarianism, a centralized system run by an oligarchy of bureaucratic leaders who command little respect and who seem conservative plodders. Over the years inequalities in the system have increased, inefficiency has mushroomed, and widespread corruption has set in. Economic progress has been agonizingly slow, and the society has become increasingly rigid. Soviet culture has languished, with many talented writers and artists repressed or in exile. In the view of some observers, postwar Soviet society had opportunities for progressive change but somehow "missed the boat." In this chapter tracing Soviet internal history from 1945 to 1985, we will try to see how and why that happened.

Reconstruction and Renewed Stalinism

The central domestic issue facing the Soviet Union in 1945 was finding a way to recover from the staggering losses and devastation of the war, which resulted in widespread hunger and deprivation in 1946–47. A second question was whether the relaxation of Stalinist repression that had occurred as part of the war effort—the slight leeway given artistic and personal expression, the encouragement of the Orthodox religion, the resuscitation of Russian nationalist heroes and traditions— would carry over into the postwar era. Many Soviet citizens believed that reconstruction would take place at a moderate pace, given the enormous sacrifices they had made in the war, and that the wartime allies of the USSR, particularly the United States, might assist in this endeavor. They also hoped that as a reward for their devotion and loyalty that had helped make victory possible, Stalin might make life a shade freer and more pleasant.

The Soviet people did not have to wait long to have their hopes dashed. On 9 February 1946, in the form of an electoral speech on behalf of his candidacy as a deputy to the Supreme Soviet, Stalin announced his harsh and forbidding program for the postwar Soviet Union. He called for sacrifice, superhuman work, and rigid conformity. He made clear the Soviet government would rebuild the country by its own exertions, with minimal help from the West, whose capitalist system Stalin plainly distrusted. Soviet citizens were stunned but had no choice but to settle grimly to the task.

In 1946 and 1947 several developments underscored the completeness and the severity of the renewed Stalinism imposed on the country. As soon as the war was over, the Soviet government made strenuous efforts to recover its citizens who had fallen into Western hands. Some of these were prisoners of war (POWs) captured by the Germans and liberated by the Allies; others were civilians whom the Germans had taken to Germany for forced labor or who had retreated with the German armies when they pulled out of Russia rather than fall under Soviet rule again. In a tragic and terrible blunder the Western governments at first cooperated with Soviet authorities in repatriating both POWs and civilians, many of whom strongly resisted going back. Once they were home Stalin had many of them shot, imprisoned, or sentenced to forced labor.

Other repressive measures Stalin took near the end of and immediately after the war were directed against non-Russian nationalities. He snuffed out further expressions of nationalism and autonomy among groups like the Caucasian peoples and the Ukrainians, who had been permitted during the stress of war to revive a sense of self-identity and traditional values as a means of encouraging them to make an all-out effort in the struggle against Germany. Some smaller national minorities who were accused of collaborating with the Germans, such as the Volga Germans (who immigrated to Russia in the late eighteenth century), the Crimean Tatars, and the Chechen-Ingush, a mountain people in the Caucasus, Stalin eliminated altogether, sending their leaders to forced labor camps and deporting the rest of the population from their areas of residence to Central Asia.

Another problem—much like that after the Napoleonic wars that had spawned the Decembrist movement—that Stalin faced was that hundreds of thousands of Soviet citizens, mostly as officers and soldiers of the Red Army, had visited Europe in 1944–46 and could compare, generally unfavorably, Soviet life with the standard of living they found in such countries as Rumania, Hungary, and even war-torn Germany. To prevent such potential disaffection from spreading, Stalin cut off relations between the Soviet Union and Europe and the United States. By imposing this "iron curtain," as Winston Churchill dubbed it, Stalin prevented Soviet citizens from traveling in the West and blocked the inflow into the USSR of Western people and ideas.

Stalin also instituted the Fourth Five-Year Plan, with high goals for total output and strong emphasis on heavy industry. Not only did this require substantial exertions by the population, but the slighting of housing and consumer industry meant that living conditions for the average citizen improved only slightly and slowly from the stringent level of wartime. The Soviet people were expected to work hard but to benefit little. Nevertheless, by the early 1950s, with the help of reparations from Germany, Eastern Europe, and Manchuria, the country was largely rebuilt, and production surpassed prewar levels.

Finally, Stalin launched a virulent ideological attack on capitalism abroad and on deviations from Stalinist orthodoxy at home. During the wartime Grand Alliance, Stalin and the Soviet government had played down the Marxist-Leninist view that the socialist and capitalist systems were inherently antagonistic, but in 1947 Stalin reaffirmed strongly that the world was divided into two camps, a peace-loving socialist one led by the Soviet Union and a war-mongering, aggressive one led by the United States. He called upon the Soviet people to make sacrifices to ready the Soviet Union for defense against threatened attacks by American imperialism, and he appealed to all "progressive" people in the world to rally to the Soviet cause. At the same time, as we shall see in chapter 14, political and diplomatic relations with the West were deteriorating into a "cold war," and Stalin was imposing puppet regimes on Eastern Europe (see Map 9).

The domestic implications of this ideological hardening were a crackdown in Soviet intellectual life and a new emphasis on Stalinist orthodoxy. A number of Soviet writers, composers, and artists were attacked for "bourgeois cosmopolitanism," that is, for not adhering closely enough to socialist realism in their work and to the Stalinist line generally in their attitudes. Since a large proportion of those castigated were Jews, there was an undertone of anti-Semitism in this campaign.

As he grew older, Stalin became increasingly suspicious, isolated, and irrational. He ruled virtually alone, acting through a personal secretariat and through a set of party and government officials who were expected to carry out his orders unquestioningly and who were too

MAP 9

frightened to suggest alternative policies. Consequently, we know little about the motivations for Stalin's policies or what was occurring behind the scenes. In 1952, for reasons that are unclear, Stalin convened a Party Congress, the first since 1939. He also made some slight shifts in foreign policy. Whether these moves presaged a major change of direction and the initiation of new programs, as some have speculated, or whether they were simply the groundwork for a violent new purge, as others have concluded, is simply not known. Muddying the situation was the "Doctors' Plot," charges that were published a few weeks before Stalin died accusing a group of physicians, including several who worked in the Kremlin, the seat of the government and the party, of attempting to poison high officials. Many of the doctors were Jews, but whether this story was an omen of a new reign of terror with a strong anti-Semitic tone is not clear. After Stalin's death the doctors were exonerated.

The Succession to Stalin and the Khrushchev Era

On 5 March 1953, Stalin, who was then seventy-four years old, died, apparently from natural causes. Rumors that he was poisoned seem to be pure speculation. With Stalin gone and no arrangements for the succession, the Communist leaders who had surrounded him in his last years appealed, in rather apprehensive tones, for the Soviet public to remain calm and for support for "collective leadership," that is, for rule by the members of the Politburo (at that time called the Presidium). At the same time they began jockeying for position, hoping to capture the supreme power that Stalin had wielded. Two of the chief contenders were Georgi Malenkov, a party secretary, and Lavrenti Beria, the head of the secret police (known as the KGB after its Russian initials). The struggle for power seemed to end in a victory for Malenkov, when Beria was arrested dramatically at a meeting of top leaders in July 1953 and later shot. Apparently his colleagues feared that with his control over the police and what he presumably knew about them, Beria was a threat to them all.

The main challenges Malenkov faced were consolidating his power as first among equals and finding a way to reduce the rigidity and constriction of the Stalinist system without endangering the absolute control of the party over the government and society. Something had to be done about the Stalinist system because it had become increasingly inefficient and unproductive in its latter years. The population as a whole was cowed by the threat of terror and exhausted from the continuing demands Stalin imposed upon them. Party officials and government bureaucrats had been paralyzed from making decisions or introducing new ideas because they were unsure of Stalin's views and opinions and because he might decree at any time a new orthodoxy or policy that would put them in the wrong—and hence at a minimum demoted and disgraced and at the worst packed off to a forced labor camp. At the end of the Stalinist era, the system was creaking to a halt, with productivity, commitment, and progress all faltering.

The first steps Malenkov took were tentative but promising. Police terror was relaxed, many political prisoners were released, and Soviet citizens were assured that arbitrary arrests were a thing of the past. The party emphasized "strict Leninist legality," which gave people a clear idea of where they stood and the boundaries of how far they could go in thought and action before running afoul of the regime. Intellectuals were encouraged to be more creative and to innovate to some extent. Managers and bureaucrats were instructed to think of new ideas and to participate more actively in economic decision making. Malenkov proposed greater emphasis on consumer goods and on agriculture. Finally, he began to make changes in foreign policy.

In the months that these first concessions were being implemented, however, the political struggle behind the scenes was continuing. In February 1955 Malenkov was ousted as prime minister, and Nikita Khrushchev (Hroosh-choff) emerged as the new dominant figure in the party and government. Khrushchev was entirely a self-made man (see Figure 18). Born the son of a peasant turned coal miner in southwestern Russia, he had risen by grit and ambition through the party, which educated him along the way, to become party boss in the Ukraine. Ebullient, coarse, and independent-minded, he had managed to escape Stalin's wrath and, through his strong connections in the party, gained ascendancy after 1955. In the early summer of 1957 his opponents combined against him, and the ruling Presidium (Politburo) voted to remove him. Khrushchev, however, outmaneuvered his foes, calling a meeting of the Central Committee of the party, in which he controlled

Figure 18. *Nikita S. Khrushchev, Soviet leader, 1956–63, talking with Yugoslav leader Tito at the United Nations in 1959. (Courtesy of the United Nations)*

a majority, to overrule the Presidium and to denounce what he called the "antiparty group" of his enemies. Unlike the days of the purges or even the recent fate of Beria, Khrushchev's opponents were not shot but merely demoted to minor positions or allowed to retire on pensions.

As leader of the Soviet Union Khrushchev faced two extremely difficult challenges. In foreign affairs he had to adjust both Marxist-Leninist ideology and day-to-day Soviet foreign policy to the entirely changed conditions of the postwar world: the advent of nuclear weapons; the world dominance of the two superpowers, the United States and the USSR; and the emergence of Communist China. Much of the next chapter will be devoted to the ways that he coped with these issues.

On the domestic scene Khrushchev also had to make a major readjustment: Stalinism was out of date, and new methods were required if the Soviet system were to function efficiently and to have any hope of competing with the United States. Moreover, much like the situation Lenin faced in 1921, the Soviet Union could not count on revolutionary help from abroad. Europe was recovering rapidly from the war, the Third World was busy achieving independence, and the chances of imminent world revolution were dim. Nor, given the suicidal danger of nuclear weapons, could the spread of communism be forced by the Soviet Union as long as the United States was prepared to counter Soviet expansion. Consequently, the effort to improve Soviet life and to move toward the ultimate goal of full communism would have to come from within.

In these circumstances Khrushchev took a daring gamble. To rejuvenate Soviet society (and perhaps also to tarnish his political opponents who were closely associated with Stalin), Khrushchev decided to attack Stalinism and then to replace it with a reformed system. This was risky strategy not only because Khrushchev himself had been one of Stalin's loyal henchmen but because to tear down Stalinism might lead, by a not very long leap of logic, to destroying also the system Stalin had built up, which in its dependence on the party's monopoly over ideology and governance still existed. Khrushchev hit upon the clever idea of focusing his criticism not on the system as a whole, but on Stalin himself. The party could thus be right, even though Stalin had been wrong. Of course, many Soviet citizens undoubtedly said to themselves, "If the party is right and acts in our interests, how could it have permitted Stalin to misbehave so outrageously?" But that was a danger Khrushchev was willing to risk.

The campaign of "de-Stalinization" was launched in February 1956 at the Twentieth Party Congress, to which Khrushchev delivered a long "secret speech," castigating Stalin for a number of errors and crimes. The speech was secret only in the sense that it was not published and was intended primarily for party officials, but Western governments soon obtained a copy, and Soviet citizens were shortly apprised of its gist by word of mouth. Khrushchev acknowledged Stalin's achievements in the party before 1934 and his success in industrializing the Soviet Union. But he went on to charge Stalin with having nurtured "a cult of personality" for his personal aggrandizement. This course had violated well-established party norms and had led to grievous mistakes, including the murder of guilty and innocent alike in the purges, the failure to prepare the Soviet Union adequately for the German attack in 1941, poor military leadership during World War II, and repression and foreign policy errors in the postwar era.

Khrushchev also gave a chilling description of working with Stalin:

> Stalin was a very distrustful man, sickly suspicious. . . . He could look at a man and say: "Why are your eyes so shifty today?" or "Why are you turning so much today and avoiding to look me directly in the eyes?" The sickly suspicion created in him a general distrust even toward eminent party workers whom he had known for years. Everywhere and in everything he saw "enemies," "two-facers," and "spies." Possessing unlimited power he indulged in great willfulness and choked a person morally and physically. A situation was created where one could not express one's own will.[1]

Some of the individuals Stalin had falsely accused were rehabilitated in the speech itself, when details of their cases were discussed. Others were restored to a place of Bolshevik honor in succeeding months, and in particular almost all the military leaders Stalin purged were subsequently vindicated. The attack on Stalin was renewed at the Twenty-Second Congress in 1961, at which time his body was removed from Lenin's mausoleum on Red Square and places named after him were renamed.

To a considerable extent de-Stalinization succeeded in its domestic purposes. In Eastern Europe, however, it created some problems, to be discussed in Chapter 14. Because Soviet citizens were finally convinced that mass terror was over and that life could be lived within fairly clearly established boundaries, some energy and initiative were pumped back into the system. In Soviet culture there was a marked "thaw," during which artistic works with a little more verve and imagination appeared. In 1962, Khrushchev even personally approved publication of Alexander Solzhenitsyn's damning indictment of the forced labor system, *One Day in the Life of Ivan Denisovich.* At the same time party control of public and intellectual life was strictly maintained. A slight easing of restrictions and an encouragement to be somewhat innovative were definitely not a license for free expression and political disagreement.

With characteristic vigor and optimism Khrushchev tackled the problems of stimulating production and productivity in Soviet industry

---

[1] Basil Dmytryshyn, *USSR: A Concise History,* 4th ed., (New York: 1984), 544.

and agriculture. He urged development for farming of so-called virgin lands in the central part of the country and in the republic of Kazakhstan, and he promoted introduction of new, hardier seeds; improved agricultural methods; and better organization of agriculture. Yet after some increases in output agriculture was soon lagging again. In industry Khrushchev tried a new method of managing the various sectors and fostered the introduction of new technologies. Once more, early improvement was followed by a falling off of the rate of growth of the Soviet economy.

On a visit to the United States in 1959 Khrushchev had declared jubilantly to his capitalist hosts, "We will bury you." He did not mean that literally socialism would conquer capitalism, but rather that with the gains he believed the Soviet Union was making, the day was not far off when the Soviet Union would outproduce the United States and would thus win over the rest of the world to the socialist way of organizing modern industrial life.

For the Soviet people Khrushchev improved housing and provided modest annual increases in their standard of living while promising much more within twenty years. He also accelerated the Soviet space program, which resulted in the launching of the first space satellite, *Sputnik,* in 1957. In ideology he argued that the Soviet Union had now completed the phase of building socialism and was in "the transition to communism." He talked about some of the characteristics of that future utopia but admitted that it might not arrive until the time of "our grandchildren." In foreign policy Khrushchev pursued a policy of peaceful coexistence, and the Soviet Union had a few modest successes, but by the early 1960s it suffered several setbacks, culminating in the Cuban missile crisis and its divisive quarrel with China, as we shall see in Chapter 14.

What had seemed like a rosy picture in the late 1950s had considerably dimmed only four or five years later. Laboring under the burden of faltering progress at home and clear defeats abroad, Khrushchev found himself in October 1964 ousted from power in much the same fashion he had won it. A colleague, Leonid Brezhnev, rallied a majority of top party leaders against Khrushchev and then blocked his efforts to appeal to the party's Central Committee. Khrushchev was retired to a comfortable apartment in Moscow and a villa just outside the city, while his erstwhile comrades denounced him for reckless experimentation, attempting to establish a new "cult of personality," and "hare-brained scheming."

In his almost ten years as dominant leader of the USSR Khrushchev implemented de-Stalinization, largely successfully; experimented brashly, with limited results; and created for the outside world a new image of the Soviet Union as a dynamic society. Yet, much like the nineteenth-century tsars, Khrushchev had tinkered with the system, rather than changing fundamentally its structure or principles. The Soviet Union was still a bureaucratic, authoritarian state dominated by one party that was in turn run by a handful of top leaders. Probably Khrushchev could not have gone further without endangering the party's monopoly of power. He had made unlikely a return to Stalinism, but he had not opened the door to a more creative and responsive system.

Bureaucratic Stability Under Brezhnev and His Successors

The succession to Khrushchev proceeded smoothly, despite the predictions of some outside social scientists that in a system that concentrated authority at the very top a change of leaders was bound to result in intense political struggle and perhaps violence. Leonid Brezhnev (see Figure 19), who dominated Soviet politics for almost twenty years, from 1964 to 1982, was a workers' son who had become an engineer. He rose through the ranks of the party as a protégé of Khrushchev, serving in supervisory positions in industry, in agriculture, and, during the war, in the army. Stolid and cautious, he used his bureaucratic experience and his ties in the party to bolster his position. He pursued moderate, low-key policies and was careful not "to rock the boat." For the first decade after Khrushchev's ouster Brezhnev had to maneuver among potential rivals, emphasizing the collective nature of the party's rule and playing the role of first among equals. After 1975, he openly became the sole leader and even permitted a minicult of personality to grow up around him.

At first Brezhnev and his colleagues largely continued Khrushchev's policies, although they dismantled some of his organizational experiments. Under pressure from the armed forces, they soon began a major build-up of Soviet military capabilities, both in conventional weapons and in nuclear missiles and submarines. This program created a further strain on the Soviet economy, and Brezhnev wrestled unsuccessfully with the problems of increasing Soviet productivity and arresting the decline in the rate of Soviet economic growth, which dropped from 8 to 10 percent in the 1950s to 3 to 4 percent in the 1970s. Brezhnev struggled, also in vain, with the deficiencies of Soviet agriculture.

After a period of some uncertainty the Brezhnev regime, beginning in 1968, cracked down hard on cultural creativity and intellectual dissent. The party kept a tight rein on the arts and literature, while the secret police harassed dissidents, many of whom were either forced into exile or imprisoned. The sciences and education continued to be liberally financed and encouraged, but their role was confined to serving the needs of the state.

Figure 19. *Leonid Brezhnev, Soviet leader, 1966–81, with then Soviet foreign minister, Andrei Gromyko. (Courtesy of United Nations/Tass)*

No basic changes were made in the system, and no daring policies were attempted. The result was a continuing modest improvement in the standard of living of the population, though far from what people hoped for; a sense of stability and predictability; and growing military strength and international power. Against this progress must be weighed continuing bureaucratic authoritarianism, widespread inefficiency and corruption, calcification of ideas and the system as a whole, and rapid increase in apathy and cynicism among the Soviet people.

When Brezhnev died in 1982, Yuri Andropov, reputedly the ablest member of the ruling Politburo, succeeded him. Although Andropov espoused greater efficiency and labor discipline and tentatively put forth

some economic reforms, his poor health and early death in 1984 prevented him from making any substantial impact. Andropov's successor,
Konstantine Chernenko, a nonentity in his mid-seventies, was clearly a
transitional figure. He was in power only a little over a year, dying in
early 1985. Chernenko cautiously continued the policies of the Brezhnev years, introducing no innovations or reforms.

Michael Gorbachov, who succeeded Chernenko, represented a different generation and moved quickly to consolidate his position. In his
late fifties, and therefore almost twenty years younger than the Brezhnev group, Gorbachov soon appointed political allies to the Politburo,
ousted a potential opponent, Grigor Romanov, and replaced the aging
Soviet foreign minister, Andrei Gromyko, with his own man. He projected a vigorous, open, and dynamic image, promising to tackle the
Soviet Union's economic problems and agreeing to a summit meeting
with President Ronald Reagan in the fall of 1985.

Issues in Contemporary Soviet Society

Ever since Lenin's time the party has revealed almost nothing about
the mechanisms by which policy is formulated and implemented in the
Soviet system and its leaders are selected and groomed for rule. We know
little about the operations of the Politburo or about the views and responsibilities of most of its members. Moreover, many basic social and
economic data about the Soviet Union are secret, and Western visitors
and observers are limited in what they can investigate and study. Consequently, to a much greater extent than in regard to any major Western society, statements about contemporary life in the USSR are tentative and to some extent speculative. Nevertheless, specialists in Soviet
affairs generally agree that there are several major areas of tension and
potential change in Soviet society today.

Generational Change and the Leadership Question. Surprisingly
perhaps, given the condemnation of the Soviet system by many Western politicians and critics, most specialists expect no major change in
the basic features of the system. Neither revolution, radical evolutionary transformation, nor economic collapse is considered likely. Bureaucratic rule by the party through an authoritarian political process will
probably persist for some time. This stability, or, as some prefer, stagnation, derives in part from the absence of any competing center of
power and in part from the tight control, buttressed by modern technology and force, exercised by the party, which effectively prevents any
significant opposition from arising. Two related possibilities, both unknowns for the moment, bear watching, however. One is the generational change now taking place across almost the whole population. Dying
out are the people who can remember, even as youngsters, the early

revolutionary years full of enthusiasm and hope; who experienced the rigors of industrialization, the purges, Stalinism, and World War II; and who saw the promise of the postwar years dim. Soviet citizens under the age of forty know Stalin only as a memory and have grown up entirely in the era of mediocrity and stability associated with Stalin's successors. Today, as they begin to assume senior positions in the party and in every aspect of Soviet life, what are their attitudes and goals? They are better fed, housed, clothed, and educated than their parents and grandparents. Is this enough, or do they want more? In per capita income they lag behind all other major industrial nations. Will they put enormous pressure on the regime to become more efficient, to raise dramatically the standard of living, and to provide greater opportunities for themselves and their children? If so, are they willing to work harder to achieve these goals? What are their spiritual and intellectual aspirations? Will they be forever satisfied with the dreary uniformity and deadening orthodoxy of Soviet culture? It is impossible to answer these questions, but indications of what the under-forties generation will demand should begin to emerge over the next five years.

Closely related is the puzzle of what the new leaders of the party and the Soviet Union will be like. Michael Gorbachov came to power in early 1985 representing a younger generation, but little was known about his outlook and projected program. He brought with him several colleagues in their fifties and sixties, thus marking the first step in the long expected generational change among the Soviet leadership. Yet these men are largely unknowns; outsiders have no information about their vision of the Soviet future, about how they hope to solve the problems confronting Soviet society. Moreover, within the next decade a half dozen even younger leaders, as yet unidentified, will have to be brought into the Politburo. What are they thinking? How will they act?

Perhaps, as skeptics insist, Gorbachov and his future colleagues, survivors of a bureaucratic culture, will simply be Brezhnev clones, unimaginative managers tinkering with the Soviet system and ensuring that it staggers along at about its present low level of performance. Another speculation is that the brokering of interests among powerful groups in Soviet society that now takes place informally in the Politburo will become more formalized, resulting in some sort of pluralistic system. In this way Soviet citizens, although not represented in governance directly, would nonetheless have their interests served through specialized groups. In this indirect way a more participatory structure might emerge. In any case the next ten years should see new faces and perhaps new policies, if not radical reform.

Demographic Change. The Soviet people are not only better educated and slightly better off, with only dim memories of sacrifices and war, but they are less Russian. Because birth rates among the Baltic and Slavic peoples, including the Great Russians, have dropped sharply in the past twenty years, as fertility rates among the Moslem Central Asian peoples have remained high, the proportion of Russians in the total population is falling. It is estimated that by the year 2000 the Slavs will have decreased from three fourths to two thirds of the Soviet population, and the Russians to about 46 percent, whereas the percentage of Moslems will have climbed to over one fifth. Since this change will be particularly apparent among younger age groups, it means that by the end of the century one in three young people entering the labor force, embarking on higher education, and being drafted into the army will be Asian, with a native language and culture that are not Russian. This can hardly be a pleasing prospect to Soviet leaders, especially to the military authorities. The government has adopted pronatalist policies in selected regions, which may be having some effect since there was a slight upturn in Slavic birth rates in the 1980s.

Another significant aspect of demographic change is a shortage of labor during at least the next decade, because of birth deficiencies that are the longterm result of the population losses of World War II. Some estimates predict that although 11 million people reached working age between 1976 and 1980, only 2 to 3 million will enter the work force between 1986 and 1990. Although the burgeoning Moslem population could help make up some of the short labor supply, most of the jobs are in Siberia and European Russia, and the Moslems do not want to move there from Central Asia. Finally, the rural population keeps shrinking, and the urban population growing: roughly one third and two thirds, respectively, today. That would be all right if the productivity of those left down on the farm were increasing fast enough to keep feeding the increasing number of city mouths. But overall this has not occurred, so there may well be a severe shortage of agricultural labor in coming years.

Disaffection Among the Non-Russian Nationalities. Since extremely limited information is available on the subject of disaffection among the non-Russian peoples and Western scholars are discouraged from studying it first-hand, we can only estimate how important a challenge this issue is for future Soviet leaders. Several aspects of the situation of the non-Russian minorities are, however, clear. Over the years despite efforts of Soviet authorities to minimize or eliminate religious and nationalist feelings among the nationalities such feelings have persisted. For example, Catholicism remains strong in Lithuania and Islam in Central Asia. Baltic peoples still regret the loss of their independence in 1940 and believe they are more Westernized and sophisticated than their Russian rulers. In recent decades several cases reflecting Ukrainian nationalism have become public, and anti-Russian riots have erupted in Georgia. Second, in every republic and national region the party, dominated by Russians, continues to control economic and political life. Third, the nationalities have greatly benefited under Soviet rule, obtaining a higher standard of living and more cultural and educational opportunities than they ever had in tsarist times.

What is not known is how the minority peoples themselves weigh and assess these contradictory facets of their position in the Soviet system. Do they greatly resent being under Russian tutelage and only occasionally having a chance to rise to top positions? Are they satisfied with the share of the Soviet economic pie they are getting, or do they believe they could do better economically if they had greater autonomy? Is the considerable leeway in cultural development offered them enough of an outlet for religious and nationalistic attitudes? Do they feel themselves primarily Uzbeks and Estonians, or Soviet citizens and socialist toilers?

Some specialists believe that disaffection among the nationalities is widespread, though subterranean, and may pose the single greatest threat to the future cohesiveness and viability of the Soviet system. Others believe that the grievances of the non-Russians are fairly minor and that they are being steadily and effectively socialized as members of Soviet society and adherents of Soviet nationalism. Almost everyone agrees, however, that there are tensions in the minority regions of the USSR; the question is how serious and divisive they are.

Economic Deceleration. The problem with the Soviet economy is not that it is about to collapse or even that it has stopped growing, but rather that its rate of growth has slowed down at the very moment when the demands on the economy are increasing rapidly. With military expenditures, the total population, and consumer demand all rising, the economy has either to grow faster or to become more efficient. The former is unlikely because the Soviet Union is short of both the labor and capital needed to expand the economy at a high rate. Moreover, the continuing shortfalls in agriculture act as a brake on the economy as a whole.

The major goal, therefore, is to increase rationality and efficiency. Most observers, including commentators in the Soviet Union, believe that this can best be achieved by substantial decentralization, that is, by giving individual factories and enterprises greater control over production and simultaneously giving them incentives to produce more and better-quality goods. Whether economic reforms of this kind can in fact be implemented, even if Soviet leaders decided on them in the near future, is a moot point. Opposing such reforms would be not only custom and inertia but a wide range of powerful bureaucrats with a vested interest in the present system, including central planners and supervisors, as well as middle-level executives and intermediaries. As the economy continues to decelerate, necessity may finally force a major alteration of the economic system, but it will take inspired leadership to drive it through.

The agricultural sector presents special problems (see Figure 20). Although since the 1960s collective farmers have fared quite well, with such concessions as a guaranteed annual income and encouragement to sell produce from their private plots, three inherent factors make agricultural output and productivity unlikely to advance spectacularly in the near future. One is bad weather, to which the Soviet farming sector is extremely vulnerable. Between 1980 and 1984 there were three disastrous crop years, primarily due to unfavorable weather. Each time the Soviet Union was forced to buy grain on the world market, reducing the capital available for investment or for the purchase abroad of much-needed advanced technology.

Second, the Soviet Union, because of its northerly location, has a limited amount of arable land, and it is unlikely that further extension

Figure 20. *The layout of a Russian village, now a Soviet collective farm, showing the private plots of the farmers behind each house. (Courtesy of Sovfoto/Eastfoto)*

of agriculture, similar to Khrushchev's virgin lands project, can do much to raise output.

Third, the collective farm system, even after all the tinkering with it over the past thirty years, appears to be an inefficient way to organize agricultural production. There is inadequate incentive for individual members of the collective to work hard, as they do on their small private plots. The result is that Soviet agricultural productivity is considerably behind that of Western Europe and eight to ten times lower than that in the United States. The only solution would seem to be a reversion to individual farming, an ideologically difficult step for the Soviet leaders to take.

As the economy falters, the grumbling of Soviet citizens over shortages, long lines in stores, inferior-quality merchandise, and poor service grows louder, and the hand-wringing of Soviet economists, journalists, and party officials increases. Everyone agrees that something has to be done, but no one is quite sure whether effective reform is possible.

Cynicism and Corruption. Public morale in the Soviet Union, most observers agree, is at its lowest ebb since the death of Stalin. Soviet citizens appear convinced that not much will change in the present; nor do they have hope for the future. The achievements of Soviet cosmonauts in space and of Soviet athletes in sports are honored and give momentary flashes of pride and pleasure, but there is little else to cheer about. The blankness of life leads to several socially disruptive attitudes and reactions. At one extreme, discouragement and despair are reflected in social misbehavior. Crime, including violent crime, burglary, and theft of state property, has risen markedly in the past decade. Absenteeism, long a labor problem in the USSR, is reportedly on the upswing. Also many observers and even the Soviet press report on-the-job absenteeism, that is, widespread loafing or working only the barest amount possible. Finally, there is a sharp increase in alcoholism. Although this has long been a significant problem in Russia, dating back to prerevolutionary times, it seems to be getting worse. Apart from the social consequences of these manifestations of civic disillusionment, the economic costs are high. Drunkenness on the job, absenteeism, and stealing state property together act as a significant drain on the performance and productivity of the Soviet economy.

At another extreme, low morale shows up as cynicism and as self-interest. Many Soviet citizens drop out of the system, going through enough of the motions in some routine job to stay alive and being inconspicuous enough socially to escape party pressure or censure, but spending almost all their time, energy, and thought on purely personal pursuits and pleasures, from family affairs and hobbies to private artistic and literary creations. Few people take Soviet ideology or the promises of the regime seriously, and many, even those who are not "drop-outs," try to minimize their contacts with the system.

Between antisocial behavior and personal withdrawal is a huge middle ground on which almost all Soviet citizens meet: doing better for yourself by working outside the system, "on the left," as it is called, a phrase roughly equivalent to the American "under the table." Because regular procedures are so inefficient and often inequitable, it is frequently easier and more effective to get things done illegally or semi-legally, through bribery, favoritism, or "pull." From tipping the door-man to get inside a restaurant to exchanging goods stolen from work for a piece of meat the butcher has kept under the counter, many aspects of life in the Soviet Union depend on corruption of a petty but demoralizing sort. Since many of these transactions have economic consequences, Western economists who study the Soviet Union have speculated that a substantial portion of the total goods and services produced and exchanged in the USSR are not reflected in official statistics but are part of this underground or "second" economy. Moreover, since almost everyone does it, few condemn it, and the whole society has learned to wink at widespread dishonesty and corruption.

From the viewpoint of Soviet leaders the catastrophic decline in public morale is a serious problem. Besides the direct economic and social consequences noted, the system as a whole probably cannot move ahead effectively unless people believe in it, work hard for it, and provide their talents and creativity to improve it. That none of these processes is happening now helps to explain why the Soviet system is faltering. Yet it is hard to see what new faith, what promises, what inspiration Soviet leaders can devise that will appeal to the population and spur them to contribute again. Few people take the utopian dream of socialism seriously, particularly when they compare their standard of living to the affluence of the West; few now put credence in promises of improved material well-being in the near future; and few see the Soviet Union as having any particular mission or calling for the future. Soviet citizens would defend themselves and their homeland, if attacked, but the upcoming generation of younger leaders has to find a positive ideal to inspire the Soviet people and to give them something to work and live for.

Political Apathy and Dissidence. The issue of dissidence and political disaffection is listed last because it is perhaps the least significant. The Soviet Union does not need democracy or political freedom, however much Americans might wish it were so, in order to be an efficient, dynamic, forward-moving society. Hence political reform is undoubtedly low on the list of changes one would consider necessary to rejuvenate the Soviet system.

Nevertheless it is a problem. When people have no stake in their governance, it is easier for them not to care and not to contribute. Apathy about the Communist party and the Soviet system is another side of the coin of low public morale. Moreover, the monopoly of power exercised by the party may be a major block to making the changes needed to revitalize Soviet society, just as the tsar's autocratic power served to prevent reform in the decades before 1917. At the same time it is difficult to see how the party could make the system more representative without endangering its own dominant position—and it is unlikely to do so. One possible direction of movement is through representation at the top of the party of economic and social interest groups, as noted.

The dissidents, that tiny group of courageous men and women who defy the intellectual and authoritarian restraints of the Soviet system, are to be admired greatly for their determination and integrity. Some observers believe that the Western press overplays them; this may be so, but it would be wrong to ignore their symbolic dissent from a crushingly powerful and pervasive bureaucratic system. It is important that the dissidents keep alive the spark of traditional Russian resistance to repression.

At the same time the dissident movement, as a political force, poses no threat to the government, although it is an embarrassment in the outside world. Most Soviet intellectuals, although bitterly resenting that they cannot travel freely outside the Soviet Union, that they are denied Western information and publications, and must submit their own work to various levels of censorship, do not side with the dissidents. If Soviet intellectuals are disaffected, they believe they can do more working within the system than publicly defying the authorities and being cut down. Moreover, by a combination of tactics, including permitting some discontented intellectuals and a small percentage of Jews to emigrate, the government has managed to pare down the number of dissidents and to fragment or undercut any effective opposition.

Conclusion

Three times in the four decades since the end of World War II the future of Soviet society looked bright. Right after the war Soviet citizens hoped that the reward for their sacrifice and survival might be a higher standard of living and a freer society. Instead Stalin imposed a return to forced industrialization and renewed Stalinism.

In the late 1950s when Nikita Khrushchev announced his de-Stalinization campaign, loosened the bonds of intellectual orthodoxy, and proclaimed that the Soviet Union would overtake and surpass the economy of the United States by 1980, almost anything seemed possible and realizable. An American journalist, Robert Kaiser, who revisited the Soviet Union in 1984, reported that spirit of optimism in the following conversation with a Soviet citizen:

"Stalin died some thirty years ago," an elderly Muscovite observed recently, "and our hopes soared." He raised his arm in an arc to demonstrate. "For a while things did change, there was excitement and creativity and we dreamed of a better future. But now," he went on, completing the arc he drew in the air so it became a circle, ending where it began, "we're back to here again."[2]

Even in the 1960s there was a third upsurge of sanguine expectation, as some thought that Brezhnev and company would build Soviet strength, solve the economic dilemma, and provide a stable and happy future. They were able to do only the first, and today Soviet society is in the doldrums.

At the same time we should not forget that during the postwar era Soviet citizens have lived at peace, have slowly but noticeably improved their standard of living, and have taken advantage of wide-ranging educational opportunities. Soviet power and influence in the world have grown, and the achievements of Soviet science are universally recognized. Although the future is uncertain, it would be a mistake to underestimate the creativity and resilience of the Soviet people.

FURTHER READING

Bialer, S. *Stalin's Successors: Leadership, Stability, and Change in the Soviet Union* New York: 1980.

Brumberg, A., ed. *Russia Under Khrushchev*. New York: 1962.

Byrnes, Robert F., ed. *After Brezhnev: Sources of Soviet Conduct in the 1980s.* Bloomington, Ind.: 1983.

Campbell, Robert W. *The Soviet-type Economies: Performance and Evaluation.* Boston: 1974.

Fletcher, W. *Soviet Believers: The Religious Sector of the Population.* Lawrence, Ks.: 1981.

Goldman, Marshal. *The USSR in Crisis: The Failure of an Economic System.* New York: 1983.

Hoffman, Erik and Laird, Robbin, eds. *The Soviet Polity in the Modern Era.* New York: 1984.

Lapidus, Gail. *Women in Soviet Society.* Berkeley: 1978.

Leonhard, W. *The Kremlin Since Stalin.* New York: 1962.

Millar, James. *The ABCs of Soviet Socialism.* Urbana, Ill.: 1981.

Pond, E. *From the Yaroslavsky Station.* New York: 1982 (good journalistic account of Soviet life).

Reshetar, J. S. *The Soviet Polity: Government and Politics in the USSR* (2d ed.). New York: 1978.

Smith, Hedrick. *The Russians* (rev. ed.). New York: 1983.

Tatu, M. *Power in the Kremlin: From Krushchev to Kosygin.* New York: 1969.

Tokes, R., ed. *Dissent in the USSR.* Baltimore: 1975.

[2] Robert Kaiser, "The U.S.S.R.: A Generation That Failed," *East-West Outlook,* 7, no. 4 (Autumn 1984), 5.

14

The Soviet Union
As a World Power, 1944–85

Throughout the almost four decades since the end of World War II the Soviet Union has played a major role in world affairs. At times its expanding influence and the concomitant spread of communist revolution seemed almost unstoppable. Increasingly, however, in the past decade the Soviet position has appeared much less powerful, as differences with its huge Communist neighbor, the People's Republic of China, have remained unresolved; tensions have mounted among its allies in Eastern Europe; Soviet relations with the West have deteriorated; the arms race has accelerated; and only a few small countries in the developing world have chosen Marxism-Leninism as their route to development. If anything, the tide of history, which Khrushchev, not without justification, believed was flowing with the Soviet Union in the late 1950s, now seems to have reversed itself and appears to be ebbing against any Soviet bid for world domination.

Moreover, the ability of the Soviet Union to assert itself in world affairs has been steadily eroded in recent years by developments inside the country. Neither the leaders nor the citizens seem to have the zeal for and commitment to world revolution that existed before World War II and perhaps even in the 1950s and early 1960s. Most of them are much more interested in and concerned about the array of domestic problems discussed in Chapter 13 than they are in promoting socialist upheavals abroad. Rejuvenating the Soviet economy and Soviet society is perforce demanding more and more of their time, energy, and attention.

Strange Bedfellows in the Grand Alliance, 1941–45

The Soviet Union joined Great Britain and the United States (and later Free France) in a Grand Alliance against the Axis, even accepting in 1942 the Atlantic Charter worked out by Franklin Roosevelt and Winston Churchill, with its vague humanitarian and democratic war aims. Nevertheless, as we saw in Chapter 12, there were strains within the alliance, first over military questions and subsequently over diplomatic issues. Neither the Western democracies nor the Communist Soviet government changed their basic ideological positions, merely shelving them for the duration of the war, which made them strange bedfellows indeed.

Stalin, in particular, apparently never gave up his fear of the capitalist system and his distrust of the Western powers. As a result, he viewed the postwar world as a dangerous place, and his main objective in negotiations for a peace settlement was to ensure maximum security for the Soviet state. This goal meant especially acquiring as much territory along Soviet borders and as many resources as possible. If, also, socialism could be promoted and expanded, so much the better, but the safety of the Soviet Union was his paramount concern. Although Churchill harbored no illusions about Stalin's intentions, he went along with Roosevelt, who believed, until just before his death, that the Western allies had to assume that the Soviet Union would cooperate in postwar arrangements; to suppose that Stalin would be hostile would be an act of bad faith and might endanger their combined effort to defeat Germany (see Figure 21).

Figure 21. *Prime Minister Churchill of Great Britain, President Roosevelt of the United States, and Soviet leader Stalin during their summit meeting at Yalta in the Soviet Union, February 1945. (Courtesy of UPI/Bettmann Newsphotos)*

Moreover, contrary to much popular belief and even some history writing in the West, the Soviet Union did not at first pursue an obstructionist course in the discussions concerning the shape of the postwar world that began in earnest at the first major meeting among the members of the Grand Alliance, the Teheran Conference in November 1943. Soviet intransigence became manifest only later, between the Yalta and Potsdam conferences in February–July 1945.

On general issues concerning the postwar world, Soviet negotiators were reasonably cooperative. They accepted the idea of a United Nations organization as a forum for international discussion and cooperation. At the same time they insisted its Security Council be dominated by the great powers and that each of them, including the Soviet Union, have a veto there. Soviet leaders acknowledged Allied Lend-Lease aid, which eventually totaled $11 billion and whose trucks and logistical equipment were crucial to the Soviet counteroffensives against Germany in 1943 and 1944, and indicated their willingness to repay this debt (they eventually did so only in part). They supported the idea of easing trade restrictions after the war, and they agreed to joint occupation and control of Germany after its defeat. At the Yalta Conference, which American critics have called a "betrayal" of Eastern Europe by the United States, the Western powers in fact obtained from the Soviet Union a promise to hold free elections in the nations of that region after the war (although the promise was not kept).

With the advantage of hindsight we can see that two issues began to disrupt the Grand Alliance even before its victory: the way to handle Germany once it was defeated and the political alignment of Eastern Europe. In my view, the Soviet leaders wished to treat Germany primarily as a resource for the restitution and recovery of the Soviet nation, while the Western powers wanted to permit gradual restoration of the German economy and polity so that it would not be a drain on the postwar world. These differing objectives soon led to clashes over specific issues, even though in principle the four powers (USSR, Great Britain, the United States, and France) had agreed to cooperate in administering their individual zones of occupation in Germany and in controlling Berlin jointly.

In Eastern Europe the Soviet leaders decided that they did not want to run the risk of free elections' bringing to power governments that were not fully aligned with the Soviet Union. From the Soviet point of view it was essential to the security of the postwar Soviet Union that "friendly" (i.e., not anti-Communist) countries exist throughout the territory between itself and the Western capitalist powers. As a result, Soviet representatives cooperating with local Communist parties exerted pressure on opposition parties, interfered in elections and the formation of governments, and in general worked for Communist control in each nation of the region, a course that the Western countries increasingly opposed.

The Cold War, 1946–55

These Soviet policies toward Germany and Eastern Europe bridged the last year of the war and the first few years of peace. They contributed importantly to the rift between the West, particularly the United States, and the Soviet Union that came to be known as the cold war. Substantial historiographic debate has developed over the origins of the cold war. "Revisionist" scholars have attacked the dominant Western view that Soviet expansionist policies and self-interested refusal to cooperate with its former allies caused the break. Instead, they have contended, economic and anticommunist considerations in American foreign policy spurred a drive for United States' dominance in Europe and the rest of the world designed to surround the socialist bloc and to ensure Western control of vital resources and trade routes. In the face of this American-led "imperialism," the Soviet Union reacted defensively, taking steps to safeguard its security and its economic independence.

As with so many heated historical issues, elements of truth exist on both sides. There is little doubt that Stalin viewed the Soviet takeover of Eastern Europe not only as enhancing Soviet security but also as fulfilling the Marxist-Leninist prediction that the socialist revolution would eventually spread westward across Europe. Moreover, Stalin encouraged activist policies by the Communist parties of Western Europe and Communist-led uprisings in Asia in the immediate postwar years. In short, the Western powers had good reason to resist what seemed to be a Soviet propensity to expand wherever the opportunity arose. On the other hand, Stalin and his advisers were justifiably concerned by Western efforts to establish pro-Western governments in Eastern Europe, to weaken Communist parties in the West, and to build "areas of strength" around the Soviet Union as part of the policy of "containment" that was officially adopted in the United States in 1947.

It is fruitless to attempt to assess blame for the cold war. The breakdown of joint action and policy, the mutual recriminations, and the growing hostility between the Soviet Union and the West were rooted in deep ideological mistrust, each side believing the other to be intrinsically committed to worldwide dominance. Marxism-Leninism taught that as the capitalist system neared its death throes, it would do everything possible to crush socialism and thus stave off its inevitable demise. To Stalin, Western efforts to "encircle" the Soviet Union must have seemed full confirmation of this postulate. Conversely, American and Western leaders believed the Communists were bent on world revolution and could be checked only by vigorous counteraction and countervailing force. Unfortunately, little has been done since the 1940s to bridge this ideological gulf and to test whether a basis for genuine coexistence of the two systems exists. Perhaps both sides should consider adopting Khrushchev's peasant dictum: "let us agree not to poke our pigs' snouts into each other's gardens."

Two important milestones of the cold war were announced in 1947. First was the *Truman Doctrine,* American President Harry Truman's statement, directed to Turkey and Greece but with wider implications, that the United States would aid and support governments committed to defending themselves against internal subversion and outside pressure. The practical result was that British and American assistance facilitated the triumph of conservative government forces in Greece over Communist rebels in a fierce three-year civil war.

A second major step was the Marshall Plan, a program of massive American economic aid to Western Europe designed to buttress reconstruction and economic stability there in the hope of lessening the danger of a Communist takeover. In principle, Marshall Plan assistance was available also to the countries of Eastern Europe, but Stalin, after brief hesitation, decided not to participate, branding the Marshall Plan a subterfuge for United States "imperialist" exploitation and domination of Europe. In the years after 1947 the Marshall Plan worked exceedingly well, greatly boosting European economic recovery and reducing the influence and attraction of Communism in Western Europe.

In Eastern Europe a turning point in the cold war was reached in early 1948, when a Communist-dominated government came to power in Czechoslovakia and shortly afterward the respected Czech foreign minister, Jan Masaryk, committed suicide. By the end of 1948 all the countries of Eastern Europe were under Communist rule or Communist-run governments. The Western powers protested violations of the Yalta agreement, but to no avail. Although the Red Army was not used directly in this political conquest, it was obviously an ominous force "in the wings." Political maneuver by indigenous Communist parties or fronts and economic pressure from the Soviet Union were the main instruments of the subjugation of Eastern Europe, and there was little the United States and the west European countries could do about it. Some historians have suggested that the United States should have offered extensive economic aid to the USSR in exchange for political concessions in Eastern Europe, but it is unlikely that Congress would have supported such a gamble. Military intervention was out of the question since the Western countries had been demobilizing while the Red Army remained a powerful force in Eastern Europe.

Almost before it had been established, Soviet hegemony over Eastern Europe was broken by the defection of Communist Yugoslavia under its wartime hero-leader, Josip Broz, known as Tito. The Yugoslav Communists had come to power on their own, as a result of a long guerrilla struggle against conservative opponents and the Germans, and Tito and his comrades had no intention of submitting completely to Soviet domination. Angered at Tito's resistance to Soviet orders, Stalin in 1948 expelled Yugoslavia from the *Cominform*, the organization of Communist parties that had replaced the Comintern. Stalin reportedly said that he would wiggle his little finger, and that would be the end of Tito. But Tito opposed Soviet subversion staunchly, and Stalin apparently decided that military occupation of Yugoslavia would be too costly. Under Khrushchev and subsequently, Soviet leaders have tried to repair the breach with Yugoslavia, but today, although relations between the Soviet Union and Yugoslavia are correct and cordial, Yugoslavia continues to pursue an independent course in both domestic and foreign policies, balancing between the West and the Soviet Union in defense of its own interests.

A decisive landmark in the cold war was the collapse of efforts by the wartime allies to pursue a common policy toward Germany. As noted earlier, a main Soviet concern was to extract reparations and other economic restitution from Germany as quickly as possible. A secondary goal was undoubtedly to prevent the rebuilding of a strong unified Germany, which, perhaps under Western influence, could again threaten the Soviet Union. In any case as early as 1946 the Soviet authorities began to treat their zone of occupation in Germany as a resource to be depleted, in violation of joint policies agreed to earlier that the German economy should be allowed to recover to a moderate level. The Soviet government shipped German factories back to the Soviet Union, took heavy reparations, and in general acted independently in Germany. By 1948 the de facto division of Germany had occurred, with an eastern zone under Soviet occupation and a western zone under British, French, and American occupation. These two zones soon emerged as separate German states, the German Democratic Republic (East Germany) allied with the Soviet Union and the Federal Republic of Germany (West Germany) allied with the West, as they still are today.

Before Germany was formally divided, a serious crisis in the cold war arose over Berlin, the former German capital. Primarily for military reasons Soviet forces had been designated to capture Berlin, and the West had agreed to joint postwar occupation of the city, even though it was situated over a hundred miles inside the Soviet zone of occupation in East Germany. In the early summer of 1948 Soviet authorities tried to force the Allies out by cutting off overland routes to the city. Stalin apparently hoped to remove an irritant inside the Soviet bloc of power in the east and at the same time to test the mettle of the Western powers. The latter responded to the Berlin blockade by mounting an intensive air lift of supplies to their sectors of the city and making clear their determination to stay there. After eleven months the Soviet Union called off the blockade, but Berlin has remained a sensitive point in East-West relations.

The height of the cold war was reached in 1949 and 1950. In the former year the Western powers banded together in a mutual assistance alliance known as the North Atlantic Treaty Organization (NATO). Several years later the Soviet Union responded by creating an eastern alliance system, the Warsaw Pact. Also in 1949 the Chinese Communists came to power, winning a civil war waged off and on since 1927 and intensively since 1945. Their opponent, Chiang Kai-shek, was forced to retreat to Taiwan, and the Soviet Union gained a major ally in Asia. In a later section of this chapter we will trace the stormy course of relations between the Soviet Union and the People's Republic of China, the new Chinese state.

Next door to China the Korean peninsula, like Germany, had been divided into two zones of occupation after the defeat of Japan, a northern one under Soviet control and a southern one under American control. As the cold war intensified, these two zones had followed the German pattern, and embryonic separate states had been set up. In June 1950 a Communist army from North Korea invaded South Korea. Evidence of the role of the Soviet Union in this affair is lacking. Whether the North Koreans attacked at Soviet instigation or merely with Soviet acquiescence, it was an evident attempt to extend Communist influence over the whole country, and the United States responded vigorously, heading a United Nations (UN) military force to repulse the invasion. After the North Koreans had been driven back, General Douglas MacArthur, head of the UN armies, unwisely decided to pursue the enemy deep into North Korea. This action brought Chinese Communist "volunteers" into the fray, and MacArthur was forced to retreat. A stalemate was reached, roughly along the line of the division of the country before hostilities began.

Taken as a whole, Stalin's foreign policy after the war achieved some important Soviet objectives. Except Greece, which aligned with the West, and Finland, which remained independent but was careful not to antagonize the Soviet Union, the whole belt of states in eastern Europe lying between the Soviet Union and western Europe became Communist, although Yugoslavia (and later tiny Albania) rejected Soviet direction and dominance. Through the Council of Mutual Economic Assistance these countries were closely linked to the Soviet Union economically, usually on terms favorable to the latter. East Germany was incorporated into the Soviet bloc, Communist control was established in North Korea, and a Communist revolution took place in China, albeit with minimal help from the Soviet Union.

On the other hand, Soviet actions in Eastern Europe and Germany and the invasion of South Korea provoked a strong reaction from the

Western powers, leading to their rearmament and formation of an anti-Soviet alliance, NATO. Moreover, the Soviet Union, with establishment of a pro-American state in West Germany, lost any chance to extend its influence in Germany as a whole, and the position of Communist parties in France and Italy weakened. The Soviet government faced continuing hostility in the West, and its prospects in the rest of the world did not seem bright. Still, the Soviet Union was secure and had a strong base from which to extend its influence in Asia and Africa.

Peaceful Coexistence and Détente, 1956–80

A major problem that Stalin failed to resolve before he died was how the Soviet Union should react to the American monopoly of nuclear weapons. Stalin had ordered a crash program to develop Soviet nuclear capabilities, but he had not reconsidered the overall strategic and foreign policy position of the USSR in this light. Khrushchev and his colleagues soon tackled the issue. Given the enormous destructive power of atomic and hydrogen bombs, it was suicidal, the Soviet leaders realized, to predicate Soviet doctrine and external actions on the Leninist premise of a "frightful collision" between the socialist and capitalist systems. Instead Khrushchev propounded an extension of the Leninist principle of peaceful coexistence, arguing that capitalism and socialism could live side by side until the time when socialism, by nonviolent means such as economic example, political competition, and propaganda, would win over the world's peoples, and a global system of socialist states would be established. Or to put it another way, for socialism to triumph, as it was bound to according to the laws of history, war was not inevitable. The victory could come by peaceful means.

The new theory of "the noninevitability of war" was developed in 1954–55 and enunciated at the Twentieth Party Congress in February 1956. Even earlier, however, Stalin's successors had begun to ameliorate the confrontational policies of the cold war era, and there is some evidence that Stalin himself was beginning to soften his foreign policy line on the eve of his death. In the mid-1950s the Korean War was formally ended by conclusion of an armistice agreement. Also, the Soviet Union and the Western powers agreed to terminate their postwar occupation of Austria and to recognize its independence. In 1958 the Soviet authorities ended the closure of their country that had existed since World War II, and the first Western tourists, scholars, and businessmen were admitted to the USSR. Khrushchev and his comrades vigorously sought trade with the Western world and promoted cultural exchange agreements with the United States and other countries. Soviet performing arts groups, exhibits, students, and academicians came to the West and vice versa. Finally, the Soviet government developed closer diplomatic, political, economic, and cultural ties with the countries of Asia, Africa, and Latin America and was delighted when Fidel Castro, the leader of a revolution in Cuba, finally declared in 1961 that he was a Marxist-Leninist and would establish a socialist system in Cuba.

Although the new policies associated with peaceful coexistence (or peaceful competition as it should more accurately be called) did much to refurbish the Soviet image and to enhance Soviet influence in the world, Soviet foreign policy also ran into marked setbacks in the 1950s and 1960s, some within the socialist bloc itself and some in relations with the Western powers. Stalin had encouraged the view that international socialism was a monolithic bloc wisely modeled on the Soviet experience and benevolently directed by the Soviet government. Many critics of the Soviet Union and most Western leaders unhesitatingly accepted this picture of socialist unity and Soviet control. Yet as early as 1948 the myth was shattered, when the Yugoslav Communists chose to pursue their own course free of Soviet dictation.

After Stalin's death it became increasingly difficult to maintain unanimity within the bloc and direction by Moscow. As part of his de-Stalinization policies Khrushchev relaxed the Soviet grip on Eastern Europe slightly, and some Eastern European leaders persecuted in Stalinist times were rehabilitated. This was not enough, however, and in 1956 open opposition to Soviet domination erupted in Poland and in Hungary. The Polish assertion of greater independence was spearheaded by Wladyslaw Gomulka, a popular Polish Communist, and other party leaders. In a dramatic showdown in Poland in October 1956 Gomulka and his colleagues reportedly told a visiting Soviet delegation headed by Khrushchev that if Moscow tried to enforce greater conformity on Poland, the Polish people—down to the last man, woman, and child—would fight. The Soviet leaders backed down, and Gomulka was permitted to initiate reforms in state and party affairs in Poland.

Events in Hungary had a less benign outcome. For a number of months in 1956 there had been growing restiveness among Hungarian intellectuals and party members, but no individual or group emerged to focus and direct this discontent, as had occurred in Poland. Instead the mood of disaffection spread to the general populace, and in November 1956 a popular rebellion against the existing government and against Soviet dominance in Hungary broke out in Budapest, the capital. After several days of street fighting the old regime was toppled, and a new government was formed. The revolutionary leaders indicated that Hungary might withdraw from the Warsaw Pact and might institute a multiparty system. This suggestion was considered so threatening to Soviet interests that Soviet leaders ordered in the Red Army after ten days, and the Hungarian Revolution was crushed. Since almost everyone, including many people within the socialist bloc and the Soviet Union, knew that the rebels were just average citizens—not counterrevolutionaries and hooligans as the Soviet media charged—the suppression of the uprising gravely damaged the image of the Soviet Union as a defender of the rights of the masses, and many Communists in the West left the party at that time.

In the 1950s the tiny Communist state of Albania rejected Soviet control and became a continuing quirky critic of Soviet policies. At the same time relations between the Soviet Union and China deteriorated and the first precursors of the later split between them appeared, as we shall see shortly.

Flare-ups of the cold war broke through the calmer atmosphere of peaceful coexistence on occasion during the late 1950s and 1960s. Germany continued to be a touchy issue between Moscow and Washington, with Soviet leaders' charging that the West was rearming Germany as a future aggressor against the USSR. Although not resorting to a blockade again, several times the Soviet Union applied other pressures in regard to Berlin, but the United States and the Western powers made clear their determination to maintain their presence in the city. A dramatic moment in the continuing crises over Berlin occurred when President John F. Kennedy visited the former German capital and proclaimed publicly in broken but crowd-pleasing German, "Ich bin ein Berliner; I am a Berliner." The Soviet and East German authorities, alarmed by the continuing defection to the West of educated and skilled East Germans, including doctors, engineers, and technicians, finally erected a high wall between the eastern and western sectors of Berlin and established a no-man's-land along the whole border between East and West Germany. The Berlin Wall succeeded in virtually ending defections, but it harmed the image of socialism and the Soviet Union. In an agreement signed in 1972 the Soviet Union and the Western powers clarified the position of and arrangements for Berlin, but the city remains divided.

The gravest crisis of this period, and indeed of the entire postwar era, occurred in October 1962. In the late 1950s the Soviet Union had begun to reorient its military capability and its strategic doctrine around "rocket forces," that is, long-range ballistic missiles equipped with nuclear warheads. The United States, however, had substantial superiority over the Soviet Union both in missiles and in total numbers of nuclear weapons, including those delivered by planes and those launched from submarines. In what was apparently a daring but foolhardy effort to overcome this inferiority before the United States knew what had happened, Khrushchev undertook to place medium-range Soviet missiles in Cuba, whence they could threaten the southeastern United States. American intelligence soon discovered this Soviet gambit, and President Kennedy after several days' somber discussions with his advisers ordered a blockade of Cuba to prevent further Soviet missile shipments to the island and asked the Soviet government to withdraw the missiles already in place.

It was a tense confrontation. If the Soviet Union refused to back down, the United States would have to invade Cuba, and a Soviet-American war, with the likelihood of devastating nuclear exchanges, could hardly be averted. At first, Soviet ships continued steaming toward the American naval forces stationed off Cuba, but at the last minute they either turned back or, if they had no military cargo, submitted peacefully to being stopped and searched. Khrushchev communicated his willingness to withdraw the missiles in exchange for an American pledge not to invade the island. Kennedy agreed, and the latter face-saving device permitted Khrushchev to claim that he had thwarted the aggressive designs of American "imperialism." He failed, however to convince his critics in the Politburo, and two years later, as we saw, they ousted him from power because of this and other failures in foreign policy and because of his flamboyant style and unpredictable changes of direction in domestic policy.

The Cuban missile crisis sobered both sides in the East-West struggle, and in the following year the Soviet Union and the Western powers signed a treaty banning all but underground tests of nuclear devices. The Soviet and American governments also agreed to establish a "hot line" of direct communications between Moscow and Washington, permitting the top leaders of each country to talk promptly and without intermediaries in the event of another major crisis. In 1984 the hot line was upgraded and remains an important device for preventing misunderstandings between the superpowers at a time of stress.

During the remainder of the 1960s Soviet-American relations were tested by the war in Vietnam. After World War II an indigenous revolutionary movement led by the Communist Ho Chi Minh sprang up in Indochina, which the French had colonized in the nineteenth century and which the Japanese had occupied in 1941. Both nationalists and Communists fought against reestablishment of French rule, in a broadly based movement that the Soviet government encouraged but aided directly only slightly. In 1954 the Soviet Union and the Western powers agreed to establish the independent states of Laos and Cambodia in part of Indochina and to partition the remainder, called Vietnam, into a northern Communist-dominated zone and a southern anti-Communist zone. At the end of the 1950s the United States gradually assumed the responsibility of assisting South Vietnam in the civil war that it was waging against Communist insurgents who received extensive assistance from North Vietnam. This commitment led finally to massive American armed intervention in Vietnam. Since North Vietnam was an ally of the Soviet Union and South Vietnam was an ally of the United States, there was always the risk that Soviet support of Ho Chi Minh and his forces would create friction in Soviet-American relations. During the course of the war, however, both the Soviet and American governments, although highly critical of each other's stance in the Vietnam struggle, tried to minimize the deleterious impact of the war on their political relationship. Washington played down Soviet aid to the North Vietnamese, and Moscow conveniently overlooked the American military assault on its Indochinese ally.

In the summer of 1968 peaceful coexistence and Soviet foreign policy in general suffered a serious setback when a new crisis erupted inside the socialist camp. A group of Communist reformers in Czechoslovakia led by Alexander Dubček had begun during the preceding six months to introduce changes designed to "humanize" Czech socialism. The reforms were almost entirely related to internal party affairs and domestic policies, and Dubček and his followers were careful to stress that they had no intention of altering Czechoslovakia's adherence to the Warsaw Pact or its close alliance with the Soviet Union. Why these assurances failed to satisfy the Soviet leaders is not entirely clear. The most likely explanation is that they feared not only how far the Czech reformers might go and what impact this might have within the Soviet Union but also the possibility of growing pro–West German sentiment in the Czech party.

In any case the Red Army, supported by other Eastern European forces (but not Rumania), invaded and occupied Czechoslovakia in August 1968. Unable to resist, the Czechs soon found themselves back under a Communist government run by pro-Soviet hard-liners. Yugoslavian and Italian Communist leaders protested the brutal repression of independent socialism in Czechoslovakia, as did Western leaders, but Soviet leader Brezhnev was unfazed, announcing instead that the Soviet Union had the obligation to interfere in the affairs of Communist societies that appeared to be "damaging either socialism in their own countries or the fundamental interests of the other socialist countries," a precept subsequently known as the Brezhnev doctrine.

Despite this claim of Soviet hegemony over international socialism the major Communist parties in Europe and in several other countries around the world asserted in the 1970s their right to adopt independent positions and policies in accord with their own domestic situations and strategies. This movement, often called Eurocommunism, was led by the Italian Communist party, but the Spanish party and important elements in the French party also supported it.

In the early 1970s the Soviet Union embarked on a new phase of coexistence, usually called détente. In international parlance the word means relaxation of tensions, but the Soviet leaders pushed it further in a consistent effort to reach agreements with the United States and the Western European nations on several important issues. The most significant by far was arms control. In the late 1950s and through the 1960s both the United States and the Soviet Union had tacitly agreed to a nuclear stalemate, called by its critics a "balance of terror." Each side made sure it had enough nuclear weapons that could survive an attack by the other side to permit it to launch a devastating retaliatory strike. The certainty that retaliation would occur prevented, or deterred, the other side from attacking. This strategy of deterrence seemed to work, but it depended on neither side's getting far ahead of the other in the arms race.

Consequently, in the late 1960s Soviet-American negotiations on arms control had been initiated, but these had been frozen during the frigid Western reaction to the Soviet invasion of Czechoslovakia. In the early 1970s progress was made, and in 1972 Brezhnev and President Richard Nixon signed an agreement banning antiballistic missile systems and a treaty limiting strategic weapons on both sides, The Strategic Arms Limitation Treaty, known as SALT I. To be sure, the treaty mainly structured rather than curbed the arms race, as both the Soviet Union and the United States sought to improve the quality and survivability of their nuclear arsenals. A second agreement, SALT II, was signed in 1979, but it was not ratified, although both countries informally abided by its provisions. From the Soviet point of view pursuit of arms limitation accords had two important advantages. It helped reduce tension between the superpowers and presented the Soviet government as essentially peace-loving and accommodating. Second, it helped retard the Western military build-up and extension of the West's superiority in advanced technology and sophisticated military hardware.

At the height of détente Soviet policy scored a considerable success with the signing of the Helsinki Declaration in 1975. After World War II the Soviet Union and the Western powers had been unable to agree on peace treaties for Germany, Poland, and Czechoslovakia. Therefore, there was no formal recognition or international sanction of the new boundaries that had resulted from the war and the Soviet reorganization of Central Europe afterward (see Map 9). At a meeting in Helsinki, Finland, in the summer of 1975 the Western powers agreed to recognize the sensitive borders between Poland and East Germany and between Poland and the Soviet Union, as well as other boundaries in the region, in exchange for a Soviet promise to increase trade, cultural contacts, and the protection of human rights across all Europe. Despite the Helsinki accords, détente began to break down at the end of the 1970s, as we shall shortly see.

The Sino-Soviet Split

After Stalin's advice to the Chinese Communists in 1927 to cooperate with Chiang Kai-Shek had resulted in their near destruction by Chiang, the Communist revolutionary movement in China went its own way, fighting mainly on its own against the Nationalists and then, after the Japanese invasion of China in 1936, against the Japanese as well. Until near the end of World War II the Soviet Union maintained rather distant relations with both Nationalist China and the Communist Chinese in order not to offend Japan, with which it had signed a nonaggression treaty in 1941 designed to prevent the Red Army from being caught in a two-front war. Soviet entry into the war against Japan in the summer of 1945, after the defeat of Germany, made the Soviet government a cobelligerent with Nationalist China, and it reached an agreement with Chiang Kai-shek in August 1945. Because Stalin wanted to maintain this relationship and because he was not eager to see an independent Communist movement come to power, the Soviet Union provided little direct support to Mao Tse-tung and his comrades as they battled to victory in China. Instead Soviet authorities helped indirectly by turning over to the Chinese Communists Manchuria, which the Red army had occupied in August 1945, as well as the Japanese war materiel captured there. They also provided some logistical support to the Chinese Communist armies.

Nevertheless, the Chinese Communists could feel justifiably that they had made their own revolution and were not beholden to anyone, least of all to Stalin and the Soviet comrades. Mao apparently resented the niggardly Soviet assistance to his revolution, and these feelings were intensified when the aid provided to the new Communist Chinese government in 1950 was limited and required repayment with interest. In addition, the Soviet government drove a hard bargain in the diplomatic and territorial arrangements that accompanied signing of a formal alliance between the two largest socialist countries. Finally, in what was clearly a personal affront, Stalin refused to treat Mao as an equal when the latter visited Moscow in December 1949.

Despite these inauspicious portents relations between the USSR and the People's Republic of China were ostensibly close in the 1950s. From the Soviet point of view it was important to keep the Chinese as allies during the Korean War, for which the Chinese supplied "volunteers," and while Moscow was having difficulties elsewhere in the socialist camp, notably in Yugoslavia, Poland, and Hungary. For their part the Chinese modeled their system and pattern of rapid development on the Stalinist experience. Moreover, the new government needed Soviet economic and military assistance, no matter how limited, and it wanted Soviet diplomatic backing in its efforts to oust the Nationalists from Taiwan and to win admission to the United Nations.

As the 1950s progressed, however, frictions increased. Mao was displeased with Khrushchev's de-Stalinization campaign, both because he had not been consulted about its advisability and because he thought it implied too "soft" a line in international affairs. After Stalin's death Mao considered himself the senior Communist leader and the chief Marxist theoretician in the world. Yet, Khrushchev treated him as a junior ally, and Mao was further offended by Khrushchev's brash and informal style. Quarrels developed over the amount and quality of Soviet aid, and the Chinese bitterly resented the high-handed manner and methods of Soviet advisers and technical assistance personnel in China.

Lying behind these surface irritants, however, were more deepseated and divisive issues. The two most significant were territorial and political-ideological. Ever since the seventeenth century, when Russian expansion eastward reached the border of the Chinese empire, the regions lying between these two great countries and the exact boundaries between them have been in dispute. The Chinese believe that in the late-nineteenth century and in the first half of the twentieth century, when China was weak, the Russians, whether tsarist diplomats or Soviet comrades, took advantage of its relative decline in power to extract unfair territorial concessions from China. The Soviet authorities, on the other hand, argue that their position in the Far East is historically justified and that since 1949 they have been more than generous in trying to make boundary adjustments that would satisfy the Chinese. A number of territorial questions are still in contention between the Soviet Union and China, and these will have to be resolved before a genuine rapprochement between the two Communist giants can occur.

The political-ideological questions centered in part on sibling rivalry within the international socialist movement. The Soviet leaders assumed they should head the movement, given their revolutionary seniority and greater power. The Chinese, historically sensitive on issues of precedence and ruling the largest Communist country in the world, resented the Russians' self-proclaimed role and in any case believed that the Soviet leaders often erred in their direction of the socialist bloc. Moreover, in Southeast Asia and in South Asia, the Soviet Union and the People's Republic of China competed for influence directly, the Soviet Union supporting the North Vietnamese against China and the Chinese backing Pakistan against the Soviet Union's friend, India, for example.

The ideological dispute arose in part over Khrushchev's new doctrine of the noninevitability of war and his policy of peaceful coexistence. The Chinese insisted that these ideas were violations of true Leninism, making the Soviet leaders guilty of the serious ideological crime of "revisionism" (changing Marxist orthodoxy). The Chinese ideologists took a "hard" line, maintaining that the world Communist movement should actively foment revolutions in the Third World and should aggressively undermine world imperialism at every opportunity. They insisted that it was wishful thinking to believe socialism could be achieved peacefully, by parliamentary or other nonviolent means, and that coexistence was only a trap designed by the imperialists to lull the socialist states into passivity while the capitalist armies prepared to encircle and destroy them. In retort, the Soviet leaders accused the Chinese of being

adventurists and warmongers and of endangering the security of the
socialist system in the nuclear age. Along these lines the debate and
bickering continued and deepened.

By 1960 the differences between the Soviet Union and China
erupted into public denunciations and direct action. The Soviet side cut
off aid to China and withdrew its advisers and technicians, including
those who had been assisting the Chinese to develop nuclear technology. In 1964 the Soviet Union also had the Chinese expelled from the
world socialist movement, although some individual parties and the
government of Albania sided with the Chinese. In the mid-1960s the
split widened, and in 1969 fighting broke out along the Sino-Soviet
border, with some casualties on each side. Since the death of Mao Tse-
tung and criticism of "the gang of four" in the mid-1970s desultory negotiations between the two sides have slightly improved relations, but a
legacy of bitterness remains, and many issues are still unresolved.

This tension means that the Soviet Union, in addition to contending with the United States and its allies, must constantly bear in mind
the long-range danger from China. Almost one third of the Red Army
is deployed on the Chinese border, and a substantial portion of Soviet
military expenditures are allocated to defense against China. Politically,
China actively opposes the influential role of Vietnam, backed by the
USSR, in Southeast Asia and supports Pakistan and the Afghan rebels
against Soviet intervention in Afghanistan. In Africa and other parts of
the world Soviet and Chinese representatives work at cross-purposes,
rather than cooperating. Improving relations with China is a pressing
problem for future Soviet leaders.

Soviet Foreign Policy in the 1980s

China is only one of several major issues that the Soviet government must deal with in this decade. These questions can be most easily
discussed by grouping them in three general categories: possibilities for
the expansion of socialist revolution or of Soviet influence, relations
within the socialist bloc, and relations with the nonsocialist world. In
each the challenges seem greater than the likely successes, particularly
if one keeps in mind that the ability of the Soviet government to act in
world affairs will be circumscribed by its need to settle the serious domestic issues discussed in Chapter 13.

Beginning in the late 1950s the Soviet Union pursued a "forward,"
or expansionist, policy in its effort to promote socialist revolution in Asia,
Africa, and Latin America. The greatest impact of this endeavor has
been to frighten anti-Communists in the West; the actual gains for socialism have been small. After its radical revolution in 1959 Cuba be-

came a socialist nation allied to the Soviet Union, in part because the United States refused to aid or even deal with Castro, whereas the USSR promised all-out support. But the victory of socialism in Cuba has been a mixed blessing for the Soviet leaders. Because of its weak, one-crop economy and considerable mismanagement by Castro and his comrades, Cuba has been a costly ally, requiring hundreds of millions of dollars annually in Soviet assistance. It has provided a base from which to try to spread revolution elsewhere in Latin America, but the results are not impressive. Outside of a Marxist government in Chile in the 1970s and the Sandinista revolution in Nicaragua in the 1980s, socialism has had little success in the Western Hemisphere. Moreover, its prospects in the future in any major Latin American country appear dim.

The Vietnamese revolution also succeeded in the postwar decades, but it did so largely on its own. Although Vietnam is now allied to the Soviet Union and has spread its brand of socialism to Cambodia (Kampuchea) by force, it does not now seem likely that socialism will advance elsewhere in Southeast Asia.

Marxist governments have come to power in Angola and in Ethiopia in Africa, with Soviet and Cuban assistance, but neither seems very strong; nor are the chances that socialist revolution will succeed elsewhere in Africa very good. In the Middle East Syria is an ally of convenience for the Soviet Union, but the twin forces of Arab nationalism and Islamic religion militate against socialist revolution's occurring in any major country in that region, including North Africa.

In South Asia the Soviet Union is engaged in a brutal genocidal war against the Afghan people, which has lasted over five years and may continue for some time. As a result of a revolutionary upheaval in Afghanistan in 1978 a weak Marxist government came to power there. Undercut by popular resistance, it was on the verge of collapse when the Red Army invaded Afghanistan in December 1979. Apparently the Soviet leaders believed—quite erroneously according to all available evidence—that the revolutionary government would be replaced by an anti-Soviet Islamic government closely linked to the United States and China. To preserve "socialism" in Afghanistan and to enhance Soviet security by making sure a pro-Soviet government ruled Afghanistan on the Soviet Union's southern border, Moscow ordered in its forces, expecting to overcome Afghan resistance and set up a puppet government in a matter of weeks. What a stupendous miscalculation!

The Afghan people, with a long history of opposition to British and Russian interference in their country and with a fervent dedication to their land and to Islam, have fought a bitter, wasting guerrilla struggle against over one hundred thousand Soviet troops. The country has been devastated, hundreds of thousands of Afghan citizens have been killed, and three to four million Afghans have fled to Pakistan and Iran. Eventually, by driving out or killing much of the population, the Soviet

Union may be able to impose socialism on Afghanistan. It will be a hollow victory, for the whole affair has seriously undermined the Soviet position in the Third World and among all Islamic peoples.

If a series of socialist revolutions around the world seems highly unlikely, what about the possible expansion of Soviet influence? Again, the prospects do not seem bright. Although Communist parties remain active in France, Italy, and Spain, they are mainly national or Eurocommunist parties and seem unlikely to follow Soviet dictation. Nowhere else in Western Europe is Soviet influence strong. Japan remains critical of the Soviet Union, in part on ideological grounds and in part because of the Soviet refusal to return the Kurile Islands in the north Pacific taken from Japan at the end of World War II. Because of Afghanistan and because of its antireligious ideology, the Soviet Union has limited influence in the Islamic world, and even its efforts to reinsert itself into the continuing Arab-Israeli conflict will probably not succeed.

In our second category, the socialist bloc, the Soviet leaders face four major challenges. The difficulties with China we have already discussed. In Eastern Europe pressures within Hungary for greater independence and for closer economic and cultural relations with the West are increasing, while Yugoslavia continues to follow its own path. Somehow the Soviet leaders must develop a means of accommodating the desire of East Europeans to develop their own domestic policies and to have greater influence in foreign policy decisions that affect the Warsaw Pact. It also seems probable that in the next decade the role of the German Democratic Republic in the socialist camp will have to be redefined. It is already establishing closer ties with West Germany, raising for Soviet leaders the specter of a resurgence of German power in central Europe. A way of keeping the East Germans in the socialist movement while still permitting them their historic connections to the West will have to be found.

Finally, the future of the socialist movement remains clouded by the problem of Poland. In the summer of 1980 an independent workers' movement, Solidarity, arose spontaneously as a protest against economic inequities and government mismanagement and corruption. In only a few months ten million Poles were enrolled in Solidarity trade unions, and a smaller rural Solidarity movement was started. The government made concessions while the Polish Communist party virtually disintegrated. In the resulting confusion, power diffused among the government, Solidarity, and the Catholic Church, and the economy neared collapse. Emboldened by the apparent weakness of their opponents and calculating that the Soviet Union would not risk armed intervention, Solidarity leaders began to discuss going beyond demands for a share in economic decision making and structural reforms to a direct political role. This system would have been a clear threat to the socialist model developed by the Soviet Union: a one-party system in which the Communist party does not share political power with any other nationally organized interest group.

As a result, General Wojciech Jaruzelski, probably with Soviet encouragement, led a military coup in December 1981. He imposed martial law for eighteen months and banned Solidarity. He, together with other senior officers and a few remnants of the Polish party, has ruled Poland since. General Jaruzelski has hinted that he "saved" Poland by forestalling Soviet intervention, but the great majority of Poles has passively opposed his regime. The Soviet leaders have had to provide extensive economic aid to Poland, and the new leadership in Poland will have to figure out how to square a restored Polish socialism with Polish nationalism, the influential role of the Catholic Church, and the Solidarity tradition of workers' self-determination.

Our third category of challenges for contemporary Soviet foreign policy is relations with the nonsocialist world, primarily the United States. For American leaders détente soured in the late 1970s, partly over minor Soviet actions but predominantly because of Soviet promotion of socialist regimes in Ethiopia and Angola, the Soviet invasion of Afghanistan, and alleged Soviet support for revolutionaries in Nicaragua and El Salvador. American disillusionment puzzled the Soviet leaders, since they had never assumed that détente meant that the two sides would stop competing in the world arena. Soviet policy makers always intended to keep their prerogative to make trouble for the imperialists wherever they could. For them, détente meant reducing tensions where possible and striking deals of mutual self-interest, but not friendly, trusting relations forever, as some Americans thought détente implied.

As détente collapsed, President Jimmy Carter imposed a grain embargo against the Soviet Union, which mainly damaged American wheat farmers, since the Soviet government bought what it needed elsewhere. He also decided to boycott the 1980 Olympic Games in Moscow and not to send the SALT II treaty to the Senate for ratification.

With the election and reelection of Ronald Reagan as American president, the Soviet leaders have found themselves in a quandary. As a strong critic of Soviet ideology and practice, President Reagan has made clear that he wishes to deal with the Soviet Union as little as possible and then mainly on his own terms. Reacting to the Soviet military build-up under Brezhnev, the Reagan administration has greatly increased American defense outlays and, from the Soviet viewpoint, seems determined to establish and maintain military superiority over Soviet forces. Although the Soviet leaders might wish to respond to American policy forcefully, that course is too dangerous; yet they cannot ignore the actions of the Reagan government without falling far behind in the race for power and influence. Consequently, they condemn Reagan but also seek ways to reduce tensions with the United States.

Two goals appear paramount in the minds of the Soviet leaders. They want the American government and people to acknowledge that the Soviet Union, in power, status, and achievement, is on a par with the United States and should be treated with respect and as an equal. Second, the Soviet leaders very much want to find a way of controlling the arms race, which they consider highly dangerous and extremely costly at a time when the Soviet economy is struggling; further, it could well end with an overwhelming American advantage built on advanced technology and know-how. In the importance they attach to limiting further development of nuclear and high-technology weapons, the Soviet leaders are probably correct. Neither the Soviet nor the American people can possibly benefit from the huge expense and great instability that escalation of the arms race will bring.

For several compelling reasons Soviet-American relations should become less antagonistic in the long run. Since the end of World War II neither country has had much success in controlling events in Asia, Africa, and Latin America and in imposing its views or system on other nations. As a result, perhaps Soviet and American leaders will come increasingly to accept that neither the world revolutionary predictions of Marxism-Leninism nor the dreams of universal democracy and freedom are likely to be fulfilled. Instead peoples everywhere, driven by national pride, seem determined to find their own way of organizing their societies without Soviet or American interference and dictation. Consequently, Soviet-American rivalry in the Third World may peter out to be replaced by an attitude of "live and let live."

At the same time, if the arms race can be checked and if the stability of Europe can be assured, leaders and citizens in the United States and the Soviet Union should gradually feel less threatened by "the other side," with a concomitant growth in commercial, educational, and cultural exchanges and a lightening of the political atmosphere. Both societies confront important domestic problems, and establishment of more open and cordial relations between the United States and the USSR should encourage efforts to solve pressing issues on the home front.

How Soviet society will evolve in the remainder of this century is unclear, but the form it takes will, in considerable measure, reflect the demanding and varied historical experience that we have reviewed briefly in this book.

FURTHER READING

Blasier, Cole. *The Giant's Rival: The USSR and Latin America*. Pittsburgh: 1983.
Brzezinski, Z. *The Soviet Bloc: Unity and Conflict*. New York: 1960.
Cohen, Stephen. *Rethinking the Soviet Experience*. New York: 1985.
Donaldson, R. H., ed. *The Soviet Union in the Third World*. Boulder, Colo.: 1980.
Edmonds, Robin. *Soviet Foreign Policy: The Brezhnev Years*. New York: 1984.
Hammond, T. *Red Flag over Afghanistan*. Boulder, Colo.: 1984.

Holloway, David. *The Soviet Union and the Arms Race.* New Haven, Conn.: 1983.

Hutchings, R. L. *Soviet–East European Relations: Consolidation and Conflict, 1968–80.* Madison, Wisc.: 1983.

Quested, P. K. I. *Sino-Russian Relations: A Short History.* Winchester, Md.: 1984.

Shulman, M. *Stalin's Foreign Policy Reappraised.* New York: 1965.

Talbott, Strobe. *Endgame: The Inside Story of SALT II.* New York: 1979.

Ulam, Adam. *Titoism and the Cominform.* Cambridge, Mass.: 1952.

———. *Dangerous Relations, the Soviet Union in World Politics, 1970–82.* Oxford: 1983.

Valenta, Jiri. *Soviet Intervention in Czechoslovakia, 1968.* Baltimore: 1979.

Yergin, Daniel. *Shattered Peace: The Origins of the Cold War.* Boston: 1978.

Zagoria, Donald. *The Sino-Soviet Conflict, 1955–61.* Princeton, N.J.: 1962.

Zinner, Paul. *Revolution in Hungary.* Cambridge, Mass.: 1961.

Index